Internal
Migration
in
Contemporary
INDIA

Thank you for choosing a SAGE product!
If you have any comment, observation or feedback,
I would like to personally hear from you.
Please write to me at **contactceo@sagepub.in**

Vivek Mehra, Managing Director and CEO,
SAGE Publications India Pvt Ltd, New Delhi

Bulk Sales

SAGE India offers special discounts
for purchase of books in bulk.
We also make available special imprints
and excerpts from our books on demand.

For orders and enquiries, write to us at

Marketing Department
SAGE Publications India Pvt Ltd
B1/I-1, Mohan Cooperative Industrial Area
Mathura Road, Post Bag 7
New Delhi 110044, India

E-mail us at **marketing@sagepub.in**

Get to know more about SAGE

Be invited to SAGE events, get on our mailing list.
Write today to **marketing@sagepub.in**

This book is also available as an e-book.

Internal Migration in Contemporary INDIA

EDITED BY

Deepak K. Mishra

⑤SAGE www.sagepublishing.com
Los Angeles I London I New Delhi I Singapore I Washington DC I Melbourne

First published in 2016 by

SAGE Publications India Pvt Ltd
B1/I-1 Mohan Cooperative Industrial Area
Mathura Road, New Delhi 110 044, India
www.sagepub.in

SAGE Publications Inc
2455 Teller Road
Thousand Oaks, California 91320, USA

SAGE Publications Ltd
1 Oliver's Yard, 55 City Road
London EC1Y 1SP, United Kingdom

SAGE Publications Asia-Pacific Pte Ltd
3 Church Street
#10-04 Samsung Hub
Singapore 049483

Published by Vivek Mehra for SAGE Publications India Pvt Ltd, typeset in 10/12.5 pt Minion Pro by Diligent Typesetter India Pvt Ltd, Delhi and printed at Chaman Enterprises, New Delhi.

Library of Congress Cataloging-in-Publication Data
Name: Mishra, Deepak K., editor.
Title: Internal migration in contemporary India / edited by Deepak K. Mishra.
Description: Thousand Oaks : SAGE Publications India Pvt Ltd, 2016. |
    Includes bibliographical references and index.
Identifiers: LCCN 2015049017| ISBN 9789351508571 (hardback : alk. paper) |
    ISBN 9789351508564 (epub) | ISBN 9789351508588 (ebook)
Subjects: LCSH: Migration, Internal—India—History—21st century.
Classification: LCC HB2099 .I58 2016 | DDC 304.80954—dc23 LC record available at http://lccn.loc.gov/2015049017

ISBN: 978-93-515-0857-1 (HB)

The SAGE Team: Supriya Das, Guneet Kaur Gulati and Rajinder Kaur

Contents

List of Tables   vii
List of Figures   xi
List of Abbreviations   xiii
Acknowledgements   xv

CHAPTER 1
Introduction: Internal Migration in Contemporary India—An
Overview of Issues and Concerns   1
Deepak K. Mishra

CHAPTER 2
Nature of Migration and Its Contribution to India's Urbanization   26
R.B. Bhagat

CHAPTER 3
Women's Mobility and Migration: An Exploratory Study of
Muslim Women Migrants in Jamia Nagar, Delhi   47
Meenakshi Thapan, Anshu Singh and Nidhitha Sreekumar

CHAPTER 4
Migration and Marginalization: A Study of North East Migrants
in Delhi   71
Babu P. Remesh

CHAPTER 5
Labour Migration in the North East   96
S. Irudaya Rajan and Rikil Chyrmang

CHAPTER 6
Educational Migration among Ladakhi Youth   154
Elizabeth Williams-Oerberg

CHAPTER 7
Migration in Agrarian Classes: A Study Based on Nine Villages
in Andhra Pradesh 180
R. Vijay

CHAPTER 8
Migration from Contemporary Bihar 204
Amrita Datta

CHAPTER 9
Migration and Punjab: Some Perceptions 222
Surjit Singh

CHAPTER 10
Seasonal Migration from Odisha: A View from the Field 263
Deepak K. Mishra

CHAPTER 11
Internal Labour Migration in India: Emerging Needs
of Comprehensive National Migration Policy 291
Anjali Borhade

About the Editor and Contributors 337
Index 340

List of Tables

1.1 Percentage of internal and international migrants based on place of last residence, India, 1971–2001   9

1.2 Size and growth rates of migrant populations by type of movement, India, 1971–2001   9

1.3 Size and growth rates of migrant populations by migration stream, India, 1971–2001   10

2.1 Percentage of internal and international migrants based on place of last residence, India 1971–2008   32

2.2 Per cent distribution of migration by steams of migration and gender, 2007–08, India (all duration)   33

2.3 Per cent distribution of migration by distance categories and steams of migration 2007–08, India (all duration)   34

2.4 Reasons of migration into rural and urban areas by gender, India, 2007–08   34

2.5 Birth, death and natural increase rate per 1,000 population by rural and urban areas, 1971–80 to 2001–10, India birth, rural and urban areas   41

2.6 Contribution of the components of urban growth, India, 1971–2011   41

5.1 Projected population in the North East, 2020   99

5.2 State-wise literacy rate, 1951–2011   100

5.3 Educational development infrastructure index and its rank, 2010–11   101

5.4 Enrolment in higher education by stages, 2001–02 to 2005–06   102

5.5 Total number of universities in the North East and girl enrolment, 2011–12   104

5.6 State-wise annual exponential growth rate of net state domestic product (NSDP) at constant (2004–05) prices, (1981–82 to 2011–12)   106

5.7   Sectoral allocation of expenditure to total development
in the North East in the 11th Five-year Plan, 2007–12   111
5.8   Growth in employment, 1983–94, 1994–2000 and 2004–10   113
5.9   Population by age group, 2011   114
5.10   Trends of public and private employment in the organized
sector, 1981–2011   115
5.11   Distribution of workers as cultivators, agricultural
labourers and other workers   117
5.12   Unemployment in the North East (per cent of labour force)   118
5.13   Average daily wages for rural casual workers engaged
in public and non-public works (rupees)   119
5.14   Net migrants rate (1991–2001)   121
5.15   Reasons for migration, 2007–08   125
5.16   Uses of remittances in selected north-eastern states, 2007–08   126
5.17   Uses of remittances in North East, 2007–08   127
5.18   Migration by place of last residence   133
5.19   Reasons for migration   134
5.20   Uses of household remittances   134
A5.1   Socio-economic profile of the north-eastern region   137
A5.2   Estimated birth rate, death rate, natural growth rate and
infant mortality rate, 1997–2010 (selected years)   139
A5.3   Number of persons living Below Poverty Line (BPL),
1983–84 to 2004–05   142
A5.4   Distribution of usually employed by category of
employment (rural/urban), 1993–94 to 2004–05   144
A5.5   Usual principal status unemployment rate among
the youth   146
A5.6   Distribution (per 1,000) of migrants in different MPCE
quintile class for each state   149
7.1   Location, number of households and sources of irrigation
in the surveyed villages   184
7.2   Distribution of owned and operated area in the study
villages (land in acres)   185
7.3   Principal crops cultivated in the surveyed villages
(land in acres)   188
7.4   The distribution of households and owned land in
different study villages   190
7.5   Migration rates HHs and individuals   193

7.6   Distribution of migrant households over classes in
      the study village   193
7.7   Correlation coefficient between percentage of households
      witnessing at least one migrant and different classes   194
7.8   Distribution of households with at least one migrant over
      classes in the surveyed villages   195
7.9   Options open to agricultural labour households and poor
      peasantry in the surveyed villages   199
A7.1 Land-based importance of NCPHs in the surveyed villages   201
A7.2 Distribution of leased-in area and leased-out area across the
      study village (land in acres)   202
8.1   Workers disaggregated by sex and residential status,
      age 15–59 years   206
9.1   Decadal change in population: Punjab   223
9.2   Some features   225
9.3   Trend in migration in Punjab   227
9.4   Trend in urban migration in Punjab   229
9.5   Trend in rural migration in Punjab   230
9.6   Migration streams for top ten states for intrastate
      migration by last residence (duration 0–9 years) in
      India: 2001   231
9.7   Migration profile (0–9 years) Punjab: 2001   233
9.8   Reasons for migration in Punjab: 2001   235
9.9   Proportion of migrants (per 1,000)   237
9.10 Distribution (per 1,000) of migrants by educational level 238
9.11 Migration rate (per 1,000 persons)   240
9.12 Migration rate (per 1,000 persons) in different MPCE
      quintile class: Punjab   241
9.13 Distribution (per 1,000) of migrants by nature of movements
      in Punjab   242
9.14 Distribution (per 1,000) of internal migrants by four types
      of rural–urban migration streams   243
9.15 Per 1,000 distribution of migrants by location of last usual
      place of residence   244
9.16 Distribution (per 1,000) of migrants by reason for migration:
      Punjab   247
9.17 Distribution (per 1,000) of migrants by their usual principal
      activity status before and after migration: Punjab   248
9.18 Number of return migrants per 1,000 migrants   250

9.19   Number of out-migrants per 1,000 persons (rural)   250
9.20   Per 1,000 distribution of out-migrants by present place of
       residence   251
9.21   Distribution (per 1,000) of out-migrants by reason for
       out-migration   254
9.22   Number of economically active (per 1,000)
       out-migrants   255
9.23   Number of remitter out-migrants (per 1,000)   256
9.24   Net migration rate (per 1,000 of population)   256
9.25   Impact of labour migration on wage rate for different
       agricultural operations in Punjab: 2011   259
10.1   Poverty in Odisha and India, 1973–74 to 2004–05   269
10.2   Seasonal migrants, all states/UTs   273
10.3   Seasonal migration, Odisha (rural)   273
10.4   Seasonal migration, region-wise Odisha (rural)   274
10.5   Seasonal migrants by social category, Odisha (rural)   274
10.6   Seasonal migrants, by destination during longest
       spell (rural)   275
10.7   Seasonal migrants, by household type (rural)   275
10.8   Seasonal migrants, by total land possessed (rural)   276
10.9   Short-term migrants, by literacy status (rural)   276
10.10 Seasonal migrants, by UPAS of those in labour force at
       origin (rural)   277
10.11 Seasonal migrant households in different MPCE decile
       classes   277
11.1   Existing central/state government policies and
       programmes for migrants   314

List of Figures

2.1 Percentage of migrants in selected million plus cities 39
5.1 Average annual exponential growth rate of population,
     1951–61 to 2001–11 98
5.2 Sectoral share to the total North East NSDP, 1980–81
     to 2011–12 109
5.3 Public and private employment in the organized sector,
     1981–2011 116
5.4 Distribution of land possessed (area in hectare) (in per cent) 123
5.5 Mean age 123
5.6 Percentage distribution by religion 124
5.7 Percentage distribution by social groups 124
5.8 Percentage distribution by religion 131
5.9 Percentage distribution by social group 132
5.10 Percentage distribution by language spoken 132
8.1 Sources of income for non-migrating households 207
8.2 Sources of income for migrating households 208
8.3 Destination: Rural or urban 211
8.4 Where do migrant workers go? 211
8.5 Distribution of migrant workers by state 212
10.1 Seasonal migration in India: NSS regions 268

List of Abbreviations

BPL	Below Poverty Line
BTAD	Bodoland Territorial Area District
BTC	Bodoland Territorial Council
CAGR	Compound Annual Growth Rate
CBR	Crude Birth Rate
CDR	Crude Death Rate
CMR	Convention of Migrant Workers
GSDP	Gross State Domestic Product
HE	Higher Education
HYV	High Yielding Variety
IAS	Indian Administrative Services
ICDS	Integrated Child Development Scheme
IHD	Institute for Human Development
IIT	Indian Institute of Technology
ILP	Inner Line Permit
IMDT	Illegal Migration Determination by Tribunal
IMR	Infant Mortality Rate
JMI	Jamia Millia Islamia
JNNURM	Jawaharlal Nehru National Urban Renewal Mission
KAS	Kashmir Administrative Services
LAMP	Learning and Migration Programme
MGNREGA	Mahatma Gandhi National Rural Employment Guarantee Act
MPCE	Monthly per Capita Expenditure
MWS	Muslim Women's Survey
NCR	National Capital Region
NCRL	National Commission on Rural Labour
NCEUS	National Commission for Enterprises in the Unorganized Sector
NER	North Eastern Region

NEIGRIHMS	North Eastern Indira Gandhi Regional Institute of Health and Medical Sciences
NELM	New Economics of Labour Migration
NESC&H	North East Support Centre & Helpline
NFS	Non-farm Sector
NIT	National Institute of Technology
NRLM	National Rural Livelihoods Mission
NSSO	National Sample Survey Organisation
NSDP	Net State Domestic Product
NTFPs	Non-Timber Forest Products
NUEPA	National University of Educational Planning and Administration
OBC	Other Backward Classes
PDS	Public Distribution System
PG	Paying Guest
PPA	Participatory Poverty Assessment
PPP	Public–Private Partnership
PSM	Purposive Sampling Method
PURA	Provision of Urban Amenities in Rural Areas
RAY	Rajiv Awas Yojana
RGIIM	Rajiv Gandhi of Indian Institute of Management
RSBY	Rashtriya Swasthya Bima Yojana
SCs	Schedule Castes
SECMOL	Students' Educational and Cultural Movement of Ladakh
SSA	Sarva Shiksha Abhiyan
STs	Scheduled Tribes
TISS	Tata Institute of Social Sciences
ULB	Urban Local Bodies
UPR	Usual Place of Residence
UPAS	Usual Principle Activity Status

Acknowledgements

This book is the outcome of a collective engagement with India's fascinating and complex transformation, and many individuals and institutions have contributed significantly in this collective journey. While there exist many significant contributions that look at India's remarkable journey from diverse vantage points, this book is about internal migration in contemporary India and its manifold linkages with the dynamics of development. First and foremost, I would like to thank Dr G. Mohan Gopal, Director, Rajiv Gandhi Institute of Contemporary Studies (RGICS), for initiating and supporting this endeavour. He not only took an active interest in the study, but also contributed to it significantly through his incisive comments and suggestions. This study was prepared under the aegis of the Rajiv Gandhi Institute of Contemporary Studies. However, the institute does not necessarily subscribe to the views expressed here. I am grateful to Dr Reshmi Banerjee, the coordinator of the project at the RGICS, New Delhi, for all her support and help in organizing the study as well as the two-day national conference at RGICS, in which the papers were presented and discussed. Dr Rakhee Bhattacharya, with whom my association predates our association with our respective current institutions, took over the coordination of the project at a critical stage, and I am thankful to her for all her constructive comments and unwavering support.

I am truly grateful to the scholars who have contributed to this book. In spite of the constraints of time, all of them responded favourably to our request for submission of the papers well in time and also participated in the conference where all the papers were presented. In particular, I am grateful to eminent scholar late Dr Surjit Singh, whose untimely death has left a void in the academic world. A keen observer of rural transformation in India, Dr Singh was generous enough to share his insights and comments on various aspects of this work.

I am grateful to the *Economic and Political Weekly* and its editor for the permission to include the work of Thapan, Singh and Sreekumar

(Chapter 3), an earlier version of which appeared in the journal. Various scholars and representatives from civil society, NGOs, trade unions, politicians and others, who actively participated and commented upon the papers presented in the conference, have significantly contributed to the development of several ideas presented in the book. Although it would not be possible to thank them all individually, I would like to place on record my gratitude to Professors T.S. Papola, Atul Sarma, Saraswati Raju, S. Irudya Rajan, Soumendra Patnaik, R. Vijay, Anuradha Banerjee, Partho Ghosh, Jesim Pais, Neetha N. Pillai and Shareena Banu for their participation, comments and observations. I am grateful to the parliamentarians—Mr Oscar Fernandez (Karnataka), Mr Bhakta Charan Das (Odisha), Mr Manicka Tagore (Tamil Nadu) and Mr Hamdullah Sayeed (Lakshadweep)—who took time out of their busy schedule to listen to various scholars and also presented their own insights on various aspects of migration. Last but not the least, I would like to acknowledge the support of my students at the Centre for the Study of Regional Development, JNU—Dinesh K. Nayak, Nishikant Singh, Rukmini Thapa, Satyam Kumar Yadav and Abha Gupta—whose support was crucial for the completion of the study. I am also grateful to the editorial team at SAGE, New Delhi for their excellent support and help.

While no single book might be adequate to understand the complexities associated with internal migration, if this collection could contribute a little in carrying forward the struggle to make migration a more inclusive and less painful experience for the poor and the marginalized, it would be a great satisfaction to me and all those who were involved in this humble effort.

Deepak K. Mishra
New Delhi, December, 2015

1

Introduction: Internal Migration in Contemporary India—An Overview of Issues and Concerns

Deepak K. Mishra

Introduction

Migration is expected to increase as a result of economic growth. The relatively low migration rate in India that has been widely discussed in the literature was expected to be replaced by the new dynamics of migration and urbanization, particularly after the neo-liberal economic reforms. However, notwithstanding some discernible changes in mobility patterns in urban settings, the expected transformation of migration is not yet visible, at least in the macro-context. On the one hand, expansion of economic opportunities for some has expanded the aspirations for many, and there has been a desire for economic betterment that has induced many to migrate. On the other hand, there have been new barriers, vulnerabilities and anxieties for the migrants. Increasing the scope for some migrants to access jobs anywhere in India has to be seen along with rising tides of chauvinist, anti-migrant and nativist politics in many parts of India. Increasing violence against women, both in urban and rural areas, often as a reaction to the increasing visibility and mobility of women, is another crucial dimension having significant implications for migrants and their well-being. Further, the continuing significance of the informal economy, recruitments based on caste and kinship networks, labour bondages of various kinds and exploitative labour relations even in globally integrated sectors necessitate further probing of the constitutive contexts of migration decisions.

This introductory chapter attempts to provide an overall background to the subsequent chapters dealing with specific issues related to internal migration in India. In the first section of the chapter, a brief discussion on three distinct perspectives on economic development that have implications for understanding contemporary issues in labour migration in India have been presented. These three perspectives are: (*a*) the agrarian question under globalization, (*b*) the questions of uneven development, poverty and migration and finally (*c*) the informal sector perspective. In the second section, broad empirical patterns of migration have been summarized and in the final section the key insights from the chapters of the volume have been presented.

Contextualizing Internal Migration in Globalizing India

The mainstream literature on migration, essentially, portrays migration as an inevitable and largely beneficial outcome of economic transformation. In the literature on structural transformation, for example, increasing spatial mobility in response to the spatial unevenness in the demands for labour and supply of labour is seen as a key stylized feature of economic development. While migration has been credited with the role of reducing interregional and inter-sectoral gaps in living standards, the 'crucial question is whether, and to what extent, migration has been able to play this role in the Indian context' (Srivastava, 2012, p. 2). In an effort to understand the trends and patterns of migration in contemporary India, we have selectively presented three different perspectives, which help us to look at contemporary experiences of migration and associated socio-economic changes on a larger canvas of development and economic transformation. These three perspectives have been articulated by scholars in many different contexts, cutting across disciplinary boundaries, and also have strong historical roots.

The Agrarian Questions of Labour

'The agrarian question' has always had a central place in the Marxian theories of development (of capitalism). In the words of Karl Kautsky

(1889/1988, p. 12), 'Is capital, and in what ways is capital, taking hold of agriculture, revolutionising it, smashing the old forms of production and of poverty and establishing the new forms which must succeed?' T. J. Byres (1996, p. 26) has defined the agrarian question as 'the continued existence in the countryside, in a substantive sense, of obstacles to an unleashing of accumulation in both the countryside and more generally—in particular, the accumulation associated with and necessary for capitalist industrialisation'. The three significant 'problematics' of Byres' agrarian question are 'accumulation', 'production' and 'politics' (Bernstein, 1996). While the accumulation problematic refers to the understanding of the 'extent to which agriculture can act as a basis for surplus accumulation, the second explores the extent to which capitalism has been able to transform the countryside, the forms that it takes, the barriers which may impede its development' (Byres, 1991). The third problematic, 'politics' involves 'the impact of political forces and forms on the evolution of rural change explicit in both the accumulation and production problematics' (Akram-Lodhi, 1998, p. 138). Akram-Lodhi (1998, p. 146) argues that since Byres associates agrarian transition with the overall development of capitalism and its ultimate dominance, 'agrarian transition may occur without necessarily requiring changes within the individual spheres of accumulation, production and politics'. Thus, the capitalist transformation may be facilitated through changes in rural production and politics, even without any apparent net contribution to accumulation being made by agriculture.

Recently, Henry Bernstein's controversial argument that agrarian question has been either resolved or bypassed has sparked off a lively debate on the nature of agrarian transition in the developing world, including India (Akram-Lodhi and Kay, 2010a, 2010b; Bernstein, 2004, 2006; Lerche, 2010, 2011, 2013). Bernstein's key argument is that the 'classic agrarian question'—the agrarian question of capital—has already been resolved or bypassed. Henry Bernstein argues:

> [D]ue to land reforms and other dynamics of capitalist restructuring and accumulation in the post-war period…predatory landed property had largely vanished as a significant economic and political force by the end of the 1970s. This was one marker of the end of the agrarian question of capital *on a world scale*, [and hence] there is no longer the agrarian question of [global] capital, nor of 'national' capitals [and states] in poorer countries today. [What remains is] crisis of labour as a crisis of reproduction. (Bernstein, 2006, pp. 452–53, *emphasis in original*)[1]

In India, for example, capitalist development is no longer dependent on accumulation from agriculture to a significant extent. Hence, the continuing agrarian crisis has been explained by the neglect of agriculture by both capital and the state. This has several implications for the way rural households survive within and outside agriculture. Lerche (2011, p. 105, *emphasis added*) has outlined the key aspects of the agrarian question in contemporary India in the following terms:

> To what extent has capitalism developed in the countryside in India, including through processes of class differentiation within the peasantry? What are the obstacles to a more dynamic development? To what extent, and how, has agriculture contributed to overall capitalist accumulation and development in India? *How has this changed the position of rural labour?*[2]

The full implication of these questions facing rural India is beyond the scope of the chapter. It is important to in the context of the chapter that the prolonged agrarian crisis in India could be a result of the fact that both Indian 'big' capital and the state have not invested in agriculture, as the sector has become less important for them (Lerche, 2011). As agrarian accumulation is no longer a binding constraint for capital, there has been less interest in productive investment in it. The gap between earnings from agricultural and non-agricultural occupation has been widening. On the other hand, notwithstanding the recent talks about a revival in agriculture, farm households in vast areas of rural India increasingly find it difficult to survive on agriculture alone. Non-agricultural livelihoods are increasingly central to both accumulative and survival strategies of the rural households. The surplus is increasingly invested outside agriculture, and the non-agrarian characteristics of rural elites are being noted in diverse contexts (Harriss-White, Mishra and Upadhyay, 2009; Vijay, 2012). Wherever some dynamism has been noted within agriculture, it is less labour-absorbing and is often marked by seasonal labour or piece-rate labour contracts. Thus, the scope for survival within agriculture, either as self-employed, or petty commodity producer or as casual labour seems limited. The growth of rural non-farm sector, though important for livelihood diversification, has not been significant enough. To the extent that the relatively better-off section of the rural society sees education and salaried employment as a source of upward social mobility, there has been a steady growth of out-migration for education and employment. On top of that, through various mechanisms, such as accumulation by dispossession, degradation of livelihood resources, such as land, water, forests and pastures, large number of people are being driven out of the rural labour market. Thus, a vast section of the rural population depending upon rural, agrarian livelihoods is likely to be deagrarianized in future. Where and under what conditions this vast labour force gets absorbed in globalizing India (witnessing jobless growth) is certainly among the most difficult questions facing Indian economy and society. Migration in general and rural–urban migration, in particular, needs to be anchored to this broader understanding of the agrarian questions of labour rather than being seen as an outcome of individual choices or in narrow sectoral terms. Several recent studies have brought out the precariousness of employment in the informal sector, where a large proportion of seasonal and circular migrants are engaged. The fragmented nature of the migrant labour market, the continued existence of unfreedom and bondage in labour markets of various kinds and the dependence on multi-local, multiple livelihoods point to the need to interrogate the concept of 'classes of labour', as put forth by Bernstein (2010) and Lerche (2010).

Uneven Development, Poverty and Migration

Regional variation in per capita income has increased in the post-reform period. Though the literature is vast, by and large, studies conclude that in the period of rapid growth of the Indian economy, regional inequality, as captured through interstate variation has increased significantly. In contrast to the emphasis on 'convergence hypothesis' that has been one of the cornerstones of the neoclassical optimism on market-led growth, empirical analysis, suggests that there is hardly any move towards convergence of any kind; most studies conclude that inter-regional disparities, as measured by interstate differences in growth performance have increased in the post-reform period (Ahluwalia, 2000; Baddeley, McNay and Cassen, 2006; Bhattacharya and Sakthivel, 2004; Dasgupta et al., 2000; Nagraj, Varoudakis and Veganzones, 1998; Shetty, 2003).[3] One of the ways through which relatively less developed regions are getting integrated into the circuits of global capitalism is through labour flows from less developed to developed regions. Migration for employment and economic reasons, thus, is not just about individual or household-level decision-making and welfare maximization, there are structural aspects of such labour flows that need scrutiny. Without in any way de-emphasizing the agency of migrants, it should be possible to understand migration as part of the dynamics of uneven development under global capitalism, which creates, strengthens and also occasionally destroys centres of growth.[4] As an inevitable outcome of this process of uneven economic transformation, labour from less developed regions tends to migrate to areas of relative prosperity. However, this is not a simple process of Lewisian transformation. Economic transformation in the origin areas, including agrarian differentiation and socio-cultural factors, such as the role of kinship, caste and community networks also work in facilitating or constraining migration flows. The nature of the growth process and technological change, as manifested in the varying demand for labour and availability of employment of different kinds, also influences migration.

Palmer-Jones and Sen (2003), for example, have argued that much of the variations in per capita income could be explained by variations in agricultural productivity, which in turn could be explained in terms of some basic geographical factors such as ecological conditions and availability of irrigation. Since there is little scope for increasing agricultural productivity in such zones, the two major policy options are expanding non-farm sector employment and migration. New literature on migration has attempted to show that migration is beneficial for the poor. Increasingly, migration is viewed as part of the livelihood strategies of the poor, and there is some evidence to suggest that over time, with expansion of social networks, increasing access to information and communication networks, even the poor migrant could afford to go for accumulative migration (Deshingkar and Start, 2003). Given the absence and imperfections in rural markets (Mishra, 2008), migration has been described as the preferred choice of labour households. This is the basis of the increasingly popular description of migration as a poverty eradication strategy that works with the market rather than against it.

The relationship between migration and poverty is far from uniform. While many studies have reported that it is the relatively better-off section that migrates more than the poor and disadvantaged, there is some evidence to argue that when the poor migrate, they usually migrate under distress, are paid less and are exploited through a variety of means (Breman, 2007). While migration brings some income and contributes significantly to consumption smoothening, its impact on poverty is highly contextual.

Informalization and Migration

The classic Lewis-type migration that assumes a smooth transfer of labour from agriculture to industry has not been found in developing countries, including India. Most of the migrants to urban centres instead got employed in the urban informal sector. The expanding informal sector has drawn a great deal of attention in past decades. It is increasingly recognized that informal sector, far from being a residual or a transitory sector is, in fact, the core of the economy in terms of its contribution to output and employment. Given the slow expansion of employment opportunities in the formal or organized sector, in general, and organized manufacturing, in particular, the informal sector has been attracting migrants from smaller towns, cities and rural areas, alike. With globalization and growth of a particular kind, the informal sector has not been replaced by the formal/ organized sector, rather new changes in production organization, such as flexible production and globally integrated commodity chains, has given new lease of life to several informal sector enterprises. There are increasing linkages between formal and informal sector enterprises through sub-contracting. Further, a process of informalization of the formal sector activities is underway, which has blurred the dividing line between formal and informal sectors. Many of the workers in organized and formal sectors are informal workers without any social security and are recruited through layers of intermediaries. Most of those working in the urban, non-agricultural, informal sector are migrants. Some sectors, like construction, are heavily dependent on informal labour drawn from distant places through middlemen. Thus, migration from rural areas is increasingly through these informal channels that lead workers to informal sector jobs. These jobs are often less remunerative and require longer hours of work.

Migration to informal sector also involves social networks of diverse kinds. These networks are often based on caste-, religion- and language-based affinities. The modes of recruitment are highly diverse, and the migrant labour market for informal work is another example of the continuing significance of identities of various kinds in the labour market. Several researchers have noted this fragmented nature of these migration contracts. On the one extreme, millions of rural migrants are being integrated into circuits of labour, which work as the foundation of globalizing India; while on the other, there are increasing work opportunities for the educated, middle class women and men, in salaried employment as well as in self-employment. The dynamics and outcomes of migration in contemporary India are being shaped by the way the informal economy is reacting to the stimuli of neo-liberal growth.

The inter-linkages between the three aspects of the economy—the agrarian context, the linkages between uneven development, poverty and migration and finally the informal economy—are crucial for understanding contemporary issues in migration. There are several sector and region-specific issues within migration. The role of gender, caste, ethnicity, religion and region in differentiating the outcome of migration has been brought out by several studies (Banerjee and Raju, 2009; Mosse et al., 2002). The context specific nature of migration, its diverse underlying causes and outcomes undoubtedly require more nuanced and disaggregated methods of analysis. In the following sections, we summarize the findings from earlier studies to bring out the key aspects of internal migration in India.

Internal Migration in India: An Overview of Trends and Patterns

Historically, internal migration in India has been low (Davis, 1951), and a declining trend in mobility is noticed till about the 1990s (Kundu and Gupta, 1996). National Sample Survey data for 1992–93 and 1999–2000 suggest an increase in mobility during the last decade (Srivastava and Sasikumar, 2003). It has been argued that a range of factors such as the stranglehold of the caste system, externalities associated with local cultural and social mores, joint family system, lower levels of educational attainment and slow agrarian transformation are responsible for such low levels of mobility (Davis, 1951; Munshi and Rosenzwig, 2009). Even in the post-reform period, contrary to early expectations, migration has not increased drastically. Nevertheless, the recent upsurge in the growth of the Indian economy, development in transport and communication infrastructure, increasing educational standards and associated rise in aspirations has led to higher levels of mobility in recent times (Bhagat, 2010). According to

Table 1.1

Percentage of internal and international migrants based on place of last residence, India, 1971–2001

Census	Total Population	Internal Migrants	Percentage (Internal Migrants)	International Migrants	Percentage (International Migrants)	Percentage of Total Population
1971	548.1	159.6	29.1	8.1	1.4	30.6
1981	659.3	200.5	30.4	6.0	0.9	31.3
1991	814.3	220.7	27.1	5.9	0.7	27.83
2001	991.8	300.9	30.3	5.0	0.5	30.8
	(1028.6)	(309.3)	(30.0)	(5.1)	(0.4)	(30.4)

Sources: Census of India, 1971, series 1, part II, D(i), migration tables; Census of India, 1981, series 1, part V, A and B(i), migration tables (tables D1 and D2); Census of India, 1991, series 1, Part V, D series, migration tables, vol. 2, part 1 (table D2); Census of India, 2001, table D2, compact disk. All censuses published in New Delhi by Ministry of Home Affairs, Registrar General and Census Commissioner, India, in Bhagat, 2010.
Notes: The census was not conducted in Assam in 1981 and in Jammu and Kashmir in 1991. The figures for India from 1981 to 2001 exclude these two states. The figures for the 2001 Census including Assam and Jammu and Kashmir are given in parentheses.

Table 1.2

Size and growth rates of migrant populations by type of movement, India, 1971–2001

Type of Movement	Size 2001 (Millions)	Percentage Distribution (2001)	Growth Rate (Percentage) 1971–81	1981–91	1991–01
Intra-district	193.5	61.6	24.9	8.3	37
Inter-district	74.6	23.7	44.3	13.7	26.3
Interstate	41.1	13.1	28.1	11.7	53.6
International Migrants	5.1	1.6	–9.1	–6.1	–13.4
All migrants	314.3	100	27	9.8	34.7
Total population	1028.6	–	24.7	23.7	21.4

Sources: Same as Table 1.1.
Note: Migrants unclassifiable by type of movement were excluded.

2001 census out of the 1.2 billion people in India 307 million are migrants as per place of birth criteria.

There has been a significant increase in the absolute number of migrants (it has doubled since 1971), but the proportion of internal migrant has continued to be about 30 per cent since 1971, except for the 1991 census, according to which it declined to about 27 per cent of the total population (Table 1.1). The proportion of international migrant constituted only about five per cent of India's population in 2001—a decline of three percentage points from the level of 1971.

Some key features of migration in India are as follows: majority of migrants are intra-district migrants (62 per cent; Table 1.2). Most of the intra-district migrants are females who customarily change their parental households and join their husband's households after marriage (Srivastava and Sasikumar, 2003). Compared with previous decades the growth rate of interstate migrants was very high (54 per cent) during the period 1991–2001, which was also the period of economic reforms, but the magnitude of this growth was not substantial enough to upset the general features of migration in India (Bhagat, 2010). The rural-to-rural stream of migration constituted 68 per cent of all intrastate migrants, compared with 28 per cent in the case of interstate migrants (Table 1.3). Rural-to-urban migration accounted for 15 and 39 per cent of intrastate and interstate migrants, respectively. As far as growth of migrants across different streams is concerned, there has been a significant increase in the interstate

Table 1.3

Size and growth rates of migrant populations by migration stream, India, 1971–2001

Migration Stream	Size 2001 (Millions)	Percentage Distribution	Growth Rate (Percentage)		
			1971–81	1981–91	1991–01
Intrastate					
Rural-to-rural	161	68.6	19.8	10.7	16.8
Rural-to-urban	36.3	15.3	45.1	20.1	16.4
Urban-to-rural	11	4.7	32.9	10.1	−4.3
Urban-to-urban	25.8	11	57.9	5.2	43.1
Interstate					
Rural-to-rural	11	28.2	13.8	9.1	46.6
Rural-to-urban	15.3	39.3	42.5	16.6	76.4
Urban-to-rural	1.9	4.9	15.9	11.4	1.5
Urban-to-urban	10.7	27.4	28.4	15.5	28

Sources: Same as Table 1.1.
Note: Migrants unclassifiable by rural–urban status were excluded.

rural-to-rural and rural-to-urban streams in the post-economic reform decade of 1991–2001, in comparison to earlier decades.

Migration for Economic Reasons

Migration for economic reasons has increased in recent years, both according to the Census and NSS data. As per the Census data, the share of economic migrants in total population increased from 2.4 per cent in 1991 to 2.8 per cent in 2001. The percentage of migrants who migrated for economic reasons in the decade preceding the Census year increased from 1.16 per cent of the population to 1.33 per cent of population.

Similarly, estimates from NSS data show that overall migration rates for an economic reason has remained unchanged at around three during 1993 to 2007–08. However, urban male migration rate has gone up from 12.73 per cent in 1993 to 13.17 per cent in 1999–2000 and to 14.36 per cent in 2007–08. This steady increase has been accompanied by a decline in male economic migration rate in rural areas, keeping the overall male economic migration rate around five.

In 2001, 30.1 per cent migrants for economic reasons were intra-district migrants, 33.3 per cent were inter-district and 36.3 per cent were interstate migrants. In 2001, among male migrants, the share of those migrating to destinations in other states was 38.1 per cent, and there has been an increase over the 1991 figure of 30.6.

The share of economic migrants who went to urban destinations was 68.7 per cent in 2001, up from 65.3 in 1991 and in the case of male economic migrants the figures were 68.1 in 1991 and 72 per cent in 2001. Among the various streams, rural–urban migrants account for as high as 45.4 per cent of the total economic migrants in 2001.

So far as interstate variations are concerned, Srivastava (2011) notes that both gross and net migration rates are strongly and positively correlated with per capita Net State Domestic Product (NSDP). The correlation between the gross out-migration rate and per capita NSDP is also positive but low. Thus, while economic migration is more towards the relatively developed states, out-migration is from the less as well as more developed states.

Several studies have reported that migration rates are positively associated with educational attainment, social group status and per capita consumption (Kundu and Sarangi, 2007; Srivastava, 2011; Srivastava and Bhattacharya, 2003). de Haan and Dubey (2006) report that for 1987–88 and 1999–2000 poverty rates among migrants were much lower than among non-migrants, and the average years of schooling was higher in the case of migrants than in the case of non-migrants. This finding has also been supported by village studies (Connell, 1976). Several studies have documented the lower participation of lower castes in migration (de Haan and Dubey, 2006). However, it is important to note that caste is among the major axis around which migration is segmented (de Haan, 2011).

This is further elaborated by Srivastava (2011) by examining the in-migration and out-migration data from 64th round of NSS. Among out-migrants for economic reasons, the highest quintile accounts for 35 per cent of migrants, while the lowest quintile accounts for 11 per cent. Among the in-migrants for economic reasons, 39.4 per cent are in the highest quintile, while the bottom quintile account for only 7.2 per cent. Further, between 1999–2000 and 2007–08, the share of top quintiles among rural–urban economic migrants increased from 31.2 to 34.5 while that among urban–urban migrants increased from 52.9 to 54.7 per cent. Thus, there is a distinct possibility that high-end mobility has increased during this period (Srivastava, 2011).[5]

While mobility is generally associated with better employment outcomes, an analysis of the employment status of migrants before and after migration does not necessarily reflect this: Srivastava (2011, p. 419) finds 'different prospects for different types of migration across different streams with comparatively better prospects for urban migrants'. The main general outcome is a decline in unemployment rates and the percentage of 'out of labour force' migrants. However, the evidence does not provide an indication of economic mobility of migrants over the years.

The evidence on the characteristics of migrants further establishes the fragmented nature of the migrant labour market in India. It was found that an out-migrant for economic reason is more likely to be from urban areas, in the higher quintiles, from the younger age group (15–34), much less likely to be female, most likely to be in a salaried household than a cultivator household followed by self-employed in non-agriculture or casual labour, more likely to be a Muslim or a Christian, most likely to be an OBC and least likely to be an ST, more likely to be in a low-income state or a high income state as compared to a middle income state (See Srivastava, 2011 for detailed results).

Similarly, an economic in-migrant is more likely to be from rural areas but more likely to end up in an urban area, much less likely to be from lower quintiles as compared to the highest quintile, most likely to be in a salaried household than a casual labour household followed by self-employed in non-agriculture, more likely to originate in agriculture and end up in non-agriculture, most likely to be in a low-income state and less likely to be in high income state, as compared to the reference category of medium-income states (Srivastava, 2011).

However, the picture alters completely when short-duration migrants are considered. A short duration out-migrant is less likely to be from urban areas, more likely to be from the lower quintiles, most likely to be in a casual labour household as compared to a self-employed household, more likely to be an ST as compared to an OBC, more likely to be from a low-income state as compared to a middle income state (Srivastava, 2011). Similar results have also been reported by Keshri and Bhagat (2010, 2012) and Mishra and Bose (2013).

Post-reform India has opened up new economic opportunities for certain sections of the population, at the same time; it has also created barriers to entry for some others. Migration is at the centre of this process of reallocation of labour across space as well as across sectors.

Internal Migration in Contemporary India: The Book

The chapters in this book address some of the key issues concerning the migration process in contemporary India. It is not attempted here to provide a comprehensive overview of migration trends and patterns in India, which is available from various other sources, but to selectively examine the contemporary dynamics of migration.

Bhagat in Chapter 2 presents the changes in internal migration in India, on the basis of data from the population census and the NSS. There has not been much change in the share of migrants in the total population. Rural-to-rural stream dominates the migration pattern. The relative insignificance of interstate migration has been linked to the ideology of nativisim in different parts of India. The high transaction costs of living and earning a livelihood in a different state, often with a very different language and culture, act as a deterrent for prospective migrants. Moreover, a few states, such as Delhi, Goa, Maharashtra, Haryana, Punjab, Gujarat and Karnataka account for a majority of interstate migrants. Rising regional chauvinism and hostility towards migrants, Bhagat argues, has slowed down internal migration in India. To the extent that mobility brings in flexibility in the labour market and out-migration results in a net inflow of remittances to the areas of origin, this lack of mobility is associated with a welfare loss as well. The relationship between poverty and migration is complex. While short-duration and seasonal migration are clearly poverty-driven, the same cannot be said about long-duration, permanent or semi-permanent migration. At the state-level, there is a weak relationship between poverty and migration. Similarly, migration rates are at relatively high in the highest monthly per capita expenditure (MPCE) classes and the relatively better-educated groups. The poor, and particularly those at the bottom of the socio-economic ladder, do not have the threshold level of capital, both physical and human, risk-taking ability as well as access to institutions, information and networks to migrate out of rural areas. On the other hand, the exclusionary nature of urban growth tends to discourage migrants to come to large cities, in particular. The contribution of migration to urbanization, Bhagat argues has been rather limited.

There are various sources and types of exclusion, but two distinct processes could be singled out for analysis. The neo-liberal restructuring of the urban space, as a process, as a framework and as a shared ideology, puts in practice a set of policies, programmes and priorities that discriminates against the poor and the underprivileged (Banerjee-Guha, 2009; Gooptu, 2009). The privileging of corporate interests in land-use, privatization of public utilities, creation of modern day enclosures and disenfranchisement of sections of population go hand in hand with selective withdrawal of the state from crucial public utilities and support systems. As costs of basic needs such as housing, education, health and transport increases, it becomes difficult for the poor to survive in the urban areas. The spatial reorganization of the urban centres through programmes for city beautification, slum demolition and 'development' and reallocation of certain activities to the fringe areas create further barriers for the poor to live and work in the urban spaces. The other notable feature of the recent phase of growth is the continuing significance of the urban informal sector. Contrary to expectations that globalization and the consequent restructuring of the economy would lead to an expansion of the formal economy at the expense of the informal economy, it has been found that the informal economy and the social regulation that underpins its growth has found newer ways of integration with the formal sector, during a period of relatively faster growth. India's economic growth story remains incomplete without that of the informal economy that remains a source of cheap labour, whose services are crucial for keeping the costs low, even in the sectors that are globally integrated. Not only that the informal sector is not showing any signs of being replaced by the formal sector, rather there are clear signs that the formal sector—both public and private—itself is being informalized in significant ways (NCEUS, 2006). A fallout of this, from the perspective of the migrant workers, is the shrinking space for any access to social security provisions, in the backdrop of privatization of public utilities. While such access to insecure informal 'jobs' in the globally integrated spaces, such as in shopping malls, call centres and IT firms and so on, has opened up the scope for the migrants to 'dream big', this has also led to increased insecurity and vulnerability for many of them (Harriss-White, Olsen, Vera-Sanso and Suresh, 2013).

The other source of exclusion and adverse inclusion of migrants is the categorization of the migrants as the 'others' by the host population. Identity-based discrimination, however, has many deeper and structural dimensions. The rising tides of intolerance that has created a particular kind of chauvinist, nativist politics, has been widely commented upon; but the experiences of migrants belonging to different categories are far from uniform and also the diverse range of experiences cannot possibly be reduced to the binaries of exclusion or inclusion. Many authors have linked these discriminatory attitudes, practices and movements both to the long-existing biases and antipathies as well as to the increasingly fierce competition for resources, jobs and living spaces under neo-liberal economic growth. Three chapters in this volume pay close attention to these varied experiences of migrants in the cities, in a context where identities remain a key axis in the interactions between migrants and non-migrants. Firstly, Thapan, Singh and Sreekumar in Chapter 3 explore the multiple and complex interactions among identities based on gender, religion and location through the experiences of Muslim women in Delhi. By 'linking mobility and migration to the idea of agency on the part of the migrant women', they bring out the layered experiences of women through their 'difficulties, problems and dilemmas of being a migrant women in a metropolis'. Among the key insights that they bring out from their primary research is the feeling of freedom that the respondent feel when they escape the violence experienced within the domestic sphere as well as outside, such as during the communal riots in Bhagalpur, Bihar. While they negotiate to live, study, earn and even acquire property, they negotiate with the urban social landscape, on a day to day basis—an experience that is shaped by their multiple identities based on gender, class, region, religion and language. Contesting the pervasive generalizations based on the 'victimhood' of women in general and Muslim women in particular, the authors put forth the need to develop a nuanced understanding of women agency, not just as an academic tool but also to design relevant social policy.

In the subsequent chapter, Remesh (Chapter 4) examines the case of migrants from the North East, who, individually and collectively, have been subjected to various forms of racial violence in Delhi and in other parts of India. The distinctive nature of migration from the North East has been well captured through the primary survey. In the backdrop of higher literacy levels, insecurities and vulnerabilities due to insurgency and political violence and high levels of youth unemployment in the North East, a large number of youth migrants have started to migrate out in search of education and employment. Notwithstanding the fact that most of the migrants from the region are better educated, financially well-off and have better skills than migrants from some other parts of the country, their distinct looks and 'culture', as perceived by the host population, make them vulnerable. The othering of the migrants from the region and stereotyping them in particular ways has a firm economic basis—they often have to pay higher rents and advances for accommodation, higher prices for many goods and services and are treated in less favourable terms in various transactions, including bribes. Notwithstanding the efforts to learn Hindi and local culture, the discriminatory attitudes persist. The discriminatory attitudes pervade the workplace as well, often resulting in sexual harassment of migrants.

In her ethnographic study of Ladakhi youth who have migrated for educational purposes, Williams-Oerberg in Chapter 6 brings in the complexities associated with educational migration of the youth. On the one hand, access to education opens up new opportunities, but the fact that there is hardly any option for obtaining higher education in Ladakh, and the experience of being seen as an 'outsider' within and outside the academic space creates certain degree of anxieties among the students. Easily confused with migrants from the North East, Ladakhi youth migrants also face certain problems, bottlenecks and discriminatory attitudes, when they move out to distant cities. These experiences, she argues, make migration for education a 'contradictory resource'.

The migration experience of people is not just to be contexualized in relation to their life and livelihoods at the destinations, the conditions at origins also shapes the trajectories of mobility. Several chapters in this volume, point to the analytical limitations of categorizing the determinants of migration decisions as push or pull factors. What makes some of the pull factors attractive enough at particular points of time and in particular contexts, for example, is the changing fall-back position of households. Although at what spatial scale do the drivers of migration operate in the areas of origin is largely an empirical question, there is a need to focus on migration patterns in specific regional settings. Five chapters in this volume focus on migration in four different regional contexts: the North East (Chapter 5), Andhra Pradesh (Chapter 7), Bihar (Chapter 8), Punjab (Chapter 9), and Odisha (Chapter 10), although there is a lot of variation in the focus of these specific studies.

Rajan and Chyrmang (Chapter 5), after discussing the broad contours of economic development in the North East, present the key aspects of migration in the region, drawing upon an analysis of both secondary and primary data. The uneven regional development, particularly in the post-reforms phase has widened the gap between the North East and the rest of the economy, and the underdevelopment as well as low employment-generating potential of the regional economy that creates the context of in-migration as well as out-migration in the region. The public sector provides more jobs in the organized sector than the private sector, although 'job creation did not improve much during 1981–2011 for both the sectors'. Analysis of migration rates across MPCE classes, on the basis of NSS data, suggests that out-migrants from the North East belong to relatively better off sections, although anecdotal evidence suggest a relatively recent surge of out-migration from amongst the low-income, less educated strata as well. The findings of the primary survey by the authors reveal the significance of remittances in meeting consumption requirement. Another aspect of mobility in the region that is not captured well by large-scale surveys and official statistics is the phenomenon of temporary involuntary migration for a variety of reasons, including ethnic conflicts, natural calamities, such as floods and also reduced access to natural resources.

While the diversity of different streams of migration has been well recognized in the literature, Vijay (Chapter 7), on the basis of primary research in Andhra Pradesh, brings out the diverse motivations and implications of migration across different agrarian classes. Distinguishing between migration by labour-supplying (who migrate out to sell their labour-time) and land-owning households (households with agrarian surplus and non-cultivating households), he argues that the migration of one class often impedes or facilitates the occupational mobility of another, a feature that is under-investigated in the migration literature. The agrarian origins of rural-to-rural and rural-to-urban migrants are important not only to understand the implications of migration for rural transformation as such but also for the outcomes labour relations at destinations and also for migrant households. Differential asset holding positions, debt burdens and distribution of labour-time across various activities and occupations often have significance for the bargaining strength and risk-taking ability of migrant labour households and the way the migrant labour market functions.

Based on a long-term research on socio-economic development in rural Bihar, Dutta (Chapter 8) presents the significant contribution of remittances as livelihoods in rural Bihar. The study brings out the heterogeneity in migration experiences of different classes of migrants and notes the significance of migration as a driver of rural development and reduction of poverty. However, Dutta also points out the vulnerabilities of the migrant population and argues in favour of proactive interventions by the state to ensure the rights and dignity of the migrant population. Singh (Chapter 9) presents a broad overview of migration in Punjab, both as a key driver as well as an outcome of the development process in one of the most prosperous states of India. On the one hand, out-migration from Punjab to other parts of India as well as to other countries has helped in the rapid transformation of the state's economy. Remittances have played a significant source of productive investment in agriculture as well as in the non-farm economy and have also helped to expand the market for consumption goods. In-migration of labour, from the relatively backward areas of India, particularly to the agricultural economy, on the other hand, has resulted in significant changes within and beyond the rural economy of the State. While this migration of agricultural labour from states, like Bihar and Uttar Pradesh, is often credited for diffusion of agricultural technology and farming practices in the relatively backward regions of origin, Mishra (Chapter 10) presents a case study of seasonal migration from interior Odisha, where such benefits seem to be rather limited. While some streams of migration do offer a scope for better earning opportunities and an escape route from poverty, particularly over time, in the case of the dominant type of seasonal migration, (that is, to brick kilns in Odisha, Andhra Pradesh and elsewhere), no such discernible trend is visible. The study brings out the precariousness of seasonal migration as a livelihood, and argues that policies aiming at strengthening the livelihood base at origin areas, through interventions in labour market, agricultural input and output market, and ensuring access to formal credit, pubic distribution system and better delivery of welfare schemes, goes a long way in eliminating some forms of distress migration.

These case studies on migration bring out some of the challenges for state intervention and policy making in the context of a developing economy, like India. While all available indications suggest that migration and remittances are going to play an increasingly significant role in many parts of India, it is also amply clear that migration patterns and outcomes are hugely diverse for different segments of the economy. Economic prosperity, emergence of certain key centres of growth, increasing skill specificity and skill intensity in a number of different sectors and industries and better transport and communication facilities have definitely facilitated the migration of many middle class individuals, including women and persons belonging to Dalit, tribal and other marginalized groups. Unevenness in levels of development across the country has given a further boost to such economic migration. However, at the same time there are a set of factors that operate in the origin areas that cause distress migration, and a large segment of migrant workers work as a reservoir of cheap labour in the informal economy. The urgent need for developing a comprehensive framework for policy intervention to address the problems of the disadvantaged migrant workers can hardly be overstressed. Borhade (Chapter 11) presents a comprehensive summary of the existing policy frameworks and the various implementation issues concerning the protection of the basic rights of the migrant workers. With detailed case studies of specific policy interventions in diverse contexts, she has presented a nuanced framework for state interventions, within the federal structure that remains a key aspect of policy making in India. The rich details of the lessons from interventions at the international, national and state levels, with significant cooperation between state and non-state agencies, brings out the need for a comprehensive national migration policy, an endeavour that must harmonize the overall objectives of inclusive growth and protection of human and labour rights of the migrant workers.

Since exploitative migration contracts are ultimately linked to the limited livelihoods opportunities of the migrant workers, such policies necessarily should address the question of development and livelihoods in relatively backward regions and sections.

Summing Up and Policy Concerns

While migration is undertaken both by the rich and the poor, in recent years, particularly in the urban labour market, there is a greater mobility of the urban, educated and better-off sections. The picture, however, changes dramatically as we consider short duration migrants. Thus, there is an urgent need to move away from discussions on general trends in migration to context-specific, segmented streams of migration. de Haan (2011) observes: While macro-level data suggests that 'migration is selective with opportunities biased against the poorer', a process that might be reinforced with technological change', 'micro-studies often show very high rates of migration amongst poorest and socially marginalised groups, and over-representation of migrants... amongst the bottom layer of the working class'. Resolving this gap in the understanding between micro- and macro- studies is a key research challenge.

With economic growth migration is expected to increase, but given the historically low levels of migration in India, there is a need to examine the ways urban labour markets are being structured. Concerns have already been expressed regarding 'exclusionary urban growth' that has created barriers—economic and non-economic—for migrants to enter into megacities (Kundu and Saraswati, 2012). The way cities are being organized as gated communities, the securitization of key aspects of urban life, shrinking access of common people to urban spaces and private provisioning of amenities, the rising costs of urban transport, beautification programmes that target slum dwellers are all manifestations of the neo-liberal restructuring of urban space. It is interesting to note that these very processes of restructuring and creation of global cities have brought in migrant workers from even the remotest and poorest regions of India, but the labour relations are structured in a way that migrant workers remain a floating, mobile labour force. They act as part of a reserve army of labour that depresses wages in the informal labour market, but they are not expected to be a part of the cities.

The politics of identity and cultural anxieties that have resulted in conflicts between host and migrant population in cities, like Mumbai also, acts as a barrier for migrants. There are new studies that confirm that caste, religious and racial prejudices are very much prevalent in urban labour and housing markets. Migrants from the North East and Ladakh have been victims of racial stereotyping and violence. Above all, the rising trend in violence against women not only creates insecurities for women, but it also restricts their freedom of mobility and employment. Migrant women, particularly those belonging to the poorer section, have become easy targets of such violence.

As more and more people are likely to look for and find jobs outside their home states, there is a need for the creation of a basic framework for minimum economic citizenship rights which are universally applicable. Such a set of rights—such as the right to seek employment and settle anywhere—already exists in our constitutional framework. The need of the hour is to reaffirm these commitments through effective implementation of constitutionally guaranteed universal economic rights and expansion of their scope to take care of migrants' rights.

The cornerstone of migrants' rights would be the institutional structures, which are being created to provide social security to the informal sector workers. Although the reports of the National Commission for Enterprises in the Unorganized Sector (NCEUS) have very clearly laid down the basis of such entitlements, there has been very little progress in terms of creating a social security mechanism for informal sector workers. However, unless the provisioning of such social security measures are made universally applicable, delinked from the domicile status of the workers and the possibility of worker's mobility is factored into the design of delivery mechanisms, there is a strong possibility that migrant workers would not be able to access these services.

The rights of the migrant workers are not only based on state action; but experience also shows that civil society actions have been often crucial in safeguarding their rights and saving them from some of the worst forms of exploitation. The need for unionization of the migrant workers can hardly be overstressed. However, it is extremely important to have collective bargaining mechanisms for migrant workers, particularly in sectors, like construction and domestic work.

Notes

1. Akram-Lodhi and Kay (2010b) have emphasised the continued relevance of the agrarian question in the following words:

   The renewed relevance of the agrarian question is witnessed in postsocialist repeasantisation through decollectivisation; semi-proletarianisation and fragmentation without full proletarianisation as livelihood strategies reconfigure; the remarkable stability in the absolute number of peasant farmers over the last 40 years; the continued importance of smallholder food production to rural livelihoods in much of the South; the deepening of the market imperative and the law of value across the world capitalist economy under neoliberal globalisation, with implications for capitalist agriculture and petty commodity producing peasant farming; the expanded commodification of natural resources, including land, labour power and genetic resources; the strong spatial specificities to these processes, as cross-border mega regions transcend the state in driving substantial shares of global capital accumulation; and the global resurgence, in response, of peasant movements in Chiapas, Brazil, India, China, and Indonesia, amongst others, as well as, of course, the critical, pivotal transnational response of La Via Campesina (Borras, Kay, and Lahiff, 2008)'.

2. There are two agrarian questions raised in the contemporary literature on capitalist transformation and agricultural development: the first, classical question 'concerns the capitalist transformation of agriculture and its many trajectories and distributional consequences', while the second concerns 'the economic roles that agriculture must play to service the development of the rest of the economy', during the very process of the first agrarian transition (Harriss-White, 2008).

3. Kar and Saktivel (2007, p. 27) have linked the rising regional disparity and the reform process in the following way: 'Firstly, in the pre-reform period, the public sector had played a crucial role in maintaining regional equality in the Indian economy by directing resources to backward areas. With a change in the focus of the public sector following the reforms, this process has become weaker. Secondly, the reforms gave greater freedom and impetus to the private sector and export-oriented production. These sectors, which were attempting to reduce costs and become competitive, were attracted to the areas that were relatively more developed. As a result, investment and activity shifted to these areas, strengthening the forces of divergence'. The reasons behind such widening inter-regional difference, which have been noted in the literature include infrastructure/infrastructural investment (Ghosh and De, 1998; Majumdar, 2005; Nagraj et al., 2000), foreign direct investment (Bajpai, Nirupam, and Jeffrey, 1996; Nunnenkamp and Stracke, 2008), skewed distribution of public expenditure (Rao et al., 1999), deliberate industrial policy at the state-level, differential domestic private investment, human capital (Ghosh, 2008), prior agricultural growth (Das and Baruah, 1996; Shand and Bhide, 2000) and governance. For a more elaborate discussion on this see Mishra (2015).

4. The emergence of Noida and Gurgaon as new industrial hubs, for example, has attracted migrants in large numbers. The decline of manufacturing in several Indian cities and towns such as Ahmedabad, Jalandhar, Kanpur, and so on has forced labour to migrate to other towns or find new occupations.

5. These figures do not take into account circular migrants.

References

Ahluwalia, M.S. (2000). 'Economic performance of states in the post-reform period'. *Economic and Political Weekly, 35*(19), 1637–48.

Akram-Lodhi, A.H. (1998). 'The agrarian question: Past and present'. *Journal of Peasant Studies, 25*(4), 134–49.

Akram-Lodhi, A.H., and Kay, C. (2010a). 'Surveying the agrarian question (Part 1): Unearthing foundations, exploring diversity'. *Journal of Peasant Studies, 37*(1), 177–202.

———. (2010b). 'Surveying the agrarian question (Part 2): Current debates and beyond'. *Journal of Peasant Studies, 37*(2), 255–84.

Baddeley, M., McNay, K., and Cassen, R. (2006). 'Divergence in India: Income differential at state level'. *Journal of Development Studies, 42*(6), 1000–22.

Bajpai, N. and Sachs, J.D. (1996). 'Trends in inter-state inequalities of income in India'. Development Discussion Paper No. 528. Harvard University, Cambridge, USA.

Banerjee-Guha, S. (2009). 'Neoliberalising the "urban": New geographies of power and injustice in Indian cities'. *Economic and Political Weekly, 44*(22), 95–107.

Banerjee, A. and Raju, S. (2009). 'Gendered mobility: Women migrants and work in urban India'. *Economic and Political Weekly, 44*(11), 115–23.

Bernstein, H. (1996). 'Agrarian questions then and now'. *Journal of Peasant Studies, 24*(1), 22–59.

———· (2004). 'Changing before our very eyes, agrarian questions and the politics of land in capitalism today'. *Journal of Agrarian Change, 4*(1–2), 190–225.

———· (2006). 'Is there an agrarian question in the 21st century?' *Canadian Journal of Development Studies, 27*(4), 449–60.

———. (2010). *Class dynamics of agrarian change.* Halifax: Fernwood Publishing.

Bhagat, R.B. (2010). 'Internal migration in India: Are the underprivileged class migrating more?' *Asia-Pacific Population Journal, 25*(1), 27–45.

Bhattacharya, B.B. and Sakthivel, S. (2004). 'Regional growth and disparity in India'. *Economic and Political Weekly, 39*(10), 1071–77.

Borras, S.M., Jr., Kay, C., and Lahiff, E. (eds.). (2008). *Market-led agrarian reform: Critical perspectives on neoliberal land policies and the rural poor.* London: Routledge.

Breman, J. (2007). *Labour bondage in West India: From past to present.* New Delhi: Oxford University Press.

Byres, T.J. (1991). 'The Agrarian Question'. In T. Bottomore, L. Harris, V.G. Kiernan and R. Miliband (eds.), *A Dictionary of Marxist Thought* (pp. 9–12). Oxford: Basil Blackwell.

Byres, T.J. (1996). *Capitalism from above and capitalism from below: An essay in comparative political economy.* London: Macmillan Press.

Connell, B.D. (1976). *Migration from rural areas: The evidence from village studies.* Delhi: Oxford University Press.

Das, S.K. and Baruah, A. (1996). 'Regional inequalities, economic growth and liberalisation: A study of the Indian economy'. *Journal of Development Studies, 32*(3), 364–90.

Dasgupta, D., Maiti, P., Mukherjee, R., Sarkar S., and Chakrabarti, S. (2000). 'Growth and interstate disparities in India'. *Economic and Political Weekly, 35*(27), 2413–22.

Davis, K. (1951). *Population of India and Pakistan.* New Jersey: Princeton University Press.

de Haan, A. (2011). 'Inclusive growth: Labour migration and poverty in India'. Retrieved from repub.eur.nl/pub/22201/wp513.pdf

de Haan, A. and Dubey, A. (2006). 'Are migrants worse off or better off? Asking the right questions'. *Margin—Journal of Applied Economic Research, 38*(3), 9–26.

Deshingkar, P. and Start, D. (2003). *Seasonal migration for livelihoods in India: Coping, accumulation and exclusion*. Working Paper No. 220. London: Overseas Development Institute.

Ghosh, M. (2008). 'Economic reforms, growth and regional divergence in India'. *Margin—The Journal of Applied Economic Research*, 2(3), 265–85.

Ghosh, B. and De, P. (1998). 'Role of infrastructure in regional development'. *Economic and Political Weekly*, 33(47–8), 3039–48.

Gooptu, N. (2009). 'Neoliberal subjectivity, enterprise culture and new workplaces: Organised retail and shopping malls in India'. *Economic and Political Weekly*, 44(22), 45–54.

Harriss-White, B. (2008). 'Introduction: India's rainfed agricultural dystopia'. *The European Journal of Development Research*, 20(4), 549–61.

Harriss-White, B., Mishra, D.K., and Upadhyay, V. (2009). 'Institutional diversity and capitalist transition: The political economy of agrarian change in Arunachal Pradesh, India'. *Journal of Agrarian Change*, 9(4), 512–47.

Harriss-White, B., Olsen, W., Vera-Sanso, P., and Suresh, V. (2013). 'Multiple shocks and slum household economies in South India'. *Economy and Society*, 42(3), 398–429.

Kar, S. and Sakthivel, S. (2007). 'Reforms and regional inequality in India'. *Economic and Political Weekly*, 42(47), 69–77.

Kautsky, Karl (1899/1988). *The Agrarian Question*, Vol. I. London: Zwan Publications (originally published in 1899 in German).

Keshri, K. and Bhagat, R.B. (2010). 'Temporary and seasonal migration in India'. *Genus*, LXVI(3), 25–45.

———. (2012). 'Temporary and seasonal migration in India: Regional pattern, characteristics and associated factors'. *Economic and Political Weekly, Vol. XLVII*(4), 81–88.

Kundu, A. and Sarangi, N. (2007). 'Migration, employment status and poverty: An analysis across urban centres'. *Economic and Political Weekly* 42(4), 299–306.

Kundu, A. and Saraswati, L.R. (2012). 'Migration and exclusionary urbanisation in India'. *Economic and Political Weekly*, 47(26–27), 219–27.

Kundu, A. and Gupta, S. (1996). 'Migration, urbanisation and regional inequality'. *Economic and Political Weekly*, 31(52), 3391–98.

Lerche, J. (2010). 'From "rural labour" to "classes of labour": Class fragmentation, caste and class struggle at the bottom of the Indian labour hierarchy'. In Barbara Harriss-White and Judith Heyer (eds), *The comparative political economy of development: Africa and South Asia* (pp. 64–85). London: Routledge.

———. (2011). 'Agrarian crisis and agrarian questions in India'. *Journal of Agrarian Change*, 11(1), 104–18.

———. (2013). 'The agrarian question in neoliberal India: Agrarian transition bypassed?' *Journal of Agrarian Change*, 13(3), 382–404.

Majumdar, R. (2005). 'Infrastructure and regional development: Interlinkages in India'. *Indian Economic Review*, 40(2), 167–84.

Mishra, Deepak K. (2008). 'Structural inequalities and interlinked transactions in agrarian markets: Results of a field survey'. In S.K. Bhaumik (ed.), *Reforming Indian agriculture towards employment generation and poverty reduction* (pp. 231–68). New Delhi: SAGE Publications.

———. (2014). 'Agrarian relations and institutional diversity in Arunachal Pradesh'. In Barbara Harriss-White and Judith Heyer (eds.), *Indian capitalism in development* (pp. 66–83). London and New York: Routledge.

———. (2015). 'Regions and capitalist transition in India: Arunachal Pradesh in a comparative perspective'. In Elisabetta Basile, Barbara Harriss-White and Christine

Lutringer (eds), *Mapping India's capitalism: Old and new regions* (pp. 87–112). London: Palgrave Macmillan.

Mishra, D.K. and Bose, D. (2013). *Seasonal migration from rural India: Emerging patterns and characteristics*. New Delhi: CSRD, JNU.

Mosse, D., Gupta, S., Mehta, M., Shah, V., Rees, J., and The KRIBP Project Team (2002). 'Brokered livelihoods: Debt, labour migration and development in tribal western India'. *Journal of Development Studies*, 38(5), 59–87.

Munshi, K. and Rosenzweig, M. (2009). 'Why is mobility in India so low? Social insurance, inequality and growth'. Retrieved from http://www.econ.brown.edu/fac/Kaivan_ Munshi/rural17.pdf (accessed on 28 January 2016).

Nagaraj, R., Varoudakis, A., and Veganzones, M.A. (1998). *Long-run growth trends and convergence across Indian states* (Technical Paper No. 131). OECD Development Centre. Retrieved from http://www.oecd.org/dev/1922509.pdf (accessed on 28 January 2016).

NCEUS (2006). *Social security for unorganised workers*. New Delhi: National Commission for Enterprises in the Unorganised Sector, Government of India.

Nunnenkamp, P. and Stracke, R. (2008). 'Foreign direct investment in post-reform India: Likely to work wonders for regional development?' *Journal of Economic Development*, 33(2), 55–84.

Palmer-Jones, R.W. and Sen, K. (2003). 'What has luck got to do with it? A regional analysis of poverty and agricultural growth in rural India'. *Journal of Development Studies*, 40(1), 1–31.

Rao, M.G., Shand, R.T., and Kalirajan, K.P. (1999). 'Convergence of incomes across Indian states: A divergent view'. *Economic and Political Weekly*, 34(13), 769–78.

Shand, R. and Bhide, S. (2000). 'Sources of economic growth—Regional dimensions of reforms'. *Economic and Political Weekly*, 34(42), 3747–57.

Shetty, S.L. (2003). 'Growth of SDP and structural change in state economics: Interstate comparisons'. *Economic and Political Weekly*, 38(49), 5189–5200.

Srivastava, R. and Bhattacharya, S. (2003). 'Globalisation, reforms and internal labour mobility: An analysis of recent Indian trends, labour and development'. *Labour and Development*, 9(2), 31–55.

Srivastava, R. and Sasikumar, S.K. (2003). *An overview of migration in India, its impacts and key issues*. Paper presented at Regional Conference on Migration, Development and Pro-poor Policy Choices in Asia, Dhaka. Retrieved from http://www.eldis.org/ assets/Docs/upload/1/document/0903/Dhaka.CP_2.pdf (accessed on 3 October 2009).

Srivastava, R.S. (2011). 'Labour migration in India: Recent trends, patterns and policy issues'. *Indian Journal of Labour Economics*, 54(33), 411–40.

———. (2012). 'Internal migration in India: An overview of its features, trends and policy challenges'. In UNESCO and UNICEF (2013) *Workshop Compendium Vol 2: Workshop Papers,* National Workshop on Internal Migration and Human Development in India, 6–7 December 2011 (ICSSR), New Delhi, India. Retrieved from http://www.unesco. org/new/fileadmin/MULTIMEDIA/FIELD/New_Delhi/pdf/Internal_Migration_ Workshop_-_Vol_2_07.pdf (accessed on 23 January 2016).

Vijay, R. (2012). 'Structural retrogression and rise of "new landlords" in Indian agriculture: An empirical exercise'. *Economic and Political Weekly*, 48(5), 37–45.

2

Nature of Migration and Its Contribution to India's Urbanization

R.B. Bhagat

Introduction

Demographically speaking, migration is one of the three basic components of population growth of any area along with fertility and mortality. Whereas both fertility and mortality operate within the biological framework, migration does not. It influences the size, composition and distribution of population and also the social, political and economic life of the people. Indian Constitution under Article 19 provides basic freedom to move to any part of the country, right to reside and earn livelihood of their choice. A number of economic, social, cultural and political factors play an important role in the decision to move. The effects of these factors vary over time and place. Analysis of migration pattern is important to understand the changes taking place in the people's movement within the country. It is the most volatile component of population growth and most sensitive to economic, political and cultural factors. Proper understanding of the patterns of migration would help in understanding not only the nature of population redistribution, but also regional inequality, labour market and the process of urbanization, modernization and development.

Migration from rural to urban areas has historically played a key role in the rapid growth of cities, and along with the reclassification of rural localities into urban centres, it continues to be an important component of city growth. At the global level as a whole, migration along with rural–urban classification is not the overriding contributor of urbanization. On the other hand, in many countries, natural increase (the difference of births minus deaths) accounts for a larger share in urban population growth (United Nations, 2011, p. 1). Further, there are significant variations in the urbanization levels across the world regions. Seventy-eight per cent of the people of the more developed regions lived in urban areas in 2011 compared to just 47 per cent in the less developed regions (United Nations, 2012).

The urban population in India, which was 62 million in 1951, increased to 377 million in 2011. While the urban population increased by six times during 1951 to 2011, the level of urbanization hardly doubled from 17 per cent in 1951 to 31 per cent in 2011. In terms of annual growth the average was 2.32 per cent during 1951–61 which accelerated up to 3.79 per cent during 1971–81, that is the highest urban growth since independence. After that it consistently decelerated 2.75 per cent per annum during 1991–2001. However, the declining growth rate was slightly reversed during 2001–11 as the urban population grew at the rate of 2.76 per cent per annum during 2001–11. The level of urbanization in the country as a whole increased from 27.7 per cent in 2001 to 31.1 per cent in 2011.

If compared with the historical urban population growth rates of advanced countries in Western Europe and Japan, about 3 per cent urban growth that India has experienced during 2001–11 could be considered as a rapid urbanization[1] (Kojima, 1996, p. 356). Sometimes scholars attribute this rapid urban growth to the distress migration from the rural areas as a result of the agrarian crisis (Sainath, 2011). An understanding of the changing pattern of migration and the demographic decomposition of the urban growth to its various components will throw light on the migration and urbanization linkages in a scientific manner. Thus, to what extent this rapid urban growth in India has been contributed by migration is a matter of interest to all those who are interested in understanding India's urbanization over the decades.

Although migration data from 2011 Census is not yet available, the National Sample Survey Organization (NSSO) 64th round provides enough data pertaining to year 2007–08 which also coincides with the mid-year of the census decade 2001–11. This chapter attempts to throws light on the historical nature of migration in India and analyzes the various streams of migration, namely rural to urban, urban to rural, rural to rural and urban to urban. Migration to the cities is also studied with available data. This study attempts to study the entire components of urban growth more specifically, in order to understand the contribution of rural to urban migration in India's urbanization.

Migration in India: A Historical Perspective

Historically looking, migration is closely associated with evolution of culture, social organization, colonization of new areas and search for food, pilgrimage, trade and invasion. In more recent times, migration played an important role in the process of industrialization and urbanization.

India has a long history of migration into the subcontinent since the time immemorial. J.H. Hutton, the Census Commissioner of 1931 Census of British India writes:

> [I]f there is one fact which impresses upon us strongly in connection with the migration history of India, it is this that all the great racial movements into India from the dawn of history up to the modern 18th century have been from the regions of the west and north-west of the Indian peninsula and they have been into India and not out of India. (Hutton, 1986, p. 610)

In pre-colonial times, the reasons of circulation of human population were mainly for religious and trade purposes. Sometimes, the spread of religions was a by-product of the circulation of ancient traders. This was true for all major religions of the world, from Buddhism to Islam, which were initially propagated along the trade routes, partly by merchants and partly by itinerant holy men (McNeill, 1984, p. 9). Migration on account of the movement of military was also important. People also moved in search of pastures with cattle. Nomadic migration, although short distance, was an important feature in the regions outside the Gangetic valley. This practice is still found in parts of Rajasthan and Madhya Pradesh located in central India. The Census Commissioner of 1931 Census, J.H. Hutton, gives a very long historical account of migration of various castes and tribes in Central India. According to him:

> In the early times climatic changes, desiccation of certain regions setting in motion movements of nomads, pressure of population, disturbed political conditions, conquest and colonization have all played their part in varying degrees. In more recent times, famines, religious persecution and colonization have influenced migration. Generally, all movements are primarily due to food. (Hutton, 1986, p. 61)

It is not true that urbanization is a feature of modern industrial civilization alone. In ancient India, there were many great urban centres. For example, around 300 BC, it is estimated that *Patliputra* (present Patna) had 270 thousand people, Mathura had 60 thousand, 48 thousand people lived in Vidisha, 40 thousand each in Vaishali and Kaushambi and 38 thousand lived in Ujjain (Sharma, 2005). Such a large concentration of population was not possible without rural to urban migration.

India at the death of Akbar had a population of 100 million and Agra was perhaps one of the largest cities in the world. The movement of population was for various purposes, more importantly for military and trade purposes. The Mughul emperors used to set out with an army and camp in several places during their military expeditions. It is mentioned that it was a tremendous affair and the camp sometimes was spread over a circumference of 30 miles and with a population of half a million. This not only included the soldiers but also a vast number of other people who were manning the hundreds of bazaars (market). Such military expeditions themselves were forming temporary cities which were constantly on the march (Nehru, 1965, p. 325).

When the British came to India the old feudal order was breaking up. The fall of the Mughul Empire produced political chaos and disorder in many parts of India. But even so, India in the eighteenth century was a great manufacturing as well as a great agricultural country, and Indian handloom supplied the markets of Asia and Europe (Nehru, 1965, p. 43). But in the face of machine based garments produced in the mills of Lancashire and Manchester in Britain, the Indian fabric (both silk and cotton) and allied industry (carding, dying and printing) could not survive. The British also imposed transit duties (octroi) in the internal movement of goods within India. This further crippled the Indian hand-based industries. A vast number of Indian weavers and artisans became jobless and unemployed. India experienced a massive deindustrialization between the periods 1757 to 1857 when East India Company of Britain ruled the country. Most of the weavers and artisans lived in town and cities. As consequences of deindustrialization, a large number of people of the artisan class and their dependent families migrated to the country side. Thus, India during the second half of eighteenth century to the first half of nineteenth century has experienced urban to rural migration unlike many European countries experiencing massive rural to urban migration during the same time. As a result, cities and towns declined and languished and people became more dependent on agriculture (Nehru, 1965, p. 433). The economic hardship or economic disturbances were other important reasons of movement of people in the late eighteenth and early nineteenth century. In eastern Uttar Pradesh and also in Hissar in Haryana widespread depopulation occurred, probably in the period 1762–70. High revenue rates and climatic disturbances combined to stimulate out-migration mostly into neighbouring Nepal or Champaran in Bihar. Thus, in the face of military and economic disturbances, communities proved to be highly mobile. However, this was not the case of people migrating from countryside to towns. There are indications that mobility from countryside to town was also limited through the operation of guild or guild-like restrictions on employment in urban trades. Further, the structure of production and consumption patterns that guided urban output have placed a major barrier to the growth of a rural-urban migratory process on account of the limited access to the unskilled and casual labourers (Commander, 1989, p. 50).

After the great mutiny of soldiers in 1857, British Government took direct charge of India. In the post 1857 periods, the development of plantation agriculture, like tea, rubber, jute, cotton, indigo, and mining and quarrying was an important factor of internal migration. The two areas of plantation agriculture emerged—namely Assam in North East and Travancore and Mysore in south India which were dependent on migrant labour. The nature of labour migration was that of indenture. They were generally placed under five-year indenture by a contract containing penal provisions for breach of the agreement. Since plantations were located in remote wilderness with very little communication between them and the rest of India, the workers were virtual prisoners for the duration of their contact. On the other hand, growth of plantation agriculture and mining and quarrying led to the development of railways and ports, which established trade relations with the other colonies of British Empire and Great Britain. This has reorganized the space relations and pattern of circulation mostly directed towards new foci in the western, southern and eastern India. Port centres like Bombay, Calcutta and Madras came into existence. These new cities were not in prominence either in medieval or ancient times but greatly influenced the pattern of circulation and migration in the Indian sub-continent during the colonial and post-colonial India.

Recent Trend and Pattern of Migration

It is now possible to study the trend and pattern of migration with the official data on migration available from the census. The census, started during the colonial period around 1872, included a question on migration, based on place of birth, which continued in all successive censuses, and later a question on place of last residence was introduced since 1971 census. The migration data based on place of last residence is also available from the various rounds of National Sample Surveys. The question on the place of last residence (also the place of birth) is able to capture the size of migrants who may be characterized to have moved on either permanent or semi-permanent basis. From demographic point of view, this data on migration is relevant as they clearly tell us the net addition in the place of destination or net subtraction at the place of origin. On the other hand, in addition, National Sample Surveys also try to ascertain temporary and seasonal migration by asking a separate question whether a household member who stayed away from his or her village or town for two months (in 55th round) one month (64th round) or more but less than six months in the last 365 days for employment or in search of employment. As temporary and seasonal migration is determined in relation to the place of origin and not counted at the place of destination, it is hardly relevant in assessing population change, in general and urban population growth, in particular. As such, this study is confined to the migration ascertained either based on the place of birth or place of last residence only.

In a historical study of migration in the Indian sub-continent based on census data, Davis (1951) has shown that Indians living outside the province or state of birth in 1931 was 3.6 per cent compared to 22.4 per cent in United States. From this Davis, concluded that the population of the Indian sub-continent like that of most peasant regions is relatively immobile. He attributed this to the prevalence of caste system, joint families, traditional values, diversity of language and culture, lack of education and predominance of agriculture and semi-feudal land relations (Davis, 1951, p. 107, 122).

Urbanization is crucially linked to migration. Whether migration is a strong or a weak force in urbanization, much depends upon the nature and pattern of migration. In India, migration occurs not only due to economic reasons, but also host of social-cultural and other factors as well. Before the contribution of migration in urban growth is discussed, it would be worthwhile to throw some light on the recent trend and pattern of migration. Similar to the conclusion of Davis for colonial India, later studies also observed the relative immobility of India's population in the latter half of the twentieth century (Kundu, 2007; Skeldon, 1986). The 2001 census estimated the total number of internal migrants at 309 million based on place of last residence, representing nearly 30 per cent of the total population. Although the number of internal migrants has doubled since 1971, the proportion has continued to be about 30 per cent since 1971, except for the 1991 census, when it declined to about 27 per cent of the total population. It is generally accepted that migration slowed down during the decade 1981–91 as a result of increased unemployment and sluggish growth in the Indian economy followed by increased mobility during 1991–2001.

It may be noted from Table 2.1 that the NSSO-based migration rate was 28.5 per cent for the year 2007–08, lower than the census-based migration rate in 2001. However, this is not comparable as census is based on complete enumeration compared to the sampled nature of NSSO based migration rates. Also there is a difference in the criterion of defining a migrant between the Census and NSSO.[2] On the other hand, if NSSO migration rates of 2007–08 are compared with 1999–2000 round of survey, there was an increase in migration rates into the urban areas. Compared with men, women showed higher increase in mobility during the same period. It is worthwhile to mention that the much of the increase or decrease in migration rates depends on the base year selected. In contrast to internal migrants, the international migrants (immigrants)

Table 2.1

Percentage of internal and international migrants based on place of last residence, India 1971–2008

Census	Total Population (in Million)	Internal Migrants (in Million)	Percentage (Internal Migrants)	International Migrants (in Million)	Percentage (International Migrants)	Percentage of Total Population
1971	548.1	159.6	29.1	8.1	1.4	30.6
1981	659.3	200.5	30.4	6.0	0.9	31.3
1991	814.3	220.7	27.1	5.9	0.7	27.83
2001	991.8 (1028.6)	300.9 (309.3)	30.3 (30.0)	5.0 (5.1)	0.5 (0.4)	30.8 (30.4)
2007–08	1009*	287.8	28.5	4.4	0.4	28.9

Sources: India, Census of India, 1971, series 1, part II, D(i), migration tables; India, Census of India, 1981, series 1, part V, A and B(i), migration tables (tables D1 and D2); India, Census of India, 1991, series 1, Part V, D series, migration tables, vol. 2, part 1 (table D2); India, Census of India, 2001, table D-2, compact diskette, Registrar General and Census Commissioner, New Delhi. The census was not conducted in Assam in 1981 and in Jammu & Kashmir in 1991. The figures for India from 1981 to 2001 exclude these two states. The figures for the 2001 census including Assam and Jammu & Kashmir are given in parentheses.

Note: * Estimated population. See NSSO (2010), p. A-100.

constitute a small number of four to five million, that is, less than half per cent of India's population, and the volume has been declining due to depletion by death of those who migrated during the partition of the country in 1947. The proportion of immigrants was about 5 per cent of India's population in 2001, which declined by three percentage points in 2001 from the level of 1971.

It is important that the types of migration be disaggregated into streams of migration in order to assess the role of migration in urban growth. The streams of migration are: from rural to rural, from rural to urban, from urban to rural and from urban to urban areas. From the viewpoint of urbanization, it is rural to urban migration that adds to the urban population, whereas urban to rural depletes the urban population. The net balance of the two streams is actually the contributor to the process of urbanization.

Table 2.2 presents that rural to rural is the most dominated stream (about 62 per cent) of migration predominantly comprised of females. On the other hand, rural to urban migration constitutes only about one-fifth of migrants. Urban to rural is the weakest stream of migration having less than 6 per cent migrants. It would be interesting to know how within each stream of migration people travel long and short distances. Table 2.3 shows the distribution of internal migrants by type of movement namely intra-district and inter-district. Both are short distance movements and interstate movements by streams of migration. The intra-district movement comprises the largest share of migration that is about 53 per cent and is dominated by rural to rural migration. Table 2.3 also indicates that the people are more mobile within the district of current residence followed

Table 2.2

Per cent distribution of migration by streams of migration and gender, 2007–08, India (all duration)

Migration Stream	Male	Female	Persons
Rural to rural	27.2	70.0	61.7
Rural to urban	39.0	14.9	19.5
Urban to urban	24.8	10.0	13.1
Urban to rural	8.9	4.9	5.7
All	100	100	100

Source: Same as in Table 2.1.

Table 2.3

Per cent distribution of migration by distance categories and streams of migration, 2007–08, India (all duration)

Migrants	Intra-district	Inter-district	Interstate	All
Rural to rural	72.4	23.2	4.4	100
Rural to urban	41.2	33.6	25.2	100
Urban to urban	48.8	33.8	17.5	100
Urban to rural	27.9	49.2	22.9	100
Total	53.3	32.0	14.7	100

Source: Based on NSSO data (2007–08).

by inter-district and interstate migration. Only about 15 per cent migrants moved from one state to another. Of those who moved across states, one-fourth and one-fifth moved from rural to urban and urban to rural areas, respectively.

Table 2.4 presents reasons of migration for those who migrated into rural and urban areas by gender. Employment is the most important reason of migration in urban areas. About 56 per cent male migrants reported employment as a reason of migration and another 25 per cent reported moved with parents and family members as a reason of migration in urban areas compared to 28 and 22 per cent respectively in the rural areas. On the other hand marriage is a reason of migration for about 61 per cent female

Table 2.4

Reasons of migration into rural and urban areas by gender, India, 2007–08

Reasons	Migrated in Rural Areas		Migrated in Urban Areas	
	Male	Female	Male	Female
Employment-related reasons	28.6	0.7	55.7	2.7
Studies	10.7	0.5	6.8	2.2
Marriage	9.4	91.2	1.4	60.8
Movement with parents/family members	22.1	4.4	25.2	29.4
Others	29.2	3.2	10.9	4.9
Total	100	100	100	100

Source: NSSO (2010).

migrants in urban area and about 91 per cent in rural areas. Studies turn out to a reason of migration for very few migrants (around 10 per cent). While almost equal percentages of males and females migrate accompanying their parents and family members in urban areas, there is a strong gender bias in the associational migration in case of males migrating into the rural areas. This shows that girl children are left behind by migrant parents/family members when they move into rural areas. In the nutshell, it is obvious that male migrate to urban areas largely due to livelihood reasons.

Interstate Migration and Ethnic Conflict

The interstate migration is not huge. About 15 per cent of all internal migration has crossed state boundaries. In numerical terms, about 45 million people were enumerated in the states other than their place of last residence, in the middle of the last decade. Among all interstate migrants about two-thirds moved to urban areas. However, the figures are too low for India as a whole which enumerated population of 1,210 million in 2011 census. The issue of interstate migration, in general, and within state migration, in particular, has been a topic of intense contest since 1970s. In one of the early writings, Myron Weiner (1978) surveyed the nature of migration and the emergence of the ideology of *sons of soils* leading to ethnic conflict in different parts India. He presented three types of conflict in three distinct regions- that is Assam, Chota Nagpur and Hyderabad. In Assam—the reason of conflict was the success of migrants, while the natives failed; in Chota Nagpur, the case was unique where tribals encountered the migrants leading their subjugation and displacement, and in Hyderabad the basis of conflict was an effort to protect the middle-class *Mulki* from the competing migrants. In all three cases, Weiner (1978) argued that the sons of the soil met the challenge of outsiders by advancing themselves into elitist positions in an effort to oust their non-indigenous competitors. This process has accelerated rather than subsiding with economic development and modernization. In the 1980s and later, the ideology of nativism further bolstered and spread into others areas like Mumbai, Goa, Meghalaya inciting conflict and violence against migrants (Rajan, Korra and Chyrmang, 2011). The hatred against migrants in case of Mumbai is more organized and violent as some political parties based on sons of the soil ideology articulated strong voice and threat to the migrants (see Hansen, 2001 for details). All these happenings and developments in different parts of India do not augur well for the potential migrants as promised in the Indian Constitution under Article 19.

It is an irony that among the 28 states and seven union territories, a large number of states are migrant sending states compared to few prominent migrant receiving states. Among the states which receive large number of migrants, Delhi tops the list followed by Goa, Maharashtra, Haryana, Punjab, Gujarat and Karnataka. On the other hand, among out migrating states, Bihar tops the list followed by UP and Manipur. It may be noted that Manipur in recent years has emerged one of the important out migrating states due to ethnic conflict and law and order problem in the state. In contrast, Kerala is in fact a net in-migrating state so far internal migration is concerned but when we take into consideration the emigration it turns out to be a net out-migrating state as most out-migrants set off abroad (NSSO, 2010).

In nutshell, the pattern of interstate migration influenced by the militant ideology of sons of the soil is not conducive for the rapid urban transition and economic growth for India; it also violates the fundamental right enshrined in the Indian Constitution.

Migration, Development and Poverty

The relationship between migration, development and poverty is complex which also varies with the forms of migration, namely, whether we are interested in temporary/seasonal migration or permanent/semi-permanent migration. Earlier studies show that poor and those with lower socio-economic background such as illiterates, scheduled castes and scheduled tribes are more prone to seasonal and temporary migration (Keshri and Bhagat, 2011; 2013). On the other hand, permanent and semi-permanent migration is dominated by the socio-economically better-off people (Bhagat, 2010). At the state level, there exists an insignificant relationship between rural poverty ratios and out-migration which indicates that push factors were not very effective in accelerating out-migration from rural areas (Bhagat, 2010). This may be due to several factors, including the low level of education and skill among the rural population combined with the high cost of living in the cities, the lack of squatting places where the poor can encroach, particularly in large cities and hostile authorities who may pass eviction orders against those that they declare are illegal occupants of city spaces on public litigation petitions. The public opinion on migration in cities tends to be very hostile towards poor and unskilled migrants, who are often blamed for many city woes, including those related to deteriorating transport facilities, environment and sanitation. In this situation, it is often difficult for poor and uneducated migrants to survive in cities. Several studies have also pointed out that it is not the poor who move out of the rural areas, but those with some education and capital (Oberai and Singh, 1983; Skeldon, 1986).

The NSSO data provide information on migrants by monthly consumer expenditure of the households. The migration rate was as high as 50.5 per cent in the highest MPCE decile class compared to 23 per cent in the lowest MPCE decile class in urban areas in 2007–08. The same was true for those moving into rural areas with corresponding percentages of 36.6 and 20.9, respectively. This shows that migration rates were higher in higher expenditure/income groups and vice versa (NSSO, 2010). Although census does not collect data on MPCE, it provides information migration by educational levels. For example, about 14 million people had migrated for reasons related to work/employment during the period 1991–2001. The literacy rate among those rural-to-urban migrants who reported work/employment as a reason to migrate was much higher compared with the rural literacy level, in general. For example, the literacy rate was about 85 per cent among intrastate and 75 per cent among interstate rural-to-urban migrants, compared with a rural literacy rate of 58 per cent at the national level. The level of education of migrants was also found to be higher than that of non-migrants. For example, among migrants moving from rural areas, the percentage of migrants with 10 years or more of education was 41 per cent among intrastate and 30 per cent among interstate migrants compared with 18 per cent among non-migrants in rural areas in 2001. This indicates that the migrants belonged to higher educational status categories compared with their non-migrant counterparts. It is also because those who have higher levels of education or economic assets tend to find it easier to establish linkages with the urban economy through socio-cultural channels, to find a foothold in the city and to avail themselves of the opportunity offered by migration (Kundu, 2007).

Migration in the Context of Urbanization

As migration into urban areas is an important component, it would be interesting to mention some of the broad features of India's urbanization in order to understand the linkages between migration and urbanization. The 2011 Census enumerated an urban population of 377 million, spread over about 8,000 cities and towns. These cities and towns are hierarchically linked with each other, but predominantly embedded in the spatial organization of national economy. The spatial structure of the Indian economy is shaped by three port cities namely Kolkata, Mumbai and Chennai, planted during colonial rule (Raza and Habeeb, 1976). Delhi also played an important role after it became the capital city in 1911. Together these cities dominated the urbanization process and the interregional flow of migration. The 2011 census shows that the urbanization process is vibrant in north, west and south India with the three largest cities, namely Delhi, Mumbai and Chennai forming a nucleus in their respective regions. Hyderabad, Bangalore and Ahmadabad are another group of big cities that shaped the regional pattern of urbanization. On the other hand, eastern and north-eastern India lagged behind with the declining importance of Kolkata and due to the lack of any other megacity in the region. The next ranking city in east and North East India is Patna, which is about seven times smaller than Kolkata. The exclusion of eastern and north-eastern India on the map of urbanization is also evident in the fact that the region as a whole is characterized by high interstate out-migration, which is largely due to the lack of vibrant cities in the region. The same is also true for the central region, consisting of the states of Uttar Pradesh, Madhya Pradesh, Chhattisgarh and Rajasthan which are not only having low level of urbanization but also have many pockets with high out-migration.

Historically, migration towards cities became more important as the million plus cities acquired prominence in the urbanization of India. At the beginning of the twentieth century, Kolkata acquired the status of a million plus city, followed by Mumbai in 1911. By 1951 Delhi, Chennai and Hyderabad joined the ranks of the million plus cities. By 2001, there were 35 million plus cities in India, in which about 38 per cent of the total urban population was residing. The number of million plus cities has gone up to 53 and population residing in them increased to 43 per cent by 2011. The rising importance of million plus cities both in numbers as well as huge concentration of urban population in them shows the significance of migrants in the city space. The share of in-migrants (all durations of

Figure 2.1

Percentage of migrants in selected million plus cities

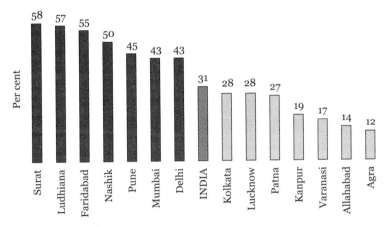

Source: Census of India, 2001.

residence) in the entire population varies from less than 15 per cent in million plus cities, like Allahabad and Agra to 55 per cent and more in cities, like Surat, Ludhiana and Faridabad. Mumbai and Delhi have about 45 per cent of migrants in 2001 (see Figure 2.1). When we look at the share of the migrants across million plus cities, it is quite evident that this share is closely related to the economic position and vibrancy of cities (Bhagat, Das and Bhat, 2009).

Migrants in cities and urban centres are predominantly engaged in the informal sector, working as construction workers, hawkers and vendors, domestic servants, rickshaw pullers/drivers, electricians, plumbers, masons, security personnel, etc. The majority are either self-employed or casual workers. About 30 per cent of migrant workers, working as casual workers, are quite vulnerable to the vagaries of the labour market and lack social protection. Only 35 per cent of migrant workers are employed as regular/salaried workers (NSSO, 2010).

India has launched a policy of economic liberalization since 1991. During the post-liberalization phase, the importance of cities and urban centres has been growing in India's economic development. For example, the contribution of urban areas to India's GDP has increased from 29 per cent in 1950–51 to 47 per cent in 1980–81, to 62 to 63 per cent by 2007, and is expected to increase to 75 per cent by 2021 (Planning

Commission, 2008, p. 394). It is also being emphasized that 9 to 10 per cent of growth in GDP depends fundamentally on making Indian cities more liveable and inclusive (Planning Commission, 2008, p. 394). However, with increasing economic growth, wealth is getting concentrated in cities and urban centres, and the rural–urban gaps in income levels, wages and employment opportunities are widening. Further, increasing economic growth is also associated with growing regional disparity and lopsided urbanization. Many have argued that the process of urbanization during the post-liberalization phase has been exclusionary which is also evident in the decelerated trend of migration (Bhagat, 2010; Kundu, 2007).

Contribution of Migration in Urban Growth

In many developing countries, the lack of adequate data on rural to urban migration as well as reliable data on natural increase precludes the disaggregation of urban growth by its various components (Brockerhoff, 1999). There are mainly four components of urban growth namely the natural increase, net migration to urban areas and the reclassification of settlements as towns or its declassification as a result of changes in the nature of economic activities, availability of infrastructure or acquisition of urban characteristics and the extension of boundaries of cities and towns within their jurisdiction.

The trend in natural increase for the last four decades ending with year 2010 is presented in Table 2.5. The natural increase in urban areas remained 19 per 1,000 during 1970–80 and 1980–90. On the other hand, rural natural increase in fact slightly increased during this period. The reason for the constant natural increase in urban areas until 1990 is that urban birth rate and death rates have declined in the same magnitude. On the other hand, urban birth rate declined faster during the 1990s compared to a small decline in urban death rate. As a result, the urban natural increase declined to 15.8 per 1,000 during the 1990s compared to 19.3 during the 1980s. It further declined to 13 during the 2000s. In fact there has been widening urban–rural differentials in natural increase over last four decades. This could slow down the urbanization if migration and rural-urban classification do not compensate the decline in natural increase. Table 2.6 throws light on the relative contribution of each component of urban growth for the last four decades.

Table 2.5

Birth, death and natural increase rate per 1,000 population by rural and urban areas, 1971–80 to 2001–10, India birth, rural and urban areas

Years	Birth Rate (per 1,000)	Death Rate (per 1,000)	Rate of Natural Increase (per 1,000)	Urban-rural Differentials in Natural Increase Rate
1971–80				
Rural	35.8	15.8	20.0	
Urban	28.5	9.2	19.3	–0.7
1981–90				
Rural	33.9	12.6	21.3	
Urban	27.0	7.7	19.3	–2.0
1991–2000				
Rural	29.4	9.9	19.5	
Urban	22.3	6.5	15.8	–3.7
2001–10				
Rural	25.7	8.4	17.3	
Urban	19.3	6.0	13.2	–4.1

Sources: Sample Registration System, Various Years, Registrar General and Census Commissioner, India (www.censusindia.gov.in); Sample Registration System Bulletins of various volumes published by the Office of the Registrar General, India.

Table 2.6

Contribution of the components of urban growth, India, 1971–2011

Components	Population in Million				Percentage Distribution			
	1971–81	1981–91	1991–2001	2001–11	1971–81	1981–91	1991–2001	2001–11
Urban increment	49.9	56.8	68.2	91.0	100.0	100.0	100.0	100.0
Natural increase (of initial population plus inter-censal migrants)	24.9	35.4	39.3	39.9	50.0	62.3	57.6	43.8
Net rural-urban migration	9.3	10.6	14.2	18.7	18.6	18.7	20.8	20.6
Net reclassification from rural to urban including jurisdictional changes and out growths	15.7	10.8	14.7	32.3	31.4	19.0	21.5	35.6

Source: Bhagat, 2012.

The natural increase in the initial population as well as the inter-censal migrants in the urban areas continues to be the largest contributor to the urban growth (58 per cent) during the 1991–2001, although its share has declined by about five per cent compared to previous decade. The net migration to urban areas based on the data from place of last residence derived from the migration tables of census shows that its share in urban growth remained around 18 to 20 per cent during the last three decades from 1971 to 2001. Why it is that in spite of decline in the growth of migration during the 1981–91, its share has remained about 18 per cent, that is, almost same, estimated during 1971–81. It is worthwhile to point out here that while rural to urban migration had declined during 1980s, the counter stream of urban to rural migration had also declined more drastically. As a result, the net migration to urban areas increased from 9.3 million in the decade 1971–81 to 10.6 million in the decade 1981–91. Thus, as far as the contribution of migration is concerned, it remained unaffected in the 1980s. On the other hand, slowing down of urbanization may be correctly attributed to the reclassification of towns and much more to the little geographical expansion of the existing towns by jurisdictional changes. The share of net reclassification (population of new towns minus declassified towns compiled directly from census sources) has declined from nearly 19 per cent in the decade 1971–81 to 17 per cent in 1981–91, on the other hand the contribution of jurisdictional changes (estimated here as residual) declined from 13 per cent in 1971–81 to nearly two per cent in 1981–91. In the decade 1991–2001, the slowing down of urbanization may be attributed to the decline in the share of natural increase.

The components of urban growth, on the other hand, show a very different pattern during 2001–11. As noted above, the declining trend in urban growth was stalled and the speed of urbanization accelerated during 2001–11. As a result, the contribution of each component is likely to show some departure from the earlier trend. Assuming that the contribution of migration remained constant at about 20 per cent during 2001–11 that is similar to that of the decade 1991–2001, the absolute numbers the net rural to urban migration increased from about 14 million during 1991–2001 to about 19 million during 2001–11. On the other hand, the speeding up of the urbanization during 2001–11 is mainly the result of net rural to urban classification during 2001–11 (see Table 2.6). This is evident in the fact that the 2011 Census reported that the number of towns at the national level increased from 5,161 to 7,935; a net addition of 2,774 towns (2,532 census towns and 242 statutory towns) in 2011 compared to the net additions of 763 and 693 towns in 1991 and 2001, respectively. A fourfold increase of new towns mostly small towns (less than 20,000) shows the overriding importance of spatial changes reorganizing the rural–urban space and produced faster urbanization during the 2000s. Many of these new small towns have emerged as part of urban agglomerations of million plus cities.

Out of the nearly 20 to 21 per cent share of net migration in urban growth at the national level, about eight per cent was contributed by interstate net migration and another 12 to 13 per cent by intrastate migration. However, the share of migration in the urban growth of some of smaller states and UTs is observed much higher. Among the major states, Gujarat tops with 36 per cent contributed by migration closely followed by Maharashtra with 35 per cent and Haryana and Odisha 34 per cent in their respective urban growth. Punjab stands at par with national average in the contribution of migration in urban growth. Most of northern and north-eastern states reveal much below contribution of migration in urban growth than the national average (Bhagat and Mohanty, 2009). The most important fact that is emerging from the analysis of the components of urban growth is that migration is not playing a dominant role in India's urbanization but the factors like rural to urban classification and changes in the municipal boundaries are most important.

Concluding Remark

India has been urbanizing faster with higher contribution of rural to urban classification compared to rural to urban migration. This is very much evident during the decade 2001 to 2011. The push and pull factors dominated much of the understanding of migration and its linkages with urbanization. But the available evidences do not show that push factors are associated with high out-migration rates from rural areas. On the contrary, pull factors in urban areas are selective and exclusionary (Bhagat, 2010; Kundu, 2007). Many studies also point out that it is the relatively better off people from the rural areas with some education and capital who are migrating more (Bhagat, 2010; Oberai and Singh, 1983; Skeldon, 1986). As a result, the out-migration from rural areas is not as pervasive as thought to be, particularly in case of permanent and semi-permanent migration. However, circulation and temporary migration remain the most dominant form of spatial mobility between rural to urban areas (Keshri and Bhagat, 2013).

Faster urbanization in India co-exists with huge urban deprivations. This is nowhere better manifested than in the facts that 25 per cent of the urban households have no access to drinking water within their premises, 22 per cent have no bathroom, 15 per cent have no access to a drainage facility and 11 per cent do not even have any toilet facility (Bhagat, 2011). However, for the present urban predicament, migrants cannot be blamed for urban policy and planning failures. On the other hand, while slums are integral part of the cities, both migrants and non-migrants live in slums due to lack of housing. It is also wrong to attribute that slums are entirely the product of rural to urban migration and urban poverty is entirely the spillover of rural poverty (Mitra, 2010).

At the city and town level, the rising importance of million plus cities, both in numbers as well as concentration of population, shows the significance of migrants in the city space. When we look at the share of the migrants across the million plus cities, it is quite evident that the share is closely related to the economic position and vibrancy of cities.

Migrants' contribution to the city has always been underestimated in spite of the fact that migrants provide cheap labour to the industrial sector and cheap services to the urban elites. On the other hand, migrants are blamed for every woe of the city inviting strong abhorrence of the so-called urban natives. The strong negativity against migrants particularly found in megacities is the result of failure of urban and city planning and also due to lack of involvement of people in planning and governance. Cities are bureaucratically planned and governed in spite of the 74th amendment to the Constitution that made provisions for the democratic and decentralized functioning and governance of the urban local bodies.

Government policies and programmes are silent on the issue of migration and protecting the rights of migrants. This is evident in the Five Year Plan documents. Both the 11th Five Year Plan (2007–12) and the Draft Approach Paper to the 12th Five Year Plan (2012–17) recognize urban transition in a positive framework, yet no reference has been made to the migration issue in these documents, let alone to the safeguarding of migrants' rights in the city. It is pointed out many times that urban development is a state subject in India, whereas various policies and programmes are being formulated by the Centre. Some of the policies and programmes, like The Jawaharlal Nehru Urban Renewal Mission (JNNURM) and Rajiv Awas Yojana (RAY), did address the issues of urban poor and slum dwellers, but not the conditions of migrants in the cities perhaps under the assumption that migrants and poor are the synonymous categories. While this may be partly true, on the contrary this assumption has obstructed the mainstreaming of migration into the urban development strategies. Also, the issues like denial of economic, political, social and cultural rights of migrants do not figure in our policy and programme documents.

Notes

1. Kojima (1996) identified four patterns of urbanization based on a study of urban population growth rates of a number of countries.

    (i)   Hyper–hyper urbanization (six per cent and over)
    (ii)   Hyper urbanization (three to six per cent)
    (iii) Rapid urbanization (one per cent to less than three per cent)
    (iv)   Stagnant urbanization (less than one per cent).

    Kojima observed that the fastest urban growth in Western Europe during period of its economic rise was 2.5 per cent and for most of the period it was one to two per cent. On the other hand, urban population growth was faster in Japan reaching 4.3 per cent during the 1920s and six per cent during the 1930s (p. 356). As per the above classification, India falls under the category of rapid urbanization at the moment with urban growth rate of 2.76 per cent observed during the decade 2001–11.

2. In both Census and NSSO, a migrant is defined if place of last residence (POLR) is different from the place of enumeration (POE). However, in NSSO surveys, the POLR is defined as a place (village or town) where the migrant has stayed continuously for a period of six months or more before moving to the place of enumeration. In contrast, censuses do not limit the duration of residence in defining the POLR. In both censuses and NSSO, there is no limit of duration at the POE to qualify as a migrant.

References

Bhagat, R.B. (2010). 'Internal migration in India: Are the underprivileged migrating more?' *Asia Pacific Population Journal, 25*(1), 31–49.

———. (2011). 'Urbanisation and Access to Basic Amenities in India'. *Urban India, 31*(1), 1–13.

———. (2012). 'A turnaround in India's urbanization'. *Asia Pacific Population Journal, 27*(2), 23–39.

Bhagat, R.B. and Mohanty, S. (2009). 'Emerging Pattern of Urbanization and the Contribution of Migration in Urban Growth in India'. *Asian Population Studies, 5*(1), 5–20.

Bhagat, R.B., Das, K.C., and Mari Bhat, P.N. (2009). *Pattern of urbanisation and metropolitan growth in India*. Unpublished Project Report, International Institute for Population Sciences, Mumbai.

Brockerhoff, M. (1999). 'Urban growth in developing countries: A review of projections and predictions'. *Population and Development Review, 25*(4), 757–78.

Commander, S. (1989). 'The mechanics of demographic and economic growth in Uttar Pradesh, 1800–1900'. In Tim Dyson (ed.), *India's historical demography: Studies in famine, disease and society* (pp. 49–72). London: Curzon Press.

Davis, K. (1951). *The population of India and Pakistan*. Princeton, NJ: Princeton University Press.

Hansen, T.B. (2001). *Wages of violence: Naming and identity in postcolonial Bombay*. Princeton: Princeton University Press.

Hutton, J.H. (1986). *Census of India 1931: With complete survey of tribal life and system* (Vol. 1). Delhi: Gian Publishing House.

Keshri, K. and Bhagat, R.B. (2011). 'Temporary and seasonal migration: Regional pattern, characteristics and associated factors'. *Economic and Political Weekly*, *47*(4), 81–88.

———. (2013). 'Socio-economic determinants of temporary labour migration in India: A regional analysis'. *Asian Population Studies*, *9*(2), 175–95.

Kojima, R. (1996). 'Introduction: Population migration and urbanization in developing countries'. *The Developing Economies*, *34*(4), 349–69.

Kundu, A. (2007). Proceedings of Dr C. Chandrasekaran memorial lecture on migration and exclusionary urban growth in India. *IIPS Newsletter*, *48*(3 and 4), 5–23.

McNeill, W. (1984). 'Human Migration in Historical Perspective'. *Population and Development Review*, *10*(1), 1–18.

Mitra, A. (2010). 'Migration, livelihood and well-being: Evidence from Indian city slums'. *Urban Studies*, *47*(7), 1371–90.

Nehru, J. (1965). *Glimpses of world history*. Bombay: Asia Publishing House (reprinted in 1965 with 50 maps by J.F. Horrabin).

———. (2010). *Migration in India*. New Delhi: Ministry of Statistics and Programme Implementation, Government of India.

Oberai, A.S. and Singh, H.K.M. (1983). *Causes and consequences of internal migration: A study in the Indian Punjab*. New Delhi: Oxford University Press.

Planning Commission. (2008). *Eleventh Five Year Plan, Vol III: Agriculture, rural development, industry, services and physical infrastructure* (pp. 394–422). New Delhi: Oxford University Press.

Rajan, S.I., Vijay K. and Chyrmang, R. (2011). 'Politics of conflict and migration'. In S. Irudaya Rajan (ed.), *Migration, identity and politics* (pp. 95–107). London: Routledge.

Raza, M. and Habeeb, A. (1976). 'Characteristics of colonial urbanization: A case study of satellitic 'primacy' of Calcutta (1850–1921)'. In S. Mazoor Alam and V.V. Pokshishevsky (eds), *Urbanization in developing countries* (pp. 185–218). Hyderabad: Osmania University.

Sharma, R.S. (2005). *India's ancient past*. New Delhi: Oxford University Press.

Sainath, P. (2011). 'Census findings point to decade of rural distress'. *The Hindu*, 25 September, Chennai edition.

Skeldon, R. (1986). 'On migration patterns in India during the 1970s'. *Population and Development Review*, *12*(4), 759–79.

United Nations. (2011). *Population distribution, urbanisation, internal migration and development: An international perspective*. New York: Department of Economic and Social Affairs/Department of Population Division.

———· (2012). *World urbanization prospects: The 2011 prospects*. New York: Department of Economic and Social Affairs/Department of Population Division.

Weiner, M. (1978). *Sons of the soil: Migration and ethnic conflict in India*. Princeton: Princeton University Press.

3

Women's Mobility and Migration: An Exploratory Study of Muslim Women Migrants in Jamia Nagar, Delhi

Meenakshi Thapan, Anshu Singh
and Nidhitha Sreekumar

Gender and Migration

One aspect of mobility is migration, both internal and international, that results in the movement of women from one place to another, from one way of life to another, from one experience of being a woman in a particular socio-cultural setting to another different experience. It would not be an overstatement to argue that migration has been an aspect shaping women's lives in different ways for over a hundred years. In fact, Glick-Schiller and Salazar (2013, p. 185) argue that, 'Across the millennia, migration or seasonal movements of people have been a significant aspect of the human experience of space and time'. It has also been suggested that people and their cultural practices are not confined to a fixed territory but are parts of multiple spatial networks and temporal linkages (Glick-Schiller and Salazar, 2013, p. 186). People are, therefore, not territorially fixed or sedentary beings; they move, for seasonal work, for education, for better employment opportunities and for a host of accompanying reasons.

Tumbe argues that India has been witness to a 'culture of migration' for over a century. that the impact of this culture covers roughly 20 per cent of the population, which is equivalent to 200 million people (Tumbe, 2012, p. 87). This long history of migration tells us that women have been accustomed to the out-migration of men when they have had to take care of the family and its holdings over long periods of time while the men are away. In more recent times, women have been the pioneers in out-migration in search of better livelihood options and upward mobility. This is in addition to their migration through marriage to men in different cities or towns in search of upward mobility and improved life opportunities for themselves and their families. Forced migration, as a consequence of conflict, war or violence, has been one avenue for migration, exile and refugee-hood for both men and women in the Indian subcontinent. It has been particularly poignant in the case of women as they have been the victims of such migration first when the partition of India took place in 1947 and then, each time, there has been conflict or war or violence triggered by communal forces in different parts of the country (see, for example, Bhasin and Menon, 1998; Behera, 2006; Bannerjee, 2010).

Statistics about Women's Migration

Migration and gender is a deeply complex area of knowledge owing to the conjunction 'and', which brings together the concepts of 'migration' and 'gender', but at the same time maintains them as distinct categories within the broader discourse (Palmary et al., 2010, p. 1). So far, studies on migration have either viewed the phenomenon as a response to economic pressures or as a negotiation between two cultures that of the migrant and the host (Chopra, 2004, p. 44). In itself, migration is no doubt a 'physical and social transaction', but it is also 'an instrument of cultural diffusion and social integration' (Bannerjee and Raju, 2009, p. 115). It is only when we move away from an approach that views migration from a male-dominated perspective, purely in economic terms, that we can hope to uncover other factors that both impact and are an outcome of women's migration. We need to consider women's migration as being not merely compatible with male migration (that is, a consequence of marriage and therefore, movement) but also as an independent feature, albeit dependent on several different factors. As researchers, our method in collecting and examining migration-related data plays a role in the ways in which we draw our conclusions about male and female migration.

One of the most salient findings of the 64th and the most recent round (2007–08) of the National Sample Survey Organisation (NSSO) is:

> [The] magnitude of male *migration rate* was far lower than female *migration rate*, in both rural and urban areas. In rural areas nearly 48 per cent of the females were migrants while the male *migration rate* was only 5 per cent, and in the urban areas, the male *migration rate* was nearly 26 per cent compared to female *migration rate* of 46 per cent.[1]

Such high figures for female out-migration would apparently signify migration as a consequence of marriage. However, Agnihotri, Mazumdar and Neetha (2012, p. 24) point out, basing their conclusions on a simultaneous consideration of census data, that the NSSO data does not indicate female out-migration as a consequence of marriage but that 'larger proportions of women are migrating for marriage'. Their analysis provides an exhaustive critique of existing databases and the tendency to conflate or confuse different sets of issues primarily because of a failure to recognize women as workers and independent actors in their own rights. In the authors' words:

> We believe that it is the mono-causal approach (i.e., the attribution of a single reason for migration) followed by the macro surveys that has been a major factor in camouflaging at least some economic or labour based decisions in women's migration under other apparently non-economic social reasons. For example, some implicit or actual labour migration by women may appear in the data as marriage migration or as other forms of associational movement by women simply because both may coincide, but the social reason is presumed to be all important. (Agnihotri, Mazumdar and Neetha, 2012, p. 18)

In a similar vein, Bannerjee and Raju (2009) assert that usual practice considers those women as working who report 'employment' as the reason for migration; however, women may have migrated for any reason but those who are working at the time of migration must also be counted in the universe of working migrant women (Bannerjee and Raju, 2009, p. 116). Moreover, as pointed out by Shanthi (2006, p. 5), 'The woman may be working prior to marriage and intend to get married with an urbanite to enhance her potential for employment but it does not get captured'. This inherent bias in the data sets make them a somewhat dubious basis for analysis but they are none the less the ground on which analyses of women and migration routinely take place.

Perspectives on Women's Migration

Migration in more recent times has received an impetus owing to the forces of globalization that have created both demand and supply in different contexts and in multifarious ways. It is also important to recognize that in most cases of migration, the complexities and layering of the migrant's existence are rolled and flattened through the apparatus of law. The basis of the legal system may partially lie on a coloured perception of migrant women as victims who are vulnerable, need to be 'protected', and lack agency of their own. This coloured vision is especially true with reference to the case of migrant Muslim women. Such a viewpoint compels policy framers to categorize migrant women as victims and rarely sees their decision to immigrate as a choice to escape, for example, an existing patriarchal society or seek better livelihood opportunities for themselves.

It is also noteworthy that there occurs differential treatment of women even in migrant families. Nair (2007a) brings to light the markedly different treatment meted out by the family to men and women who migrate for the upliftment of the standard of living of their family. 'Like in many other matters, a double standard prevails when it comes to the beliefs and practices of treatment of migration of both genders by the families.' The migration of a male member is considered to be a matter of pride and is valourized as a sacrifice on his behalf, whereas a similar step take by a female is considered to be nothing more than carrying out of one's basic duty (Nair, 2007a, p. 3).

In view of these facts, some scholars have attempted to provide a more nuanced understanding of what transpires between and during migration. Sociologically, it is interesting to understand how contested meanings of more broadly gendered constructs of home, nation, the political and the domestic impact both embodied migrants and how symbolic understandings of home and abroad (*desh aur videsh*, in popular parlance) have been interrogated in the context of migration (see, for example, the work of Thapan, 2005; Arya and Roy, 2006; Behera, 2006).

Over time, family traditions of migration affect the values and behavioural systems of communities, forming a 'culture of migration'. Migrant women play an important role in carrying their indigenous traits to the new settlement. It is here that the sociological frame helps in comprehending the importance of community sentiment, the role of the 'we' feeling and a sense of belonging, and the different practices that act as coping mechanisms for a migrant in the host society (Bal, 2003, p. 255).

The Case Study

This essay takes into consideration the aspects of migration among Muslim women as a heterogeneous category.[2] At the very outset, it is important to note that though there are issues that concern all women, the case of Muslim women becomes special because of their minority status. As Hasan and Menon (2005, p. 2) observe, 'The community has emerged as a formidable force, which many Muslim women believe seeks to restrict their rights.' They argue that the status of Muslim women, in particular, usually remains hidden under the cover of the 'Muslim' minority issue. The common rights of freedom to marry and divorce, given to Indian women by the law, does not apply to the Muslim women as their rights are the under the jurisdiction of the Muslim personal law. Hence, it becomes important to analyze their experience as a special case. Siddiqi and Zuberi (1993) and Kumar (2002) have also pointed out that despite being one of the most marginalized sections of our society, scholars, policy makers and government officials have ignored the concerns of Muslim women. They have discussed the suffering of Muslim women in the context of them being socially and economically backward, a condition worsened by the interference of Muslim personal law in all matters of their family life.

Migration as a social act is also closely related to the individual's decision-making power and the freedom to be mobile. Indian women, Hindu or Muslim, are largely dependent on their husbands or on their family to take decisions regarding their movement outside home. Given this scenario, it is important to note that the agency of a woman's mobility is closely related to the perception and ideas of her family. While going through the MWS-2000, we find that although lives of the majority of women, Hindu or Muslim, are controlled by their family, mainly the men, and Muslim women are more subjugated and controlled (Hasan and Menon, 2004). Scholars have argued that there is a very close relation between Islam and the subjugation of women. Engineer (2013) and other scholars note that it is the social atmosphere that determines the subjugation of women in Islam, not the religion itself, because Islam provides equal rights to men and women. However, Muslim women in India and many South Asian countries do not seem to enjoy these rights. Gill and Thiara (2009) have noted that women in South Asian societies are often vulnerable to various forms of violence which is not justified only by arguing that they are part of religion or culture. Women, according to them, in South Asian societies face 'multiple and intersecting forms of violence' (Gill and Thiara, 2009) and can be seen at the receiving end of various violent crimes within the family and outside it. Their case is more peculiar because, unlike Hindu women, Muslim women cannot directly go to court for redressal of their grievances. They are governed by Muslim personal law that limits and curtails their position as free citizens of a democratic nation.

Hasan and Menon (2004) have argued that women, despite their educational achievements, are not the primary decision-makers; especially in the spheres that are not directly related to the household. However, younger women are showing more willingness and interest in taking decisions. Within the context of migration 'decision-making' is quite an important factor. Hasan and Menon (2004) have noted that 86 per cent of women in India, Hindu and Muslim, need permission from their fathers or husbands to engage in most of the activities that require them to go out of home, even if it means to the nearby market or the doctor. It clearly reflects the importance of the family in the lives of women. Mobility to work and to get education is also largely dependent on the family, and so is the case with marriage. However, with new players of education and occupation in the market, the demands and the expectations from women as a large part of the labour force, are expected to change.

Based on a case study, this chapter will deal with some of the issues pertaining to migration by Muslim women, their choices, their aspirations and problems.[3] Apart from general labour migration, the case of Muslim women also provides us the opportunity to study migration stemming from violence in the domestic and public sphere, which presents a specific case within this group. We note how Muslim women, given the Muslim personal law guiding them through married life, deal with unwanted, violent or second marriages. Along with this, migration due to violence on the community, like the Mumbai riots (1992) or Bhagalpur riots (1989), is specific to the Muslim population in India.

Violence is one of the major reasons for migration around the globe. Forbes and Tirman (2009) have pointed out that the majority of this population is comprised of women and children who face enormous violence during the processes of migration and relocation in contexts of conflict. Behera (2006) notes that the large population of women who migrate due to reasons of conflict are the least observed and analyzed section of South Asian societies. She has pointed out that conflict situations have to inform themselves of the gender issues which have been largely ignored. Since independence and the partition of India, Muslims have faced violence in different parts of India. We may note that the discourses around communal violence or violence against Muslims have largely been oblivious to 'gendered' violence (Hasan and Menon, 2005). Kumar (2002) has pointed out that Muslim women are not viewed as gendered subjects of violence; their identity is overshadowed by their communal identity. Our study seeks to examine the lives of these women as gendered subjects: their struggles, their journey, their quest to find a safe territory and their efforts to recreate a fresh life at a new place.

The argument in this chapter is developed by linking mobility and migration to the idea of agency on part of the migrant woman as well as what enunciates the difficulties, problems and dilemmas of being a migrant woman in a metropolis. Apart from secondary sources, data collected through fieldwork, at Jamia Nagar, Delhi, has been included to substantiate this argument. The fieldwork, being preliminary in nature, takes only a very small sample of Muslim women and providing vignettes of their experience, in their own words, is designed to take into account the reasons for migration that also results in the experience of being part of the process of ghettoization of this particular community. There is an effort to examine the processes through which women belonging to this community have sought to incorporate their individual aspirations independently as well as within larger familial goals.[4] As the sample is of a limited size, no broad generalizations are being offered and it is hoped that this initial exercise will lead to an interest in further micro-level and qualitative research around migrant women, particularly from marginalized communities so that policy perspectives may be better informed from a subaltern standpoint that is not necessarily present in large data sets.

Migrant Muslim Women in Jamia Nagar, Delhi

Jamia Nagar has always been a Muslim-dominated area; however, the influx of the population became higher during the times of communal conflict like the partition of India in 1947 or the violence against the Muslim community in Gujarat in 2002. Jamia Nagar is home to many Muslim families and single men and women who have migrated from all over India for various reasons that include the search for opportunities for employment and education and for finding a better life. This area is considered a Muslim ghetto by many sociologists of urban India (see, for example, Gayer, 2011, especially 213 ff.).[6] An important point to note here is that Jamia Nagar is a special type of ghetto. Though culturally dominated and spatially designed to suit the needs of the Muslim population, it is not a very poor city space, as ghettos are usually described in the popular literature. In this aspect, it does not account for only low-income groups as its inhabitants, it is in fact home to all classes of Muslims who have moved for reasons of social security, which according to them, can only be found in a Muslim-dominated area. The study has taken this factor into account and women from a variety of social classes were interviewed to understand the idea of ghettoization due to migration in this area.

Migration, Freedom and Social Mobility

We found that women account for almost half of the migrated population in the area. They have migrated from various parts of the country to Jamia Nagar. Interestingly, their reasons for migration are closely related to the migration of the men of their family, be it divorce, domestic violence or the will of the male members of the family to move away from a disputed area. The women interviewed, belonging to the age group 21 to 60 years, are residents of Batla House and Abul Fazl localities of the Jamia Nagar area of Delhi. In the context of this fieldwork, a migrant woman has been defined as a woman who has moved from any other state than Delhi or a place within Delhi to Jamia Nagar area due to any reason and wishes to stay there for a considerable period of time.

As observed by scholars, it is important to note that Islam has pre-defined the role of women in society and the family (Engineer, 2013; Hasan and Menon, 2005; Kumar, 2002; Siddiqi and Zuberi, 1993). As one 35-year-old woman (working as a domestic help) said:

> I went to a local *madarasa*. *Maulwiji* used to train us in reciting Quran and we were told about the prescribed role of women in society and the household. Women are meant to take care of the home. They are responsible for the household.

In the interviews, women have resonated the perspective that family plays an important role in their lives; so much so that the decision of moving from one place to another, that is migration, is largely dependent on the family. This respondent added, 'I came here at the age of 16, just after my marriage, my husband used to work here in the university (Jamia Millia Islamia). He lived in the same place as I am living now'. Another respondent, who is an engineer by profession, said:

> I was married to my husband through a channel of relatives. It was an arranged marriage, with the complete involvement of both families. I agreed to get married as the groom was working in Delhi and I thought moving out to Delhi will be fun.

Women migrating for better education and employment options agree that Delhi has more opportunities for higher education and good jobs. Education in Delhi appears to act as a tool for empowerment for them. It not only helps to convince the family in favour of migration of women but also becomes handy in making women financially and socially independent. This is similar to the observations made by Virk (2004) with respect to women construction workers in Amritsar city, where economic problems like famines and scarcities, indebtedness and lack of sufficient employment opportunities in their native places may push women out of their villages.

It is important to note here that the Muslim-dominant regions in India, like Bihar and Uttar Pradesh, are underdeveloped and migrant women in Delhi experience a change of culture that is closely related to the 'city culture' or 'metropolitan culture'. The interviewees have explained how they have experienced 'freedom' after coming to Delhi. This refers to the freedom to move around, to take financial decisions, and to dress in other ways, to mention a few. In this context, Nair (2007b) discusses the migration of women nurses from Kerala to Delhi and highlights various personal goals such as the desire to travel and see the world, learn new languages and, most importantly, 'to earn their living and become self-reliant' (Nair, 2007b, p. 140). This indicates their strong sense of seeking independence and freedom from familial and other regional constraints. In our study, a 21-year-old student respondent, who migrated to Delhi for education and has now decided to settle here after marriage points out that:

> It was fun coming to a new place. I have always heard about Delhi, the buildings, the fun. Delhi lived up to its expectations. My brother was busy in his work, and I had lots of friends who used to take me to various places here. We just had to be careful about the timings of returning, as it is not safe at night, but otherwise it was all fun. The best part is that my friends live near my house, so whenever I wish I can meet them to make plans. Travelling alone is fun too. My finances are handled by my parents and

my brothers, and interestingly after my brother started earning I have to answer less about my expenditure. Also, it is the first time I interacted with boys, and I enjoyed it thoroughly.

Independence here is also linked to interaction with young men which is otherwise prohibited. However, it is migration to Delhi after marriage that is viewed as a very empowering experience by all the interviewed women. All married women have noted that moving to Delhi after marriage was an important reason that determined their choice of their present husbands. This view can be substantiated by the relation between marriage and migration in the case of women, as Palriwala and Uberoi (2008) have observed. In the context of women's 'marriage migration', they argue that 'migration within or as a result of marriage, may often be the most efficient and socially acceptable means available to disadvantaged women to achieve a measure of social and economic mobility' (Palriwala and Uberoi, 2008, p. 23). While marriage for many women may act as a push towards migration, it may not, at the same time, be an enabling experience or the main reason for migration. Migration is often also a refuge from the experience of domestic and other forms of violence.

Migration to Delhi also involves freedom from violence in the domestic sphere and from communal violence, for example, in Bhagalpur, Bihar.[7] Women who were suffering domestic violence or were abandoned by their husbands had moved to Delhi to obtain education and jobs, overcoming the dependence on their family or the families of their husbands. This is in contrast to the popular belief that Muslim women find it difficult to move out of marriage, a point also made by Hasan and Menon (2004). For instance, a 23-year-old woman who shifted to Delhi, with her two children, to attain education and a job after being left by her husband, told us:

Those were sad times, my *sasu ma* (mother-in-law) suggested that I should continue my education, and get settled somewhere. She was suffering from guilt because of her son. My father decided to send me here to my mother's brother and his family. My father accompanied me and my kids by train. *Mamu Jaan* (mother's brother) told him that it will be good if I could be educated and support myself. The idea clicked with me and my father. I am living here for the past four to five years now. I completed my graduation and B.Ed from Jamia a year ago. Now I am looking for a job.

We, therefore, find that for this respondent, migration has been a very empowering experience and has resulted in greater mobility for her in terms of educational and livelihood options. The significant role of the family in supporting her and helping her attain her goals is a factor that must be taken into account as well. Respondents have also mentioned that if they had continued to live in their native place, they would have had to face atrocities and dependence. Migrating to a metropolitan city gives them a sense of distance from the social, cultural and religious obligations which were not supportive of their independent lifestyle and which is alien to their lives in the small towns and rural areas of India. Many women said that though the decision to move out from the native place was taken by the family or a male member of the household, migration has helped them to progress in life. They are beginning to make independent decisions about their food, clothes, household needs, daily chores and overall movement outside the home in general. Most of the respondents have asserted their will to stay in Delhi and work for personal betterment. The students who have moved for education, argue that moving out has helped them have a say in choosing their life partner and the kind of life they wish to lead after marriage.

The Ghettoization of Community Spaces

While moving to Delhi, all our respondents decided or were forced to live in Jamia Nagar and nearby places. This area is overwhelmingly dominated by the Muslim population which, for Muslim women, makes it a comfortable place to live in. They can easily practice their religion and tend to feel safe about the communal forces. Once they interact with new societies, migrant communities construct their own social worlds (Bal, 2003). Migrant women in particular play an important role in carrying their indigenous traits to the new settlement. Nair (2007a) for example discusses the manner in which networking helps maintain linkages between the place left behind and the new one. This also helps migrant women acquire a place to live in, which is otherwise very difficult in Delhi. In our study, we have noted that women migrate to Jamia Nagar through their links with family members and others from their villages already living there.

Migrant women who shifted to Delhi after the Bhagalpur riots noted that the family decided to move to Patna and then to Abul Fazl Enclave (Jamia Nagar), as it is a Muslim-dominated area which will keep them safe in times of communal riots in the future. A 26-year-old IT professional asserts that shifting to a Muslim-dominated region was the main priority after the retirement of her father. '…This is a Muslim-dominated place. My parents thought it will be good to live in an area with other Muslim people, instead of living amongst other religions.' This emphasis on finding refuge and safety by residing amongst the larger minority population brings out the poignancy of the situation and at the same time results in the ghettoization of the community and the urban space.[8] Family and community honour rests upon the security of women which is assured by enclosing them in a 'Muslim-dominated area' where they can easily move in and out without coming in to contact with men of other religions. Most of the women interviewed also affirmed that they feel more secure in Jamia Nagar than any other area. However, it may also be argued that due to their already existing connection inside the community and the area, and dependence on the family, they are unwilling to explore other places of residence.

Restricting women to one particular, culturally dominated place is not only specific to women of the Muslim community. As Bal puts it:

> The migration of women has a special significance for community life. In order to transform itself to an ethnic community, it is essential to have regenerative abilities among them. The presence of wives and families of the migrants provides this assurance of continuity. The community life perpetuates the tradition, norms and values of the society of origin in a foreign land, thus providing them an identity in an alien culture. (Bal, 2003, p. 255)

Therefore, the tendency in most ethnic enclaves is to build a strong community with women and children at the core so as to ensure the continuity of the community through the reproduction of cultural, religious and ritual norms, values and practices that lie at the heart of community life.

Living in a Muslim-dominated area might be a choice for most migrants. However, not everyone in the Muslim community has willingly migrated to Jamia Nagar. Often, the conditions around a communal situation force people to move and this is also an outcome of the fear among Hindu landlords of keeping Muslims as tenants. As a result, young Muslim families who wish to move out of the ghetto cannot do so. In the words of a woman who works as an engineer in Delhi:

> It was in the year 2008–09 when we were searching for a home. My husband did not want to live in any Muslim ghetto, but we were having trouble in finding a home anywhere else. He contacted many property dealers, and

we could afford a home in any good locality but no deal could be finalized. Property dealers told us that finding a home for a Muslim couple is not easy because the Hindu landlords are uncomfortable renting a home to Muslims, be it in any area. No amount of money could have convinced the landlords as the problem was that of religion. So my husband suggested that we could find a home in New Friends' Colony and Jamia Nagar. I have no idea why he did not want to come here in the first place. Since I have lived in a Muslim dominated area of Bhopal and I don't find it to be a problem. However, the property dealer could not find any house in Jamia Nagar or New Friends' Colony. This was the time when the Batla house encounter took place in 2008 in Jamia Nagar, so even the Muslim landlords were not convinced to take new tenants.[9] Once again money was not a problem. The major problem was that people were scared of Muslims; it was just the wrong time to find a new house.

Old women and the women who are living alone do not want to move out of the Muslim-dominated area; they believe that they are safe here. This willingness to stay depends on the family and its needs, that is, if there is a family. The same place offers different material prospects to different members of the Muslim population. Women coming from economically backward places find Jamia Nagar to be a developed area but the women who have moved in here from more developed parts of India consider it to be a backward area. For example, an upper class woman moving in from Darbhanga says:

This place is dirtier than Aligarh but is more expensive as it is located in Delhi. When I came here it was relatively more spacious but there is a foul smell now and it is as if there has been an explosion in the population, and everyone wants to live here. I can, however, understand that the reason is that this place is safe for the Muslims and Delhi has a lot of work opportunities.

The engineer woman who migrated in to Jamia Nagar from Chanakyapuri in New Delhi, however, elaborated,

By looking at the accommodation in Batla house and accommodation in Chandni Chowk, I understood why my husband was not willing to shift in here. The place is so congested, and there is no space on the streets. While living in Chanakyapuri I used to travel comfortably after 8.00 p.m.; here, I am afraid, and my husband comes to pick me from Maharani Bagh bus stop. But on the other hand, it seems that the place is livelier than Chankyapuri. You can easily spot people roaming around, shopping and having fun even late at night. The student population is the life of the place, they are always around. But with unlit streets and sometimes goons around, I don't feel safe in this part of Jamia Nagar. Not to mention the bad state of construction here. The Yamuna river is close by, the place easily gets flooded with even a little rain and the dampness never goes away. See the damp patches in the wall, they never go away. There is never enough light in the house, as the buildings around are made in such a way that no fresh air and sunlight can enter the home. No wall putty helps here. Though there is no problem of electricity and water because the MLA makes sure that these necessities are available to all, sadly the same cannot be said for the sanitation works. The meat shops do not dispose off their wastes properly, they then rot and smell.

This migrant woman's social class background and sensibilities bring out her aversion to the smells and difficulties of life in damp, crowded spaces although she accepts the liveliness of living in the midst of the community. Social class is an important factor in the lived experience of the Muslim women in the Jamia Nagar locality. A domestic help from Motihari says, 'Now life is different, I have grown up and matured, I wish I could go back home. But I can't, this place is addictive, the freedom is addictive'. Depending on social class backgrounds, women acknowledge and appreciate different standards of living in the community. What appears to be a stifling, smelly environment for one upper class woman is freedom and independence for another.

Migration to Delhi might have provided small town women the freedom to choose and move, but Jamia Nagar does not score as a liveable place as complaints about the lack of space and cleanliness are unanimously voiced by everybody. Despite these factors, there are women who have purchased property on their own. Having a home of one's own adds to the willingness to stay on in the area. There is more likely a will for returning to their 'own home' (parents' home in most of the cases) if the woman does not own property. Acquiring property provides a sense of belongingness which for women has been a motivation for continuing to stay in Jamia Nagar. The dirty and noisy Jamia Nagar is liveable for the women who own property here, irrespective of their class position.

A riot survivor of Bhagalpur who now owns a publishing firm says:

They (her father-in-law and husband) had bought a property here. This place was chosen due to the fact that this is a Muslim-dominated area. I had no idea before I came here, about the place. They decided that this will be good for living and also for the education of the children. We, the ladies of the house, came only after the construction of the ground floor of this home. It was an unauthorized colony at that time so land was cheap but constructing a house was difficult. The men took turns to come here for the construction. We didn't have much money to construct the whole house so we used to live in three bedrooms on the ground floor when we came here. Some more families bought homes here after the riots. That gave us moral support…It was like starting a new life altogether. We had no household goods when we came here and no jobs for people starting from scratch. My father-in-law worked on his contacts from Bihar to re-establish his business here…For me this place is different and for my mother-in-law it was alien but my children have grown up quite well here and they don't find any problems in living here. We are comfortable now, though it is very congested, at least it is safe. During the bad time of violence, threat was not from rioters but the property mafia. Though not well planned and very congested, this place is secure and safe for all Muslims.

Another respondent, a 35-year-old woman, mother of two, says, '…I will think of returning to my parents' house after my children have completed their education. I cannot manage to marry them off all by myself. It is a lot of work'. Delhi, generally, and here, Jamia Millia Islamia (JMI) provides better opportunities for education and employment but for this woman, even the financial independence does not make up for social independence. An important decision like getting their daughters married requires the support of the extended family. In the midst of all the lifestyle change post-migration, it is also true that women face difficulties in living and travelling alone. The respondents reported cases of the stalking of women by acquaintances and other men which results in their not wanting to live alone. The need for security is closely related to the need for having support from male kin or family, their mental support or their physical presence, which has been voiced by every respondent irrespective of age, class and occupation. A young woman emphasises that it is because of the family support she has received that she has journeyed alone without fear.

In addition, the field data contributes to a nuanced understanding of migration through the concepts of 'culture of migration' and the 'we'—feeling—sense of belonging through living together in one place as one community. This sense of solidarity arises through the ghetto formation among the Muslim women in Jamia Nagar. Ghettos are meant to be associated with the identity of 'we' in contrast to the 'other' and are constructed not only to belong to a group but also to stand against an 'other'. Abdo's work (2006) on ghettos in America provides the argument that after the crisis of 9/11, the Muslim population has faced discrimination. Abdo argues that ghettos are then looked upon by Muslims as an alternative to escape embarrassment and stigmatization. Muslims choose to live in the places with the majority of their population and send their children to Muslim schools. At the same time, this results in the stigmatization of the community as a whole.

Almost all the work on ghettoization shows that the process of living together in one place is a reaction to fear, a strategy to deal with the terror. As Bourdieu (1990) says, human subjects strategize to play the social game, and it not only needs knowledge of the common rule of the game but also personal creativity. However, Bourdieu also argues that resistance to a type of structure leads one to conform to other stereotyped structures of society. Muslims strategize to walk out of the given structure of society and build their lives. But it all results in them being cut off from the mainstream, hence reproducing the hegemonic culture. Scholars argue that ghettoization is decided by a family and under the circumstances, the entire family moves together from one place to another, but this statement lacks a perspective on the gender dynamics in ghettoization and migration. In the case of women migrants in Jamia Nagar, we have attempted to examine ghettoization from a gendered perspective of migration and find autonomy and freedom in women's lives in what appears to be a closed off and constrained social space.

Seeking Change

Our fieldwork findings manoeuvre around the 'women as victims approach' and show the manner in which Muslim women who have migrated to Jamia Nagar are leading a more fulfilling life in their new locality, as is evident from the fact that they claim to have migrated for social security, well-being, better opportunities and higher education. In fact, the younger women express their joy towards the new-found freedom in all aspects of living. It is observed that many women are fleeing from small-town prejudices, dangerous and overbearing fathers and male relatives. Home can therefore be a suffocating place. This argument provides a contrast to the popularly held conceptions regarding the predicament of migrants, women in particular (Agustin, 2005). The respondents have also noted that if they had continued to live in their native places, it would have resulted in continued suffering and dependence. One such respondent is of the opinion that Jamia Nagar has made them more independent:

I never thought of living alone in an unknown place. I was married at the age of 15. I grew up with the thought of being with a person all my life. Then things change, now here I am living, studying, trying to support myself. It is difficult for a small town girl like me; never in my dreams would I have done so. I have never seen anybody do this. The surroundings help you grow; here the environment is quite supportive.

Similarly, a 21-year-old student observes that:

Patna is a reserved place, and while living there, I could not think of roaming around this freely. I lived here for three years, my brothers were very supportive and so were my parents. I completed my school and went back to Patna. It was to be decided whether I should continue my education or get married. My father was in favour of further education. So I came back to JMI.

Again, the role of the family in helping women gain independence can be seen clearly. Another woman notes that migration also acts as a break from the cultural baggage that they carry by living in a small town:

It was the decision of the men in my life whether or not I have to migrate. I was asked and I agreed because I know they are my well-wishers. For a woman leaving *maika* (mother's home) is natural but leaving *sasural* (in-laws home) alive is a shame. Here people are not concerned; else I could have died of shame.

Though most of the interviewed women migrated for reasons stemming from decisions taken with the support of the men in their family, the women have exercised their agency in their decision for staying on. The factors that motivated migration ranged from the men deciding to migrate for work, marriage leading to migration and women being compelled to migrate owing to atrocities by the male members of their family. At the same time, women have migrated for higher education and employment opportunities with family support.

Over time, family traditions of migration affect the values and behavioural systems of communities, forming a 'culture of migration'. As the number of migrants increase, migration becomes deeply ingrained into the repertoire of people's behaviour, and values associated with migration become part of the community's sense of identity. When migration was dominated by males, young men perceived migration as a rite of passage to adulthood. Later, as migration became more feminized, it also affected female values and behaviour, and this forges a new culture of migration

(Oishi, 2005). 'Culture as a "way of life" is a crucial construction, and the argument is that by its very nature, migration challenges the idea of a unitary or single way of life' (Iyer, 2004, p. 45). There are many cultures and ways of life and there is no homogeneous understanding of the experience of belonging and identity as a consequence of migration.

Women's migration within India takes place as a result of several factors identified in the course of the chapter. We need to, however, take into account the fact that there is great disparity in women's migration strategies ranging from employment, education, career moves and marriage, and this does not in any way undermine their need to seek mobility. Our focus on Muslim women migrants is an effort to open up the space for understanding women's migration goals and strategies within an overall framework of mobility, family and territorial space. Muslim women, belonging to different socio-economic backgrounds seek mobility but this is often achieved within the rubric of familial and community strategies of both migration and of living together as members of the same community in a territorial space marked out as their own. This has certain implications that both facilitate as well as impede their need for employment, safety and autonomy.

Concluding Comments and Policy Recommendations

This essay has emphasized that Muslim women have remained invisible in the larger discourse on migration. Their presence has been acknowledged, but very few scholars are looking at them as a distinct category. Engineer (2013) has shown that the vulnerability of Indian Muslim women cannot be rooted only in Islam. It is the social context coupled by the practice of Islam that makes them a vulnerable group. They are denied various rights, for instance property rights, which though are part of Islam, are not acceptable in the Indian social milieu dominated by patriarchy. The superimposition of communal identity over the gendered identity often results in overlooking the gender specific problems of women in the community. The social and economic backwardness, the dominance of Muslim personal law that is interpreted and implemented by the men of the Muslim community, and the religious profiling in the worldwide discourse on terrorism also add to the layers of vulnerability of Muslim women.

Scholars believe that there is an urgent need to look at the Muslim women as a separate category and produce findings that can help Muslim women in various spheres of their life (see the works of Siddiqi and Zuberi, 1993; Kumar, 2002; IIJ, 2003). This chapter has examined aspects of Muslim women's lives in a localized context of their own, shaped by their anxieties and desires, located in the family and community. It is observed that lives of women are focused around their family and the decisions, major or minor, are largely taken by the men of the family. However, it cannot be argued that they have no control over their own lives. As shown by Bodman and Tohidi (1998), Muslim women try to adjust and adapt to modern culture but they do not take extreme measures to do so. Rather, they adjust themselves in both private beliefs and public sphere opportunities without losing their ability to assert their decisions and identities. This is similar to the observation by Hasan and Menon (2004, p. 147),

> [T]here is a hierarchy of the significance of decisions, and women can-and do-exercise the option *not* to decide, selectively. By this strategy, they may simultaneously maintain a public image of submissiveness while actually gradually increasing their influence and participation in the home.

This is seen in the fact that Muslim women, with the help of their family, undertake migration. It is a step taken to release themselves of the social submissiveness and indecisiveness that is associated with their gendered subjecthood. They move to certain pre-determined places, with the help of familial or other contacts, largely through marriage, to get on with their lives. Though they compromise on some quarters of their migration, being in a new place amongst new people helps their growth in terms of building self-confidence and in taking day-to-day decisions about their lives. In this manner, migration for women can be seen as a way to break away from the depressing situation at the native place. Most of our respondents reported to be free from the cultural norms and societal values that held them back in their native places. These situations are also complicated by the violence that is perpetrated upon women.

In cases of domestic violence, or moving on in a marriage, our respondents show a great deal of free decision-making, but this is also partly influenced by a consideration of familial perspectives. Muslim women are also subject to violence in public spheres like communal riots and massacres. Forbes and Tirman (2009), Behera (2006) and Gill and Thiara (2009), have shown in their work that women and children are the most vulnerable groups in any violent act. Owing to the fact that we have a long history of communal riots in India, the significance of violence in changing the lives of women by allowing them to migrate and setting up a whole new life cannot be ignored. Here also family plays a crucial role in deciding the ways to keep their women and the honour of the family, which is vested in the women, to be safe and secure.

Through the primary and secondary findings of this chapter, it emerges that vulnerability is constructed through representations of female suffering and the consequences of naming certain groups as vulnerable and as victims. Thus one may infer that the labelling of certain groups as vulnerable is a social construct, which is then perpetuated by law, administration and all other citizens follow suit. It is in this manner that covertly gendered but explicitly gender-free notions of culture, domestic violence and 'race' work to exclude women's experience although, on the façade there may exist the portrayal of a gender-neutral dimension (Palmary et al., 2010, p. 8). It is striking that in present times women should be seen as so overwhelmingly pushed, obligated, coerced, or forced when they leave home to get ahead through work. 'But, so entrenched is the idea of women as forming an essential *part* of home, if not actually *being* it themselves, that they are routinely denied the agency' (Agustin, 2005, p. 224). As researchers, we, therefore, need to be open to the idea of viewing women as making choices even when they are encircled by the family and the community. Their desire for education, employment, and above all, freedom, must be recognized as increasingly contributing factors for their mobility.

Legal and policy frameworks, both globally and in India, have failed to pay sufficient and serious attention to women migrants. This lacuna needs to be urgently addressed at both the state and national levels if India seriously wants to develop a gender-sensitive policy orientation towards migrants. In order to so, the need of the hour is to generate first class micro-level data, based on qualitative study among the most marginalized migrant communities, understanding the experience, problems and dilemmas of migrant women and their families. In addition to fieldwork at the ground level in slums, ghettos and shanty towns of large metropolitan cities, it is important to recognize innovative perspectives for research that take into account the voices of women without losing the larger socio-economic picture and political conditions, within which all movement takes place.

In the process of this study, it was observed that scholars and government organizations have largely ignored the questions related to Muslim women and migration. Keeping this in mind, it is recommended that a database on this theme should be developed. Efforts must be made to undertake more research, like the Muslim Women's Survey (MWS). There is also a severe dearth of data on migration due to different forms of violence in India. If such information can be generated, more studies can be undertaken. The database could include, for instance, data pertaining to people from minority communities who have left their homes after an act of violence, or whether these are communal riots, wars or conflicts of different kinds and what their outcome is for different kinds of marginalized communities. Their migration and resettlement details also need to be recorded. In addition, gendered data on violence is still lacking. Under the present conditions, there is an urgent need for generating statistical details and records of death, rape, sexual assault and medical conditions of women victims of violence.

Notes

1. Source: http://pib.nic.in/newsite/erelease.aspx?relid=62559 (accessed on 5 September 2013).
2. Acknowledging the role of migration in shaping the discourse around women's mobility and agency, this chapter is based on primary data collected at Jamia Nagar as well as existing literature on the issue. The exploratory study has been analyzed within the broader context of gender and migration with an emphasis on dimensions of freedom and ghettoization that have emerged from the survey data. The narratives have proved to be a rich source of data that enable making recommendations that might be useful at the legal and policy levels.
3. Our survey was conducted in Jamia Nagar that includes Abul Fazal Enclave, Batla House, Zakir Nagar, Shaheen Bagh, Johri Farm and Jamia Millia Islamia. The respondents were all females in the age bracket of 17–60 years, contacted through acquaintances and friends. An interview schedule was prepared before venturing into the field. It included open-ended questions about reasons for migration, conditions of life in the native place and destination, struggles resulting from expected gender roles, among other matters. All the interactions were conducted in an informal environment, either at the place of residence of the respondent or their workplace.
4. Women from eight households were interviewed in Hindustani; all the interviews were conducted in Jamia Nagar. The women have migrated from Bihar and Uttar Pradesh to Delhi with the permission of their family, and mostly along with them. All the women are educated; contrary to popular belief, only one of them has been educated in a *madrasa*. All the others are educated in government or private schools. Two of them are working

in multinational corporations (MNCs) and one owns her own business. Two women who are still pursuing their higher studies are keen to work afterwards.

5. Bhagalpur riots took place in 1989; Bhagalpur is a district in the state of Bihar, which faced violence in 1989. Its causes are closely related to the *Ayodhya Janam bhumi* debate. During the riots Muslims were targeted in Bhagalpur, and many Muslim men and women lost their lives in the riots. Many mosques and Muslim property were also destroyed.

6. It has been argued that the migration of the Muslim population is closely related to the ghettoization of the Muslim population in some pockets of the country due to fear of communal violence or for the reasons of social security, that is, feeling comfortable while practising their religion. See Gayer and Jaffrelot (2011).

7. Officially known as Operation Batla House, this took place in September 2008. Delhi police claims that in this particular operation they were trying to get hold of the terrorists responsible for the Delhi blasts of September, 2008. The claims are yet to be proved but the operation faced criticism for falsely targeting and profiling young innocent Muslim boys for terrorist activities. See Jamia Teachers' Solidarity Association (2009).

8. Writers of poetry and fiction, Lahiri (1999, 2003) and Alexander (2003), for example, provide rich and nuanced descriptions of the fraught experience of belonging in alien cultures.

References

Abdo, G. (2006). *Mecca and main street: Muslim life in America after 9/11*. United Kingdom: Oxford University Press.

Agnihotri, I. Mazumdar, I., and Neetha, N. (2012). *Gender and migration. Negotiating rights. A women's movement perspective*. Delhi: Centre for Women's Development Studies.

Agustin, L. M. (2005). 'Still challenging "place": Sex, money, and agency in women's migrations'. In W. Harcourt and A. Escobar (eds), *Women and the politics of place* (pp. 221–23). Bloomfield, CT: Kumarian.

Alexander, M. (2003). *The shock of arrival. Reflections on postcolonial experience*. US: South End Press.

Arya, S. and Roy, A. (eds). (2006). *Poverty, gender and migration*, Vol. 2 of *Women and migration in Asia*. New Delhi: SAGE Publications.

Bal, G. (2003). 'Transnational migrants: Punjabi women in Canada'. In Paramjit S. Judge, S.L. Sharma, S.K. Sharma and Gurpreet Bal (eds), *Development, gender and diaspora: Context of globalization* (pp. 253–74). Jaipur: Rawat Publications.

Bannerjee, A. and Saraswati, R. (2009). 'Gendered mobility: Women migrants and work in urban India'. *Economic and Political Weekly of India, XLIV*(28), 115–23.

Bannerjee, P. (2010). *Borders, histories, existences. Gender and beyond*. New Delhi and Thousand Oaks: SAGE Publications.

Behera, N.C. (ed.). (2006). *Gender, conflict and migration*, Vol. 3 of *Women and migration in Asia*. New Delhi: SAGE Publications.

Bhasin, K., and Menon, R. (1998). *Borders and boundaries: Women in India's partition*. New Delhi: Kali for Women.

Bodman, H.L. and Tohidi, N. (eds). (1998). *Women in Muslim societies: Diversity within unity*. Boulder: Lynne Rienner Publishers.

Bourdieu, P. (1990). *The logic of practice*. Stanford: Stanford University Press.

Chopra, R. (2004). 'Maps of experience (narratives of migration in an Indian village)'. In Gopal Iyer (ed.), *Distressed migrant labour in India: Key human rights issues* (pp. 44–65). New Delhi: Kanishka.

Engineer, A.A. (2013). *Islam: Gender justice: Muslim gender discrimination*. New Delhi: Gyan Publishing House.

Forbes, S. M. and Tirman, J. (2009). *Women, migration, and conflict: Breaking a deadly cycle*. Washington, D.C.: Springer.

Gayer, L. (2011). 'Safe and sound. Searching for a "good environment" in Abul Fazl Enclave, Delhi'. In Laurent Gayer and Christophe Jaffrelot (eds), *Muslims in Indian cities. Trajectories of marginalisation*. New York: Columbia University Press.

Gayer, L. and Jaffrelot, C. (eds). (2011). *Muslims in Indian cities. Trajectories of marginalisation*. New York: Columbia University Press.

Gill, A., and Thiara, R.K. (2009). *Violence against women in South Asian Communities: Issues for policy and practice*. UK and USA: Jessica Kingsley Publishers.

Glick-Schiller, N., and Salazar, N.B. (2013). 'Regimes of mobility across the globe'. *Journal of Ethnic and Migration Studies*, *39*(2), 183–200.

Hasan, Z. and Menon, R. (2004). *Unequal citizens: A study of Muslim women in India*. New Delhi: Oxford University Press.

———. (eds.) (2005). 'Introduction'. *In a Minority: Essays on Muslim women in India*. New Delhi: Oxford University Press.

IIJ (International Initiative for Justice). (2003). *Threatened existence: A feminist analysis of the genocide in Gujarat*. Retrieved from http://www.onlinevolunteers.org/gujarat/reports/iijg/2003/ (accessed on 19 September 2010).

Iyer, K.G. (ed.). (2004). *Distressed migrant labour in India—Key human rights issues*. New Delhi: Kanishka Publishers.

Jamia Teachers' Solidarity Association. (2009). *'Encounter' at Batla house: Unanswered questions report*. Retrieved from http://document.teacherssolidarity.org (accessed on 19 September 2010).

Kumar, H. (2002). *Status of Muslim women in India*. New Delhi: Aakar Books.

Lahiri, J. (1999). *The interpreter of maladies*. Boston, NY: Houghton Mifflin.

———. (2003). *The namesake: A novel*. Boston, NY: Houghton Mifflin.

Nair, S. (2007a). *Migrants and the urban landscape of Delhi—Experiences of women nurses from Kerala*. Paper presented in National Seminar on Women and Migration organised by Centre for Women's Development Studies, New Delhi.

———. (2007b). 'Rethinking citizenship, community and rights: The case of nurses from Kerala in Delhi'. *Indian Journal of Gender Studies*, *14*(1), 137–56.

Oishi, N. (2005). *Women in motion. Globalization, state policies, and labor migration in Asia*. California: Stanford University Press.

Palmary, I., Burman, E., Chantler, K., and Kiguwa, P. (eds). (2010). *Gender and migration: Feminist interventions* (pp. 1–11). London: Zed Books.

Palriwala, R., and Uberoi, P. (eds). (2008). *Marriage, migration and gender*, Vol. 5 of *Women and Migration in Asia*. New Delhi: SAGE Publications.

Shanthi, K. (2006). *Female labour migration in India: Insights from NSSO data* (Working Paper No. 4). Madras School of Economics.

Siddiqi, Z.A. and Zuberi, A.J. (1993). *Muslim women: Problems and prospects.* New Delhi: M. D. Publications.

Thapan, M. (ed.). (2005). 'Introduction', in *Transnational migration and the politics of identity*, Vol. 1 of *Women and migration in Asia.* New Delhi: SAGE Publications.

Tumbe, C. (2012). 'Migration persistence across twentieth century India'. *Migration and Development*, *1*(1), 87–112.

Virk, R. (2004). 'Women construction workers in Amritsar city'. In Gopal Iyer (ed.), *Distressed migrant labour in India: Key human rights issues* (pp. 162–77). New Delhi: Kanishka.

4

Migration and Marginalization: A Study of North East Migrants in Delhi

Babu P. Remesh[1]

Introduction

Out-migration of youth from the North Eastern Region (NER),[2] on a large scale, towards far-off cities in other parts of the country is a recent phenomenon. The region is traditionally considered as a receiving pocket of migrants and accordingly most of the research on migration pertaining to the region is confined to issues and dimensions of in-migration. However, with a steady and steep increase in out-migration since 1980s,[3] a trend that further strengthened in the immediate past,[4] there has been growing concerns over the determinants and implications of such migration (Shimray, 2007; Singh, 2007).

National Capital Region (NCR)—or broadly 'Delhi Region'—is one of the most favoured destinations of migrants from NER. Estimates suggest that currently in Delhi region, there are 90,000 to 100,000 north-eastern ethnic residences. The other major urban centres include Bengaluru, Mumbai, Kolkata, Chennai, Chandigarh, Pune and Hyderabad. Along with these city-bound movements, some proportion of the migrants also moves to smaller towns and suburbs of far-off states within the country.[5]

In this backdrop, a field-based study was conducted, covering 402[6] working migrants[7] from four selected localities (Vijay Nagar, Munirka, Moti Bagh and Kotla Mubarakpur) in Delhi,[8] to explore various dimensions of the out-migration from the North East to the Delhi region.[9] This chapter, based on the findings of this study, captures some of the crucial dimensions of out-migration. The specific dimensions explored include: determinants and processes of migration; profile of out-migrants and unique aspects of migration from the North East, formation and detailing of migrant-neighbourhoods, emerging occupational patterns, vulnerabilities and insecurities of migrants in the city, and their continuous struggle of negotiating the city life. The identity crisis and racial discrimination experienced by the migrants in the city are also briefly discussed to capture some of underlying determinants of their insecurities in the alien-urban landscape. The role of social and institutional/agency networks in facilitating migration and negotiating the life in the city is yet another aspect discussed in the chapter.

Profile of Migrants

Out of the 402 respondents, 214 (52.24 per cent) were men. Around three-fourths (74.8 per cent) of the respondents were from the age cohort of 25–30 and 15.2 per cent of the respondents were even younger (18–25 age group). These strongly indicate the 'youth' aspect of the migrants. Out of the total respondents, 93.03 per cent of the respondents were unmarried. A small proportion of them (1.24 per cent) were either separated/deserted. This pattern can be explained as follows. As the influx of North East youth to the new economy occupations are fairly new, the age profile is rather young. Partly, recruitment of youth is also an objective function of the firms in new service sector occupations. Further, as most of the respondents are within the first five years of their migration or entering into work, they are mostly single and sharing the same residential premises mostly with their friends from the North East (same locality or same tribe).

Out of the total, 44.3 per cent of the respondents were from Manipur.[10] This was followed by Mizoram (17.2 per cent), Assam (16.2 per cent), Nagaland (7 per cent), Arunachal Pradesh (6.2 per cent), Tripura (6.0 per cent) and Meghalaya (3.2 per cent). There was no respondent from Sikkim.[11] Almost 57.2 per cent reported that they belong to semi-urban areas of their state. This is followed by urban (30.3 per cent) and rural (12.4 per cent) areas.[12]

Majority of the respondents reported as Christians (49.75)[13] or Hindus (45.02 per cent). Forty eight per cent of migrants from Arunachal Pradesh reported that they belong to Buddhism. A few respondents from Manipur and Tripura (6 per cent and 4.2 per cent respectively) also reported themselves as Buddhists. Respondents belonging to the Muslim community were only 0.2 per cent of total (or 1.5 per cent of Assamese), who all stayed in Moti Bagh. Fifty seven per cent reported themselves belonging to STs and 35.2 as forward castes. Six per cent were found to be from other backward classes (OBCs) and other 1.7 per cent from scheduled castes (SCs).

Educational profile of the respondents is impressive. There are no illiterates among the respondents and those who are with less than intermediary (plus two) education are less than 3 per cent. Around 84 per cent of the respondents have at least graduation/professional diploma or similar higher qualification. Almost 47.3 per cent reported as graduates, 30.3 per cent as postgraduates and 6.6 per cent as professionals with diploma and higher vocational skills. Apart from this, several of the respondents were found studying for some other courses along with their present employment.

Determinants and Unique Aspects of Migration

The reasons/determinants of migration could also be grouped as 'push' and 'pull' factors, as done by North East Support Centre and Helpline (NESC&H) (2011). Such binary segregation allows to classifying the emerging situation of migration within the broad categories of 'compulsions' and 'attractions'. An important reason behind the migration of youth from NER to urban centres is 'educational and employment considerations'. It is widely understood that despite a high literacy rate,[14] the region is characterized by a visible lack of adequate avenues for higher or technical education or vocational training. There is also a felt mismatch between the demand in the job market and the weak local educational system, especially to meet the requirements of the new economy occupations and professional service sectors (Lyndem and De, 2004). These conditions, coupled with inadequate economic infrastructure, may have definite implications on the migration decisions of educated and ambitious youth to urban centres for higher learning. It widely understood that a good proportion of this youth continue to live in urban centres after education, for employment.[15]

The bleak employment prospect in the local labour markets is a critical determinant of migration of youth from NER to urban centres. Increasing educated and youth unemployment in the North Eastern states owes considerably to the abysmally lower level of industrialization and lower expansion of modern service sector occupations in the region. The recent saturation in the government/public sector jobs also intensifies the unemployment situation. Lower labour absorption capacity of local labour markets and perceived employment prospects in the urban centres together prompt the aspirant youth in NER to migrate to cities (at least for some time) to explore better opportunities.

The political unrest, violence and poverty of the region also often influence the decisions of youth in favour of migration (Shimray, 2004, 2007). Most of the states in the NER have unrests and tensions (which include: religious/ethnic/communal clashes, tensions between local and infiltrated population, insurgency, tensions between people and army, insurgency and so on). Due to these tensions, the normal life of the people in the region is affected. For instance, reports suggest that in Manipur, life has become a nightmare for the ordinary people in recent years. With 100 days of public strikes a year, markets shut, schools closed and public transportation off the road, it is difficult to pursue studies and livelihoods in the state. Such tensions together with bleak educational infrastructure and employment prospects in the region are found prompting the youngsters to try their luck in urban centres in other parts of the country.

Charm of working in cities and in new economy jobs and possibilities of getting jobs in the city also add to their decision regarding migration. The relatively better command over English (among educated) and friendly attitudes of the youth from NER often help them to easily find a job in the cities, especially in hospitality and care works. Further to this, it is commonly perceived that getting a central government job in the migrated destinations is relatively easy for those belonging to scheduled caste or scheduled tribe (SC/ST) communities as many of them are rightly qualified for reserved jobs both in higher and lower positions.

Migration from NER to urban centres is distinct from the usual patterns of migration of rural poor to urban centres. As discussed earlier, as compared to the migrants from other parts of the country, these migrants are from better economic and educational backgrounds.[16] Due to this, a large chunk of migration is not due to abject poverty or in search of low-paid manual employment in the city. For instance, in Delhi, it is hard to find a rickshaw puller or urban street vendor from NER. Further, the presence of North East population is also very minimal in factory works in NCR.

Seasonal migration, which is a prominent pattern with those migrants from other North Indian states is almost absent in the case of migration of NER youth. Compared to migrants from Bihar, Haryana and Uttar Pradesh, the North Easters stay for more months and a larger portion subsequently opts for permanent stay in Delhi region.[17] Given the better financial status, educational profile and better human resources of the migrants, this pattern needs to be understood in detail. The preference for continuing in the city largely owes to the tensions in native states. Almost all the states in region are crippled with some tensions—be it insurgency, ethnic clashes or tensions between natives and infiltrated. This prompts those who have some resources to migrate to the cities, especially for education of their children. As the North Eastern states lack higher educational infrastructure (but are endowed with good educational system up to secondary level), such migration for educational pursuit is prominent among aspirant youth who have completed some level of education at their native places. Further, after obtaining better education in the city most migrants choose to continue living in the city in order to 'best utilize' their capacities. Thus, while tensions and lack of educational infrastructure jointly act as the driving force for first-stage of migration, it is lack of employment opportunities (which is also related to tensions) that deter the return of migrants.

Most of the youth came to the city as single migrants, without their family or friends, in a group. As per the survey data, 93.2 per cent of the respondents reported as single migrants. But many of them had someone (family members, relatives, friends or someone from the same community/ locality) to provide initial support and help. Thus, a lower share of marriage migration is a unique aspect of the migration from NER to urban centres.

The patterns of savings and remittances showed interesting results. Unlike the migrants from other states to Delhi region (for example, those from Bihar or Kerala), the North Easters are not found remitting considerable portions of their income to their family in the native states.[18] A majority rely on formal banking system for saving and remitting money back home. Despite the difficulties narrated apropos opening bank accounts, 93.3 per cent reported that they do have a bank account in Delhi with more than two-thirds actually using the formal banking system on a regular basis. A reason for this particular aspect is the higher level of education and awareness of the migrants.

From the survey, it was evident that given their unique cultural background, most of the youth are found spending a good proportion of their income on outfits, food, travelling and organizing frequent gatherings of friends and community members. This feature is quite distinct from the migrants in Delhi belonging to other parts of the country. Another uniqueness found is in terms of investment on educational pursuits. Several of the respondents were studying for higher qualifications, in correspondence courses or in evening/weekend classes.

Yet another aspect that needs mention is the absence of institutional/ community networks or agency networks in migration process. Mostly the migrants are not coming to the city through agents or with the help of institutions/community organizations (for example, church), which is prominently seen in migration of workers from other regions (for example, in construction sites, or migration for domestic work).[19]

Emerging Occupational Profile and Process of Accessing Jobs

Owing to the better educational background, migrants from NER are more inclined towards pursuing higher studies or entering into office jobs/white-collar occupations in government or private sector firms. The proliferation of jobs in the modern service sector industries, in the recent years also opened up considerable occupational avenues for the youth from the North East, who have 'right' aptitudes for the customer-oriented service economy.

Till the early years of the present century, a major proportion of the migrants in Delhi from the North East were found working in government jobs. Since there is some reservation for those belonging to SC/ST communities, the North Easters belonging to tribal communities found these jobs easily accessible, given their better educational backgrounds and fluency in English. But, in the recent years, with the emergence of new occupations in the globalized era, there are more avenues coming in the private sector and service sector occupations (NESC&H, 2011). Accordingly, a major chunk of youngsters were found working in a host of private sector occupations (including administrative and office jobs, business process outsourcing (BPO) jobs, customer care activities, hospitality jobs—waiters/waitresses, receptionists, sales executives and so on).[20] In the four pockets (Vijaya Nagar, Munirka, Moti Bagh and Kotla Mubarakpur) selected for detailed case studies, most of the people were found working in such private sector or MNC occupations (in office-based white-collar jobs) and in a variety of service sector occupations in the new economy, ranging from sales persons to air hostess.

Almost 67.3 per cent of the respondents reported that the present occupation is their first job, which pointed towards the phase-wise shift from studentship to worker status. Around 81.1 per cent reported their job as permanent. But from detailed probing, it was evident that the permanency is a notion, as most of them worked in projects/contracts or with term-based appointments. In view of this, it is more appropriate to conceptualize them as regular but semi-permanent.

A prominent pattern of getting access to city jobs was through referrals. This is truer for those who work in new service sector occupations. '[T]he company promotes a "bring your own buddy" policy and it was easy for me to find a job as my cousin was working there', said a Mizo girl who works in a BPO firm. Several others got the job by applying to the firms, of which they had some understanding through their kith and kin. Other important means was to apply directly in response to advertisements (especially in newspapers and the Internet) and to appear for direct/telephonic interview.

There were also instances where the employees were recruited directly from North East, in recruitment *melas* organized by the company or through placement agencies/training centres, where they got basic knowledge about the jobs. During the visit to North Eastern states, it was noticed that several of the BPO firms had some arrangements with training centres in Shillong, Kohima, Dimapur and Guwahati to recruit candidates with right aptitudes.

Irrespective of the mode of selection, the respondents had to undergo several rounds of testing which include aptitude tests, group discussions, telephonic/direct interview, written tests and so on. More than academic qualifications, the respondents feel that it is their positive aptitudes and attitudes that were counted by the firms. The pleasing appearance, fluent English, trendy dressing styles and free mingling nature of the youth often help them to find a job in the hospitality sector. For instance, during the

Common Wealth Games period, thousands of youth from the region got temporary but nicely paying jobs in the reception and hospitality-related sections of the organizing committee.

The docile but committed and hard-working nature of the North Easters is often preferred by the employers. 'They are hardworking, honest and committed', 'pleasing appearance', 'soft-spoken and with nice behaviour', 'They won't group against the interests of the company'—These are some of the typical and oft repeated responses of the owners and managers of the firms. Yet another attraction is the higher retention rates (or longer period of continuance) of North East workers. The survey data suggests that more than 50 per cent of the respondents continued in their present occupation for more than a year. Almost 28.4 per cent was employed for more than 2 years. The Mongoloid features of the north-eastern migrants are also preferred by the employers (for example, Chinese restaurants, Momo stalls in multiplex shopping malls,[21] star hotels and hospitals) as it helps the firms to give some international/cross-cultural/ethnic ambience to their establishments.

Patterns of Migration and Migrant Neighbourhoods

A prominent pattern of migration involves two stages. In the first stage, the youth will come to the city as students and after the completion of their course or after few years of study, they get into some suitable jobs available in the city. Confirming this pattern, several of the respondents of the study initially came for education in prominent education institutions (such as the University of Delhi [DU], Jawaharlal Nehru University [JNU] and Jamia Millia Islamia) and during their stay in Delhi found a suitable job and continued in the city. While most of these migrants came for post-graduate education, in most recent years, several of the youngsters are found coming for undergraduate studies or even for basic schooling. In such cases, the migration often becomes family migration. For instance, some of the respondents pointed out that their primary aim of migration to the city was to educate their children. A closer examination suggests that migrants from certain states (for example, Manipur) show stronger cases of such two-stage migration.

Migrants are found living in pockets where there are more people from the same region/locality/tribes. Sharing of same residence/room by 2–4 persons is the most prominent form. In the survey, 44.2 per cent of the respondents reported that they stay with their friends or colleagues. Another 17.6 per cent also reported staying in groups—but with close relatives or family members. In the former category also, the preferred arrangement is to stay with those people who are from the same community/ tribe or region. When the group becomes that of close relatives, even the number goes up. During the survey, the study team saw many such groups where 8–10 members of the same family (or close relatives) stay together. This pattern of staying in groups inter alia has led to the emergence of migrant neighbourhoods with high concentration of population from NER. All the four selected study regions of the study are such migrant neighbourhoods.

Several of the groups that the study team came across were that of either single migrant girls or boys. Very rarely mixed groups constituting boys and girls were found—these groups were mostly of close relatives/ family members. Staying all alone and with spouse/fiancé was also noticed, though not very frequently. But, even such smaller units preferred to stay in a locality with more concentration of people from their own region/ community. Some of the respondents (17.6 per cent) were also reported staying independently in rented accommodations. A few also reported staying as paying guests (2.2 per cent). Even those were with single accommodation status reported that they prefer to stay in pockets, with concentration of North East people.

Staying in close groups and in migrant neighbourhoods was preferred by most of the respondents on various counts. To quote typical responses: 'As we do share common food habits, eating habits and cultural background, being together means a kind of mutual support to each other'; 'We can understand the problems and puzzles of other person, as we also face those of same sort'. Migrant neighbourhoods provide other advantages apart from having a feeling of togetherness and understanding. There are shops run by people from their locality or sometimes shops that sell the goods from their native states. For instance, a restaurant being run by a Manipuri in a migrant-locality in South Delhi is one of the most frequented eating joints by people from all parts of North East. The food provided is a mix of food from different regions within NER. Within migrant neighbourhoods, the members also get opportunities for having get-togethers on occasions, such as festivals and state formation days, and so on. It also helps them to closely work with community-based collectives.[22]

It was highlighted by most of the respondents that migrant neighbourhoods provided them a feeling of security and many of their tensions back home are forgotten. For instance, members from communities which are at conflict in Manipur, live harmoniously in a Delhi settlement. Thus, these neighbourhoods provide the migrants a feeling of togetherness and binding, which is often lacking in their native places.

Negotiating the City Life: Insecurities and Vulnerabilities

Most of the respondents found the city 'tougher than expected' and opined that they felt 'more insecure' in Delhi. The same observation was maintained by the respondents, even when it was pointed out that many of them had to leave their native places due to insurgencies and disruption in normal life.[23] 'There is a huge difference between what we expected and what we are experiencing', said a respondent. 'The insecurity that we felt in our home state is different compared to that we face here. We cannot compare both', adds another respondent.

Right from climate, eating habits, customs and costumes—everything in Delhi is different for the migrants and adjusting to all these changed situations is the first challenge confronted by the North Easters. Many of them pointed out that all these make them insecure in the city—and that is suggested as the major reason for the strong preference for sharing accommodation with friends/relatives/colleagues from North East in localities which are predominantly inhabited by North Easters.[24] 'It is the strong feeling of loneliness and isolation that prompts us to stay together in localities where the residents share same issues', says a Naga respondent from Kotla.

In quite a few cases, the respondents reported that they tried to adjust with the changed situations to break their 'outsider' status. Picking up bits of spoken Hindi, familiarizing themselves with North Indian food items, dress styles, participation in local festivals, and so on are pointed out as some of the activities towards 'acquiring basic skills for day-to-day life in the city'! But even after these adjustment efforts, many of them find that their Mongolian features and fair skin often made them distinct in public spaces. A number of unsuccessful attempts to become insider were reported by the respondents. Staying at Munirka, a BPO employee from Arunachal Pradesh said:

> Even after wearing sari or salwar-kurta it is very easy to recognise our difference due to our fair skin and wrongly pronounced Hindi by everyone—be it auto drivers, street vendors or eve teasers. And sooner we will fall prey to discriminatory treatment.

Quite often the distinct identity of the migrants adds to their vulnerabilities in the urban alien land. The calm nature and friendly attitudes of North Easters are often mistaken as signs of docility and helplessness. To quote a respondent: 'Basically our people are peace loving and friendly and sometimes we find these qualities as misfit in the harsh city life. Our smiling faces and soft-spoken mannerisms are often read as signs of vulnerability.'

Cultural Gap, Faulty Notions and Social Labelling

Majority of the respondents reported that the root of insecurity lies with the attitude of the society towards people from North East. It is visible that here the issue is that of a 'cultural gap'. The land and people of Delhi differ drastically from the North East in every aspect (climate, culture, food habits, faith and social systems, physical features, personality traits and so on). Due to this cultural difference, quite often the host community find the migrants from NER strange and their social behaviour non-confirming to accepted 'social values'. 'It is quite strange to expect a north eastern tribal youth, who was brought up with the values of a particular tribal community, to behave confirming to the values and ethos entertained by the caste-based society shaped along patriarchal lines', explained a university teacher from North East, while responding to this cultural gap.

As most of the migrants belong to tribal societies in North East, their norms of social behaviour are distinctly different from the north Indian population. The social life in most of the tribal societies is with more gender equality and, thus, the friendly mingling of youth from North East, without inhibitions based on gender divisions often prompt the local population to perceive the North Easters as people with loose moral values.

Compared to an average North Indian, the people from North East are more fluent in English. Their dressing styles and modes of entertainment are also different (more close to those of South East Asian and Western societies than mainland India). All these aspects lead to the formation of faulty notions regarding the social life of the migrants from the region, which inter alia are used for labelling them as socially inferior.[25] During the survey, many respondents pointed out that their calm nature and positive attitudes are often taken as vulnerabilities and due to these qualities, often they fall prey to various discriminations in their day-to-day life.

Discriminations in Daily Life

Discriminatory treatment reported by the respondents ranged from violation of basic rights of living to larger issues of citizenship. A common issue cited by majority is related to discriminatory practices related to rented accommodation.

It is interesting to note that out of the 402 respondents, only one reported to be staying in own accommodation. Getting a room/flat on rent is the most difficult task for migrants from North East. A good chunk of the local landlords are not even considering North Easters as potential clients to rent out their rooms/flats—as they look down at North East people citing differences in culture. 'They have loose morals', 'they eat pigs and dogs', 'their presence will pollute our children', and so on are the justifications given by many of the local room/flat owning people (as reported by some of the respondents. Some of the respondents got the rented accommodation only after ensuring that they will cook and eat only vegetarian food in their rooms. A very few also shared instances of eating 'smuggled' non-vegetarian food in their rooms, without information of landlords.

Yet another set of property owners charge exorbitantly extra rents from the North Easters. The middlemen and the property dealers also demand more money from the North Eastern people.[26]

The rent charged to North Easters is found fairly high compared to the ongoing market rates. The survey data suggests that on an average, the respondents pay ₹6,535 per month. If we juxtapose this data with the fact that most of them are staying in groups show the exorbitantly higher levels of rent. 'We normally pay about two times rent than people from other parts of the country pay', a migrant resident of Vijaya Nagar points out.

The advance amount collected from North Easters related to renting of residential space is also found exorbitantly high. On an average, the respondents paid ₹8,930 as advance amount. Maximum average advance amount was reported in Kotla (₹13,825) followed by Munirka (₹11,430), Moti Bagh (₹6,725) and Vijay Nagar (₹4,417). The average commission/ brokerage amount paid by migrants was found to be ₹2,632, for 11 months for the present staying arrangement. Mostly these renting activities and advance payment are carried out informally and several instances of denial of repayment and withholding of the deposits are reported.

Apart from high rent rates and advance amounts, in several instances, the landlords refuse to ensure continued support in terms of ensuring basic facilities (such as water supply) and to take care of basic maintenance and repair of the living space. A distraught Mizo resident in Munirka remarks:

> This is my third year in this room; even when I got it no maintenance or white wash of the room is done. The owner won't do it so long as we stay here, though the rent is increased every year. They know that we have not much options than continuing as per their terms.

Many of the respondents reported that they had to change the residences against their will and consent, even before the term of the contract (be it is written or oral), as the owners did not take them serious enough to be consulted before taking such decision of eviction. A good chunk of respondents reported that they have shifted their residences two to three times.[27] Several of the respondents reported that there is a constant fear they might be given notice any time to move out. The lease agreement in many cases is a formality and thus does not provide any protection. Even if there is a written agreement, it is only for a year or less than that, leaving enough scope for periodic revision of the rents. 'Even after taking good care of the house, it's really sad that every now and then the rents are revised or we are asked to move out, which is not happening to tenants from other states.'

Another oft-reported complaint by the migrants is related to extraction of high charges for electricity supplied to the tenants. A typical complaint in this direction is as follows: 'They fix faulty meters and read them according to their wish. Every month they demand to increase some money in any case.' In few cases respondents pointed out that the landlords used to charge extra when guests or visitors from native place come.

The most insulting aspect, according to some of the respondents, is intrusion into their personal lives and 'moral policing' by the landlords.

Many of them reported that landlords use to visit their rooms/flats any time without any prior intimation. Even in the presence of visitors, rude comments are passed such as: 'we don't like you to bring your friends', 'you people do not have any manners', 'you are uncivilized people' and so on.

The inability of migrants to speak Hindi fluently often gives a false impression to the local people that the former are ignorant/dumb on some aspects. This too also leads to a situation of locals dominating over the migrants. Apart from this, the respondents expressed their woes apropos many other aspects, which include charging of higher rates (on a par with foreigners) by auto rickshaw drivers and street vendors to denial of equal rights in common forums. All the respondents had several stories to substantiate the imposition of higher rates (on account of their distinct features) in every aspect of day-to-day living. 'Even after mastering Hindi and changing dress styles, with this fair skin and distinct physical features, it is difficult to avoid "skin tax" by auto drivers and shop keepers!' says a youth from Tripura.

Most of the migrants felt that they do face discriminatory treatment when it comes to participation in social activities—for example, in collectives of residents. While the North Easters are asked to contribute more than locals at times of pooling of resources, the flow of benefits are in the reverse order—according to most of the respondents. 'Even in the matter of collection of bribes, authorities expect more from the North East people'—adds another respondent.

Illegality as a Means of Exploitation

It is widely pointed out that the vulnerability of the migrants is often perpetuated and maintained carefully by locals and authorities by not granting them legal rights and formal status in many cases. In an interview, a restaurant owner from North East, who runs a very popular eating joint for North Easters in Munirka pointed out that the local authorities have been systematically stalling all his attempts to get a formal license to run the establishment for the past several years. 'They know that giving license to me is losing a permanent client', said the respondent. He added that due to his non-confirming status, he ends up paying in exorbitant rents apart from meeting recurring demands for bribe to concerned officials from all relevant Municipal Departments.

Viewing the migrants from North East as terrorists and those involved in anti-national activities is also yet another aspect of labelling them. In many cases, wrong portrayal of facts by media and erroneous conceptualizations by the urban middle class often leads to situations of isolating and ill-treating the migrants.

Several respondents from Munirka and Vijaya Nagar informed that the local politicians and flat owners discouraged or practically objected to them enrolling themselves in the voter list, despite the fact that they have been staying there for several months. It is widely understood that with voter rights in the locality, the bargaining power of the migrants will considerably increase. Moreover, in many of these pockets, migrants have decisive share of votes that can influence the results at least in local self-government elections. In view of all these, there is a planned resistance from locals, while the migrants want to get their names enlisted in the voter list. An agitated youth in Moti Bagh pointed out, 'they even denied us to enroll ourselves in the Population Census. That means we are not Indian citizens!'

Unlike the average migrants in Delhi, the migrants from North East are more educated and conscious about their civic rights and about obtaining the minimum documents that are essential for surviving in the city (such voter identity card, ration card, bank account, and so on). However, majority of the respondents testify that they had to spend lots of money, time and resources to obtain these documents. This bleak status itself shows the prominence of politics of illegality, in the lives of migrants from the North East.

Opening a bank account, getting a driving license and so on are reported as major hurdles by most of the respondents. Many of them told that the authorities simply refused to entertain their applications, even when they had supporting documents. 'Some more compassionate approach from the authorities would have provided formal address and some bargaining power to the migrants', opined a social activist.

Verbal Abuse, Racial Discrimination and Violence

Use of obscene language by local people is one of the most prominent forms of insult faced by the migrants in the city. Almost all the respondents had something to tell about the verbal abuse they have faced in the city.

All the respondents told that several times they were addressed publically as 'chinki'[28] by the local people and even by officials and authorities. Similarly, many a times the respondents were addressed as 'Nepali'. Some of the women respondents told that words like 'chinki monkeys', 'Thapa' (Thai Bar) 'Chini Malai', are very commonly used by eve teasers. 'If we react, they openly mock at us and rudely tell us to go back to China', tells a Mizo girl from Munirka.

Discrimination here often takes the form of racial abuse, as it is primarily based on appearance and characters (colour, figure and facial features) due to the East Asian ethnic origin of the migrants. Most of the respondents remarked that they used to avoid confrontations and neglect such abuses to the extent possible, as a reaction of same kind may sometime lead to more undesirable outcome. Minority feeling always deters the victim from fighting back or reacting to such abuses with similar responses.

Many of the respondents always anticipated some kind of lewd remarks from the local people and those from mainland India and thus they have been sceptical about the usage of each and every term. The term migrants itself upset many of the respondents and key resource persons. Although the terms such as migration and migrants are frequently used in the study of internal migration, for the first time the researchers felt that the respondents are not comfortable with the term. Some of them openly questioned the use of such a term by sending that 'we are very much Indians, and still you call us migrants'. The report released by NESC&H (2011) also reflects this uneasiness. To quote from the report: 'The term migrant is used when a citizen of the country goes and lives in another country but terming the same citizen who goes and lives in another city of different state within the country, the term becomes questionable.'

Such situations of verbal abuse often lead to loss of dignity and many of the respondents pointed out that even in their own national capital, they find themselves as strangers. To quote a typical observation: 'At times, we do not feel that we too are Indians. We are treated as foreigners.'

A major reason for labelling and insulting is the faulty prejudices and wrong notions entertained by the host community regarding the North Easters. A typical North East person, from the perspective of common Delhiites can be summarized as 'one with "chinky" eyes, fair complexion, who follows Christianity and who eats pigs (and even dogs), and who dresses scantily but fashionably and mingles with persons of even opposite sex without any inhibition—as s/he has very loose moral values'. A few of the quotations from an Internet discussion site explain this faulty prejudices and wrong judgments by the host society:

> It is known that north east tribes, like Nagas, Mizos and Arunachalis did not wear clothes some decades back. So they have the habit of wearing short and skimpy dresses.

> North East boys also dress in a very unsmart [shabby] and third class manner, with cargo pants, half pants, tattoos and rings, spikes, and so on. Maybe because they are tribal, they do not know to dress decently. (brackets added)

In many cases, the abusers do not accept the deviations from their preconceived notions. For instance, though many of the Manipuris have typical North Indian/Hindu names and at times, they had to face some questions (sometimes innocent clarifications) regarding this. In this connection, a Manipuri respondent told that she had changed her name as she had to answer frequent irritating queries such as 'How come you have our name?'

Apart from verbal abuse, few of the respondents also reported instances of physical attack and atrocities in public spaces. While narrating an incident faced by her, a Manipuri respondent told that after that event, she lost confidence to move out alone freely. Though they were not direct victims, many had episodes to add. The frequent reports of atrocities on migrants from the North East add to their anxieties and helplessness in the city.

It was commonly complained that the authorities often do not provide adequate help and support at times of such physical violence. Reluctance in filing FIR by the police is an oft-repeated grievance. In one of the incidents, narrated by the respondents, the police took the victim in the same vehicle along with the perpetuator. In several cases, the intervention of police ended with a counselling session to victims with specific advices regarding how to conduct in the city (in terms of dressing and mingling with friends).

Discriminations and Harassment at the Workplace

In the survey, 38.2 per cent reported that they felt some sort of discrimination at the workplace, while 9.6 per cent did not respond to this question. The rest, 42.2 per cent, categorically denied any instance of discrimination. The aspects of discrimination ranged into a variety of issues, such as assigning higher work targets or long hours of work, denial of leaves, discriminations at the time of promotion, holding up of salaries and termination from jobs without prior notice.

The perceived notions of submissiveness and helplessness attached to youth from North East often prompt the authorities not to consider them seriously. 'Just because we are soft-spoken and nice, people tend to take us for granted. Our importance arises only when there is work beyond office hours and on holidays', says a BPO worker from Mizoram.

Tensions at workplace often arise when the success of the NE migrants in attractive entry-level jobs leads to some resentment among local workers. Eventually, many such discomforts lead to bullying at workplace—even with an extended tone in racial lines. To quote a typical statement: 'They are driving down salaries; stealing our jobs; driving up rents in some neighbourhoods.' Most of the respondents told that rather than sharply raising their voice against these discriminations most of them try to overcome these tensions by concentrating more on work or by simply quitting the job (and thereby the related worries!).

Company of colleagues from same region often provides mutual support and solace at workplace. Almost 80.8 per cent reported the presence of north-eastern colleagues at the workplace. Despite this, a good number of the respondents had to tell something about sexual harassment at the workplace, which happened (as per their perception) due to their disadvantageous position as migrants from the North East. Though a very few had direct and blatant incidents to narrate, many had some narratives that happened to their colleagues or to someone closer to them.

While 70.9 per cent of the workers reported no serious sexual discrimination, almost all the female respondents told that they have faced milder forms of sexual harassments (coloured remarks/jokes, touching, staring and so on) at least few times at their workplaces. Coming from a different society with more free social relations, they find this negative treatment unreasonable. But many of the victims tried to ignore such cases or kept some 'safe distance' from such persons. Only one respondent reported a clear-cut case of sexual harassment, in which the perpetuator did not get much punitive action just a simple change of workspace, away from the complainant.

Several of the respondents expressed their displeasure regarding the careless handling of sexual discrimination cases at workplace. When the sexual harassment comes from the consumers, quite often not much follow-up is made in this matter. 'If it is from a colleague you can report to team leader (TL) or higher authorities, they will warn the miscreant. But, if it is a customer quite often the TL will ask us to ignore', reports a floor walker, from Manipur, in a shopping mall. 'People here don't see the women of North East as potential workers. They look to us as commodities to be used', adds a bank executive, hailing from Morigon District of Assam. It was reported that many of the victims leave the workplaces after the incident, as the work atmosphere no longer continues to be warm and friendly.[29]

Institutional Support and Migrants' Collectives

Concerned state and central government bodies are not found to be much effective in providing support to migrants on various aspects—such as facilitation of informed migration; career guidance; provision of legal support in times of need and so on—as per majority of respondents. 'The functions of various state *bhawans* are limited to those of guest houses and restaurants', points out a social worker dealing with issues of migrants from North East. The collective of Parliamentarians from the North East (for example, North East MP forum) is also not found effectively intervening to improve the plight of the migrants (NESC&H, 2011).

Detailed discussions with the respondents revealed the presence of some social-networking activities and collectives. A major form of social networking and collectivity is in the lines of community connections. People from same tribes and communities are found meeting at common places to celebrate festivals or to discuss issues concerning that particular group. Such collectives are often organized at the behest of or with the support of church and related organizations (for example, Vai Phei Christian Fellowship; North East Support Centre and Helpline). While some of these organizations confine them mostly to religious and community-related aspects, some organizations such as NESC&H provide more detailed help including assistance in situations of discriminations and harassments, which often attain characteristics of racial abuse (for a detailed discussion on these aspects, see Remesh, 2012b). Legal support and pressure group building are also found successfully done by some of these collectives, despite their limited financial and physical resources, compared to governmental agencies.

Some of the most effective groups in addressing the issues of migrants from North East are the various student unions with respect to various states (for example, unions of Manipuri students, Naga students, Mizo students, and so on). These student organizations, based on central university campuses (DU, JNU, and so on), are the first to react to many of the atrocities against the migrant population. Contrary to community-based organizations,[30] these students' organizations are found working closely on issues of mutual interest—at least on an issue-based, case-to-case mode.

Virtual collectives are the other stronger way of collectivity that is actively present among the migrants (for example, website of epao—an Internet forum of Manipuris). These collectives provide the youth to reach to other similarly placed migrants and share their concerns. A regular following up of Internet discussions related to the issues of north-eastern migrants in urban centres reveals the efficacy of such virtual discussion forums to debate on important concerns of the migrants.

Concluding Remarks and Policy Implications

The foregoing analysis suggests that dynamics of migration of youth from the North East to urban centres (for example, NCR) is quite unique and distinct. Thus, it is wrong to conceptualize the reasons and determinants of migration of the group in the same way as of those from other parts of the country based on stereotyped assumptions of rural–urban migration. As evident from the discussion, the growing presence of youth from NER in urban centres is largely determined by the inadequacy of higher education system and the non-availability of employment opportunities that match with the aspirations of the youth in the native economies. Such a situation, coupled with the social tensions (due to multiple reasons) necessitates the massive city-bound exodus of the youth in the region. Thus, any policy measures to address out-migration from the North East have to adequately focus on strengthening the opportunities for higher education and in promoting matching employment avenues for educated youth in local labour markets.

The study finds that many of the hardships faced by the migrants in the city are essentially due to sheer lack of understanding of the members of the host society about the values and cultures of north-eastern communities. In view of this, many issues including adverse social profiling of migrants and the subsequent atrocities can be mitigated to a greater extent, through efforts and initiatives to bridge the 'cultural gap' between the migrant and local societies. Media can play an effective role in this regard, by including more programmes and news about the NER, rich cultural heritage and social values and ethos of diverse communities in the region. It is also desirable to include more information about the North East and its socio-economic and cultural aspects in the educational textbooks. Promoting internal tourism (to NER) is yet another way of orienting the city dwellers about the North East, which inter alia may lead to waning of misconceptions about the migrants from the region. Such efforts will surely help the host community to appreciate and recognize the socio-political, economic and cultural distinctions between individual states/ communities within the NER.

The centrality of migrant collectives and social networks in facilitating migration and providing support to the migrants in the city is a key finding of the study. Nevertheless, it was evident that there is lot more to be done by these organizations in terms of providing support to migrants and fighting for their genuine issues. Given the fact that most of the collectives of migrants are strongly based on certain cultural, ethnic and sub-regional identities, the first and foremost effort needs to be on forging a strong solidarity between these groups. While doing so, it is also important to effectively utilize the resources and capacities of relevant government departments, state government establishments (for example, the houses/ *bhawans* of each of the north-eastern states) and most importantly, the elected representatives (parliamentarians) from the region. Civil society organizations can also join in such efforts, which will surely help bringing more permanent institutional solutions and effective policy interventions to facilitate 'informed migration' and to address the post-migration issues of youth from the North East.

Sensitizing and orienting the city administration and police authorities is another important mode of improving the plight of migrants. In a scenario where atrocities against migrants from the North East are increasingly reported, such efforts for promoting awareness and pro-active attitudes among development functionaries and policy authorities will surely help bringing some feeling of security among migrants. It is important to mention that some positive developments are happening in this direction in the recent past. Issues of youth from the North East and the need for finding solutions was a major agenda in the recent elections in Delhi and accordingly, already there are some governmental initiatives (for example, special helpline) in place. This tempo can be further maintained, with increased participation of migrants in the electoral politics (as voters and as representatives) in the city, which is strikingly dismal at the present juncture.

Thus, on the whole, it is evident from the foregoing discussion that some positive changes for migrant youths from the North East in urban centres could be brought out only through coordinated and concerted efforts of all stakeholders, including civil society organizations (of migrants as well as the host communities), governmental agencies, collectives and so on.

Notes

1. This chapter is drawn from the report of a research study supported by the V.V. Giri National Labour Institute, NOIDA (Remesh, 2012a). Nevertheless, the views expressed do not necessarily represent those of the National Labour Institute.
2. NER comprises eight states, namely Assam, Arunachal Pradesh, Manipur, Meghalaya, Mizoram, Nagaland, Tripura and Sikkim. The assumption of homogeneity in understanding the issues of the North East is erroneous. However, the chapter uses this unified approach as an entry point to lay out some common issues of out-migration of the youth from the region to urban centres.
3. Using Census Data, Chyrmang (2011) estimates that the proportion of out-migration from NER has increased from 1.7 per cent to 2.9. per cent during 1981 to 2001. While 1981–91 period marked a steady growth in out-migration, in the next decade (1991 to 2001), the increase was double.
4. Rough estimates and reports suggest that there is a considerable expansion in out-migration from NER in the first decade of the present century. For instance, a recent report claims that in 2010 alone, around one lakh people migrated to from NER to other cities of India (Das et al., 2011).
5. For instance, a recent research suggests that there are 8,000 Assamese youth working in plywood factories in Perumbavoor, a town in far-off Kerala (Das and Chutia, 2011).
6. Though the study had not followed any strict statistical procedure, attention was given in selecting a representative sample giving due attention on various attributes such as gender, age, state of origin, occupational categories and so on.
7. As the specific focus of the present study was on migration for employment and labour-related issues confronted by migrants in the city, the sample did not include students from the North East. However, during the course of the present study, it is strongly felt that the analysis in the study could be further enriched if it is supplemented with a field study of students from the Northeast and their collectives.

8. These localities were selected on the basis of a detailed mapping of pockets with higher concentration of migrants from NER—subsequent to some pilot visits and discussions with some key resource persons. For further details on the methodology of the study, see Remesh (2012a).

9. To collect supplementary, qualitative information, 40 case studies were also prepared. Further to this, a brief field visit to some of the source regions was conducted (covering four states in NER—Assam, Meghalaya, Sikkim and Nagaland). During this visit, first-hand information/views from key informants (such as migrant families, church authorities, researchers, labour department officials, social activists and so on) were gathered.

10. While drawing the sample, due attention was given in selecting a more or less a representative sample of respondents. Thus, the higher proportion of Manipuris in all the study areas reflects the overall dominance of the people from this state among the migrants. This increased presence could be because of the increased intensity of socio-political tensions in the state, compared to other states of North East. Though many of the states in the NER have some internal tensions or the other, the intensity of such troubles is much more in the case of Manipur. Due to this, a large number of Manipuris prefer to move out of the state for educational and livelihood options. Even after continuing their education, many of these youth prefer to stay back in the city or move to some other city/destination, as they find it difficult to get suitable avenues for employment in the native states (and on account of better environment in the city for education and development of their children). Thus, it is the 'higher retention rates' of migrants from Manipur compared to their counterparts from other states that results in their predominantly higher share among the overall migrants from the North East.

11. Absence of migrants from Sikkim in the sample is partly due to the negligible proportion of people from this state among the total migrants from the North East. From the visit to Sikkim, it is evident that compared to other states in the region, there were not many acute internal tensions or instabilities in the state—which to some extent explains the lower presence of migrants from this state in Delhi.

12. The above set of information also prompted one to question the validity of available secondary data on migration with respect to the North East. For instance, the NSSO data shows higher migration rates for Sikkim people and lower rates for Manipuris, which is not in line with the pattern that one gets from the present survey data.

13. The proportion of Christians in total population varied from 98.6 per cent and 96.4 per cent in Mizoram and Nagaland to 0 per cent in Assam.

14. As per the latest available estimates, the regional literacy rate of NER is 65.7 per cent. Most states in the region are much ahead of the national average in terms of literacy rate—for example, Mizoram 88.5 per cent, Tripura 73.6 per cent, Manipur 68.8 per cent and Nagaland 67.1 per cent.

15. 'Educational considerations' is found as the second major reason for migration of youth from NER, after employment.

16. This observation is particularly true in the case of migrants in Delhi.

17. The survey data suggests that more than 50 per cent of the respondents continued in their present occupation for more than a year. Almost 28.4 per cent was for more than two years.

18. Linking this negligible amount of remittances and huge costs incurred by states in the NER, due to loss of human resources, Singh (2007) explains the migration from NER to

rest of the country as a clear example of brain-drain, where receiving regions (developed and advanced states) are reaping all benefits at the expense of states from NER.

19. However, in some cases (for example, domestic helps from Assam) some presence of private recruitment agencies is noticed.

20. In a study covering 34 women workers from six states from the North East, Shingmila (2007) also observes that majority of the new migrants are working in service sector (for example, showrooms, shops, hotels, beauty parlours, hospitals and call centres).

21. This is despite the fact that many of them had no other connection or exposure regarding Chinese cuisines or ways of hospitalities. Further, to its surprise, the study team could not find any street-side Momo stalls run by people from the North East. Mostly, such stalls are run by people from either Darjeeling, Nepal or from Tibet.

22. For instance, Munirka has a fellowship of North Easters belonging to Vaiphie Christians, the meetings of which are even used to discuss common issues and challenges confronted by migrants from the North East in the city. In Dwarka, in a north east-based church, more than one thousand people from NER are reported to attend the Sunday mass, for which people even commute from other migrant neighbourhoods such as Vijay Nagar, Munirka and Noida.

23. For instance, majority of the Manipuri respondents pointed out that their primary intention of moving to Delhi was to attain a peaceful environment for education and pursuit of better employment, which is not possible at their native state.

24. Unlike migrants from other states, the North Eastners are normally particular about choosing their room-mate from own community/state/region and about staying in pockets where they could find more migrants from their own community/state/region.

25. A recent study of NESC&H explains this aspect as 'social profiling' and hostile mindset of the locals (NESC&H, 2011).

26. In Delhi, the preference for tenants is often strongly linked to their home state. While South Indians are generally preferred by the North Indian property owners, people from the North East come as one of the least preferred categories. The reason for this strong non-preference is closely linked to the cultural gaps, faulty notions and labelling—which is discussed in the previous section.

27. Here, however, it needs to be noted that all shifting need not be of involuntary nature. As explained in the earlier section, the pattern of stay of North Easters has an element of shifting residence—alongside their progress in the city life.

28. Chinki is a racial slur referring mainly to a person of Chinese ethnicity but sometimes generalized to refer to any person of East Asian descent. The usage of the word is often considered as an ethnic insult.

29. Notwithstanding the above descriptions, it is important to mention that not all migrants from NER are discriminated against and ill-treated in the city. Those who are in better professional positions (for example, academics, bank executives and so on) are often found free from such abuses. This aspect is evident in some of the case studies, prepared as part of the study.

30. From the discussions with some key resource persons it is understood that a major hurdle for collectivity of community-based organizations of people from the North East is the lack of unity among groups representing people from different states and different tribal communities. Often these organizations compete with each other in organizing or protesting.

References

Chyrmang, R. (2011). 'Magnitude of migration from north eastern region of India'. In Rajan, S. Irudaya (ed.), *Migration, Identity and Chyrmang Conflict: India Migration Report 2011.* New Delhi: Routledge.

Das, K., and Chutia, D. (2011). 'Outward bound'. *The Assam Tribune*, A5–A11.

Lyndem, Biloris and De, Utpal Kumar (2004). *Education in North East India: Experience and challenge.* New Delhi: Concept Publishing Company.

NESC&H (North East Support Centre and Helpline). (2011). *North East Migration and Challenges in Capital Cities.* Research Report. New Delhi: Author. Retrieved 2 January 2011 from http://nehelpline.net/NE_report.pdf

Remesh, B.P. (2012a). *Migration from North East to urban centres: A case study of Delhi region* (NLI Research Studies Series No. 94). V. V. Giri National Labour Institute, Noida.

———. (2012b). 'Strangers in their own land: Migrants from the North East in Delhi'. *Economic and Political Weekly, XLVII*(22), 35–40.

Shimray, U.A. (2004). 'Socio-political unrest in the region called North-East India'. *Economic and Political Weekly, XXXIX*(42), 4637–43.

———. (2007). *Youth on move: North East experience.* Retrieved from http://www.kanglaonline.com/index.php?template=kshow&kid=1262 (accessed on 2 January 2012)

Shingmila, S. (2007). *North-East migrant women in Delhi's service sector.* Paper presented at the National Seminar on Women and Migration organised by Centre for Women's Development Studies, New Delhi.

Singh, M.P. (2007). Brain drain and the North East. Retrieved from http://www.kanglaonline.com/?template=kshow&kid=245 (accessed on 2 January 2012)

5

Labour Migration in
the North East

S. Irudaya Rajan and Rikil Chyrmang

Introduction

The North Eastern Region (NER)[1] of India spreads over an area of
2.62 lakhs km[2]. It stretches from 89.46° to 97.30° East longitude and
21.57° to 29.30° North latitude. Most of the states in the region share an
international border around 4,500 km long with Bangladesh, Bhutan,
Burma, China and Nepal. The whole region is connected to the rest of
the country by means of a 22 km land corridor through Siliguri in the
eastern part of West Bengal. The region has 213 tribal communities
and 175 languages along with numerous non-tribal communities found
mixed with the indigenous population. It has a unique cultural identity,
ethnicity, linguistic and religious profile that is totally different from
other parts of India or the world, geographically, historically and socially.
The most recent data on the socioeconomic profile of the NER hinted at
the backwardness of the region (Table A5.1). It was one of the last areas
on the subcontinent to be taken over by the British (Hanjabam, 2007).
Even after the end of colonialism, it lagged behind in terms of both the
physical and social infrastructure necessary for economic development.
The economic growth and development of the region has been lopsided
for the last four decades and its economic backwardness could explain
as to why people migrate.

In this context, the Todaro Model 'Push–Pull' theory on migration
explains the phenomenon in terms of the status of overall development
in the sending and receiving places. During the last three decades,
labour migration from the NER shows an increasing trend (Chyrmang,

2011; Goswami and Chyrmang, 2012). According to the 2001 census, 307.2 million out of 1028.6 million persons, that is, almost 30 per cent of the total population, of India were migrants. Of this, 42.1 million were interstate migrants. During the same period, the eight states of NER enumerated 39 million persons, of which 1.11 million were migrants. The states of Manipur, Nagaland, Tripura and Assam recorded out-migrants, whereas Sikkim, Arunachal Pradesh, Meghalaya and Mizoram recorded in-migrants (Krishan, 2007). Migration and its impact on economic and non-economic variables have assumed immense importance. This chapter makes an attempt to examine the economic development and the factors that determine migration, the impact of remittances on households and the economic conditions of migrant households using monthly per capita consumption expenditure (MPCE). The data sources for the analysis are: Census, Directorate of Economic and Statistics, Government of India, New Delhi, state-level reports in the North East, NSS rounds on migration and employment and our special survey in Assam.

This chapter is organized into six sections. The first section discusses the socio-demographic profile in the North East. The second section discusses the status of economic growth and development. This section sets the context in which migration is taking place. The third section elaborates on the trends and pattern of labour employment and population dynamics. The fourth section discusses the conceptual issues pertaining to labour migration. The fifth section discusses our field study report. The sixth section ends with the summary, conclusion and policy options.

Demographic Profile

According to Indian Census 2011, the NER constitutes 7.9 per cent of the country's total geographical area with a total population of 45,587,982 constituting 3.8 per cent of the total population of the country. The population includes 23,309,165 males and 22,278,817 females and has a density of 174 persons per km^2, which is much less than the national population density of 382. The decadal growth of population is 15.38 less than the national average of 17.64. There are 956 females per 1,000 males which is marginally better than the national ratio of 940. The average annual exponential growth rate of population since 1951–61 to 2001–11 has come down except for Nagaland which has increased tremendously from 1961–71 to 1991–01 (Figure 5.1).

Figure 5.1

Average annual exponential growth rate of population, 1951–61 to 2001–11

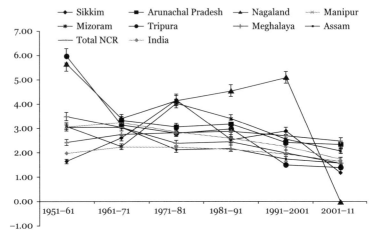

Source: Calculated by the authors from Census of India, Register General of India, New Delhi.

Assam is the most highly populated NER with a population of 31,169,272 and Sikkim is the least populated region with 607,688 people. People belonging to Scheduled Tribes (STs) comprise more than half of the total population of the region. The states that have a very high proportion of ST in their population are Mizoram followed by Nagaland, Meghalaya and Arunachal Pradesh. The crude birth rate (CBR), crude death rate (CDR) and infant mortality rate (IMR) for both rural and urban India have shown a decline from 1997 to 2010 (Table A5.2). The corresponding figures for NER are lower than those for the country as a whole, although some states of the region, such as Assam and Meghalaya have very high CBR, CDR and IMR. However, there is a vast difference with respect to the rural–urban composition. Though there is policy enhancement, in the case of Arunachal Pradesh and Nagaland the CBR, CDR and IMR for both the rural and urban areas continued to show a rising trend from 1997 to 2010.

Population is projected to touch 57 million marks by 2020 (Table 5.1). This basic fact could be important for policy formulation and perspective planning for the region. Assam's population density might rise to 471, Tripura's to 403, Nagaland's to 302, Arunachal Pradesh's to 21, Manipur's to 163, Meghalaya's to 171, Mizoram's to 68 and Sikkim's to 129. By 2020, Assam, Tripura and Nagaland could face a new challenge with a phenomenal rise in population density. Land area remaining more or

Table 5.1

Projected population in the North East, 2020

State	Population (in '000s)			Density (Persons per km²)		
	2001	2011	2020	2001	2011	2020
Arunachal Pradesh	1,098	1,394	1,723	13	17	21
Assam	26,656	31,643	36,925	340	403	471
Manipur	2,389	2,988	3,640	107	134	163
Meghalaya	2,319	3,016	3,828	103	134	171
Mizoram	889	1,139	1,424	40	54	68
Nagaland	1,989	3,231	5,002	120	195	302
Sikkim	541	715	919	76	101	129
Tripura	3,199	3,706	4,231	304	353	403
Total	39,080	47,832	57,692	149	182	220

Sources: Statistical Abstract; CSO/NEC Secretariat.
Note: Growth rate as per RGI's projection.

less inelastic, dispersal and settlement of the population would be a huge problem. This phenomena is already visible in Assam with regard to land rights. Though population is decreasing in relative terms, it shows a phenomenal increase in absolute terms. This poses new challenges for the region where the increase of population is also caused by regular and irregular migration despite the existence of an Inner Line Permit (ILP) in three states (Arunachal Pradesh, Mizoram, Nagaland) and the Illegal Migration Determination by Tribunal (IMDT) Act in Assam. Now Meghalaya and Manipur are also demanding an ILP to restrict the menace of influx. The large-scale influx of population may adversely affect ecology and environment due to possible intrusion of man into virgin land on a larger scale. It is high time that planners, social scientists and environmental scientists find workable solutions to the problem.

Enrolment in Primary and Higher Education

Education and building of skills and knowledge for the youth is the cornerstone of progress. This is the only capital that people without land and financial capital can acquire to enhance their income streams and improve their living conditions. In the development process, education

Table 5.2

State-wise literacy rate, 1951–2011

State	1951	1961	1971	1981	1991	2001	2011
Arunachal Pradesh	NA	47.90	11.30	20.80	41.60	54.74	66.95
Assam	18.30	83.00	28.70	NA	52.90	64.28	73.18
Manipur	11.40	36.00	32.90	41.40	59.90	68.87	79.85
Meghalaya	NA	NA	29.50	34.10	49.10	63.11	75.48
Mizoram	NA	NA	NA	59.90	82.30	88.49	91.58
Nagaland	10.40	20.40	27.40	42.60	61.60	67.11	80.11
Sikkim	7.30	14.20	17.70	34.10	56.90	69.68	82.20
Tripura	15.50	24.30	31.00	42.10	60.40	73.66	87.75
Total Northeast	7.86	28.23	22.31	34.38	58.09	68.74	79.64
All India	18.30	28.30	34.45	43.57	52.20	65.38	74.04

Source: Office of the Registrar General, India.

is vital to growth across all sectors. The past decade has seen visible improvement in the overall educational attainment of several of the states: male and female literacy rates have increased. The literacy level and status of elementary education in the region until 1981 lagged behind the national average. But by 1991, all the states of the region, except Arunachal Pradesh, had caught up with the nation, and had in fact, achieved literacy rates higher than the national average. Mizoram has the highest literacy rate of 91.58 per cent and Arunachal Pradesh is the least literate State with 66.95 per cent. In 2011, Tripura's literacy rate has increased tremendously to 87.75 per cent, after Mizoram. Mizoram was the second most literate State in the country in 2001 and fell to the third place after Kerala and Lakshadweep in 2011 (Table 5.2).

The educational development infrastructure index is very low in general, and in particular, at the primary and upper primary level, except for Sikkim, which ranked first among the 35 Indian states. The composite index shows Sikkim at rank 7, Mizoram at 16 and the rest of the north-eastern states at ranks much lower than other Indian states during 2010–11 (Table 5.3).

The north-eastern states have made impressive achievements in the sphere of school enrolment (NCAER, 2004). But enrolment declined considerably as the educational levels moved from the primary level to

Table 5.3

Educational development infrastructure index and its rank, 2010–11

	Primary Level		Upper Primary Level		EDI (Composite Primary and Upper Primary	
	Value	Rank	Value	Rank	Value	Rank
Arunachal Pradesh	0.429	32	0.695	21	0.598	31
Assam	0.377	34	0.479	34	0.555	33
Manipur	0.517	30	0.673	24	0.620	25
Meghalaya	0.246	35	0.295	35	0.600	30
Mizoram	0.697	18	0.727	18	0.727	16
Nagaland	0.649	22	0.671	25	0.674	20
Sikkim	0.898	1	0.969	1	0.795	7
Tripura	0.568	27	0.730	17	0.634	23

Sources: DISE 2010–11: Flash Statistics; National University of Educational Planning and Administration (NUEPA), 2012.
Note: Rank from the 35 Indian states.

the secondary and higher levels. At the primary level, the proportion of enrolment was quite high during the period, 1998–99 to 2002–03 (Shimray and Devi, 2009). However, in subsequent stages of tertiary education, starting from polytechnic up to the PhD level, a sharp decline is seen during 2001–02 to 2005–06 (Table 5.4). The overall trends from 2001–02 to 2005–06 for all the states show an increase except Manipur. Taking stock of higher education (HE) in India, the picture is gloomy, with gross enrolment ratio (GER) around 13 per cent, while global average is 35 per cent and that of the developed countries, 50 per cent. This speaks volumes for the dismal position of HE in India. The situation in the North East is most dismal, and while the GER of Manipur is quite high at 24 per cent, it much lower than the average for the rest of the North East. A matter of great concern is the migration of a large number of students from the North East to other parts of the country every year for educational purposes. Another other matter of concern is the domain of skill development of the youth in HE.

Can there be a mechanism on the part of the government to take corrective action and reverse the flow (News, 2012)?[2] About a decade ago, the supply of higher education in the NER was skewed, but the

Table 5.4

Enrolment in higher education by stages, 2001–02 to 2005–06

Year	ITI	BEd/BT	Medical	BE/BSc (Engg)/ BArch	BCom	BSc	BA	MCom	MSc	MA	PhD	Others	Total
Arunachal Pradesh													
2001–02	0	60	0	396	352	304	4,400	14	43	384	10	0	5,963
2005–06	720	59	90	672	359	391	5,756	37	58	516	29	152	8,839
Assam													
2001–02	0	2,943	2,550	4,137	18,051	33,346	139,919	1,077	3,944	7,442	744	10,351	224,504
2005–06	3,379	2,553	3,007	2,768	10,967	26,030	153,927	362	2,099	5,307	437	6,815	217,651
Manipur													
2001–02	0	332	604	0	871	6,831	16,425	90	75	851	84	1,928	28,091
2005–06	840	290	105	368	358	4,850	5,770	156	640	760	755	23,285	37,537
Meghalaya													
2001–02	0	157	0	0	1,526	2,684	11,936	54	253	806	322	0	17,738
2005–06	624	354	0	768	2,176	2,841	20,863	87	382	1,119	311	9,133	38,658
Mizoram													
2001–02	792	165	0	0	278	507	5,037	0	0	0	0	0	6779
2005–06	0	115	0	384	291	605	6,542	0	0	0	0	5,846	13,783

							Nagaland						
2001–02	0	103	0	0	834	685	7,492	26	80	315	0	0	9,535
2005–06	351	95	0	0	1,598	1,454	11,040	1,454	11,040	0	0	1,933	17,925
						Sikkim							
2001–02	0	81	199	916	210	468	1,781	0	0	0	0	195	3,850
2005–06	817	196	405	1,424	377	429	4,733	0	82	187	0	335	8,985
						Tripura							
2001–02	0	120	193	573	1,547	2,893	13,464	93	195	627	8	842	20,555
2005–06	744	472	198	915	1,288	2,871	16,072	81	285	942	11	966	24,845

Sources: Selected Education Statistics, 2005–06, Ministry of Human Resource Development, Government of India, New Delhi.

region now has 41 higher educational institutions including those of national importance and of excellence, such as the Central University, the Indian Institute of Technology (IIT), the Rajiv Gandhi Indian Institute of Management (RGIIM) and the National Institute of Technology (NIT). The other two important universities set up are the Tata Institute of Social Science (TISS), Guwahati, and the North Eastern Indira Gandhi Regional Institute of Health and Medical Sciences (NEIGRIHMS). Besides, a number of private colleges and universities have also been established. The percentage of girl student enrolment is highest in Meghalaya with 51 per cent and less in Sikkim with 39 per cent (Table 5.5).

However, these endeavours have not dissuaded student migration to other parts of the state/countries for higher education for reasons such as different socio-economic conditions, local disturbances that could affect study environment, and the lack of industrialization that could

Table 5.5

Total number of universities in the North East and girl enrolment, 2011–12

State	CT	SU	PU	DU	IIM	IIT	NIT	Total	Total Enrolment	Girl Enrolment	Girl Students (in %)
Arunachal Pradesh	1		1	1			1	4	15,864	6,504	41
Assam	2	4	3			1	1	11	310,011	133,305	43
Manipur	2		0				1	3	34,204	15,392	45
Meghalaya	1		8		1		1	11	39,536	20,163	51
Mizoram	1		1				1	3	13,223	6,215	47
Nagaland	1		2				1	4	23,185	10,897	47
Sikkim	1		4				1	6	7,778	3,033	39
Tripura	1		1				1	3	27,691	12,184	44
Total	10	4	20	1	1	1	8	45	471,492	207,693	44

Sources: Selected Educational Statistics, 2004–05, Ministry of Human Resource Development, Government of India, New Delhi; UGC (2011): Inclusive and Qualitative Expansion of Higher Education (12th Five Year Plan, 2012–17).
Notes: (a) CT: Central universities, SU: State universities, PU: Private universities, DU: Deemed to be university, IIM: Indian Institute of Management, IIT: Indian Institute of Technology, NIT: National Institute of Technology.
(b) All the central and state universities in the NER (except Tezpur University) have a number of affiliated colleges.

translate into employment opportunities. It has also been seen that the increase in the number of institutions is only in terms of quantity, not quality. More so, the youth are sceptical about the efficiency, probability of recognition of the university in terms of standards for job purposes and campus placement, because not many students can get admission into IITs, IIMs and medical institutions. Under these circumstances, the central and state governments need to improve the infrastructure of these institutions through Public–Private Partnership (PPP) and attract talented faculty so that there is a visible improvement in the quality of higher education (Singh and Ahmad, 2012). The future of the North East lies in the hands of its youth. For that matter, life-skill education should be introduced for students, as it would enable an individual to adjust and adapt himself to changing environments with no difficulty (Laskar, 2012).

Economic Growth and Development

Economic growth is a narrow concept, taking into account the state/national income, per capita income and per capita consumption. In case of economic development, one has to consider other parameters, like literacy rate, population growth, health, housing problem, law and order, and so on. Therefore, for an overall understanding of development, the growth in social infrastructure through national programmes must be complemented by the development of physical, social and economic infrastructure. There are differences among the eight north-eastern states with respect to resource endowments, levels of industrialization and infrastructural facilities. The economies of all the states remain underdeveloped and primarily agrarian with very weak industrial sectors. The industrial sector has mainly developed around tea, oil and timber in Assam and mining, saw mills and plywood factories in other parts of the region. Historically, the regions remained the most backward in the country due to poor infrastructure and lack of democratic governance combined with low productivity and market access, low levels of industrial activity and limited spread of a modern service sector. The standard of living of the people in the region, as measured by per capita gross state domestic product (GSDP), has lagged significantly behind the rest of the country. Agriculture is the main stay for the North East economy.

The Phase of Economic Growth Since Economic Liberalization

The NER per capita income growth during 1981–82 was growing at the rate of 5.9 per cent per annum, better than the national average of 1.7 per cent, but thereafter started declining sharply till it reached 0.6 per cent during 1983–84, again rose to 7.0 per cent during 1987–88 in contrast to the national average of 0.3 per cent. Since 1983–84, the region faced the challenges of globalization and low per capita income growth more than the rest of the country. Backed by history, the growth experience in the different states of the northeast after the economic liberalization of 1981 was in a sorry state of affairs.

The per capita income growth pattern of each state of the northeast has a very distinctive nature due to a variety of problems. The problem from internal and external factors, the distinct geo-physical features, the geo-politics, the economic blockade by several ethnic organizations and historical constraints could reflect in shaping the growth process since 1981–82 to 2011–12, when all the north-eastern states faced several episodes of negative growth rates. Within the two and half decades from 1981–82 to 2011–12, Nagaland experienced negative growth the highest number of times—ten times, Manipur eight times, Assam, Arunachal Pradesh and Meghalaya five times each, and Sikkim and Tripura four times each (Table 5.6).

Table 5.6

State-wise annual exponential growth rate of net state domestic product (NSDP) at constant (2004–05) prices, (1981–82 to 2011–12)

Years	AR	AS	MN	ML	MZ	NL	SK	TR	NE	IND
1981–82	11.4	9.2	3.0	1.3	NA	15.9	2.5	−4.5	5.9	1.7
1982–83	0.3	2.5	−1.0	−1.3	NA	9.1	8.6	7.3	3.5	0.7
1983–84	3.8	2.3	5.7	−0.5	NA	−1.5	0.5	−5.8	0.6	4.0
1984–85	6.4	−1.6	1.5	2.3	NA	−0.8	9.2	0.1	1.8	0.3
1985–86	9.4	4.4	2.9	1.9	NA	−1.7	5.1	−1.7	2.7	2.8
1986–87	3.6	−4.8	−0.6	−1.1	NA	7.0	13.9	2.7	2.5	0.7
1987–88	3.2	2.2	5.1	6.3	NA	7.9	16.6	9.7	7.0	0.3
1988–89	4.8	−1.5	2.3	−2.0	NA	4.0	9.2	8.9	3.4	13.4
1989–90	−0.5	4.9	−1.2	9.7	NA	0.2	6.6	3.4	3.2	3.1

(Table 5.6 Continued)

(Table 5.6 Continued)

Years	AR	AS	MN	ML	MZ	NL	SK	TR	NE	IND
1990–91	14.6	1.8	3.1	8.6	NA	−0.5	8.1	4.3	5.4	3.8
1991–92	11.2	2.0	5.9	1.8	NA	1.5	−10.3	0.1	1.6	−0.5
1992–93	0.1	−1.1	2.4	−8.3	NA	11.6	25.0	1.4	4.5	5.0
1993–94	11.7	1.7	−0.3	4.0	NA	−3.1	−7.6	8.5	1.5	3.3
1994–95	−4.5	0.4	−4.9	0.7	NA	3.1	−1.5	−3.1	−1.3	5.1
1995–96	12.1	0.4	1.0	8.6	NA	2.5	6.6	6.4	5.4	2.7
1996–97	−8.1	0.6	7.2	0.9	NA	2.4	3.7	9.3	1.7	6.7
1997–98	0.5	0.1	6.8	3.7	NA	4.1	4.3	9.4	4.0	2.1
1998–99	0.9	−1.9	−0.5	7.9	NA	−11.4	3.9	8.3	0.5	6.7
1999–2000	2.0	1.8	10.9	5.7	NA	−4.3	−0.4	7.7	3.1	3.5
2000–01	5.3	1.3	−8.3	3.9	3.8	11.3	2.8	5.8	3.3	−0.8
2001–02	14	0.7	4.0	4.1	6.3	6.0	4.2	13.5	6.8	2.3
2002–03	−5.7	4.3	−2.5	2.3	9.7	4.6	7.0	4.8	2.2	2.0
2003–04	9.5	4.6	8.7	4.9	3.2	−0.5	6.4	4.5	5.3	6.6
2004–05	11.5	2.0	7.1	5.6	4.5	−0.3	6.5	6.9	5.7	6.1
2005–06	−6.0	3.4	2.3	7.2	7.4	−1.5	7.5	8.6	3.1	8.1
2006–07	12.5	3.3	1.9	7.0	4.5	0.7	7.2	0.8	4.9	8.2
2007–08	5.5	4.2	4.9	7.0	11.0	0.3	6.3	3.6	5.3	7.7
2008–09	8.2	6.0	7.3	12.9	15.1	6.4	13.1	10.6	7.6	6.4
2009–10	12.8	8.1	7.6	8.6	10.7	4.3	26.5	9.6	8.7	8.1
2010–11	8.3	7.3	6.2	9.4	9.3	3.9	8.9	9.7	7.6	8.4
2011–12	4.1	8.6	6.4	9.6	NA	3.0	NA	9.9	1.4	6.9

Source: Reserve Bank of India.
Notes: The whole series is splicing into single base year, 2004–05. GR: Compound Annual Growth Rate (CAGR) = (((Base year/current year) $^\wedge$ (1/1))−1)*100, NA: Data not available, AR: Arunachal Pradesh, AS: Assam, MN: Manipur, ML: Meghalaya, MZ: Mizoram, NL: Nagaland, SK: Sikkim, TR: Tripura, NE: North East, IND: India.

Sectoral Contribution to Total Per Capita Income Net State Domestic Product (NSDP)

The contribution of the three sectors of an economy, that is, the primary sector, the secondary or manufacturing sector and the tertiary or service sector, play a very important role in boosting the economic growth of the state economy. All these three sectors are interlinked. Agriculture is the dominant economic activity providing employment to 64.28 per cent of the total workers in the region. The region has 3.73 per cent of the total population of the country and contributes 2.6 per cent to the NSDP (Saikia, 2001). The agricultural sector of the region is distinct from that in the rest of India in terms of its features, patterns and performance.

Figure 5.2 shows the percentage share of the primary, secondary and tertiary sector[3] in the North East NSDP at constant prices from 1980–81 to 2007–08. The share of the primary sector declined continuously from 37.9 per cent to 25.3 per cent between 1981 and 2008. The contribution of the secondary sector increased slightly from 16 per cent to 25 per cent, and services, from 46 per cent to 50 per cent. The highest contribution comes from the services and secondary sectors. The decline in the primary sector could be mainly due to the low level of investment and expenditure on agriculture and allied activities for development due to factors, such as difficult terrain, wide variations in slopes and altitude, lagging of transport facilities, communication, input supply, marketing and credit, increasing population demanding more food, deforestation, degradation and soil erosion, loss of bio-diversity, decline in land productivity, diverse land tenure systems, frequent flood and overall environmental hazards. Despite these problems, the region is endowed with some unique positive features such as rich natural resources, abundant rainfall, diverse plant and animal resources, natural beauty, placidity and serenity (NAAS, 2001; Ghosh, 2003; NEDFi, 2005). The major setback is that agriculture in the region could not benefit much from modernization and the Green Revolution. There is no location-specific and system-based technology, or the use of high yielding variety (HYV) seeds and fertilizers. Therefore, there is an urgent need for national development policies to address these location-specific issues and constraints and explore the region's potential for development.

There is wide variation in terms of the state-wise sectoral share to the total North East NSDP. The decade of 1980–81 to 1990–91 showed that the share of agriculture was greater than the shares of industry and services in the North East economy. Though there has been decline across all the north-eastern states, Assam's share is greater in comparison to the other states.

Figure 5.2

Sectoral share to the total North East NSDP, 1980–81 to 2011–12

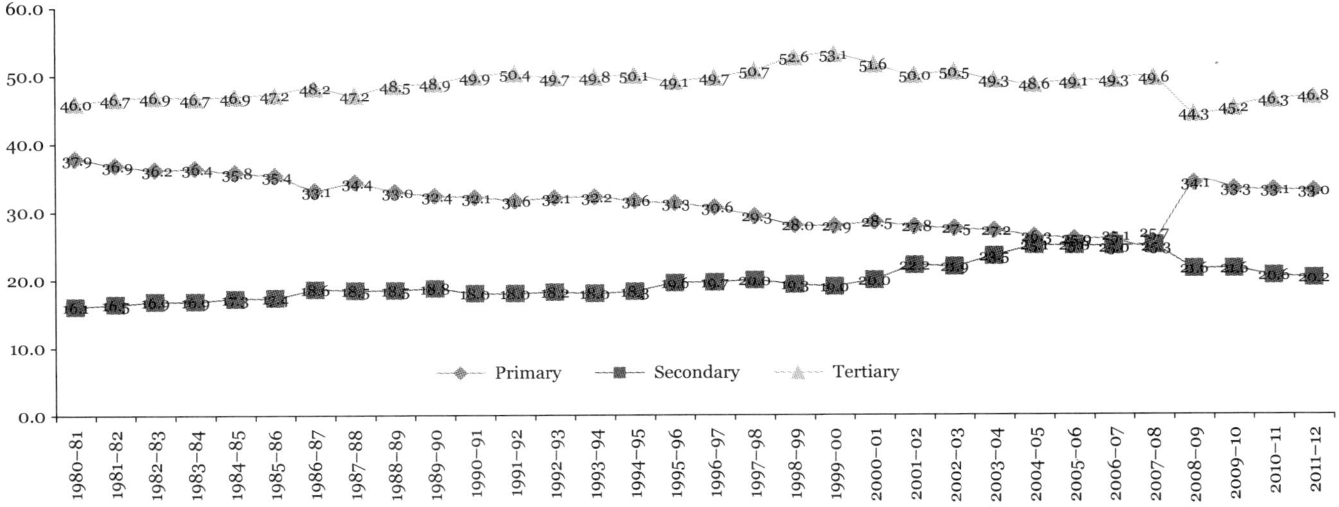

Years (x-axis): 1980–81, 1981–82, 1982–83, 1983–84, 1984–85, 1985–86, 1986–87, 1987–88, 1988–89, 1989–90, 1990–91, 1991–92, 1992–93, 1993–94, 1994–95, 1995–96, 1996–97, 1997–98, 1998–99, 1999–00, 2000–01, 2001–02, 2002–03, 2003–04, 2004–05, 2005–06, 2006–07, 2007–08, 2008–09, 2009–10, 2010–11, 2011–12

y-axis: 0.0, 10.0, 20.0, 30.0, 40.0, 50.0, 60.0

Tertiary (top line) values: 46.0, 46.7, 46.9, 46.7, 47.2, 48.2, 47.2, 48.5, 48.9, 50.4, 49.7, 49.8, 50.1, 49.1, 49.7, 50.7, 52.6, 53.1, 51.6, 50.0, 50.5, 49.3, 48.6, 49.1, 49.3, 49.6, ... 44.3, 45.2, ... 46.3, 46.8

Secondary (middle line) values: 37.9, 36.9, 36.2, 36.4, 35.8, 35.4, 36.1, 34.4, 33.0, 32.4, 31.0, 31.6, 32.2, 31.3, 30.6, 29.3, 27.8, 28.0, 27.9, 29.5, 27.8, 27.5, 27.2, 26.3, ... 34.1, 33.3, 33.1, 33.0

Primary (bottom line) values: 16.1, 16.1, 16.5, ..., 21.0, 20.0, 21.1, 20.8, 20.2

Legend: Primary — Secondary — Tertiary

Source: Same as for Table 5.6.

Income and Expenditure During the 11th Five Year Plan, 2007–12

Table 5.7 reveals the distribution of sectoral allocation expenditure to total development indicators in the NER during 2006–07. Expenditure is higher on transport (9.65 per cent), education (9.25 per cent) and energy (8.58 per cent). The expenditure is minimal on the following: communication (0.0003 per cent), science and technology (0.92 per cent) and housing (1.80 per cent).

The state-wise expenditure shows a different picture: Arunachal Pradesh spent more on transport (15.67 per cent), energy (12.62 per cent) and education (11.16 per cent) and less on communication, science and technology (0.44 per cent) and others social services (1.18 per cent).

Assam spent more on urban development (16.94 per cent), education (9.42 per cent) and transport (9.03 per cent) and spent less on communication, science and technology (0.60 per cent) and special area programmes (0.27 per cent). Manipur spent more on energy (13.11 per cent), water supply and sanitation (9.93 per cent) and irrigation and flood control (6.75 per cent) and less on communication, medical and public health (0.90 per cent) and science and technology (1.11 per cent).

Meghalaya spent more on transport (12.81 per cent), education (10.55 per cent) and energy (8.56.11 per cent) and less on communication, housing (0.95 per cent) and special area programmes (1.49 per cent). Mizoram spent more on transport (11.30 per cent), education (9.64 per cent), energy (8.81 per cent) and less on communication, science and technology, (1.12 per cent) and general services (1.22 per cent). Nagaland spent more on transport (10.49 per cent), energy (8.26 per cent), special area programmes (7.39 per cent) and less on communication, science and technology (0.70 per cent) and other services (1.75 per cent). Sikkim spent more on education (12.10 per cent), transport (8.28 per cent) and energy (7.74 per cent) and less on communication, irrigation and flood control (1.28 per cent) and special area programmes (1.58 per cent). Finally, Tripura spent more on education (8.42 per cent), transport (8.07 per cent) and other social services (7.16 per cent) and less on communication (0.003 per cent), science and technology (0.34 per cent) and general services (1.31 per cent).

Table 5.7

Sectoral allocation of expenditure to total development in the North East in the 11th Five Year Plan, 2007–12

Major Heads of Development	AR	AS	MN	ML	MZ	NL	SK	TR	NE
1. Agriculture and allied activities	7.41	1.47	3.84	5.80	5.99	6.31	4.18	5.47	4.19
2. Rural development	2.54	5.35	2.37	6.33	2.52	3.98	7.72	7.14	4.92
3. Special area programmes	4.17	0.27	2.02	1.49	0.72	7.39	1.58	3.92	2.09
4. Irrigation and flood control	5.09	8.15	6.75	1.73	2.53	1.93	1.28	4.10	5.10
5. Energy	12.62	7.41	13.11	8.56	8.81	8.26	7.74	5.02	8.58
6. Industry and minerals	1.92	1.02	5.74	2.29	2.51	4.79	3.54	2.19	2.48
7. Transport	15.67	9.03	3.52	12.81	11.30	10.49	8.28	8.07	9.65
8. Communications	0.00	0.00	0.00	0.00	0.00	0.00	0.00	0.00	0.03
9. Science and technology	0.44	0.60	1.11	1.93	1.12	0.70	2.23	0.34	0.92
10. General economic services	4.36	1.64	1.38	1.99	4.41	4.35	2.40	2.01	2.427
11. Social services	22.07	31.76	28.64	27.48	29.41	23.67	28.51	30.18	28.780
a. Education	11.16	9.42	6.55	10.55	9.64	6.44	12.10	8.42	9.25
b. Medical and public health	2.83	2.41	0.90	5.00	6.32	3.22	5.58	5.03	3.47
c. Water supply and sanitation	2.74	1.21	9.93	4.58	6.12	3.32	3.86	3.80	3.73
d. Housing	1.86	0.01	2.70	0.95	4.06	3.86	2.13	3.87	1.80
e. Urban development	2.27	16.94	2.08	2.53	1.68	5.06	1.84	1.88	7.31
f. Other social services	1.18	1.75	6.47	3.84	1.57	1.75	2.96	7.16	3.19
12. General services	1.57	1.48	2.82	2.05	1.22	4.41	3.98	1.31	2.04
Total North East	100.00	100.00	100.00	100.00	100.00	100.00	100.00	100.00	100.00

Source: Planning Commission, Government of India, Inclusive Growth, Volume 1.
Note: AR: Arunachal Pradesh, AS: Assam, MN: Manipur, ML: Meghalaya, MZ: Mizoram, NL: Nagaland, SK: Sikkim, TR: Tripura, NE: North East.

Labour Employment and Population Dynamics

The young population in the region reiterates the need for manpower planning and employment generation over the next few years. Employment generation has undergone a crisis of sorts in the aftermath of the freeze on public sector jobs in the last plan period, but surprisingly rising unemployment and underemployment are associated with high wage rates, especially in the hill states.

Employment

Creating job opportunities is a challenge in the development strategy for any State or region. Labour employment in the NER constitutes only 3.6 per cent of India's total workforce (2004–05). The labour scenario is quite unique compared to other regions of the country owing to a multitude of factors (including geographical, socio-economic and political). Employment generation is an important parameter for boosting overall economic development. The poverty ratio in all the NE States is much higher than the national average. Employment growth in India and the NE States declined during the period 1983–84 to 2004–10. The decline of growth in employment across all the north-eastern states is more pronounced among females than among males (Table 5.8).

The nexus between poverty and unemployment could lead to millions of people falling below the poverty line, though the levels of poverty declined drastically in recent decades. Still, over 23 million people in India and 6 million in the NE states live below the poverty line. The NER accounted for around 3 per cent of poverty in the Indian total (Table A5.3). The estimated number of unemployed persons according to the NSSO in 2002 was 52 lakhs of which more than 50 per cent were educated. Unemployment or lack of it directly impacts the process of economic growth. Moreover, the inability to match the rising demand for employment fuels social unrest. The North East has been experiencing such unrest for the past few decades. Sustainable employment could provide a healing touch to the anguish and sense of helplessness of the youth in the region (NEC). One of the reasons for the poor employment base is the undeveloped primary sector, particularly, the agro-horticulture sector. This sector has the potential for growth due to good agro-climatic conditions that would provide employment opportunities for the

Table 5.8

Growth in employment, 1983–94, 1994–2000 and 2004–10

State	1983–94			1994–2000			2004–10		
	Male	*Female*	*Total*	*Male*	*Female*	*Total*	*Male*	*Female*	*Total*
Arunachal Pradesh	0.5	–0.7	0.0	–	–	–	–1.0	0.4	–0.7
Assam	1.3	3.2	0.6	2.5	2.3	2.5	1.7	–3.3	–2.1
Manipur	3.6	2.9	3.3	3.2	–0.3	2.0	1.2	–6.8	–0.9
Meghalaya	3.1	4.0	3.5	2.3	3	2.6	0.2	–3.4	–1.1
Mizoram	3.1	2.5	6.3	2.9	5.9	4.0	1.0	1.1	1.1
Nagaland	9.7	4.5	2.4	4.6	5.9	8.6	–2.1	–9.6	4.3
Sikkim	2.9	0.6	2.3	1.4	9.1	3.4	1.5	–1.2	1.3
Tripura	3.3	10.4	4.3	2.7	–5.5	1.4	–0.7	–3.8	1.4
India	2.2	1.7	2.1	1.9	0.9	1.6	0.6	3.8	1.4

Source: NSSO, 38th, 50th, 55th, 61st and 66th Round on Employment and Unemployment in India.

Note: Growth in employment has been estimated as compound annual growth of people employed aged 15 and above in usual principal and sub-status.

people of the region. An effective solution to the problem of unemployment can therefore be an increase in the growth rate in the primary sector by raising the level of investment and the diversification of agro-horticulture for greater productivity.

Population Dynamics

The strategy for inclusive growth should involve skill development by increasing wage employment as well as creating self-employment opportunities for the youth. Growth of employment is crucial for development planning, as it raises the standards of living of the people, improves access to basic services, and leads to an overall improvement in social welfare. The age composition among the youth is shown in Table 5.9 where the NE states are seen to have a large young population with over 28 per cent of the people between the ages of 15–29 years against the national average of over 26 per cent during 2001–11. There is variation across the NE states. The states of Nagaland, Manipur, Mizoram and Sikkim have more youth with over 30 per cent between the ages of 15–29. Employment

Table 5.9

Population by age group, 2011

Arunachal Pradesh	133,176.20	16,029.03	20,021.04	36,050.07	12.04	15.03	27.07
Assam	3,148,480.20	346,508.88	503,233.49	849,742.37	11.01	15.98	26.99
Manipur	248,377.20	26,243.30	46,722.29	72,965.59	10.57	18.81	29.38
Meghalaya	299,407.50	35,673.91	45,551.67	81,225.58	11.91	15.21	27.13
Mizoram	107,851.70	11,353.16	19,738.79	31,091.96	10.53	18.30	28.83
Nagaland	241,364.30	33,891.74	50,555.48	84,447.21	14.04	20.95	34.99
Sikkim	64,208.90	7519.17	12,626.15	20,145.33	11.71	19.66	31.37
Tripura	359,378.10	37,831.52	63,821.17	101,652.69	10.53	17.76	28.29
NER	4,602,244.10	516,176.36	762,391.58	1,278,567.94	11.22	16.57	27.78
India	118,898,543.20	12,306,317.15	18,579,378.13	30,885,695.27	10.35	15.63	25.98

Source: Census of India, 2011.

creation for the youth is an essential element in the planning process for the development of the north-eastern region.

The region witnessed a rapid expansion of employment during the eighties and nineties, with the largest number of jobs created being within public administration. Lakhs of people in the NER are dependent on public sector employment, at the same time, the supply of manpower has been constrained by the lack of good quality professional and vocational training that would raise the skills base and boost entrepreneurial abilities (NEC). Public sector provides more jobs than the private sector. Job creation did not improve during the years 1981–2011 for both the sectors. The situation of employment in India is opposite to that in the NER in that private sector employment is greater than that in the public sector. No new jobs have been created in both the public and private sectors. Across the states, employment creation in the public sector is slowly improving except in Assam, where lakhs of people are able to find employment in the private sector (Table 5.10). Private sector employment opportunities for the people in the region are very skewed (Figure 5.3). However, most of the other states in the region find more severe in getting employment in the public and private sectors.

Table 5.10

Trends of public and private employment in the organized sector, 1981–2011

Public Sector								
Year	Assam	Manipur	Meghalaya	Mizoram	Nagaland	Tripura	NER	India
1981	3.58	0.36	0.44	0.15	0.39	0.62	5.54	155.00
1991	5.01	0.55	0.64	0.33	0.64	0.88	8.05	191.00
2001	5.37	0.80	0.73	0.40	0.74	1.10	9.14	191.40
2011	5.34	0.76	0.47	0.10	0.73	1.38	8.78	175.48
Private Sector								
1981	4.99	0.01	0.04	0.01	0.01	0.06	5.12	73.95
1991	5.49	0.01	0.05	0.01	0.02	0.10	5.68	76.76
2001	5.79	0.03	0.09	0.01	0.03	0.13	6.08	86.52
2011	5.83	0.03	0.05	0.00	0.05	0.06	6.02	114.52

Source: Employment Review for various years, Directorate General of Employment and Training, GOI.

Notes: @=Quick estimate figures, Sikkim and Arunachal Pradesh were not covered under the EMI Programme. EMI: Employment Market Information, conducted by the Employment Exchanges.

Figure 5-3

Public and private employment in the organized sector, 1981–2011

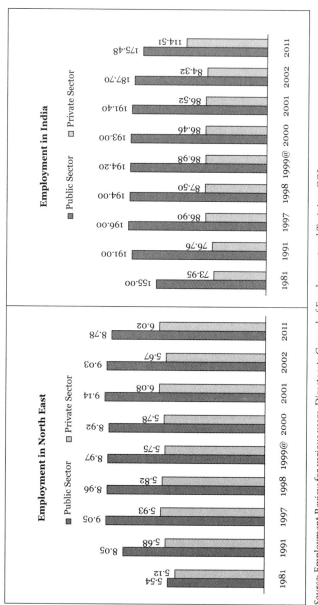

Employment in India

■ Public Sector □ Private Sector

	1981	1991	1997	1998	1999@	2000	2001	2002	2011
Public Sector	155.00	191.00	196.00	194.00	194.20	193.00	191.40	187.70	175.48
Private Sector	73.95	76.76	86.90	87.50	86.98	86.46	86.52	84.32	114.51

Employment in North East

■ Public Sector □ Private Sector

	1981	1991	1997	1998	1999@	2000	2001	2002	2011
Public Sector	5.54	8.05	9.05	8.96	8.97	8.92	9.14	9.03	8.78
Private Sector	5.12	5.68	5.93	5.82	5.75	5.78	6.08	5.67	6.02

Source: Employment Review for various years, Directorate General of Employment and Training, GOI.

Some encouraging trends are that the proportion of rural self-employed people increased between 1999–2000 and 2004–05, and the share of casual labour fell, especially in Assam, Sikkim and Nagaland. The trend in urban areas is somewhat similar during the same period, except in Assam and Meghalaya where self-employment fell, the share of regular employment increased, and casualization of labour increased marginally in Assam (Table A5.4). The region is still dependent on agriculture for employment both in the rural and urban areas, with 85–88 per cent of jobs still concentrated in this sector. The significant unused cultivable area, especially in the hill states indicates that the farm sector still has the potential to provide livelihoods (NEDFi, 2003). However, declining productivity in agriculture calls for some degree of Government intervention for creating livelihood opportunities in the region. As in the rest of the country, there was a steep decline in the number of cultivators and an increase in the number of agricultural labourers and other workers during the 1990s, but the situation in NER is exacerbated by the limited livelihood opportunities in both the farm and non-farm sectors (Table 5.11). The growing number of 'other workers' indicates that there was some improvement in the non-farm employment scenario in the year 1990.

Table 5.11

Distribution of workers as cultivators, agricultural labourers and other workers

	Percentage of Total Workers, 1981–2001								
	Cultivators			*Agricultural Labourers*			*Other Workers*		
States	*1981*	*1991*	*2001*	*1981*	*1991*	*2001*	*1981*	*1991*	*2001*
Arunachal Pradesh	71.3	60.8	57.8	2.5	5.4	3.9	26.3	33.7	37.0
Assam	NA	54.8	39.1	NA	12.6	13.3	NA	31.7	44.0
Manipur	63.6	59.9	40.2	5.0	10.3	12.0	31.4	23.8	37.6
Meghalaya	62.6	56.3	48.1	10.0	13.0	17.7	27.5	30.4	32.0
Mizoram	70.6	62.3	54.9	2.5	5.4	5.7	26.9	31.2	37.9
Nagaland	72.3	72.7	64.7	0.8	1.6	3.7	26.9	25.3	29.0
Sikkim	60.1	58	49.9	3.3	8.2	6.5	36.6	33.1	42.0
Tripura	43.3	38.7	27	24.0	24.2	23.8	32.7	35.2	46.1
India	41.5	39.7	31.6	25.1	27.4	26.7	33.4	30.5	37.5

Source: Census 1981, 1991 and 2001.

Table 5.12

Unemployment in the North East (per cent of labour force)

	1983–94			1999–2000			2009–10		
States	*Male*	*Female*	*Total*	*Male*	*Female*	*Total*	*Male*	*Female*	*Total*
Arunachal Pradesh	NA	NA	NA	1.0	0.9	0.9	4.5	9.4	5.8
Assam	2.2	2.4	2.2	3.7	8.0	4.6	7.2	8.5	1.9
Manipur	0.6	0.0	0.4	3.7	3.1	3.5	8.8	2.4	1.0
Meghalaya	1.8	0.9	1.5	0.9	0.9	0.9	2.5	1.7	5.9
Mizoram	0.3	1.0	0.4	2.5	1.3	2.0	3.3	7.4	4.7
Nagaland	0.4	0.0	0.3	4.0	2.9	3.5	2.6	3.1	4.5
Sikkim	2.6	1.3	2.2	3.6	2.7	3.4	5.9	7.8	6.7
Tripura	2.1	17.7	3.9	1.6	4.5	1.9	1.4	7.4	6.3
India	2.3	1.3	2.0	2.5	1.8	2.3	4.3	2.4	7.3

Source: NSSO, 38th, 50th, 55th and 66th Round on Employment and Unemployment in India.
Note: 1983 NSSO survey excludes Arunachal Pradesh and rural Nagaland.

Table 5.12 shows that there is a large variation in the unemployment rates according to usual status for males and females members across the NE states. The unemployment scenario improved as the percentage of the labour force marginally increased during the period 1983–84 to 2009–10. There was a marginal decline in the unemployment rate in some north-eastern states between 1993–94 and 1999–2000, though it is seen to have increased in the recent NSS survey 66th Round. The situation has been more adverse for women and in urban areas in the age of 15–29 years between 1999–2000 and 2004–05 (Table A5.5).

The unemployment rate in the northeast is very high. There is a need for proper planning to improve the quality of lives of the people in the region. The rising unemployment and underemployment has been accompanied by wages that are higher than the national average (Table 5.13). Underemployment with high wages presents a paradoxical situation. High wages could be a serious constraint to private investment, especially from outside NER, given that regulations and local conditions in some hill states restrict the free inflow of labour.

Despite richness in natural endowment, the NER is one of the most backward areas of the country and home to a very high proportion of the poor people. Agriculture is highly risky and productivity is low. The crucial message is that its abundant, rich natural resources were

Table 5.13

Average daily wages for rural casual workers engaged in public and non-public* works (rupees)

| | Public Works | | | | | |
| | 1999–2000 | | | 2004–05 | | |
States	Male	Female	Total	Male	Female	Total
Arunachal Pradesh	79.23	121.43	80.66	75.14	64.14	71.12
Assam	67.97	27.14	59.81	70.00	-	70.00
Manipur	60.15	24.74	42.31	86.23	40.00	85.00
Meghalaya	63.31	53.31	57.80	106.98	-	106.98
Mizoram	85.55	71.43	77.14	95.04	81.75	92.58
Nagaland	84.39	109.41	87.67	98.60	68.72	87.65
Sikkim	83.29	0.00	83.29	89.29	89.29	89.29
Tripura	86.59	123.88	95.64	84.43	40.00	76.71
India	48.14	38.06	45.55	65.33	49.19	56.33
	Non-public* Works					
Arunachal Pradesh	67.09	42.73	57.64	104.38	50.60	91.41
Assam	48.82	35.55	46.63	62.59	53.29	60.18
Manipur	59.46	47.40	56.88	72.62	64.41	71.33
Meghalaya	57.37	43.06	51.29	73.20	43.35	64.16
Mizoram	97.77	66.24	92.33	111.86	88.89	109.85
Nagaland	71.93	46.67	68.23	146.05	150.00	146.32
Sikkim	50.71	40.60	49.20	89.16	74.22	86.53
Tripura	49.14	38.66	47.83	64.07	43.40	61.30
India	44.84	29.01	39.64	55.03	34.94	48.89

Source: Employment–Unemployment Situation in India, NSS 55th and 61st Round.
Notes: *Non-Public works: Works other than public works (that is, NSSO activity status code 41).
The age group of casual workers in NSSO 55th Round (1999–2000) was people of age 5 and above, while the corresponding age group for 61st Round (2004–05) was between age 15 and 59.

neglected in the past, but must be put to efficient use now to catalyze the developmental process (Barah, 2001). Two important strategies for increasing employment are: (a) expanding economic activity to raise the demand for different levels of skills, which would in turn facilitate the shift to a high-growth economy; and (b) human capital development, which would essentially mean an enhancement of employable skills (NEC).

The other most important aspect of employment is labour migration, which gets complicated due to several socio-political considerations—both in terms of internal migration of population (from within and outside the region) as well as in terms of influx of labourers across national boundaries. Although there have been various initiatives taken up by the government for employment and income generation in the region, their benefits to the people at the grassroots level is still debatable. In this context, understanding the aspect of labour migration in the NER is important for skill upgradation and enhancing employment opportunities for the youth.

Labour Migration: Conceptual Issues

The NSS survey collected information on migration particulars of the households which had migrated to the place of enumeration during the last 365 days. This included information on location of last usual residence, pattern of migration and reason for migration. Particulars of out-migrants who migrated from the household to another village/town at any time in the past were also collected. Information gathered included present place of residence, reason for migration, period since leaving the household, whether presently engaged in any economic activity, whether remittances had been sent, and number of times and amount of remittances sent during last 365 days, were collected. Migrants have been defined as those for whom the last usual place of residence (UPR) is different from the present place of enumeration. In this survey, the UPR of a person was defined as a place (village/town) where the person had stayed continuously for a period of six months or more (NSSO, 2008). There are number of cases where the migrants had no choice. They may simply be forced out because of differences in economic opportunities; others are caused by injustice, violation of human rights, violent conflict, persecution at home or environmental degradation (HMI World Congress, 2004).

The Situation of Migrant Workers

Net migration is the difference between the number of persons entering the territory of a state and the number of persons who leave the territory of a state in the same period, also called 'migratory balance'. This balance

Table 5.14

Net migrant rate (1991–2001)

(in per cent)

Sl. No.	States	Male	Female	Person
1.	Arunachal Pradesh	+0.73	+0.57	+0.65
2.	Assam	−0.06	−0.09	−0.07
3.	Manipur	−0.16	−0.13	−0.14
4.	Meghalaya	+0.09	+0.04	+0.07
5.	Mizoram	−0.16	−0.35	−0.25
6.	Nagaland	+0.05	−0.41	−0.17
7.	Sikkim	+0.26	+0.16	+0.21
8.	Tripura	+0.02	+0.02	+0.02
	Total North East	+0.07	−0.03	+0.02

Source: D Series, Migration Tables 1991, 2001.

applies to both internal and international migration and is called net in migration/immigration when arrivals exceed departures and net out-migration/emigration when departures exceed arrivals (Perruchoud and Redpath-Cross, 2011). A positive value represents more people entering the state than leaving it, while a negative value means more people leaving than entering it.

Table 5.14 shows the interstate population migration rates for the inter-census period (1991–2001). Assam has a large net out-migrant. Implicit in these population movements is an origin-destination migration matrix of workers. The NER is receiving more in-migrants than out-migrants. There are various reasons why females out-migrate. Some of north-eastern states gain migration and some lose migration. In terms of gain, the states that send more out-migrants are gaining and the states receiving more in-migrants are losing. Assam, Manipur, Mizoram and Nagaland are the gainers. Arunachal Pradesh, Meghalaya, Sikkim and Tripura are loser states.

Migration is a common phenomenon seen all over the world since growth centres, which generate demand for labour, often tend to concentrate in certain areas. However, migrant workers are the most vulnerable and exploited among the informal sector workers and have not received any attention in labour policy.

In the source states which are origins of supply of migrant workers— and most of them migrate to take up some labour-intensive, low-wage occupation—an effective and large-scale effort for vocational training in labour intensive occupations is required. Furthermore, such a programme should be amenable to the special needs of the entrants to informal labour markets. In the destination states, the focus of public policy (including Labour Policy) should be to improve the conditions under which the bulk of these in-migrants live and work. In so far as the destination locations fail to provide certain basic minimum living conditions for the new in-migrants, it would be better to restrain economic growth at such locations.

In the labour and employment sector, better implementation of certain legislations pertaining to unorganized workers can protect the interests of most of the migrant workers; for example, the Regulation of Employment and Conditions of Service Act, 1976; the Building and other Construction Workers Act, 1976; the Workmen's Compensation Act, 1923, the Minimum Wages Act, 1948, and the Interstate Migrants for Workmen Act, 1979. During recent times, the Central government has taken an initiative with the introduction of 'The Unorganized Workers' Social Security Bill, 2007'.

Household Characteristics and Labour Migration

The choice of a place for migration depends not only on the socio-economic condition of the place but also on the background, contact and personal preference of the migrant. Based on the information collected for persons migrating to other states, the NSS 64th Round throws light on the different characteristics of out-migrants. The household members in the North East that possessed land in the first moving average possessed up to one hectare land area. The second moving average constituted 26.42 per cent and possessed land between 0.41–1.00 hectares, and the third moving average of 14.15 per cent possessed land of area between 1.01–2.00 hectares (Figure 5.4).

The NSS survey in all the eight northeastern states revealed that 14.42 per cent of their former member of the household migrated out any time in the past and 85.58 per cent who didn't migrate. The pattern of migration is such that 46.15 per cent are temporary migrants and 53.85 per cent are permanent in nature. The mean age of the out-migrants is around 30 years of age which shows a normal distribution curve for the youth (Figure 5.5).

Figure 5.4

Distribution of land possessed (area in hectare) (in per cent)

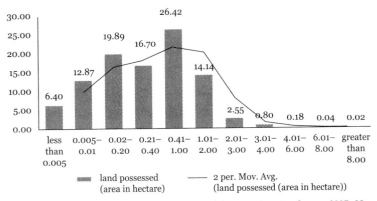

Source: Computed from NSS 64th Round, unit level data on Migration Survey, 2007–08.

Figure 5.5

Mean age

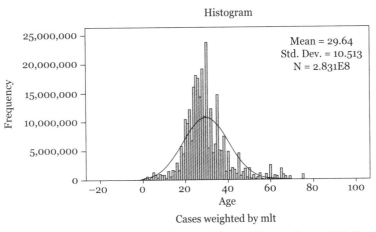

Source: Computed from NSS 64th Round, unit level data on Migration Survey, 2007–08.

The proportion of the out-migrants from both sexes is the same. Of the out-migrants, 61 per cent are found to be Hindu, 21 per cent Muslim and 14 per cent Christian, respectively (Figure 5.6). The migrants that fall in the category of others who do not want to reveal the community to which they belong are found to be highest with 37 per cent, Schedule Tribe (ST) 29 per cent and Other Backward Classed (OBC) 26 per cent, and the least among them are Schedule Castes (SC) with only 8 per cent (Figure 5.7).

Figure 5.6

Percentage distribution by religion

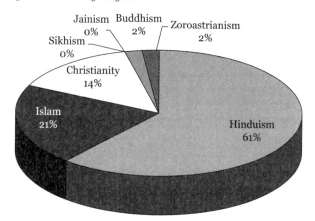

Source: Computed from NSS 64th Round, unit level data on Migration Survey, 2007–08.

Figure 5.7

Percentage distribution by social groups

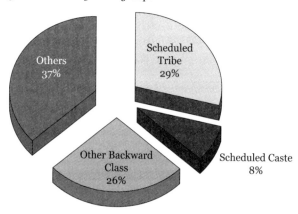

Source: Computed from NSS 64th Round, unit level data on Migration Survey, 2007–08.

Reasons for Migration

In India, the most prominent reason for female migration in both the rural and urban areas was marriage (NSS 64th Round, 2010). The reason for migration for male migrants was dominated by employment-related reasons. The higher proportion of out-migration from all the other north-eastern states for marriage was also validated by the 2001 census. Table 5.15 shows the reason for out-migration due to natural disasters (drought, flood, tsunami, and so on) is the highest at 17.69 per cent followed by migration to take up employment/better employment (15.71 per cent), transfer of service/contract (11.87 per cent), in search of better employment (11.63 per cent), and in search of employment (10.71 per cent). In all, the most important reasons for which people from the North East moved out were economic reasons (59.42 per cent).

Table 5.15

Reasons for migration, 2007–08

Reasons for Migration	In Per cent
In search of employment	10.71
In search of better employment	11.63
Business	9.50
To take up employment/better employment	15.71
Transfer of service/contract	11.87
Proximity to place of work	3.01
Studies	6.37
Natural disaster (drought, flood and tsunami)	17.69
Social/political problems (riots, terrorism, political refugee and bad law and order)	0.44
Displacement by development project	1.89
Acquisition of own house/flat	5.56
Housing problems	0.70
Health care	0.23
Post retirement	0.05
Marriage	0.62
Others	4.03
Total	100.00

Source: Computed from NSS 64th Round, unit level data on Migration Survey, 2007–08.

The Uses of 'Household' Remittances

Remittances and savings constitute a primary channel through which migrants are able to stabilize their living conditions which also have an impact on intra- and inter-household dynamics and the pattern of growth and development in the source area (Srivastava, 2011). The NSS 64th round collected information for the first time on household use of remittances.

The out-migrants from the North East presently engaged in any economic activity is 44.8 per cent, 53.5 per cent are not engaged and 1.7 per cent did not reveal the information about their activity. About 34 per cent of the out-migrants sent remittances during the last 365 days and 66 per cent did not remit money to their household. The total amount of remittances received by the north-eastern states during the last 365 days is ₹9.18 million. The broad trend across states was towards using remittances for household consumption expenditure (and within that, for food expenditure) (Tumbe, 2011). But there is distinct regional variation. The majority of the Northeastern states use remittances above 50 per cent for the education of their household members. This validated the fact that there is lack of educational infrastructure for attainment of higher learning. In Sikkim 11 per cent of remittances were used for marriage and ceremonial expenses and 17 per cent for improving housing conditions (major repairs, purchase of land and buildings) (Table 5.16).

The category of three most important uses of household remittances in the North East is shown in Table 5.17. In the first category, 66.92 per cent of remittances are used for household expenses on food items. In the second category, it is distributed towards education of household members

Table 5.16

Uses of remittances in selected north-eastern states, 2007–08

		RRHH Reporting use of Remittances (in %)	
Uses of Remittances	*North East*		*All India*
Education of household members	Arunachal Pradesh, Manipur, Meghalaya and Mizoram	Above 55	5
For improving housing condition (major repairs, purchase of land and buildings, and so on)	Sikkim	17	9

Source: Computed from NSS 64th Round, unit level data on Migration Survey, 2007–08.
Note: RRHH= Remittance receiving Household.

Table 5.17

Uses of remittances in the North East, 2007–08

Uses of Remittances	First Category	Second Category	Third Category
Household consumer expenditure: on food items	66.92	2.41	6.12
Education of household members	0.96	31.48	2.50
Household durable	1.88	23.88	11.63
Marriage and other ceremonies	1.89	2.97	1.10
Health care	9.22	18.52	24.90
Others items on household consumer expenditure	7.45	13.11	40.56
For improving housing condition (major repairs, purchase of land and buildings, and so on)	3.54	3.61	3.39
Debt repayment	1.35	1.08	1.95
Financing working capital	0.47	0.14	0.06
Initiating new entrepreneurial activity	0.04	0.10	0.24
Saving/investment	2.17	1.78	2.51
Others	4.12	0.93	5.04
Total	100.00	100.00	100.00

Source: Computed from NSS 64th Round, unit level data on Migration Survey, 2007–08.

(31.48 per cent), household durables (23.88 per cent) and health care expenses (18.52 per cent), respectively. The third category is expenses on other items (40.56 per cent), health expenditure (24.90 per cent) and expenses on household durable goods (11.63 per cent) respectively.

Distribution of Migration Rate Monthly Per Capita Consumer Expenditure (MPCE) Quintile Classes

The MPCE for a household is the total consumer expenditure over all items divided by the household size and expressed on a per month (30 days) basis. A person's MPCE is understood as that of the household to which he or she belongs. The NSSO provides migration characteristics with the 'level of living' of the household members. As it is difficult to collect reliable income data, the NSSO collects data on consumption expenditure in its surveys. The estimate of MPCE derived based on worksheet may not converge to the corresponding estimates derived through main enquiry schedules of household consumer expenditure. The abridged worksheet was used to reduce the respondent fatigue. Based on the abridged worksheet, MPCE was worked out for each sample household, which is expected to serve as a close proxy for income and facilitates the ordering the households and persons thereof in the hierarchy of their level of living.

The migration rate for any category of persons (say for rural or urban, male or female) has been estimated as the number of migrants belonging to that category per 1,000 persons in that category. To study the mobility of persons at different 'levels of living', the proportion of total migrants (per 1,000 persons) in different MPCE quintile classes for each state of all NE is presented in Table A5.6.

Quintile classes of MPCE: The population of any state/region or domain can be divided into five quintile classes of MPCE, where the 1st quintile of the distribution of MPCE means the level of MPCE below which 20 per cent of the population lies, the second quintile is the level below which 40 per cent of the population lies, and so on. The estimated MPCE quintile classes for the distribution of MPCE in the rural and urban sector and for both males and females of each north-eastern state shows that the majority of the migrants fall in the category of the top MPCE quintile class. This indicates that the standard of living is very high among the out-migrants from the North East.

A Special Survey from Udalguri District of Assam

Objective of the Study

The main aim of this special survey is to examine the economic impact of out-migration on the sending households. What have been the consequences of out-migration?

Background

Udalguri district is situated on the Indo-Bhutan border carved out of erstwhile Darrang district prior to the formation of Bodoland Territorial Council (BTC) in 2004. It is one of the four districts (Kokrajhar, Chirang, Baksa and Udalguri) of Bodoland Territorial Area District (BTAD) under the VI Schedule of Indian Constitution. The district comprises two subdivisions, nine revenue circles and 11 development blocks, two towns, seven police stations and seven police out posts. It covers a geographical area of 1,852.16 km². Under these nine revenue circles, there are 802 villages as per the 2001 census.

Udalguri district is one of the 27 districts of Assam and Udalguri town is its headquarters. It is surrounded by the Himalayan Kingdom of Bhutan in the North, the Brahmaputra River in the South, River Paasnoi that separates Darrang from Sonitpur District in the East, and the Mangaldai Sub-division in the West. According to the 2001 census, the total population of the Udalguri circle (under Darrang District) was 192,924, out of which 178,027 lived in rural areas and only 14,897 lived in the urban areas. The Scheduled Tribe (ST) population was 75,928 (32.07 per cent), the Scheduled Caste (SC) population was 3,296 (4.10 per cent), and the rest was general population. Among the STs, the majority belong to the Bodo-Kachary groups. The literacy rate is 34 per cent. The population density is 411 per km², which is slightly higher than the state average of 340 per km². About 54 per cent of the population lives below poverty line and the main occupation and livelihood options are agriculture and livestock. The categorical proportion of workers to the total workers was:

Cultivators: 38.14 per cent
Small and marginal farmers of the cultivators: 23.76 per cent
Agricultural labourers: 8.92 per cent
Artisans: 2.78 per cent
Household/cottage industry workers: 3.39 per cent
Workers in allied agro-base activities: 6.37 per cent
Other workers: 16.59 per cent

The infrastructure facilities in general, especially in the rural areas, are inadequate. A railway line facing East–West direction passes through the heart of the subdivision headquarters which has three stations, Udalguri, Rowta and Mazbat. National Highway No. 52 runs through Udalguri, touching some small towns like Kharupetia, Dalgaon, Rowta and Orang. A pucca road connects with the National Highway at Rowta in the East, Bhairabkunda town with the neighbouring Bhutan, and yet another road connects the western part and two parts of the Mangaldai Subdivision. Very few road connections of the different places and villages with the subdivision are gravelled—most of them are un-gravelled and not motorable. Some gravelled roads too are not in a motorable condition. Many factors are responsible for this condition: many rivers flow through the subdivision and erode the roads as well as bridges during the rainy season; negligence on the part of the government to take necessary steps to improve the conditions of roads and socio-political unrest leading to the destruction of some of the roads and bridges. Most of the remote villages remain cut off from the towns and other parts of the world during the rainy season. Another vital infrastructure facility that is lacking in most of the villages of the district is electricity. Only 258 out of 802 villages of the subdivision are fully or partially electrified and the rest still live in darkness. Health facilities are scant in the villages, and even if the facilities are available, the medical officers are absent throughout the year. There are a few veterinary hospitals to look after the health conditions of the domestic animals. There are 843 elementary schools, 37 high schools, 13 higher secondary schools and two colleges in the district. The number of post offices in the area is 51, out of which only five post offices had telegraph facilities until 2001. These post offices are situated at the town or in semi-urban areas. The rural inhabitants hardly use any such postal services or telephones.

The district is socially and economically backward as the number of people keep increasing but the resources remain constant and limited to feed their hungry population. This has led to pressure on the level of development, thereby encouraging people to migrate. Another problem is the continuing tradition of agitations, *bandhs, hartals,* and more, which could also have a negative impact on the socio-economic conditions and livelihood.

Sample Design and Methodology

We have used both primary and secondary information. The primary data were collected on a random basis from 210 households out of the 339 households in Kathalguri village. The household listing was based on the 2001 census—we have updated the house list. The survey period was from 20 July 2012 to 5 October 2012. The questionnaire contained nine blocks. The first block elicits the socio-demographic characteristics of the household members while the second block collects data on migration status, such as pattern of migration, duration of stay, present occupation, reason for migration, remittances and it utilization. The next two blocks collect information on the household expenses on children's education and health. The fifth and sixth blocks collect information on social capital and physical assets of the household. The seventh and eight blocks contain information on land and livestock of the households. The last two blocks give information on monthly per capita expenditure on food and non-food items and saving and investment of the household members.

The choice of the study location is based on the Purposive Sampling Method (PSM). The advantage of using this method is to study the specificity of the problem of rural people and their livelihood strategy and how remittances had an impact on their household and living conditions. Understanding the background of migration process in a disturbed and underdeveloped area from village-based household information is important. This village is selected on the basis of geographical locations and backwardness. For the purpose of conducting survey, the comprehensive qualitative questionnaire was developed. The study employed cross tabulation and simple statistical tools for analysis. This survey will be extended to another 100 households by the junior author and will be used for writing his doctoral dissertation.

Discussion

Household Characteristics

Figures 5.8 and 5.9 illustrate the distribution of households by religion and social groups. The majority of people living in the village are Hindu (63 per cent) followed by Muslim (24 per cent), Christian (12 per cent) and other religions (1 per cent).

Figure 5.8

Percentage distribution by religion

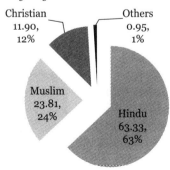

Source: Field survey, 2012.

Figure 5.9

Percentage distribution by social group

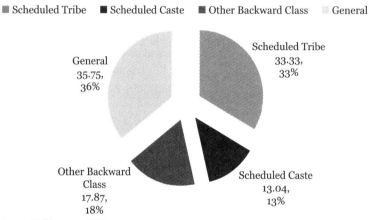

Source: Field survey, 2012.

The general category constitutes 36 per cent, ST (33 per cent), OBC (18 per cent), and SC (13 per cent). Based on language, the highest proportion speaks Boro (33.81 per cent). Bengali (28.10 per cent), other languages (20.95 per cent), Assamese (16.67 per cent) and Hindi (0.48 per cent) (Figure 5.10).

Figure 5.10

Percentage distribution by language spoken

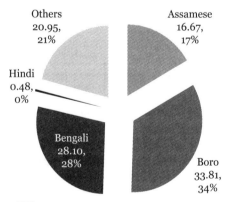

Source: Field survey, 2012.

Migration Status

The sample is a mixture of different communities living in the village. To capture the out-migrants from the household members, the basic question asked was whether any member of the household moved out of the village during the last four years. The results reveal that 17 per cent households had a migrant. Among them, 65 per cent are temporary and the remaining 35 per cent are said to be permanent in nature. The duration of migration among migrants is as follows: one week (4.17 per cent), one month (10.42 per cent), six months (14.58 per cent), one year (64.58 per cent) and others (6.25 per cent). The migrants are enumerated as per destination. In the same state and within the same district (18.75 per cent), same state but another district (50.00 per cent) and outside the state (31.25 per cent). Migration by place of last residence is found to be more from the same state but another district for both rural (14.58 per cent) and urban (41.66 per cent) areas (Table 5.18).

Reasons for Migration

A person is likely to migrate if his/her expected income is greater in a location other than at the place of his/her residence. But the wage rates and employment opportunities differ between the place of origin and destination (Sjaastad, 1962; Todaro 1969). According to the special survey, the reason for migration for the purpose of studies was the highest with

Table 5.18

Migration by place of last residence

Place of Last Residence	Rural/Urban	%
Same district	Rural	12.50
	Urban	14.58
Same state but another district	Rural	14.58
	Urban	41.66
Another state	Rural	4.16
	Urban	12.50
	Total	100.00

Source: Field survey, 2012.

Table 5.19

Reasons for migration

Sr. No.	Reasons for Migration	%
1.	In search of employment	2.08
2.	Marriage	25.00
3.	In search of better employment	4.17
4.	Business	4.17
5.	To take up employment/better employment	12.50
6.	Transfer of service/contract	14.58
7.	Proximity to place of work	4.17
8.	Studies	33.33
	Total	100.00

Source: Field survey, 2012.

33.33 per cent, for marriage 25.00 per cent, for transfer of service/contract 14.58 per cent, and to take up employment/better employment 12.50 per cent (Table 5.19). The present occupations of the migrants are cultivator (18.42 per cent), wage employment in agriculture (23.68 per cent) and wage employment in non-agriculture (57.89 per cent).

Remittances

During the last four years, 48.72 per cent of the migrant households have received remittances while 51.28 per cent did not receive any remittance. The average amount of remittances received by the household was ₹5,862. About 46.15 per cent of the remittances were used for household consumer expenditure (Table 5.20), followed by marriage and other ceremonies (30.77 per cent).

Table 5.20

Uses of household remittances

S. No.	Uses of Remittances	%
1.	For household consumer expenditure on food items	3.85
2.	Education of household members	7.69

(Table 5.20 Continued)

(Table 5.20 Continued)

S. No.	Uses of Remittances	%
3.	Marriage and other ceremonies	30.77
4.	Health care	3.85
5.	Financing working capital	7.69
6.	Other items on household consumer expenditure	46.15
	Total	100.00

Source: Field survey, 2012.

Summary and Conclusion

In this study, we have analyzed the demographic and socio-economic profile of the North East, economic growth and development after the economic liberalization, the sectoral contribution of the NSDP, the trends and patterns of labour employment and the contribution of migration to the development of households by using the existing data available from the NER as well as other secondary sources including the unit level NSS data. We have also conducted a field survey from Assam to assess the migration phenomenon in the context of conflict. The finding indicates that the largest contribution of NSDP among all the NE states comes from agriculture and the service sector. Although agriculture's contribution to the state domestic product is declining across all the NER, only Nagaland's share from agriculture and industry is increasing. It is also documented from the existing data that economic growth and development has been lopsided for the last four decades. The uneven distribution of the benefits of liberalization and globalization has widened the developmental gap between the rest of India (excluding a few economically backward states) and the NER.

It might be the case that the states with developed physical and social infrastructure attract more FDI and domestic investment. While the north-eastern states having multifaceted problems such as poor social and physical infrastructure, socio-political instabilities, frequent disturbances, lack of governance and failure to attract investment which finally lead to the decline in their economic sustainability. This scenario traps them in the vicious grip of low income, low investment and low growth. It has also been observed that in many of the north-eastern states, the human development index is far behind the rest of Indian states. Hence the need of the hour is to bridge the gap between the North East and the rest of

India. This will require speeding up of the pace of development by the building of an investment-friendly environment, and containing peace and harmony among people along with good governance practices.

The scenario of labour and employment has not shown any progress since the economic reforms. The strategy for inclusive growth should involve skill development by not only enhancing wage employment but also generating avenues for self-employment of the youth as the north-eastern states have a very large youth population. Employment growth will be crucial for development planning, as it raises standards of living of the people, improves access to basic services and leads to an overall improvement in social welfare.

The findings of the study show that the majority of the people in the North East are dependent on public sector job for gainful employment, except in Assam where more of the youth were able to find greater employment opportunities in the private sector. The underpinnings of economic backwardness could explain as to why people migrate. Migration contributes to the prosperity of both the place of origin and destination over time. The important reasons for which people from the North East moved out were employment, education and marriage. The findings show that Assam, Manipur, Mizoram and Nagaland are the gainers whereas Arunachal Pradesh, Meghalaya, Sikkim and Tripura are losers.

Migration is a common occurrence all over the world since growth centres which generate demand for labour often tend to concentrate in certain areas. However, migrant workers are the most vulnerable and exploited among the workers in the informal sector, and have not received any attention in the labour policy. With respect to labour and employment, better implementation of certain legislations pertaining to unorganized workers can protect the interests of most of the migrant workers. The recent scenario of labour migration in the North East has shown a new dimension where they use their income by sending back remittances to their household members. The findings of the field survey show that 46.15 per cent of households use remittances for consumer expenditure or day-to-day requirements. Thus, remittances enable the households to improve their economic well-being which in turn will enhance growth and development in their vicinity.

Appendix

Table A5.1

Socio-economic profile of the north-eastern region

Socio-economic Indicators	Arunachal Pradesh	Assam	Manipur	Meghalaya	Mizoram	Nagaland	Sikkim	Tripura	Total NE
Area ('000 km²)	83.74	78.44	22.33	22.43	21.08	NA	NA	10.49	262.19
Population (lakh)	13.83	311.69	27.22	29.64	10.91	19.81	6.08	36.71	455.88
Rural population (lakh)	8.7	232.16	18.18	18.65	4.48	16.36	4.81	26.53	329.87
Exponential growth rate	2.33	1.58	1.72	2.49	2.07	-0.05	1.17	1.39	1.58
Density (per km²)	13	340	107	103	40	120	76	304	–
Sex ratio	901	932	972	975	938	909	875	950	–
% of forest area to geographical area	61.55	34.45	78.01	42.34	79.3	52.05	82.31	60.01	–
Reporting area for land utilisation ('000 ha)	5,504	7,850	2,211	2,241	2,109	1,560	710	1049	23,234
Production of total food grains ('000 MT)	241	3,895	392	221	129	389	102	558	5927
Per capita consumption of electricity (kWh)	162.3	105.5	72.9	300.8	162.3	61.4	130.8	111.3	–
Road length per 100 km² of area (km)	21.93	114.09	51.21	42.65	24.07	126.79	28.45	155.41	
Road length per 1,000 population (km)	16.69	3.29	4.76	3.98	5.64	10.51	3.36	5.09	
Average population per bank branch	15,813	21,906	31,021	12,811	11,424	28,821	11,260	17,928	
Credit deposit ratio (%)	17.24	30.77	29.06	36.92	38.28	16.93	23.3	25.36	

(Table A5.1 Continued)

(Table A5.1 Continued)

Socio-economic Indicators	Arunachal Pradesh	Assam	Manipur	Meghalaya	Mizoram	Nagaland	Sikkim	Tripura	Total NE
Number of health centres functioning	485	5819	508	519	42	502	175	621	9049
Person serve per PHC	41,535	274,765	125,307	105,352	46,424	91,553	143,556	336,098	
Birth rate (per '000)	20	27	17	26	17	NA	22	15	–
IMR/000	37	70	14	61	14	NA	34	34	–
Literacy rate (%)	44.71	53.79	59.85	50.75	74.44	57.65	69.68	63.81	–
Student–Teacher ratio:									
a. HSSC	29	21	20	23	22	27	19	23	
b. High school	27	18	19	18	13	20	18	23	
Population per post office	3,574	6,672	3,444	4,705	2,208	6,142	2,596	4,468	–
Area serve by post office	274.43	19.63	32.13	45.62	52.36	50.93	34.13	14.57	–
BPL	33.47	36.09	28.54	33.87	19.47	32.67	36.55	34.44	–
PC NSDP (at price in ₹) 2010–11	15,400	91,240	8839	12,723	5177	10,680	3873	17,500	16,543
X plan outlay/per capita (₹)	35,413	3,119	11,737	12,975	25,872	11,200	30,605	13,270	

Sources: (a) Statistical Abstract of India, 2003, CSO, (b) Basic Statistics of NER 2002, NEC Secretariat, (c) Tenth Plan Document, Planning Commission, (d) Basic Road Statistics of India, mining of shipping, road transport and highway, (e) Bulletin on Rural Health Statistics in India, 2005, Minimum of HFW, (f) Sikkim Statistical Profile, (g) Eleventh Finance Commission Report.

Table A5.2

Estimated birth rate, death rate, natural growth rate and infant mortality rate, 1997–2010 (selected years)

State	Birth Rate			Death Rate			Natural Growth Rate			IMR		
	Total	Rural	Urban	Total	Rural	Urban	Total	Rural	Urban	Total	Rural	Urban
						1997						
Arunachal Pradesh	21.4	22.3	12.2	5.8	6.1	2.0	15.6	16.1	10.2	47	49	17
Assam	28.2	29.0	20.7	9.9	10.3	5.9	18.3	18.7	14.8	76	79	37
Manipur	19.7	20.5	17.6	5.9	5.8	6.2	13.8	14.7	11.5	30	21	28
Meghalaya	30.2	32.9	16.6	8.8	9.7	4.4	21.4	23.2	12.3	54	56	52
Mizoram	15.0	16.4	13.3	4.8	5.7	3.7	10.2	10.7	9.6	19	22	15
Nagaland	NA	NA	7.9	NA	NA	2.7	NA	NA	5.2	NA	NA	16
Sikkim	19.8	20.0	12.8	6.5	6.6	3.5	13.3	13.4	9.3	51	51	41
Tripura	18.3	18.9	15.5	6.8	6.9	5.8	11.6	11.9	9.7	51	53	39
All India	27.2	28.9	21.5	8.9	9.6	6.5	18.3	19.2	15.0	71	77	45
						2003						
Arunachal Pradesh	18.9	19.5	12.3	4.7	4.9	2.5	14.2	14.6	9.8	34	35	11
Assam	26.3	27.2	18.0	9.1	9.5	5.9	17.2	17.7	12	67	70	35
Manipur	15.5	16.1	14.1	4.8	4.9	4.4	10.7	11.1	9.7	16	15	19
Meghalaya	24.7	26.6	13.8	7.4	8.1	3.4	17.3	18.5	10.4	57	59	44

(Table A5.2 Continued)

(Table A5.2 Continued)

State	Birth Rate			Death Rate			Natural Growth Rate			IMR		
	Total	Rural	Urban	Total	Rural	Urban	Total	Rural	Urban	Total	Rural	Urban
Mizoram	16.0	19.4	11.7	5.1	6.2	3.6	10.9	13.2	8.1	16	18	14
Nagaland	NA	NA	11.8	NA	NA	2.4	NA	NA	9.5	NA	NA	16
Sikkim	21.9	22.3	13.4	5.0	5.1	4.0	16.9	17.2	9.5	33	33	23
Tripura	14.5	14.8	13.2	5.5	5.4	6.0	9.0	9.4	7.2	32	32	31
All India	24.8	26.4	19.8	8.0	8.7	6.0	16.8	17.8	13.8	60	66	38
2007												
Arunachal Pradesh	22.2	23.4	17.3	5.1	5.6	3.3	17.0	17.8	13.9	37	41	15
Assam	24.3	25.7	15.5	8.6	9.1	5.7	15.7	16.6	9.8	66	68	41
Manipur	14.6	14.4	15.2	4.4	4.2	4.9	10.2	10.2	10.3	12	13	9
Meghalaya	24.4	26.1	17.0	7.5	7.9	6.0	16.9	18.2	11.0	56	57	46
Mizoram	18.2	22.5	13.7	5.2	6.0	4.3	13.0	16.5	9.4	23	27	16
Nagaland	17.4	17.7	16.1	5.0	5.4	3.8	12.3	12.3	12.4	21	18	29
Sikkim	18.1	18.2	17.5	5.3	5.4	4.4	12.8	12.8	13.1	34	36	20
Tripura	17.1	17.9	13.5	6.5	6.6	6.4	10.5	11.3	7.2	39	40	32
All India	23.1	24.7	18.6	7.4	8.0	6.0	15.7	16.8	12.7	55	61	37

2010

Arunachal Pradesh	20.5	22.1	14.6	5.9	6.9	2.3	14.6	15.2	12.3	31	34	12
Assam	23.2	24.4	15.8	8.2	8.6	5.8	14.9	15.8	10.1	58	60	36
Manipur	14.9	14.8	15.3	4.2	4.3	4.0	10.7	10.5	11.3	14	15	9
Meghalaya	24.5	26.6	14.8	7.9	8.4	5.6	16.6	18.2	9.2	55	58	37
Mizoram	17.1	21.1	13.0	4.5	5.4	3.7	12.5	15.7	9.3	37	47	21
Nagaland	16.8	17.0	16.0	3.6	3.7	3.3	13.2	13.3	12.7	23	24	20
Sikkim	17.8	18.1	16.1	5.6	5.9	3.8	12.3	12.3	12.3	30	31	19
Tripura	14.9	15.6	11.5	5.0	4.8	5.7	9.9	10.8	5.8	27	29	19
All India	22.1	23.7	18.0	7.2	7.7	5.8	14.9	15.9	12.2	47	51	31

Source: Sample Registration System, Registrar General of India.

Table A5.3

Number of persons living Below Poverty Line (BPL), 1983–84 to 2004–05

State	Rural			Urban			Combined	
	Persons (Lakhs)	%BPL Persons	Poverty Line (₹)	Persons (Lakhs)	%BPL Persons	Poverty Line (₹)	Persons (Lakhs)	%BPL Persons
1983-84								
Arunachal Pradesh	2.70	42.6	98.32	0.12	21.73	97.51	2.82	40.88
Assam	73.43	42.6	98.32	4.26	21.73	97.51	77.69	40.47
Manipur	4.76	42.6	98.32	0.89	21.73	97.51	5.65	37.02
Meghalaya	5.04	42.6	98.32	0.57	21.73	97.51	5.62	38.81
Mizoram	1.58	42.6	98.32	0.37	21.73	97.51	1.96	36.00
Nagaland	3.19	42.6	98.32	0.31	21.73	97.51	3.5	39.25
Sikkim	1.24	42.6	98.32	0.10	21.73	97.51	1.35	39.71
Tripura	8.35	42.6	98.32	0.60	21.73	97.51	8.95	40.03
All India	2,519.57	45.65	89.50	709.40	40.79	1,15.65	3,228.97	44.48
1993-94								
Arunachal Pradesh	3.62	45.01	232.05	0.11	7.73	212.42	3.73	39.35
Assam	94.33	45.01	232.05	2.03	7.73	212.42	96.36	40.86
Manipur	6.33	45.01	232.05	0.47	7.73	212.42	6.80	33.78
Meghalaya	7.09	45.01	232.05	0.29	7.73	212.42	7.38	37.92

Mizoram	1.64	45.01	232.05	0.30	7.73	212.42	1.94	25.66
Nagaland	4.85	45.01	232.05	0.20	7.73	212.42	5.05	37.92
Sikkim	1.81	45.01	232.05	0.03	7.73	212.42	1.84	41.43
Tripura	11.41	45.01	232.05	0.38	7.73	212.42	11.79	39.01
All India	2,440.31	37.27	205.84	763.37	32.36	281.35	3,203.67	35.97
2004–05 $ based on mixed recall period (consumption)								
Arunachal Pradesh	1.47	17.00	387.64	0.07	2.40	378.84	1.54	13.40
Assam	41.46	17.00	387.64	0.93	2.40	378.84	42.39	15.00
Manipur	2.86	17.00	387.64	0.14	2.40	378.84	3.00	13.20
Meghalaya	3.32	17.00	387.64	0.12	2.40	378.84	3.43	14.10
Mizoram	0.78	17.00	387.64	0.11	2.40	378.84	0.89	9.50
Nagaland	2.94	17.00	387.64	0.09	2.40	378.84	3.03	14.50
Sikkim	0.85	17.00	387.64	0.02	2.40	378.84	0.87	15.20
Tripura	4.70	17.00	387.64	0.14	2.40	378.84	4.85	14.40
All India	1,702.99	21.80	356.30	682.00	21.70	538.60	2,384.99	21.80

Source: Planning Commission, Government of India.

Table A5.4

Distribution of usually employed by category of employment (rural/urban), 1993–94 to 2004–05

States	1993–94 Principal and Sub-status			1999–2000 Principal and Sub-status			2004–05 Principal and Sub-status		
	Self-Employed	Regular Employed	Casual Labour	Self-employed	Regular Employed	Casual Labour	Self-employed	Regular Employed	Casual Labour
Rural									
Arunachal Pradesh	85.4	12.3	2.3	79.3	12.6	8.1	83.3	10.8	5.9
Assam	57.8	14.4	27.8	58.2	16.6	25.2	71.0	9.1	19.9
Manipur	83.0	12.1	4.9	80.0	10.0	10.0	85.1	9.5	5.4
Meghalaya	79.7	6.3	14.0	79.6	4.4	16.0	81.0	5.0	14.1
Mizoram	91.1	7.3	1.4	89.0	8.4	2.6	91.4	6.7	1.8
Nagaland	78.1	19.2	2.7	82.1	16.6	1.3	88.3	11.0	0.7
Sikkim	57.0	27.0	16.0	62.0	26.1	11.9	67.8	25.2	7.0
Tripura	56.9	12.8	30.3	47.2	11.1	41.7	52.8	10.2	37.0
India	58.1	6.6	35.3	55.8	6.8	37.4	60.2	7.1	32.8
Urban									
Arunachal Pradesh	22.0	69.5	8.5	24.1	59.0	16.9	42.7	48.8	8.2
Assam	45.3	43.1	11.6	44.7	42.9	12.4	42.3	45.1	12.6

Manipur	63.9	33.3	2.8	60.3	30.6	9.1	65.4	29.9	4.6
Meghalaya	34.1	55.8	10.1	26.3	56.4	17.3	20.1	70.8	9.1
Mizoram	61.0	33.1	5.9	49.5	33.8	16.7	59.0	34.1	6.9
Nagaland	39.1	54.4	6.5	24.2	71.7	4.1	62.2	33.8	4.1
Sikkim	45.3	48.2	6.5	32.7	56.5	10.8	40.4	57.2	2.4
Tripura	38.8	48.3	12.9	31.3	53.0	15.7	40.7	46.0	13.3
India	42.4	39.5	18.1	42.2	40.0	17.8	45.4	39.5	15.0

Sources: NSS Report No. 409, Employment and Unemployment in India, 1993–94; NSS Report No. 458, employment and Unemployment in India, 1999–2000; NSS Report No. 515, Employment and Unemployment in India, 2004–05.

Table A5.5

Usual principal status unemployment rate among the youth

(15–29 Years, %)

Unemployment Rate, 1999–2000 (Rural)

State	Male				Female				Total			
	15–19	20–24	25–29	15–19	15–19	20–24	25–29	15–19	15–19	20–24	25–29	15–19
Arunachal Pradesh	4.1	4.3	1.1	2.5	0.9	1.1	0.0	0.4	1.8	2.6	0.7	1.5
Assam	10.3	13.8	7.2	10.2	20.3	32.9	19.4	24.5	11.4	17.1	9.3	12.5
Manipur	6.4	5.6	4.4	5.2	0.0	10.7	6.2	7.2	4.7	7.2	4.9	5.8
Meghalaya	2.2	1.5	0.0	1.1	0.0	1.6	0.4	0.7	1.2	1.6	0.2	1.0
Mizoram	0.2	2.6	10.3	4.9	0.0	0.0	4.1	1.4	0.0	1.6	8.0	3.4
Nagaland	2.9	15.3	8.3	9.9	9.2	14.5	5.3	10.0	5.3	15.0	7.6	10.0
Sikkim	7.4	8.4	13.1	10.2	0.0	10.3	2.5	5.0	4.9	8.9	9.5	8.4
Tripura	3.7	2.2	1.8	2.8	12.7	5.7	18.2	12.8	6.1	2.5	3.9	3.9
India	6.5	6.2	3.2	5.1	4.1	4.9	2.4	3.7	5.7	5.8	2.8	4.6

Unemployment Rate, 2004–05 (Rural)

State	Male				Female				Total			
	15–19	20–24	25–29	15–19	15–19	20–24	25–29	15–19	15–19	20–24	25–29	15–19
Arunachal Pradesh	2.1	3.6	3.2	3.0	0.9	1.3	2.5	1.7	1.3	2.6	2.9	2.5
Assam	10.3	11.1	5.1	8.5	19.1	17.2	10	15.3	12.1	12.3	5.8	9.7

Manipur	8.2	3.0	5.6	5.1	0.0	2.9	2.5	2.3	4.8	3	4.4	3.9
Meghalaya	0.0	0.6	0.1	0.2	0.0	2.6	1.1	1.6	0.0	1.6	0.6	0.8
Mizoram	0.7	2.4	2.2	2.0	0.0	0.4	0.0	0.3	0.5	1.5	1.4	1.3
Nagaland	8.2	26.9	19.2	20.8	8.1	15	4.1	9.5	7.8	20.1	12.4	14.9
Sikkim	10.3	13.0	3.5	8.6	0.0	6.4	3.7	4.0	7.1	10.7	3.6	7.0
Tripura	33.6	31.2	13.1	25.7	65.7	67.1	45.2	60.8	40.9	39.1	18.5	33.0
India	7.9	6.2	2.3	5.2	6.7	9.3	5.2	7.0	7.5	7.0	3.3	5.7

Unemployment Rate, 1999–2000 (Urban)

	Male				Female				Total			
State	15–19	20–24	25–29	15–19	15–19	20–24	25–29	15–19	15–19	20–24	25–29	15–19
Arunachal Pradesh	0.0	14.2	8.9	9.1	54.1	31.6	2.6	18.5	11.8	21.6	7.1	11.9
Assam	20.5	34.4	15.5	22.2	0.8	70.5	55.7	45.0	12.7	39	22.8	26.6
Manipur	8.6	21.4	23.9	22.6	61.1	6.9	29.1	24.2	30.8	17.3	25.4	23.1
Meghalaya	6.1	14.9	10.2	11.9	19.5	13.1	21.2	17.7	10.4	14.4	15.4	14.3
Mizoram	4.9	11.3	14.8	12.7	17.1	6.1	3.8	6.0	6.3	9.1	11.1	10.3
Nagaland	0.0	34.0	30.8	31.1	0.0	55.5	10.6	23.3	0.0	41	24.6	28.3
Sikkim	22.1	13.2	15.4	15.6	0.0	49.5	16.7	29.9	16.7	23.4	15.6	19.0
Tripura	1.1	35.2	23.4	22.1	0.0	35.3	6.9	17.3	0.9	35.1	21.2	21.4
India	15.4	13.9	7.5	11.5	15.5	22.6	11.5	16.6	15.4	15.4	8.2	12.4

(Table A5.5 Continued)

(Table A5.5 Continued)

	Unemployment Rate, 2004-05 (Urban)											
	Male				Female				Total			
State	15–19	20–24	25–29	15–19	15–19	20–24	25–29	15–19	15–19	20–24	25–29	15–19
Arunachal Pradesh	12.9	10.7	2.3	5.6	7.1	11.3	3.7	7.4	9.5	10.9	2.7	4.9
Assam	12.6	26.9	19.8	20.9	19.7	50.0	19.4	33.4	14.1	32.8	19.5	23.3
Manipur	5.5	22.6	19.3	19.7	1.2	11.4	28.7	18.5	2.9	19.0	22.4	19.3
Meghalaya	29.4	3.0	12.8	12.9	3.0	14.8	15.3	12.0	14.6	8.7	14.0	12.5
Mizoram	2.8	7.4	2.1	4.4	0.0	5.9	7.6	6.2	1.8	6.7	4.5	4.9
Nagaland	0.0	33.2	19.7	22.1	0.0	55.2	23.7	35.5	0.0	43.4	21.4	27.7
Sikkim	21.7	7.9	0.0	6.7	0.0	24.6	0.0	6.3	16.9	10.5	0.0	8.0
Tripura	55.4	54.0	34.0	45.4	69.1	94.8	77.6	83.7	60.7	70.3	52.6	61.4
India	14.0	12.5	5.8	10.0	15.6	25.8	15.8	19.9	14.5	15.2	7.6	11.9

Source: Employment and unemployment situation in India, 1999–2000 and 2004–05, Report No. 458 and 515, National Sample Survey Organisation.

Table A5.6

Distribution (per 1,000) of migrants in different MPCE quintile class for each state

MPCE Quintile Class	Arunachal Pradesh	Assam	Manipur	Meghalaya	Mizoram	Nagaland	Sikkim	Tripura
			Rural: Male					
0–20	178	305	214	61	224	85	85	219
20–40	15	178	75	74	238	114	89	156
40–60	32	192	55	147	155	134	129	169
60–80	338	100	225	275	94	205	193	192
80–100	437	225	431	443	289	462	504	265
All	1,000	1,000	1,000	1,000	1,000	1,000	1,000	1,000
			Rural: Female					
0–20	189	202	414	41	202	145	152	246
20–40	0	231	27	95	173	95	184	145
40–60	536	213	135	130	251	129	165	206
60–80	17	152	15	155	95	205	191	164
80–100	257	202	409	579	280	426	307	238
All	1,000	1,000	1,000	1,000	1,000	1,000	1,000	1,000
			Rural: Male + Female					
0–20	181	214	297	52	213	120	130	239
20–40	11	225	55	83	205	103	152	148

(Table A5.6 Continued)

(Table A5.6 Continued)

MPCE Quintile Class	Arunachal Pradesh	Assam	Manipur	Meghalaya	Mizoram	Nagaland	Sikkim	Tripura
40–60	170	210	88	140	203	131	153	197
60–80	250	146	138	224	94	205	192	171
80–100	**388**	205	**422**	**501**	**285**	**441**	**373**	**245**
All	1,000	1,000	1,000	1,000	1,000	1,000	1,000	1,000
Urban: Male								
0–20	153	141	0	132	133	209	210	147
20–40	**396**	134	27	118	145	172	164	126
40–60	95	134	10	49	185	124	**291**	208
60–80	133	210	**964**	344	195	240	79	208
80–100	223	**382**	0	**358**	**342**	**256**	256	**312**
All	1,000	1,000	1,000	1,000	1,000	1,000	1,000	1,000
Urban: Female								
0–20	214	203	56	172	131	185	**252**	181
20–40	241	182	0	50	165	193	123	124
40–60	121	146	0	153	189	152	212	**263**
60–80	162	187	457	274	150	**280**	205	195
80–100	**261**	**283**	**487**	**352**	**365**	190	208	237
All	1,000	1,000	1,000	1,000	1,000	1,000	1,000	1,000

			Urban: Male + Female				
0–20	176	175	40	153	132	197	233	169
20–40	337	160	8	82	156	182	142	125
40–60	105	140	3	104	187	138	248	243
60–80	144	197	603	307	171	260	148	200
80–100	237	328	347	355	354	223	230	264
All	1,000	1,000	1,000	1,000	1,000	1,000	1,000	1,000

Source: NSS 64th Round, 2007–08.

Notes

1. It consists of eight states: Assam, Arunachal Pradesh, Manipur, Meghalaya, Mizoram, Nagaland, Tripura and Sikkim.
2. The Union Minister for Development of North Eastern Region (DoNER) and Parliamentary Affairs, Paban Singh Ghatowar delivering his address at the 13th Convocation of Manipur University.
3. *Primary sector*: Includes cultivators; agriculture labourers; plantation, livestock, forestry, fishing; hunting and allied activities. *Secondary sector*: Includes mining and quarrying; manufacturing and repairs; electricity, gas and water supply and both registered, unregister manufacturing. *Tertiary or services sector*: Includes construction; wholesale and retail trade; hotels and restaurants; transport, storage and communications; financial intermediation; real estate, renting and business activities; public administration and defence; compulsory social security; education; health and social work; other community, social and personal service activities; private households with employed persons; extra-territorial organizations and bodies.

References

Barah, B.C. (2001). 'Northeastern India: Strategies for agricultural development: An overview'. In B.C. Barah (ed.), *Prioritization of strategies for agricultural development in Northeastern India* (Proceedings 9). New Delhi: National Centre for Agricultural Economics and Policy Research (ICAR).

Chyrmang, R. (2011). 'Magnitude of migration from North Eastern Region of India'. In S. Irudaya Rajan (ed.), *India migration report 2011: Migration, identity and conflict*. New Delhi: Routledge.

Ghosh, N. (2003). *Organic farming in North-East hill region in India*, 3rd Biennial Conference on 'Biodiversity and Quality of Life', 18–20 December, Kolkata.

Goswami, B. and Chyrmang, R. (2012). 'Trend and pattern of internal out-migration from India's North-East'. *Manpower Journal*, XLVI(2), 1–29.

Hanjabam, S.S. (2007). 'The youth panorama of Northeast India'. *Asia Europe Journal*, 5(4), 557–71.

HMI World Congress. (2004). Human Movements and Immigration World Congress. Retrieved from http://www.unfpa.org/press/human-movements-and-immigration-world-congress (accessed on 3 September 2012).

Krishan, G. (2007). 'India: Pattern of interstate migration, man and development'. *Centre for Research in Rural and Industrial Development*, 29(1), 182–87.

Laskar, A.H. (2012). 'Life skill education in NE'. *The Assam Tribune*, 74(275), 10.

NAAS. (2001). *Strategies for agricultural research in the North-East*. Policy Paper 9. National Academy of Agriculture Science, New Delhi.

NCAER. (2004). *East India human development report*. New Delhi: Oxford University Press.

NEC (North Eastern Council). *Vision document 2020* (Vol. 1). Report prepared by Ministry of Development of North Eastern Region and North Eastern Council, New Delhi.

NEDFi. (2003). 'Quarterly journal on north eastern states economy (Agriculture)', *NEDFi Databank Quarterly*, 4(3), 25.

———. (2005). 'Quarterly journal on north eastern states economy (Border trade sector)', *NEDFi Databank Quarterly*, 2(1), 13.

NUEPA. (2012). *Elementary education in India: Progress towards UEE*. New Delhi: Ministry of Human Resource Development, GOI.

NSSO. (2008). *64th round survey on employment and unemployment situation in India, 2007–08* (NSS Report No. 531).

News, N. (2012). 'Higher education scenario dismal in India: Ghatowar'. *The Assam Tribune*, 74(275), 10.

Perruchoud, R. and Redpath-Cross, J. (2011). *International migration law: Glossary on migration*. Geneva, Switzerland: International Organisation for Migration (IOM).

Saikia, A. (2001). 'Performance of agricultural economy of the northeastern India: Constraints and priorities'. In B.C. Barah (ed.), *Prioritization of strategies for agricultural development in northeastern India*, Proceedings 9, National Centre for Agricultural Economics and Policy Research (ICAR) (p.13). New Delhi.

Shimray, U.A. and Devi, M.D.U. (2009). *Trends and patterns of migration: Interface with education—A case of the north-eastern region* (Monograph series no. 15). Institute for Social and Economic Change (ISEC), Bengaluru.

Singh, K.P. and Ahmad, S. (2012). 'Taking stock of higher education in the North-East'. *Economic and Political Weekly*, XLVII(38), 24–27.

Srivastava, R. (2011). 'Labour migration in India: Recent trends, pattern and policy issues'. *The Indian Journal of Labour Economics*, 54(3), 431.

Sjaastad, L.A. (1962). 'The cost and returns of human migration'. *The Journal of Political Economy*, 70(5), 80–93.

Tumbe, C. (2012). 'Migration persistence across twentieth century India'. *Migration and Development*, 1(1), 87–112.

Todaro, M.P. (1969). 'A model of labour migration and urban unemployment in less developed countries'. *American Economic Review*, 595(1), 138–48.

UGC. (2011). *Inclusive and qualitative expansion of higher education* (12th Five Year Plan, 2012–17). University Grants Commission: New Delhi.

6

Educational Migration among Ladakhi Youth

Elizabeth Williams-Oerberg

Introduction[1]

A group of young Ladakhi men entered Wonderland Restaurant on a cold day in May 2012 in Leh, Ladakh and began to discuss the dilemmas they faced regarding employment, and whether or not they should migrate to other cities throughout India in order to pursue higher education. They discussed the importance of obtaining a government job emphasized by their parents, their extended families and surrounding community, yet they also acknowledged how difficult it is to actually obtain such employment. These men, although above the average age for pursuing a higher education, sat and discussed how to obtain the coveted government job, agreeing unanimously that a higher education is necessary and something they should strive to achieve. One of the men pulled out a folder with a stack of papers explaining the admission process to the different colleges in the three universities in India preferred by Ladakhis: Jammu University, Panjab University in Chandigarh, and Delhi University. A complicated mess was revealed in that folder—what to study, where, when, and more. Paradoxically, they have already obtained lucrative employment in the tourism industry in Ladakh, so why feel the need to move away from Ladakh and struggle for the sake of a university degree?

'A university degree by itself may be worth little economically, but no person is worth very much socially without one' (Béteille, 2010, p. 90).

With the rising standards and achievements in higher education[2] among Ladakhis, obtaining a university degree provides a level of status and prestige that these young men have not yet achieved. Whereas, previously a primary school education was deemed sufficient, a university degree is currently the educational standard to be strived for. As one young Ladakhi male explains, 'Without a degree you are nowhere in India' (Delhi, April 2012). It is therefore felt necessary to leave Ladakh to pursue a higher education, no matter the struggle and inconvenience. Whereas previously university education was only a reality for the wealthy and the elite, currently the middle classes are streaming to universities in order to realize those futures that a university education may offer (see Beteille, 2010). There is a widespread acknowledgement that in order to improve one's economic and social standing in India, a university degree is indispensable (also see Advani, 2009; Chopra and Jeffery, 2005; Ciotti, 2006; Froerer, 2011; Jeffrey, 2010; Jeffrey, Jeffery and Jeffery, 2010). Universities throughout India are bombarded with a drastic increase in admission applications, new colleges and universities are mushrooming up in the entire subcontinent, and youth from all over the nation are migrating in increasing numbers so that they may also participate in the education economy. As Advani explains, an English-medium education is 'a powerful driver for affluent rural and semi-rural families seeking cultural capital and claim to the professional careers which are located in urban higher education' (2009, p. 17). In order to participate in the knowledge economy and gain access to professional careers, a degree from an English-medium urban university is considered mandatory, driving a significant rural-to-urban migration among youth in the case in Ladakh.

Compared with other migrant populations in India, the primary cause for migration from Ladakh to urban areas is not for economic employment, but for the pursuit of a higher education. Most of the Ladakhi migrants are 18–30 years old and migrate alone without immediate family nearby to support them. The problems that these youth face in migrating to urban areas are not specific to their situation only, as many migrants—especially from the North East areas of India—experience similar dilemmas. Yet because of the lack of options for pursuing higher education in Ladakh itself, many Ladakhi migrants consider their educational migration outside Ladakh as forced and necessary in order to achieve the same degree-status as other Indians. This chapter addresses the problems that Ladakhi youth face in their migration pursuits and suggests possible policy measures that would aid in either curtailing this perceived forced migration or in creating the environment necessary in which the Ladakhi migrants can thrive in their educational migration endeavours.

Research Methods

The research presented in this chapter is based on 11 months of qualitative multi-sited ethnographic fieldwork among Ladakhi student migrants in mostly Delhi, but also Jammu and Chandigarh, and follows these students back to Ladakh.[3] Political and religious leaders, scholars, parents, school children, previous educational migrants, youth who did not migrate, youth who were about to migrate and students from other communities including Tibetan and North East Indian were also interviewed. Totally 134 recorded interviews in addition to numerous in-depth conversations with interlocutors make up the bulk of the information from which the discussion presented in this chapter is drawn upon. Participant observation—engaging in Ladakhi students' everyday lives and participating in cultural, religious and educational events documented in fieldnotes—also contributes significantly to the analysis, along with following Ladakhi online communities over a period of three years. Additionally, an in-depth study of relevant newspaper and magazine articles, websites, blogs and official documents provided historical as well as contemporary contextualization. The vast array of data accumulated from this work provides a triangulation of data in order to understand the migrant situation Ladakhi youth encounter, and how their situation might be improved as per the recommended policy initiatives at the end of this chapter.

Because the research upon which this chapter is based is part of a PhD project approaching Ladakhi student migrants and the negotiation of Buddhism in their everyday lives in Delhi, with Buddhism and Buddhist students as the primary focus of the PhD study, admittedly what is presented in this chapter is skewed towards Ladakhi Buddhists from Leh District, with Ladakhi Muslim students from Kargil and Leh districts, unfortunately underrepresented. I do very much hope that further work will be done among Ladakhi Muslim migrants in India.[4] That being said, Ladakhi Muslims were not completely absent from this research as a dozen Ladakhi Muslim students studying in Jammu and Delhi were interviewed repeatedly, formally and informally, and Ladakhi Muslim online communities and news reports were followed as well.

Throughout this chapter, I address the patterns of educational migration among Ladakhi youth, beginning with the historical context and development of education in Ladakh. With improvements in the financial and educational sector, an increasing number of Ladakhi youth are migrating to pursue an education, which provides for challenges in itself—both in the new migratory environments and back home in Ladakh. I suggest that the migratory experiences that Ladakhi youth encounter even through this internal, rural-to-urban migration resemble transnational migration due to a perceived change in geographic, social and cultural environment which often includes experiences of discrimination and marginalization. Policy initiatives such as those recommended at the end of the chapter would help to integrate student migrants from far flung areas and reduce feelings of alienation, possibly increasing national cohesion and inclusion.

Historical Development of Education in Ladakh

Lying in the borderlands of India nestled in the Himalayas between Pakistan and China, Ladakh[5] has often been considered to be a remote area, cut off from the rest of India and the rest of the world for at least six months a year due to high passes, heavy snow and unmotorable roads during the winter.[6] Recently the Ladakhi society has undergone a dramatic transformation caused by a number of factors which include: the secession of Ladakh as part of Jammu and Kashmir state into the Indian Union in 1947; an overwhelming military presence in the face of the disputes over the borders with both Pakistan and China; a tremendous influx of international and domestic tourists following the opening of Ladakh's borders to tourism in 1974; and the migration of a large segment of the youth population to other parts of India in order to pursue a higher education, which is the focus of this chapter. These developments combined have led to rapid change in Ladakh, including the infrastructural improvements of roads built connecting Ladakh internally as well as with the rest of India, an airport with daily flights to Leh, and increased access to water, electricity and education (see Aggarwal, 2004, p. 40; Bertelsen, 1996; Bray, 2007;

Kaul and Kaul, 2004; Kingsnorth, 2000). Throughout the past few decades, the Ladakhi society has been transforming from a land-based economy with agriculture, animal husbandry and trade, to a cash-based economy with tourism and government employment, including the army, as the main sources of income (see Bertelsen, 1996; Crook, 1995; Goering, 1990; LAHDC, 2005, 2010; Norberg-Hodge, 1991).

Historically the people of Ladakh have been characterized as simple, economically backward and in need of development and modernization (see Aggarwal, 2004, p. 35; Beek, 1999; Bertelsen, 1996). When Jawaharlal Nehru visited Leh, Ladakh on 8 July 1949, he stated in his address to the public, 'In Ladakh you are backward and unless you learn and train yourselves you cannot run the affairs of your country' (Amrita Bazar Patrika, 8 July 1949 quoted in van Beek, 1999). Nehru was not the first outsider to comment about the so-called backwardness of Ladakhis and inform them of the necessity of learning and education in order to bring them out of economic depravity. In a memorandum presented by the Kashmir-Raj Bodhi Maha Sabha to the Glancy Commission in 1932 it was declared that the economic backwardness was a result of educational insufficiency. The Sabha asserted that 'to call these helpless people dumb-driven cattle would be no exaggeration. There is no organization to represent them and that is why their grievances have remained unventilated' (Buddhist Community of Kashmir, 1932, p. 129 quoted in Bertelsen, 1997a). Furthermore, it was determined that 'their backwardness in education has led to their economic exploitation and to their being deprived of their share in public services' (Mahabodhi, 1931, p. 128 quoted in Beek and Bertelsen 1997, p. 46). Already from the 1930s onwards it was asserted that in order for Ladakhis to gain the recognition, rights and resources needed to spur economic development, education was absolutely central.

The focus on education as the most successful pathway to development and modernization has long been a main focus area for national development, as well as for international organizations such as the UNESCO, The World Bank and The UNDP (see, for example, The Task Force of Higher Education and Society, 2000). In order to bring improvements in the quality of life for the individual as well as for the society as a whole, education has been deemed essential (see Sen, 1997, 2000). In Ladakh, education is also highlighted as necessary in order to spur development, as Fatima writes: 'the lack of education is the single most important obstacle to development of society in Kargil' (1999, p. 119).

And according to the Ladakh Hill Development Council, Leh, education plays an important role in the development of the region:

> Education has a critical role to play in the development of any society. In Ladakh, the importance of education is even more marked because it was a neglected sector in the region for many years before the authorities finally woke up to its importance. There is therefore a need to make up for lost time. (LAHDC, 2005, p. 49)

In the 1970s, significant improvements in the education sector took place including an increase in the number of schools and in the number of students enrolled. Educational schemes initiated by the district-level government established new schools in even the more remote areas of Ladakh, along with many higher secondary schools and high schools (LAHDC, 2012a, p. 2). From the mid-1990s 'every small village, even that with only five or six families, boasts of a primary school, while bigger villages may have five or six schools each, including a middle and high school' (Dawa, 1995, p. 72). Enrolment in schools has increased dramatically, and according to the LAHDC Department of Education (Leh) 'almost all the children in the age group of 6–14 years were enrolled and retained in school' (LAHDC, 2012a, p. 4). This increased enrolment is reflected in the statistics for literacy development in Ladakh. According to the LAHDC Department of Education (Leh) (2012a, b), the rate for literacy in 1961 was 10 per cent, already a substantial increase from the 0.2 per cent reported in the Census of India in 1931 (Bertelsen, 1997b, p. 133). In 1981, the literacy rate increased to 25 per cent, in 2001 to 65 per cent, and as recent as 2011, the literacy rate is reported to be as high as 80.5 per cent (LAHDC, 2012a, p. 18, 2012b, p. 4). In Kargil District, the literacy rate has currently reached 60 per cent, with 80 per cent literacy in urban Kargil, and 59 per cent literacy in rural areas (LAHDC, 2013). Since the 1970s, a general consensus has augmented that education is a necessary and important aspect of a child's life, well-being and future.

Private School Migration

Even though significant improvements in the education sector have taken place, the quality of education offered at government schools has lagged noticeably behind private institutions. In 2011, 661 students attending government schools in Leh district sat for the matriculation exams and only 218 students passed, that is, 33 per cent (Chief Education Officer, 2012); comparatively a private school in Leh, Lamdon Model Sr. Secondary School, reported a 100 per cent pass-rate among the 130 students who sat for the exam (The Principal Office, 2011, p. 19). The disparity between government schools and private schools has resulted in a general distrust in the government-run education system, and an increasing number of parents are choosing to send their children to private schools. In 2011 there were 11,764 students enrolled in private institutions with only 8,641 students enrolled in government institutions in Leh District (LAHDC, 2012b). Branches of private schools are becoming established in larger villages throughout Ladakh, while a significant number of young Ladakhis have to make the move to these private school locations, thus marking the beginning of their educational migration trajectory. Some parents who can afford to do so are choosing to send their children to private schools outside of Ladakh in order to give them the competitive advantage they consider necessary to gain admission into more prestigious universities. Most of the students, who do migrate to especially Delhi, but also Jammu and Chandigarh for higher secondary and university education, have previously attended private schools in Ladakh or boarding schools outside Ladakh in places such as Delhi, Dalhousie and Dehradun, some even from a very young age.

The preference for private schools is not a unique phenomenon in Ladakh as the trend is noticeable throughout India. According to Advani, the state education system started crumbling in the 1970s, leading to a 'steady exodus of the upper middle class from local or government-aided schools to private unaided fee-charging schools…for expanding their professional aspirations and life options' (Arvind, 2011, p. 499). Subrahmanian also highlights this growing trend when she writes, 'Almost invariably, private schools are considered preferable to government schools' (2005, p. 69). For students who live in remote areas such as Ladakh, in order to attend these preferential private schools they have to move away from their homes and villages to wherever these private schools are located. While an increasing value is placed in spending on education, more families are gaining access to the economic resources required to invest in their children's education due to the increase in tourism and military employment, with families from Leh town receiving the most benefit. In June 2011, one family in Leh town explained that their main expense was supporting their children's education in Delhi. 'We have to suffer!', the father somewhat jokingly exclaimed. Parents are spending their hard-earned money on sending their children away for the sake of education, even if they have to sacrifice the close-knit family and time spent together.

That being said, only the youth whose families can afford to financially support their education and stay outside of Ladakh are those who migrate. The youth who remain in the villages at the local government schools most often do not have the opportunity to migrate for higher education- due to lower marks on the matriculation and entrance exams, but mostly due to the lack of financial resources in the family to provide for private schooling and higher education. A number of educational outreach schemes have begun in Leh, for example at the Students' Educational and Cultural Movement of Ladakh (SECMOL) and at the Lamdon Model School and the Mahabodhi School, which sponsor children from far away villages to stay at their hostels and receive a private school education. The need, however, far outweighs the availability of such hostel rooms (Education counselor, LAHDC Leh, private communication, June 2012). Thus, the increase in enrolment in private school institutions and the added advantage for gaining access to higher education has resulted in an increase in social inequality among the wealthy and the poor in Ladakh, most visible in the rural–urban discrepancy where rural families in far-flung villages are often left behind in the pursuit for higher education.

Migration for Higher Education

While major improvements in primary and secondary education in Ladakh have taken place, higher education facilities in Ladakh remain poor.[7] The best opportunity to achieve a quality higher education is to migrate outside of Ladakh to Jammu, Chandigarh, Srinagar and preferably Delhi. Educational migration is not a new phenomenon in Ladakh and can be traced back to the thirteenth century when Ladakhi Buddhist monks were sent to Tibet for a monastic education (see Bray, 1991, p. 116; Tsering, 1995). Ladakhi Muslims also travelled to places such as Kerbala Mualla, Najf Sharif and other religious places in Iran and

Iraq for a theological education, and then returned to Ladakh to work as Imams and Sheikhs (Sheikh, 1996). Educational migration among the lay population, however, is a more recent phenomenon.[8] After obtaining employment in the army in the 1960s, Ladakhis increasingly invested the income generated from these positions into their children's education and sent their children outside Ladakh to obtain a higher education. This increased educational migration became apparent in the late 1960s with the establishment of separate students' unions for Ladakhi students in Jammu and Delhi (Bertelsen, 1996, p. 182). Today many student migrants consider themselves, in their own words, 'educational refugees', feeling forced to leave Ladakh in order to attain a higher education, and the numbers are increasing every year. While one Ladakhi male interlocutor (personal communication, May 2012) estimated there to be around 80–100 Ladakhi Buddhist students in Jammu fifteen years ago, today there are said to be around 5,000[9] Buddhist students and 2,000 Muslim students; Chandigarh is said to currently house around 1,500 students, most of whom are Buddhist[10]; Delhi is said to have at least around 1,500 students[11]; Srinagar 1,500 students,[12] and throughout the rest of India approximately 1,000.[13] When we consider that the total population of Ladakh, both Kargil and Leh District is around 230,000 with an average youth population of 26 per cent (~60,000) the approximate 12,500 student migrants throughout India is significant (20 per cent) (LAHDC, 2012b, 2013).

While the lack of higher educational facilities in Ladakh itself is an important 'push factor' for the rural-to-urban educational migration pattern, there are also a number of additional factors which contribute to the increasing number of student migrants. These include improvements in economic standing of Ladakhi households, improvements in exam results, and the granting of Scheduled Tribe status to the majority of the Ladakhi population which allows greater access to higher education through the reservation system.[14] There are also more intangible conditions leading to educational migration as a desired trajectory. When inquiring as to why Ladakhi families choose to invest in education, it is generally recognized that competition among neighbours has become a major driving force for sending one's children outside of Ladakh. Education for many Ladakhi families seems to have replaced the television as a token of middle class achievement and in this way, as Osella and Osella (2000, p. 119) suggest, has become a prominent 'consumption arena'.

This highlights the perceived sense of status or prestige that not only the student attains, but also their parents and extended families when a young Ladakhi studies outside Ladakh.

Internal Migration as 'Transnational Migration'

While pursuing a higher education is the main factor initiating migration, students consider 'exposure to the outside world' to be an important benefit of migration. While most of the literature on migration address a 'transnational migration' (Basch et al., 1995) as a crossing of nation-state borders, Ladakhi students also experience a form of transnational migration even within an internal migration movement. Basch et al. define transnationalism as 'the processes by which immigrants forge and sustain multi-stranded social relations that link together their societies of origin and settlement' emphasizing the 'social fields that cross geographic, cultural, and political borders' (Basch et al., 1995, p. 7). Ladakhi students often refer to their own migration as 'studying abroad' with the felt change in environment and lifestyles they encounter in their new educational and urban environments. By somehow tapping into a global or transnational world through internal migration even, they gain new skills and outlooks which further a process of transformation, or as they say 'modernization' (see Beek, 2008). Many Ladakhi students seem to value the increased awareness and experience of being introduced to alternative outlooks and lifestyles during their stay outside Ladakh, although others express concern about an apparent loss of culture and distinct identity from the adoption of so-called Indian, or modern/Western outlooks. At the same time, the marginalization and alienation that Ladakhi students experience through internal migration within India might even be comparable to the experiences an Indian citizen might encounter in educational migration to a university in Europe. Ladakhi students also encounter a number of more practical issues similar to experiences encountered by transnational migrants, which are addressed below.

Ladakhi youth encounter a very different landscape, language, culture and lifestyle when they migrate than what they have previously been accustomed to. Even though most emphasize the benefits of this exposure, many students find the living conditions in these new places to be less than pleasant and endure a difficult transitional period during the process of settling in to their new lifestyles. Especially for the students who have spent their childhood in Ladakh, the move from a rural, sparsely-populated, high-altitude, desert-like mountainous terrain to a noisy, congested, hot and humid urban metropolis proves challenging. As one Ladakhi male relates:

> So all of a sudden we have to change our environment and everything to a society which is very alien from ours. We have to face a lot of problems in terms of language, and it takes time to understand the other society's values, customs and everything. (Delhi, April 2012)

In addition to the experience of moving from a small town in Ladakh to a big city in a different environment, students also experience marginalization due to having different facial, or as they say 'racial'[15] features. Ladakhis, similar to students from North East India, look considerably different from the Indian majority and they are often treated as foreigners, as if they do not belong. Ladakhis have not had as contentious a relationship with the Indian nation-state as, for example, North East Indians, and in comparison seem to be more proud of being Indian. Yet, even with the increased awareness and attention that Ladakh has received after the Kargil War of 1999 and the immense popularity of the Bollywood movie '3 Idiots' showcasing Ladakh and its natural beauty, Ladakhis still encounter a general disbelief that they are in fact Indians. They are frequently assumed to be foreigners by their fellow students and people they encounter on the streets, further exacerbating a sense of alienation and frustration in their new urban Indian environment. On the streets, they are often jeered at and called names such as 'chinky' and 'Gorkha' and told to go back to China or Nepal where they belong to. Ladakhi women, as north-eastern women, are often subjected to sexual harassment in public places such as crowded shopping areas and public transportation (also see Aggarwal, 2004; McDuie-Ra, 2012). Many Ladakhis experience racial and sexual harassment on a daily basis, making their experience of life in the city considerably unpleasant and alienating- more so for Ladakhi women than for men.

The lack of awareness and understanding about borderland areas such as Ladakh becomes especially obvious in the housing situation. Because hostel rooms are sparse and difficult to acquire, many Ladakhi migrants have to find their own housing. Often students will draw upon social networks established through family, village and school connections for help, yet they face considerable difficulties when inquiring about various flats and paying guest (PG) accommodation. When explaining that they are in fact Indian, from Ladakh in the Jammu and Kashmir state, many landlords when they hear this refuse to rent their rooms based on a suspicion that they might be terrorists, which is especially the case for Ladakhi Muslims. Even if they do meet a landlord who is willing to rent a room or flat to them, they often have to pay higher rentals than the other tenants, as has also been observed among other SC and ST student populations (see McDuie-Ra, 2012; Wankhede, 2008).

Based on a shared experience of prejudice and harassment in the public sphere, Ladakhis often tend to gravitate towards each other forming small pockets of Ladakhi friends' circles which often expand to include north-eastern and Tibetan students. They share the experience of marginalization and 'outsiderness' and instead of subjecting themselves to further alienation, some students prefer to keep to themselves and not interact as much with the other majority student communities. Even inspiration from popular culture models are often retrieved from East Asia rather than India. Many students explain that they prefer to watch Korean movies rather than Bollywood movies, stating they can relate more to the Korean actors than to the Bollywood actors due to similarities in body, face and hair type. The experience of foreignness or marginalization in their own country has compelled a sense of identification which is distinct from the mainstream Indian majority, yet shared with other ethnic minority students from the north-eastern borderland regions.

Academic Disadvantages

It is not only among strangers that Ladakhi student migrants encounter difficulties, it is also very much part of their classroom experience throughout their higher education pursuits. Because they enter the university typically through the reservation system due to their status as a member of a Scheduled Tribe, quite often they are not considered equal among their classmates (also see Wankhede, 2008). Based on their facial features, teachers can easily gather that they have gained entrance under the reservation system and in some cases they are not given the opportunity to prove their academic skills. As one Ladakhi student explains:

> I don't know any of the teachers. I know there are some great teachers here. I haven't talked with them because I don't have the guts to go. Because if I go before them they would think 'How is he here'? There are teachers, very good teachers, they always ask, 'Where are you from?' I say Ladakh, then he says 'Ladakhi students, they don't study.' They have this impression from also way back, that we are not intelligent. We study, all of us are hard working. (Delhi, April 2012)

He continues by explaining how if someone looks at him then they know that he has gained entrance through the 'reserved category' and assume that he is less intelligent:

> For example, for me, if someone looks at me, then he must be knowing that, 'He must have come through reserved category. He must not be good.' For me, it's fine. This other guy, I told you about, from Rajasthan… his name is Ajay Kumar Meena.[16] Meena is a tribe, they are also given this reserve category, scheduled tribe category. So he always gives the name Ajay Kumar, that's it. Without the Meena. It shows that somehow he doesn't want to show that he belongs to this category.

Unlike Ajay, Ladakhis cannot hide their Scheduled Tribe status by removing a tribal/caste name. Based on their facial features, teachers and classmates presume they have gained entrance through the reservation system and then judge them as being less apt in their studies.

Language and communication issues also provide significant hurdles upon arrival in these new urban academic environments. One woman explains:

> And also we have got some language problem. We speak in Ladakhi in Leh and after that here we are supposed to speak in Hindi… I didn't study Hindi in school. I used to study Urdu and I don't know how to speak in Hindi. So, I am trying. I try a lot. (Delhi, May 2011)

It is not only the language, but the style of communicating which is different from that which they are used to. Students, even if they know Hindi and English well, often encounter difficulties in speaking up in class. A Ladakhi student union member explains, 'First when they come here for further study they hesitate to talk to their teachers because of the language barrier, and they hesitate to ask questions to the teachers'

(Jammu, April 2011). Because students are hesitant to speak up in class, they are often mistakenly perceived as being less intelligent. One Ladakhi male student from Jawaharlal Nehru University explained how students and teachers alike view Ladakhis as less intellectual:

> Intellectual here is sometimes making a comparison with other people.... It's not that I am not intellectual in terms of my thinking capacity. But we do have some language barrier, our experience, articulation and all these things. (Delhi, April 2012).

Because of the conflation of the variance in language and communication styles along with the prejudice that Ladakhi students face based on gaining admission as a member of a Scheduled Tribe, these students often struggle with having the confidence to engage in discussions and ask questions in class.

Many Ladakhi students experience that they require additional academic help so that they can adjust to the new learning environments, as is the case for many students admitted through the reservation system (see Planning Commission, 2006). Those who have the means pay for extra coaching or private tuitions[17] in order to keep up with their fellow classmates. According to Dawa 'tuition fees are a growing problem...there is fierce competition among parents to secure tutorials for their children in various subjects...for many ordinary people, tuition fees are becoming unaffordable' (1995, p. 75). In addition to the expensive private school fees, room rates and living expenses, Ladakhis often also have to add steep coaching and tuition fees creating an increasing disparity between those families who can afford higher education for their children, and those who cannot, and further increasing the general economic burden of higher education for Ladakhi families.

Not only do students and their families face economic hardships due to educational migration, but psychological hardship is rampant among Ladakhi students. A male student union member at Jammu University explains:

> So we face lots of problems...the biggest problem is that Ladakhi students have no guardian who can guide them, who motivates them.... And there are many suicide cases in Jammu. When a student gets depressed they take very dangerous steps. (Jammu, April 2011)

According to this student, the struggles that some students face have been so difficult that a few have even taken their own lives. In addition to depression, a lack of confidence is common, especially during the first few years of their undergraduate education:

> This [university education] is making students weaker, less confident.... We should have colleges out there in Ladakh itself. Till 10th class [in Leh] I was so confident. I was the head boy of the school. I had no stage fear at all.... Here, this fear is coming, maybe frustration, maybe my confidence is getting lower and lower here.... There's no point, I don't find a point of studying here. We should rather, the Ladakhi politicians should rather focus on establishing good colleges here. (Ladakhi male student, Delhi, February 2012)

This student when considering the change in his level of confidence after migrating to Delhi expresses the desire for quality higher education to be established in Ladakh so that other students do not have to go through a similar struggle and decrease in confidence that he himself has gone through.

Unanimously students explain that a lack of guidance is the single biggest issue they face in their educational migration endeavours. There is no one to explain the university admission process to them, or what course of study they should apply for, which area of studies would be most relevant and helpful for them in order to realize their projected job prospects. Young students appear at the admission sites sometimes without even knowing what they should apply for, or without knowing what their best chances for gaining entrance might be in relation to their grades. Unfortunately, many students end up studying courses which do not match their interests, skills, or future career ambitions and potentials. Of late, the Ladakhi student unions have become more active in helping students through the admission process, taking time out from studying for exams in order to provide guidance. In 2011 they were allowed to set up a help desk around the admissions area at Delhi University; however, in 2012 they were prevented from doing so by the university.

Educational Migration 'A Contradictory Resource'

Back home in Ladakh, the drawbacks of such a seemingly large exodus of the youth population to the 'outside' are also discussed. Even though parents are investing substantially in their children's education, concern

Photo courtesy: Jigmet Rabgyas, 2012.

about the possible threat to Ladakhi culture and tradition as a result of this period spent 'abroad' are frequently expressed, among both old and young alike (also see Dawa, 1995; Palden, 1998; Tsering, 1995).

Although the pursuit of the so-called 'modern education' is in itself seen as a social good, the result or consequences of the 'modern education' is mostly seen as negative. This falls in line with Levinson, Foley and Holland's (1996, p. 2) work considering education as a 'contradictory resource' in which 'schools and education often become sites of intense cultural politics'. In Ladakh, there exists scepticism and some degree of anxiety regarding the preservation of Ladakhi culture and identity among the educated youth. In the discourse on education, these concerns are often expressed through the emphasis on the necessity of a 'moral education' based on local, traditional and/or religious understandings in order to balance out the perceived negative effects of the 'modern education'. By learning more about religion, Ladakhi students can gain a 'moral education' which is specific to Ladakh and Ladakhi culture and distinct from the mainstream Indian society. For many Ladakhi students, an active engagement with religion, either Islam or Buddhism, is a means by which the student migrant can connect to their homeland. While pursuing a 'modern education', some also try to gain a 'moral education' in order to balance the lifestyle they encounter in their new environments, which they experience as more challenging and competitive. A Ladakhi male student in Delhi explains:

> I am still struggling to survive in this modern world, when I came from a very alien society [Ladakh]. I'm just presuming, but for me modern education is getting into a system, to adapting into a system which is already created by some elite people. So first of all I am struggling to fit into that system … The meaning of education is changing… Once a great man said, 'We don't need greater educated people. We have enough education, educated people, intelligent educated people. So that leads to the destruction of the society.' (Delhi, April 2012)

For this student who has migrated to Delhi to obtain a higher education and completed his Master's Degree from Delhi University, when he takes a step back to evaluate of what use the modern education might be, he observes that the education he has obtained and that which other Ladakhi students strive to attain might be threatening traditional Ladakhi culture and leading to, in his words, 'the destruction of society'. One cannot help but wonder, 'Is the pursuit of higher education really worth it?' With the incredible expense, effort, struggle and suffering Ladakhi students and their families undergo so that the heralded university degree can be obtained, what then are the returns of such determined educational migration pathways?

Ladakhi students often express the desire to return to Ladakh return to their families, return to Leh, and some even wish to return to the small village their family is from. However, most students realize that their efforts to obtain a higher education will often not bear fruition. Many, if not most, returning educational migrants will have to find a job which does not match their educational qualifications or interests. The likelihood of obtaining the coveted government job is decreasing annually. In June 2012, for example, for an opening of 40 positions as a general teacher in the government schools more than 3,000 candidates applied, mostly women, all with at least a Bachelor degree, a large number with an MA and some even with a PhD. This felt pressure to obtain the improbable government position was discussed with ardour at the table of young Ladakhi men described in the beginning of this chapter. Furthermore, as one Ladakhi male student explains: 'In India it is very good to have a degree. That's what I am having. Somehow. And I am suffering. And somehow I am having a degree. That is what is considered' (Delhi, February 2012). The degree, nevertheless, is still valued, still 'considered', and students continue to be sent to universities throughout India in increasing numbers year after year. So while students and their families are suffering perceptible hardships of sending these young Ladakhis away, there still remains significant value placed on the attainment of the university degree. Gaining exposure and knowledge about the so-called 'outside world', attending prestigious universities and thereby participating in the Indian knowledge economy all aid in the concentrated move away from being considered as members of a 'backward' population towards being a highly educated (albeit underemployed) community who are progressively gaining economic and social development along with the rights, recognition and resources they feel should be duly allocated.

In Conclusion: Policy Recommendations to Improve the Ladakhi Student Migrant Experience

While educational migration in this case might be considered a 'contradictory resource' and comes at a price, there is still an acceptance in the Ladakhi society, at large, that the pursuit of a higher education is a societal good which should be encouraged. Even though students often gain degrees in fields in which there is little or no scope for jobs in Ladakh, the graduate and postgraduate degrees in themselves provide a considerable amount of prestige and status to both the individual and the larger family unit. However, students and families also lose something while studying abroad, especially if they have to stay away from Ladakh to find a job within their field of study. What is important, then, is to help these students in their educational endeavours so that their experiences 'abroad' and interactions with mainstream India become positive encounters that do not further exacerbate communal, ethnic and regional divides and inequalities.

> So now we need to think, Ladakh is…, India is emerging, India is growing… So, now we need to think about the kind of the policy of the government, and where actually we are getting alienated. And what are the provisions in the Indian constitution which facilitates our improvement and growth and advancement. Simply laying down in the constitution is not enough, there should be provisions. (Ladakhi male student, New Delhi, April 2012)

In order to improve the quality of life of these students who choose to go through the hardships of moving away from home to pursue a higher education, I would recommend the following policy initiatives:

Central University in Ladakh

Establishing a Central University in Ladakh would allow students who do not wish to migrate or who cannot afford to migrate to obtain a quality higher education in Ladakh itself. While currently there exists a Degree College in Leh, and plans are underway to build a State University[18] branch within the next five years, a Central University would more sufficiently fulfill the local demand for quality higher education. Ladakhis are pursuing a university education not only for the sake of a degree, but for the advantages that a higher education will provide including the possibility of qualifying for the competitive Kashmir Administrative Services (KAS) and Indian Administrative Services (IAS) exams and obtaining a position in these prestigious government institutions. A Central University in Ladakh itself will allow for increased access to quality higher education especially among the disadvantaged populations who cannot afford to send their children 'abroad'. A Central University in Ladakh would encourage education pathways which are more relevant for employment in Ladakh, perhaps also strengthening research areas specific to the environment and terrain in Ladakh which are currently underdeveloped. Students would also have the opportunity to remain in Ladakh, reducing the number of young Ladakhis who migrate, thus lessening the perceived threat to the preservation of Ladakhi culture and society. An overwhelming majority of Ladakhi students, parents and politicians expressed the necessity of a central university in Ladakh in order to reduce the hardships that Ladakhi youth, families and society as a whole undergo as a result of the significant rate of educational migration.

Awareness Campaigns about Ethnic and/or Racial Prejudice on Campus and Elsewhere

The 'racial' or ethnic discrimination that Ladakhis along with other ethnic minorities face needs to be addressed and lessened. I recommend awareness campaigns so that focus is drawn towards the wrongdoing that such harassment creates when ethnic communities are further marginalized. An overall awareness campaign in larger metropolitan cities which house increasing populations of student migrants from the borderland regions of India would help to minimize the racial discrimination they face not only in their campus environments, but in the larger urban environments.

Higher Penalty for Racial and Sexual Harassment of Ethnic Minority Men and Women

A significant penalty should be put in place for both racial and sexual harassment of people from ethnic minority backgrounds, combined with better registration of such incidences. By instilling a penalty the message is clear- it is not acceptable to harass people from your own country merely because they seem different from the majority.

Help Desks for Student Migrants at College/University Campuses

Supplemental services such as help desks for student migrants of all backgrounds would help to ease the stress of the move. For many student migrants becoming acquainted with their new environment is a demanding task and adds extra stress to their already stressful academic ambitions.

Additional Hostel Facilities

Additional hostel facilities, either through new construction or through increasing the number of rooms reserved for Ladakhi students would greatly ease the housing difficulties that Ladakhi students face. Because student migrants move away from their homes and families, they do not always have the social networks in place to provide safe and convenient housing. For minority students the housing search can be an especially frustrating experience when they encounter discrimination from potential landlords. Hostel facilities, therefore, would greatly reduce the hassle of navigating a hostile city, and, especially for women, greatly increase their level of safety.

Coaching and Guidance Services for SC/ST/OBC Students

Coaching and career guidance should be available for students who gain admission to universities through reservations. Extra coaching would provide an immense help for the SC/ST/OBC students. Obtaining extra help in gaining the social and academic competencies necessary in order to succeed in the university would go a long way in improving these students' experiences and achievements during college life. A summer course or a supplemental course in the first semester of the undergraduate education for reserved category students would also help to boost academic and social competencies in order to increase the level of confidence needed to speak up in class and approach their teachers for help when needed. Additionally, career guidance facilities would help immensely, especially for first generation students.

Centre for Internal Migration Services

A Centre for Internal Migration would benefit not only the Ladakhi student migrants, but also other migrants who for various reasons choose to uproot themselves from their homes and families in order to pursue their vision of a better life. Such a Centre would service migrants by registering complaints about harassment and discrimination, and when necessary seek the relevant officials to penalize the perpetrators. A Centre for Internal Migration could also attempt to register the migrant population in order to generate statistics about this increasing and diffuse population. In addition, wherever possible, the Centre could provide advice and assistance as to where migrants could look for housing and employment.

Internal migrants are the ambassadors from their region and demonstrate the rich diversity that India offers. By supporting these migrants, as well as promoting an inter-cultural dialogue and exchange among these various people from different backgrounds, a stronger sense of cohesion among the Indian population will be encouraged. It is, therefore, important that these migrants feel as if they belong in their own country- especially in Delhi, the seat and centre of their government and nation-state. By recognizing the work that migrants do in bringing people together from different regions, and supporting their efforts to expand their horizons and live in other parts of India, an environment of exchange and understanding may be fostered.

Notes

1. This chapter has benefitted greatly from the comments and suggestions received on earlier drafts from Dr Neetha N. Pillai, discussant at the RGICS conference on 'Internal Migration in Contemporary India', 23 February 2013, and also from Martijn van Beek, Karen Valentin, Karina Dalgas, Helene Ilkjær and Jakob Williams Ørberg.

2. Higher education, here, refers to education above the higher secondary level, mostly at colleges and universities.

3. The research was undertaken as part of a PhD study on 'The Intergenerational Transmission of Global Buddhism among Ladakhi student migrants in Delhi' at the Institute for Culture and Society, Aarhus University, Denmark. The research was funded by the Danish Research Council for Culture and Communication (FKK) as part of a larger research project, 'Buddhism and Modernity: Global Dynamics of Transmission and Translation'.

4. Sumera Shafi, a Ladakhi Muslim student at Jawaharlal Nehru University, Delhi, has been engaging in research among Ladakhi Muslim students in Delhi and her findings support what I have written here.

5. The region of Ladakh has two districts—Leh district with a Buddhist majority and Kargil district with a Muslim majority. In May 1995, both districts were granted autonomy status with the notification of the Ladakh Autonomous Hill Development Council Act, 1995. The Ladakh Autonomous Hill Development Council was established in Leh in August 1995 and in Kargil in July 2003 (http://leh.nic.in/pages/lahdcl.html; and http://kargil.nic.in/lahdck/lahdck.htm).

6. Ladakhis and outside commentators still refer to Ladakh as being cut off from the outside world for six months a year, although Leh district has become accessible year round through costly regular flights. Before the establishment of firm, closed borders with Tibet and Pakistan, Ladakh was a vivid trading centre along the Trans-Himalayan trading route with Central Asia (Beek, 1998; Bray, 1991; Rizvi, 1983; Sheikh, 2010).

7. Both Kargil and Leh have a Degree College introduced by the Government of Jammu & Kashmir. The level of education offered at these colleges suffers from a poor reputation, although significant improvements have been made during the past few years.

8. Sonam Norbu is said to be the first Ladakhi to obtain a British university degree (in engineering) from Kashmir University in Srinagar in the 1930s (Bertelsen, 1996).

9. Former Jammu student union president, personal communication, May 2011.

10. Former Chandigarh Student Union president, personal communication, December 2012.

11. Former Delhi Student Union President, personal communication, April 2012.

12. Former student Kashmir University, Srinagar, personal communication, May 2013.

13. There are no statistics generated on Ladakhi student migration; however, membership in the Ladakhi student unions throughout India is 'mandatory', so these numbers are based on membership numbers as well as estimates from student union presidents who take responsibility for the Ladakhi student community outside of Ladakh. There are no means to collect data on these migrants as they are, per definition, in flux. Students may spend anywhere from 1–20 years of their lives outside Ladakh, moving among the various destinations outside as well as inside Ladakh. Students rarely stay in the same location throughout their educational migrations and at times move back to Ladakh for a period before taking the next educational step.

14. In October 1989, eight Scheduled Tribes have been recognized in Ladakh by the Indian President in accordance with the Indian Constitution, article 342, clause 1 (see Aggarwal, 2004, p. 41; Beek, 1997; Bertelsen, 1997, p. 74). According to Government of India (2007, p. iv), 'Due to their social disability and economic backwardness, they were grossly handicapped in getting reasonable share in elected offices, government jobs and educational institutions and, therefore, it was considered necessary to follow a policy of reservations in their favour to ensure their equitable participation in governance'. The reservations of seats for Scheduled Tribe members (7.5%) and Scheduled Caste members (15%) in legislative assemblies, public sector employment and government-aided educational institutions has been a constitutional provision since 1982 (see Ambagudia, 2011; Chanana, 1993). Currently, 82% of the population in Ladakh is classified as a member of a Scheduled Tribe (LAHDC, 2012b, p. 4).

15. Ladakhis state that they belong to a different 'race', belonging to a 'Mongolian' race compared to the 'Aryan' race of North India (see also Aggarwal, 2004, p. 12). A similar view is often found among north eastern students (see McDuie-Ra, 2012).

16. I have changed the name to keep this student anonymous.

17. Tuition in this case refers to private tutorials rather than tuition fees for private school and university admission.

18. In July 2012, the ground was broken for the establishment of the branch of Kashmir University to be established in Leh, in the hope that it would be completed in the next few years.

References

Advani, S. (2009). *Schooling the national imagination: Education, English, and the Indian modern*. New Delhi: Oxford University Press.

Aggarwal, R. (2004). *Beyond lines of control: Performance and politics on the disputed borders of Ladakh, India*. Durham and London: Duke University Press.

Ambagudia, J. (2011). 'Scheduled tribes and the politics of inclusion in India'. *Asian Social Work and Policy Review, 5*(1), 33–43.

Arvind, G.R. (2011). 'Colonialism, modernism, and neo-liberalism: Problematizing education in India'. In Yong Zhao et al. (eds), *Handbook of Asian education: A cultural perspective* (p. 481). New York: London: Routledge.

Basch, L., Schiller, N.G., and Blanc, C.S. (1995). *Nations unbound: Transnational projects, postcolonial predicaments, and deterritorialized nation-states*. Basel: Gordon and Breach Science Publishers.

Beek, M. v. (1997). 'The importance of being tribal. Or: The impossibility of being Ladakhis'. In T. Dodin and H. Räther (eds), *Recent research on Ladakh 7. Proceedings of the seventh colloquium of the international association for Ladakh studies* (pp. 21–41). Ulm: Universität Ulm.

———. (1998). 'Worlds apart: Autobiographies of two Ladakhi caravaneers compared'. *FOCAAL, 32*, 55–69.

———. (1999). 'Hill councils, development and democracy: Assumptions and experiences from Ladakh'. *Alternatives, 24*(4), 435–59.

Beek, M.v. (2008). 'Imaginaries of Ladakhi modernity'. In R. Barnett and R. Schwartz (eds.), *Tibetan modernities: Notes from the field on cultural and social change* (p. 165). Boston, MA: Brill.

Beek, M.v. and Bertelsen, K.B. (1997). 'No present without past: The 1989 agitation in Ladakh'. In T. Dodin and H. Räther (eds), *Recent research on Ladakh 7*. Proceedings of the seventh colloquium of the international association for Ladakh studies (pp. 67–88). Ulm: Ulm University.

Bertelsen, K.B. (1996). 'Our communalized future: Sustainable development, social identification, and the politics of representation in Ladakh'. Doctoral thesis. Aarhus University, Denmark.

———. (1997a). 'Early modern Buddhism in Ladakh: On the construction of Buddhist Ladakhi identity, and its consequences'. In T. Dodin and H. Räther (eds.), *Recent Research on Ladakh 7:* Proceedings of the 7th colloquium of the international association for Ladakh studies (pp. 67–88). Bonn: University of Bonn.

———. (1997b). 'Protestant Buddhism and Social Identification in Ladakh'. *Archives de sciences sociales des religions* 42e Année (99), 129–51.

Béteille, André. (2010). *Universities at the crossroads*. New Delhi: Oxford University Press.

Bray, J. (1991). 'Ladakhi history and Indian nationhood'. *South Asia Research, 11*(2), 115–33.

———. (2007). 'Old religions, new identities and conflicting values in Ladakh'. Paper presented at International conference on Religion, Conflict and Development. University of Passau, Germany.

Chanana, K. (1993). 'Accessing higher education: The dilemma of schooling women, minorities, Scheduled Castes and Scheduled Tribes in contemporary India'. *Higher Education, 26*(1), 69–92.

Chopra, R. and Jeffery, P. (eds). (2005). *Educational regimes in contemporary India*. New Delhi: SAGE Publications.

Ciotti, M. (2006). 'In the past we were a bit "Chamar": Education as a self and community engineering process in northern India'. *Journal of the Royal Anthropological Institute, 12*(4), 899–916.

Crook, J.H. (1995). 'Ecology and culture in the adaptive radiation of Tibetan speaking peoples in the Himalayas'. In H. Osmaston and P. Denwood (eds), *Recent research on Ladakh 4 and 5*. London: School of Oriental and African Studies, University of London.

Dawa, D.S. (1995). 'Whither Ladakh education?' In M. van Beek and K.B. Bertelsen (eds), *Ladakh: Culture, history and development between Himalaya and Karakoram* (pp. 72–77). Aarhus: Aarhus University Press.

Fatima, K. (1999). 'Women's development and education in Kargil district'. In M. van Beek and K.B. Bertelsen (eds), *Ladakh: Culture, history and development between Himalaya and Karakoram* (pp. 119–24). Aarhus: Aarhus University Press.

Froerer, P. (2011). 'Education, inequality and social mobility in Central India'. *European Journal of Development Research, 23*(5), 695–711.

Goering, P.G. (1990). 'The response to tourism in Ladakh'. *Cultural Survival Quarterly, 14*(1), 20.

Government of India. (2007). *National commission for Scheduled Tribes: A handbook*. Retrieved from http://ncst.nic.in/index.asp?langid=1files/17294/index.html (accessed on 16 May 2013).

Jeffery, C. (2010). *Timepass: Youth, class, and the politics of waiting in India*. Stanford, CA: Stanford University Press.

Jeffrey, C., Jeffery, P. and Jeffery, R. (2010). *Education, unemployment and masculinities in India.* New Delhi: Social Science Press and Orient Blackswan.

Kaul, S. and Kaul, H. N. (2004). *Ladakh through the ages: Towards a new identity.* New Delhi: Indus Publishing Company.

Kingsnorth, P. (2000). 'Shadows in the kingdom of light: Ladakh and social change'. *The Ecologist, 30*(8), 35.

LAHDC. (2005). *Ladakh 2025 vision document.* Retrieved 12 May 2013 from http://www.leh.nic.in/VISION_DOCUMENT.PDF

———. (2010). *A 5-year perspective plan (2010–15) under MGNREGA through micro level planning for Leh District 'Gyruja'.* Tata-LAHDC Development Support Programme.

———. (2013). *District Kargil at a glance.* Retrieved from http://kargil.nic.in/glance/glance.htm (accessed on 17 May 2013).

LAHDC, Leh. (2012a). Government of Jammu & Kashmir, Ladakh Autonomous Hill Development Council, Leh. Department of Education [Powerpoint presentation]. Leh, Ladakh.

———. (2012b). *Statistical handbook of Leh, Ladakh, 2011–12.* Retrieved 17 May 2013 from http://leh.nic.in/pages/handbook.pdf

Levinson, B.A., Foley, D.E., and Holland, D. (eds) (1996). *The cultural production of the educated person: Critical ethnographies of schooling and local practice* (pp. 1–54). Albany, NY, State University of New York Press.

McDuie-Ra, D. (2012). *Northeast migrants in Delhi: Race, refuge and retail.* Amsterdam: Amsterdam University Press.

Norberg-Hodge, H. (1991). *Ancient futures: Learning from Ladakh.* San Francisco: Sierra Books Club.

Office of the Chief Education Officer, Leh (2012). *Statistical handbook of education 2011–2012.* Leh: Ladakh Autonomous Hill Development Council.

Osella, F. and Osella, C. (2000). *Social mobility in Kerala: Modernity and identity in conflict.* London: Pluto Press.

Palden, T. (1998). *After thirty years.* Delhi: Jayyed Press.

Planning Commission (2006). *Working group report of the development of education of SC/ST/minorities/girls and other disadvantaged groups for 11th Five Year Plan (2007–2012).* Government of India, New Delhi. Retrieved from http://planipolis.iiep.unesco.org/upload/India/India_wg11_scst.pdf (accessed on 18 January 2016).

Rizvi, J. (1983). *Ladakh: Crossroads of High Asia.* Delhi: Oxford University Press.

Sen, A. (1997). 'Editorial: Human capital and human capability'. *World Development, 25*(12), 1959–61.

———. (2000). *Development as freedom.* New York: Anchor Books.

Sheikh, A.G. (1996). 'Ladakh's link with Baltistan'. *Ladags Melong, 1*(4), 25–29.

———. (2010). *Reflections on Ladakh, Tibet and Central Asia.* New Delhi: Skyline Publications.

Subrahmanian, R. (2005). 'Education exclusion and the developmental state'. In R. Chopra and P. Jeffery (eds.), *Educational regimes in contemporary India* (pp. 62–82). New Delhi: SAGE Publications.

Tata-LAHDC Development Support Programme. (2010). *A 5-Year perspective plan (2010–15) under MGNREGA through micro level planning for Leh District.* District Level Report First Draft (updated 16 August, 2010). Mumbai: Tata Institute of Social Sciences

The Task Force of Higher Education and Society. (2000). *Higher education in developing countries: Peril and promise.* Washington, DC.: The International Bank for Reconstruction and Development/The World Bank.

The Principal Office. (2011). *Result at a glance. Rig-dZod 7: 19.* Leh: Lamdon Model Senior Secondary School.

Tsering, N. (1995). 'The fate of traditional education in Ladakh'. In H. Osmaston and P. Denwood (eds.), *Recent research on Ladakh 4 & 5. Proceedings of the fourth and fifth international colloquia on Ladakh* (pp. 209–13). London: School of Oriental and African Studies, University of London.

van Beek, Martijn. (1999). 'Hill councils, development and democracy: Assumptions and experiences from Ladakh'. *Alternatives, 24*(4), 435–59.

Wankhede, G.G. (2008). 'Accessing higher education: Affirmative action and structured inequality—the Indian experience'. *Social Change, 38*(1), 31.

7

Migration in Agrarian Classes: A Study Based on Nine Villages in Andhra Pradesh

R. Vijay

Introduction

Historically, people have moved from one place to another. With the advent of capitalism, migration of people has been visualized to have an important role in initiating growth and development of an economy. An indicator of the importance of migration is the recent policy-related literature, World Development Report titled *Reshaping Economic Geography* and Human Development Report titled *Overcoming Barriers: Human Mobility and Development* (United Nations Development Program, 2009). Both the reports gave prominence to human mobility and its consequence on growth and development. The theoretical literature and policy-related literature on migration has its roots in the dualistic framework of analysis of the economy. The dualism is analyzed in terms of agriculture-industry dualism and/or traditional–modern dualism framework. The predominant emphasis in both the sets of literature is on migration of 'labour' and to look at migrants as a 'homogeneous' category. The empirical literature on India, based on secondary sources, presents a case where the 'rich' dominate the migration process. The rich are highly educated, upper caste people and are permanent migrants, while the poor have lower education, belong to disadvantaged classes and are temporary migrants. Maybe one can identify the rich to be 'human capital' induced migrations, while the poor are labour-induced migrants. So, this empirical literature identifies two streams of migrants with different characteristics. The village level empirical studies largely concentrate on the migration of the labour supplying households and its consequences (Vijay, 2011). This chapter has the modest objective to study the (two) classes of migration in rural sector and the consequences of one class of migration on the potential for migration of the other class? Does migration of people in one group initiate occupational diversification in the other group? In other words, an attempt is made to study the short-run consequences of migration within agriculture on other groups.

To analyze the classes of migration and the dynamics of the migration process on different classes, the study is divided into two parts: (*a*) The village was accepted as a unit of analysis and nine villages in different agro-climatic zones were selected in the state of Andhra Pradesh and (*b*) all households in the village were given a detailed questionnaire on the resources endowment, exchanges and migration decisions. Based on this, all households were classified into farm sector and non-farm sector (based on primary occupation) households. The households in farm sector were again classified into classes based on their labour exchanges and land resources owned. A fivefold classification was adopted: (*a*) non-cultivating households, (*b*) rich peasantry, (*c*) middle peasantry, (*d*) poor peasantry and (*e*) agricultural labour households. This method of analysis has the advantage that one can see whether the labour supplying or the labour-demanding households are witnessing migrations.

As it is generally identified in the empirical literature, identifying migration (at a point of time and over time) is a complex process and has lots of problems. The particular survey, which is used in the chapter, was not addressed to study migrations but was on land and poverty and was able to capture the survival strategies used by the households in the farm sector. One of the survival strategies used by households is migration and so the survey had collected information on migration of individuals in the family. The respondents were asked a question whether there has been any migration of any member of the household in the period of enumeration. In the process, it is the respondent's construct of who is a migrant in the household that is decisive for the identification of a migrant. So, what we were able to capture is the migration of individuals for economic purposes. In the social construct, females getting married and migrating is not identified as migrants and so do not get captured as migrants. In addition, there were individuals in a household who would go to the nearby town in the morning and come back by evening and daily migrations are also not captured as migrants by the households. A second major limitation is that the households are classified into classes/groups in terms of single year's data, but there could be year-to-year fluctuations in labour exchanges; even though the criteria for classification maybe the same, but the composition of each class/group may change over time. A third major limitation is that one is trying to derive dynamic consequences based on one-year data.

The chapter is organized into four sections. The first section is a brief description of the villages and structure of the economy. The following section is on inter-village trends in migration and possible explanation of these trends. The third section is on presenting intra-level differences in migration rates and consequences of one set of migrations on the other. The last section is the conclusion section.

Description of the Surveyed Villages

Socio-economic Profiles of Surveyed Villages

Agrarian institutions, including the market institutions, have a tendency to undergo changes and transform themselves, and these changes are associated with the level of development of the region and/or sub-region. This is more so when the total economy is not well integrated within itself. Possibly, it is common to note the existence of the regions, namely Telangana, Rayalseema and Coastal Andhra, which can be seen as an illustration of non-integrated regions. However, considering the levels of development, the state is sometimes grouped into five regions (Rao and Bharathi, 2010; Rao and Subrahmanyam, 2002). In the scale of development, South Coastal Andhra comprising the Krishna–Godavari delta regions, namely the districts of East Godavari, West Godavari, Krishna, Guntur, Prakasam and Nellore occupy the top place, with a high index of output per hectare. Next in importance comes the region of North Telangana, comprising the districts of Nizamabad, Adilabad, Karimnagar and Khammam. North Coastal Andhra, which includes Srikakulam, Vizianagaram and Visakhapatnam, occupying the third place. Rayalseema comprising Cuddapah, Kurnool, Ananthapur and Chittoor comes fourth, and South Telangana comprising Rangareddy, Hyderabad, Mahaboobnagar, Medak and Nalgonda occupies the fifth place. The regional differences are partly historical and partly due to differential public investments, such as irrigation by canal water and complementary private investments. As the institutions are likely to undergo changes in terms of the level of investments and consequent level of development, the survey attempts to distribute the nine sample villages across the four regions. The attempt to cover at least two villages in each region succeeded in all regions excluding Rayalseema.

Location and Sources of Irrigation

Table 7.1 provides information regarding the *mandals*, from which the villages are selected, the number of households surveyed in the farm sector, and the sources of irrigation in the surveyed villages. The survey was conducted in the year 2003–04. Of the three villages surveyed in the West Godavari District, two (Mentipudi and Kothapalli) are irrigated through canal water and one (Seethampet), which is not part of the command area and is in the dry zone in the district with nearly 54 per cent of the land being irrigated by wells. Two villages were selected from Mahaboobnagar District, a district popularly known to be drought–prone witnessing large-scale labour migration to urban areas. One of the villages is rain-fed and the second has canal water as the source of irrigation. Karimnagar District, which is part of the Telangana area and identified as a district which had a significant intervention of CPI (PW) now called the CPI (Maoist). The two villages surveyed in this area also had a presence of this party in the past, but not in the present. One of the villages surveyed was dominantly irrigated by canal water, while in the second village, wells are the main source of irrigation. The two villages selected in North Coastal Andhra are Jonanki and B. Koduru. While Jonanki is a village with significant presence of tanks for irrigation, the other village has the presence of wells (Table 7.1).

Land Owned and Operated

The extent of land owned and operated by households residing in the village is provided in Table 7.2. The coastal irrigated districts have a smaller extent of land operated and owned when compared to all the other surveyed villages. However, the difference between the land owned and land operated is significantly different in the two canal irrigated coastal villages and in Jonanki, the dry village in Srikakulam District. In the other

Table 7.1

Location, number of households and sources of irrigation in the surveyed villages

District	Mandal	Village	Total Number of Households Surveyed in the Village	% of Land Irrigated by Different Sources			
				Canal	Tanks	Wells	Rainfall
	Veravasaram	Mentipudi	90	100	–	–	–
	Ganapavaram	Kothapalli	208	100	–	–	–
West Godavari	Koyyalagudem	Seethampet	170	–	–	54.77	46.22
	Atmakur	Arepalli	338	53.26	18.86	18.23	9.65
Mahaboobnagar	Bhootpur	Tatiparthy	216	–	12.42	32.34	55.25
	Dharmapuri	Chinnapur	216	61.47	–	16.69	21.85
Karimnagar	Dharmapuri	Nagaram	171	29.26	–	65.7	5.05
	Jalumuru	Jonanki	151	–	92.22	–	7.78
Srikakulam	Elcherla	B. Koduru	177	–	–	58.09	41.91

Source: Field survey.

Table 7.2

Distribution of owned and operated area in the study villages (land in acres)

Village	Owned Land (col. 1)	Operated Land (col. 2)	Difference (col.1–col.2)	Difference as % of Operated Land
Mentipudi	118.25	211.25	–93	–0.44
Kothapalli	114.95	302.8	–187.85	–0.62
Seethampet	415.64	405.34	10.3	0.03
Arepalli	1023.2	997.95	25.25	0.03
Tatiparthy	749.07	805.07	–56	–0.07
Chinnapur	305.51	294.635	10.875	0.04
Nagaram	395.3	422.2	–26.9	–0.06
Jonanki	267.57	196.77	70.8	0.36
B. Koduru	406.07	416.64	–10.57	–0.03
Total	3,795.56	4,052.655	–257.095	–0.06

Source: Field survey.

surveyed villages, the differences between land owned and land operated is not significant. In three villages, there is a relatively higher share of land owned when compared to the land operated, and three villages have a higher share of land operated when compared to the land owned. In case of Mentipudi, the land operated is greater by 93 acres or 44 per cent of the land operated is not enumerated as land owned. This ratio increases to 62 per cent when one considers the second canal irrigated coastal district, namely Kothapalli. In sharp contrast to the canal irrigated coastal districts, the rain-fed dry village of Jonanki in Srikakulam District has a higher extent of land owned when compared to the land operated.

A higher extent of land operated when compared to land owned could either be due to under-reporting of land owned by households as a response to the land reform legislation or as a result of the survey design. The unit of analysis in the survey was households residing in the village. There were households that lived outside the village but held land in the village, these were not enumerated. If there were non-resident households who owned land and were also cultivating the land, the land owned and operated by these households was not captured in the survey. In addition, in case of non-resident households that owned land but did not self-cultivate their land, the extent of land owned by these households was not captured in the survey; since this land is operated by the residents in the village, the data on land operated captures this data. This is a potential source for difference between the land owned and land operated. In the same vein, if the land owned is greater than the land operated, one reason could be that the land owning households are not operating land as they find it unremunerative (this might be the case in the dry village) or maybe because land owning households are leasing out land to non-resident households. In the Indian context, it might not be completely off the mark if it is assumed that a major segment of the non-resident households are earlier residents of the village (owning and maybe also cultivating) and have diversified their occupation from agriculture to non-agriculture. Village studies, Athreya, Djurfeidt and Lindberg (1990) for the delta zone in Tamil Nadu and Upadhya (1988) for the delta zone in Andhra Pradesh) clearly show the presence of this trend.

Migrations in the recent past may or may not influence the production decision in the present. If the migration is permanent and these households sell their land, land distribution will be effected during period of transition but after that influence is minimal. But if the 'past' migrations continue to own land and lease out the land the past migrations also influence the present production decision. Capturing the importance of migrations in the past which has significant influence in the present is a complex problem but an indicator of this tendency is if there is a significant difference between land owned and land operated with land operated higher than land owned (see Table A7.1, for importance of tenancy in study-villages).

At the aggregate level, the extent of land operated is greater than the land owned; this provides an indication of the presence of non-resident land owners who lease out the land. However, village-wise there are major differences. The villages presenting major differences in the amount of land owned and operated are the two canal irrigated West Godavari districts (where land owned is less than the land operated) and one dry village (where land owned is greater than land operated). In the other villages, this difference is not significant. So maybe the two coastal villages have witnessed out migrations of individual/households in the recent past but these households do continue to hold land in the village. There are three caveats to the above reasoning of attributing this difference to past migrations. One, the differences between land operated and land owned can be due to under-reporting of land owned not land operated. Two, the non-residents may not be past migrants but non-residents who want to 'park' their funds in land for speculative reasons. Three, past migrants might not be land owners but landless labour implying higher land operated when compared to land owned might be a proxy for past migrations but a proxy which is biased in favour of landed households.

Cropping Pattern

In the case of Godavari District, the two canal irrigated villages have a dominance of paddy crop while the third village has a dominance of cultivation of tobacco crop. In Seethampet village, nearly 52 per cent of the land is under tobacco crop, followed by 22 per cent under paddy crop, 9 per cent under sugarcane crop and 4 per cent under maize crop, which is part of chicken feed. Seethampet village has a much more diversified cropping pattern and the crops cultivated are inputs to the agro-industry. Arepalli, the village in Mahaboobnagar District with significant proportion of land irrigated by canal, has again a high proportion of land assigned to paddy cultivation. In the dry village of Mahaboobnagar District, the principal crop is the inferior cereal, namely jowar. The two villages in Karimnagar District have a significant proportion of land under paddy, while in Chinnapur village maize is cultivated—it is partly consumed and partly sold in the market. In Nagaram village, in addition to paddy, turmeric is grown for the market and forms a significant proportion of the crops cultivated. In the case of the two villages surveyed in Srikakulam District, the tank-irrigated village has a dominance of paddy crop while in the second village, B. Koduru, paddy is the important crop followed by pulses and chillies (Table 7.3).

Structure of the Surveyed Village Economy

It is common to present data on farm households on the basis of land classification, either land owned or operated (Haque, 2001; Murty, 2004; Vyas, 2003). The agriculture census for example presents data on the basis of land classification. Consolidation of such data is categorized into marginal, small, medium and large holdings on the basis of the size of area held. Given that labour is the predominant factor of production relative to capital, which includes the technology embodied in it, the use of labour plays an important role in determining inter-farm differences (Patnaik, 1990). The labour used by the farm sector is not only the physical, but

Table 7.3

Principal crops cultivated in the surveyed villages (land in acres)

Villages	Paddy	Tobacco	Maize	Jowar	Turmeric	Grams	Castor	Chilies	Sugarcane	Others	Total
Mentipudi	187.5 (73.02)	–	–	–	–	–	–	–	–	69.25 (26.97)	256.75 (100)
Kothapalli	272.75 (65.47)	–	–	–	–	–	–	–	–	143.85 (34.53)	416.6 (100)
Seethampet	93.74 (22.52)	215.5 (51.79)	17 (4.09)	–	–	–	–	–	37 (8.89)	52.9 (12.71)	416.14 (100)
Arepalli	537.2 (52.78)	–	–	66 (6.49)	–	–	87 (8.55)	–	–	327.5 (32.18)	1017.7 (100)
Tatiparthy	55.5 (7.40)	–	6.5 (0.87)	296.1 (39.53)	–	40 (5.34)	211 (28.2)	0.5 (0.06)	–	139.47 (18.62)	749.07 (100)
Chinnapur	139.24 (45.55)	–	34.2 (11.18)	–	2.08 (0.68)	–	4.5 (1.47)	2 (0.65)	–	123.65 (40.46)	305.64 (100)
Nagaram	145.95 (36.80)	–	40.8 (10.30)	–	69.9 (17.64)	18 (4.54)	–	24.23 (6.11)	–	97.535 (24.6)	396.5 (100)
Jonanki	193.9 (72.46)	–	–	–	–	–	–	–	–	73.67 (27.53)	267.57 (100)
B. Koduru	148.85 (45.09)	–	–	–	–	22.85 (6.92)	–	36.14 (10.95)	–	122.25 (37.04)	330.09 (100)
Total	1,774.6 (42.69)	215.5 (5.185)	98.5 (2.37)	362.1 (8.71)	72 (1.73)	80.85 (1.94)	303 (7.28)	62.87 (1.51)	37 (0.89)	1,150.1 (27.67)	4,156.1 (100)

Source: Field survey.

Note: Figures in brackets are percentage to total cultivated land in the village.

also mental–that is, the knowledge on the production process. This is important in the Indian context where, by tradition, certain caste groups have ownership and control over land, but do not engage in cultivation; and at the other extreme we have the cultivating caste who have knowledge of the process of production but whose labour cannot be productively employed, as they do not have access to land. To mitigate the difficulty that arises due to such inherent distribution of the land and labour, the system develops institutions, such as tenancy, permanent farm servants, and wage labour, to produce output from the mental and manual labour of the peasantry, for the households that have only land but cannot/do not cultivate. This is one segment of the agrarian sector with landholders on one side and labour-holders on the other. Another segment of the agrarian sector is the households that have lands as well as the necessary labour. These two segments differ significantly in the use of resources—both land and labour—and have different objective functions. In order to capture the inter-farm differences, it is essential to classify the households on the basis of resources and the use of labour on the farms. For this purpose, a fivefold classification—(*a*) non-cultivating households, (*b*) rich peasantry, (*c*) middle peasantry, (*d*) poor peasantry and (*e*) agricultural labour households—was adopted by Rao and Bharathi (2010) which is used in the following analysis by the present writer.

In a stable village economy, land and other assets needed in the production process are concentrated in the hands of the non-cultivating households, rich peasantry, and middle peasantry. The agricultural labour households and poor peasantry derive their income from the production activity undertaken by these groups. While the agricultural labour households are completely dependent on the production activity of the other groups for livelihood, the poor peasants are partly dependent on these groups for their livelihood as they also own some agricultural land. The economic relations such as tenancy and labour employment are initiated and controlled by the former classes, while the poor peasantry and agricultural labour households participate in the transactions. This gives the village the stability and reproductive capacity as all the classes have an interest in reproducing the transactions.

The number of households in the farm sector in the nine villages is 1,737, owning 3,795.56 acres. The average size of owned land works out to be 2.18 acres per household, and if one excludes the agricultural labour households, it works out to be 3.02 acres per household. These figures compare favourably with the reported figures of the Agricultural

Census. Table 7.4 provides some interesting trends on the structure of the rural economy: At the aggregate level, the economy is dominated by the poor peasantry—they form 43.87 per cent of the households and own 35.43 per cent of the land. In terms of numbers, the agricultural labour households form the second largest group in the villages and constitute 27.63 per cent of the households. Thus, the poor peasantry and agricultural labour households form 70.5 per cent of the rural households. At the other extreme are the labour-demanding households: the rich peasantry and the non-cultivating households: The rich peasants form 4.37 per cent of the households and operate 16.90 per cent of the land; while the non-cultivating households are numerically larger than

Table 7.4

The distribution of households and owned land in different study villages

Villages	Agricultural	Poor Peasants	Middle Peasants	Rich Peasants	Non-cultivating	Total
Mentipudi	16	33	20	12	9	90
	(0)	(10.7)	(27.05)	(35.5)	(45)	(118.25)
Kothapalli	98	70	31	3	6	208
	(0)	(21.35)	(57.1)	(18)	(18.5)	(114.95)
Seethampet	91	22	26	19	12	170
	(5.5)	(25.75)	(99.79)	(184.5)	(100.1)	(415.64)
Arepalli	56	201	59	8	14	338
	(8.25)	(453.95)	(297)	(146)	(118)	(1,023.2)
Tatiparthy	29	155	29	3	0	216
	(22)	(530.57)	(150.5)	(46)	(0)	(749.07)
Chinnapur	49	60	64	7	36	216
	(0.12)	(50.7)	(123.88)	(49.5)	(81.3)	(305.51)
Nagaram	38	77	39	13	4	171
	(7.5)	(120.8)	(136.7)	(107.3)	(23)	(395.3)
Jonanki	32	76	24	6	13	151
	(0)	(65.05)	(44.52)	(25.7)	(132.3)	(267.57)
B. Koduru	71	68	30	5	3	177
	(0.25)	(65.82)	(66)	(29)	(245)	(406.07)
Total	480	762	322	76	97	1737
	(43.62)	(1,344.69)	(1,002.54)	(641.5)	(763.2)	(3,795.56)

Source: Field survey.
Note: Figures in brackets indicate land owned in acres.

the rich peasantry (5.58 per cent) and own 20.10 per cent of the land. The middle peasantry constitutes 18.53 per cent of the households and owns 26.41 per cent of the land.

In terms of structures in the farm sector, the non-cultivating households have a higher share numerically as well as in terms of the land owned, when compared to the rich peasantry—the rich peasantry also forms a significant proportion in the farm sector. Over time, if the rich peasantry is increasing in importance due to their increased market interaction and scale advantage in the production system, the importance of agricultural labour households should also increase as providers of labour. An increase in the importance of non-cultivating households would lead to increase in importance tenancy.

At the village level, there are major differences in terms of structures. At one extreme is the village Seethampet (a dry village in West Godavari District), where the rich peasantry owns nearly 44 per cent of the land and cultivates crops, which are inputs to agri-industry. This village has the highest share of agricultural labour households. At the other extreme are B. Koduru village (Srikakulam District) and Jonanki village (Mahaboobnagar District), where the non-cultivating households own around 60 per cent and 50 per cent of the land, respectively. In these villages, the land is concentrated with the non-cultivating households (traditional landlords) and uses a series of permanent farm servants, who in turn employ daily wage labourers to cultivate land (the non-cultivating household in B. Koduru neither cultivates nor supervises production; chillies are cultivated in this land, and the household owns three fish tanks—whose the output is sold outside the village—as well as a movie theatre in a nearby town). The two coastal villages with a high proportion of non-resident households owning land gives the impression of a village with a dominance of non-cultivating households. The two villages in Karimnagar District have a presence of rich peasantry and non-cultivating households; but the major share of the land here is owned by the middle peasantry. In one village (Chinnapur), they own 40 per cent of the land, while in the second village (Nagaram), they own 35 per cent of the land. In the two villages in Mahaboobnagar District, the poor peasantry dominates the economy. In both the villages, the poor peasantry forms nearly 71 per cent of the households–while in Arepalli, these households own nearly 44 per cent of the land, and in Tatiparthy, they own nearly 70 per cent of the land (Table 7.4).

Inter-Village Differences in Migration

If one considers all the villages together, around 20 per cent of the households witness migrations and the migration rate (number of individuals migrating to total population) is around 8 per cent which compares favourably with all-India migration rates of economic migration for males. Firstly, let us consider levels of migrations at the village. The villages which are witnessing the highest level of migrations are Jonanki and Arepalli. In both the villages, around 34 per cent of the households have at least one migrant from the household. The migration rate is also highest for these villages and share of migrants from this village to total migrants is also high. The villages witnessing minimum migration (both in terms of share of households with at least one migrant in household to total households as well as migration rates) are Seethampet and B. Koduru. In these two villages, the share of agricultural labour households is the largest when compared to other villages but the migrations levels are low. One possibility to explain low rates of migration is the options open to households in the economic space to earn income. In one of the villages, Seethampet, the rich peasantry dominates in terms of share of land owned by this class. These households are potential demanders of labour and given the diversified cropping pattern, their demand for labour is reasonable high reducing the need for labour-supplying households to move out of the village. In case of B. Koduru, land is concentrated in the non-cultivating households with extreme extent of land concentration. The extreme concentration may be generating demand for labour for agricultural labour households. So, interestingly, a landlord-dominated village as well as rich peasant-dominated village shows low rates of migrations. In the other study-villages, it is in between these two groups (Table 7.5).

Given the differences in migration rates over villages, it would be interesting to see which are the classes witnessing migrations in the study-villages. The Table 7.6 provides information on the distribution of households witnessing at least one migrant in households as well as the migration rates. The class which has witnessed the maximum proportion of at least one migrant in a household to total households in the group as well as highest migration rate is the non-cultivating households. Second in importance in terms of migration are two classes, that is, agricultural labour households and poor peasantry the proportion of households witnessing at least one migrant to total households in class is 20.8 per cent

Table 7.5

Migration rates HHs and individuals

Villages	% of HHs Witnessing at Least One Migrant	% of Individuals Migrating (Migration Rate) to Total Population	Share of Migrants in Each Village to Total Migrants
Mentipudi	8.8	2.2	2.3
Kothapalli	17.3	5.1	10.4
Seethampet	1.1	0.5	0.5
Arepalli	34.0	14.7	33.4
Tatiparthy	25.0	7.9	15.6
Chinnapur	22.2	8.0	13.9
Nagaram	14.6	4.4	7.2
Jonanki	34.4	13.2	15.1
B. Koduru	2.2	0.6	1.1
Total	19.8	8.1	100

Source: Fieldwork.

but the migration rate is higher for poor peasantry when compared to agricultural labour households. Next in importance comes the middle peasantry and as expected rich peasantry has the lowest proportion of households with at least one migrant and also the lowest migration rate (Table 7.6). Agricultural labour and poor peasantry are suppliers

Table 7.6

Distribution of migrant households over classes in the study village

Villages	% of HHs Witnessing at Least One Migrant	% of Individuals Migrating (Migration Rate)	Share of Migrant in Each Class
Agricultural labour	20.8	6.8	28.7
Poor peasantry	20.8	8.9	46.2
Middle peasantry	16.7	5.2	15.6
Rich peasantry	3.94	0.9	10.3
Non cultivating HHs	29.8	12.7	8.4
Total	19.86	8.1	100

Source: Fieldwork.

of labour in the labour market with agricultural labourer being a pure supplier of labour in the market while poor peasantry is part suppliers of labour in the market as they also own land. The part suppliers have a higher migration rate when compared to pure suppliers of labour. The non-cultivator group has the highest migration rate and these are not suppliers of land but might need labour to organize production. So, the villages witness labour supplying as well as potential labour demanding households migrating out of the village. If this is a true picture of migration trends, then maybe it substantiates the hypothesis raised earlier in the chapter that a higher extent of land operated when compared to land owned is due to migration of households from village but these households continue to own land in the village and lease out the land to resident households.

One is witnessing two types of migrations in the village economy. One class are the labour supplying households, with a dominance of poor peasantry, and the second class comprises potential labour demanding households with a significant presence of non-cultivating households. To substantiate the above correlation between migration rate and share of households in each class group, a survey was conducted and the results are presented in Table 7.7. As the share of agricultural labour households increases the proportion of at least one migrant member in a household decreases. But this proportion is positive and is 0.67 for poor peasant households, that is, as the proportion of poor peasants increases in the village economy, migration rate increases. In the case of middle peasants, these two variables are negative but the correlation coefficient tends towards zero. But if the village economy has significant presence of rich peasantry, the proportion is negative and around 0.55. In other words, as the share of these households in village economy increases migration decreases. If one considers non-cultivating households, as their share in

Table 7.7

Correlation coefficient between percentage of households witnessing at least one migrant and the different classes

Agricultural Labour	Poor Peasantry	Middle Peasantry	Rich Peasantry	Non Cultivating Households
−0.64	0.67	−0.02	−0.55	0.08

Source: Calculation based on fieldwork.

numbers increases, migration rates decrease. So maybe the migration levels in villages on the one hand depends on relative proportions of poor peasantry in the economy and not agricultural labour households and on the other hand the proportions of non-cultivating households in the economy. Middle peasant, a stable group, does not have any important influence on migration rates and the higher presence of rich peasantry dampens the migration rates. So, one can identify two streams of migrations—one is labour-supplying households with a dominance of poor peasantry and second is labour-demanding households with dominance of non-cultivating households.

Intra-Village Trends in Migrations

Observing migration in a structural framework, an attempt is made to analyze which class of households are witnessing migrations and the impact of one class of migrants on other class of migrants at the village level. One can identify four typologies in migrations (Table 7.8).

Table 7.8

Distribution of households with at least one migrant over classes in the surveyed villages

Villages	Agricultural	Poor Peasants	Middle Peasants	Rich Peasants	Non-cultivating	Total
Case A						
Jonanki	53.1	31.5	20.8	0	46.1	34.4
Case B						
Arepalli	42.8	36.8	28.8	0	0	34.0
Tatiparthy	34.4	21.9	34.4	0	0	25.0
Case C						
Mentipudi	12.5	3.0	10.0	8.3	22.2	8.8
Kothapalli	23.6	15.7	9.6	0	0	17.3
Chinnapur	18.3	6.6	23.4	14.2	52.7	22.2
Nagaram	31.5	12.9	2.5	0	50.0	14.6

(Table 7.8 Continued)

(Table 7.8 Continued)

Villages	Agricultural	Poor Peasants	Middle Peasants	Rich Peasants	Non-cultivating	Total
Case D						
Seethampet	2.2	0	0	0	0	1.1
B. Koduru	1.4	1.4	3.3	20.0	0	2.2

Source: Fieldwork.

Case A: Migration of Labour Supply Households as well as Non-cultivating Households are High

There is one village in this group, namely, Jonanki. Here households in all class-groups are witnessing migration excluding the rich peasantry. Here migration of labour supplying households (agricultural labour households (AGL) and poor peasantry (PP)) is high and the out-migration of non-cultivating households is also high. So this appears to be a case where the village is witnessing a distress condition. An indicator of the distress is a significant decrease in land operated when compared to land owned, that is, 36 per cent of the land owned by residents in village is not operated (Table 7.2). So, when there is a distress due to natural conditions, households in all classes migrate but the rate of out-migration of agricultural labour households is the highest.

Case B: Labour Supplying Households Witness Migration with Low Migrations for Labour Demanding and Non-cultivating Households (NCHs)

There are three villages in this group: Arepalli, Tatiparthi and Kothapalli. In these villages AGL, PP and middle peasantry (MP) class groups are witnessing migrations while rich peasantry (RP) and NCH are not witnessing migrations. In these villages the migration by AGL are higher than the migration witnessed in PP. Two of the villages are in Mahaboobnagar district and have the cultivation of a single crop in a production year. Given the low of demand of labour in some periods the labour supplying households are witnessing seasonal out-migrations in the lean season. The third village in this group is Kotapalli is in canal irrigated coastal district. This village has no migration of NCHs in the present period but has migrations in the recent past which is reflected in higher extent of land operated when compared to land owned. So if one factors in this feature, Kothapalli village is not in this group but in the following group (see Table A7.2).

Case C: The NCH Households Witness Higher Migration Compared to the Rest of the Class Groups

There are four villages in this group namely Mentipudi, Kothapalli, Chinnapur and Nagaram. In all these villages NCH households are witnessing higher migrations. In these villages, two are in the canal irrigated West Godavari district and two villages are from Karimnager district in Telengana area. The processes that are generating higher migration in these two zones are different. In case of coastal districts, the expansion of non-farm sector providing households with some surplus to diversify might be a reason for migration of people from this class. While in case of villages in Karimnagar district, the combination of potential for diversification and movement led by communist parties (CPI (PW)) might have been responsible for out-migration of NCH households from the villages.

Case D: Low Migration Villages

There are two villages in this group, namely Seethampet and B. Koduru. In both the villages, there is a dominance of agricultural labour households but migrations are low. In one village, Seethampet, the rich peasantry is relatively more dominant and so are able to internalize the demand for labour in the village. While in the second village, a traditional landlord with large land concentration is able to internalize the demand for labour and in the process reduce migrations.

Implication of Different Classes of Migration on Local Structures

If a village economy witnesses migrations, by either the labour supplying households or the labour demanding households or non-cultivating households there has to be a resultant reallocation in the village economy. The emphasis in the presentation is to see the adjustment process from the side of labour supplying households. On an aggregate, nearly 70 per cent of the rural households are agricultural labour households and poor peasantry. Some villages like Seethampet have higher share of AGL, while some villages like Tatiparty have a higher share of PPs. But if one sees the options available to these households to meet their livelihood, one gets some interesting trends. Here, one is analyzing three options: (a) to lease in land, (b) to migrate and (c) Non-farm Sector (NFS). The NFS does not appear to have a major option to the AGL and PP households in the surveyed villages.

In the first group (case A), the labour supplying as well as non-cultivating households are witnessing migrations. Migration of non-cultivating households which is due to diversification of occupation creates a space which needs to be occupied by other groups, provided the land owned by these segments is not sold or kept fallow. So, agricultural labour and poor peasants enter this space and take in land on lease. So, in case of Jonanki village, 30 per cent of labour supplying households access land in the land lease arrangements by leasing in land from the non-cultivating households (Vijay and Sreenivas, 2013). So, in this village, one segment of labour supplying households enters land lease arrangement but a more significant proportion migrates out (Table 7.9).

In the case of the second group (case B), the migration of non-cultivating households is minimal (is zero) and there are indicators of past migrations, so the dominant strategy for these households is to migrate and as no space is created by out-migration of non-cultivating households entry of labour supplying households into land lease arrangements is also very low (Table 7.9).

The third group (case C) is a case of migration of non-cultivating households. The migration of this group would result in space being created in the village economy to organize production. In case of the two canal-irrigated villages there is an entry of agricultural labour and poor peasantry to occupy this space. So tenancy becomes very important for the labour supplying households in this village and migration is a relatively less important method to meet subsistence. While in the case of the two villages in Karimnagar district, maybe due to the influence of people movement, even though non-cultivating households are migrating, the land under their control is low, leasing in is low, as well as migrating out is low.

Table 7.9

Options open to agricultural labour households and poor peasantry in the surveyed villages

Villages	% of AGL	% of PP	% of AGL and PP	Options Open to AGL and PP Households			
				Share of PP and AGL in Tenancy	Share of Pure Tenants	Share of PP and AGL Households Witnessing Migrations	No of PFS
Case A							
Jonanki	21.19	50.33	71.52	29.63	14.81	37.96	2
Case B							
Arepalli	16.57	59.47	76.04	5.06	1.56	35.41	7
Tatiparthy	13.43	71.76	85.19	5.43	0.54	22.83	0
Case C							
Mentipudi	17.78	36.67	54.44	34.69	28.57	6.12	1
Kothapalli	47.12	33.65	80.77	35.12	28.57	20.83	0
Chinnapur	22.69	27.78	50.46	12.84	1.83	14.68	3
Nagaram	22.22	45.03	67.25	6.09	0.87	20.00	8
Case D							
Seethampet	53.53	12.94	66.47	8.85	4.42	1.77	10
B. Koduru	40.11	38.42	78.53	4.32	1.44	2.88	3
Total	27.63	43.87	71.50	13.53	7.49	20.69	34

Source: Fieldwork.

In the last group, as there are no out-migrations of non-cultivating households. Tenancy does not become important and a significant demand for labour dampens incentive to migrate.

Summary and Conclusion

In the recent period, policy related literature is bringing the issue of migration to the centre stage as an instrument for growth and/or development. So the need of public policy was visualized to reduce the constraints to migrations. An implicit opinion in this context is that migrants are a homogeneous group. This chapter makes an attempt to present a case of for existence of at least two different classes of migrations in the rural areas. One class of migrants is from the labour-supplying households who migrate out to sell their labour time. The second class of migrants is from households who own land but do not cultivate the land who are identified as non-cultivating households. These households have agrarian surplus and want to invest their surplus in non-agricultural sector. In the process, these households diversify out of agriculture but with interest in land. The decision to migrate for land-owning households depends on the rate of growth of the non-farm sector and the possibilities of the non-farm sector to absorb the surplus with these households. The decision to migrate of an agricultural labour households and poor peasantry depends on nature of demand of labour in the local condition or economic space in which they stay. Migrations by these two segments are significant in the village studies. Interestingly migrations of poor peasantry, when compared to agricultural labour households, have a more significant influence on migration rates at the village level. One possible explanation could be the access to credit market by the poor peasantry, which induces migration as migration also has a cost. The higher propensity to migration by these groups could be either to mobilize resources to invest on production process or to repay debt taken to organize production in the last period. The villages with a higher proportion of rich peasantry or landlord with large land concentration witness very low levels of migration as they have the potential to create large demand for labour.

Another feature studied in the chapter was the implications of migrations (of both classes) on the resultant reallocation of land and labour resources. If there is out-migration of labour supplying households there is no major change in the reallocation of resources. But if the non-cultivating households migrate there are significant changes in the reallocation mechanism. If there is migration of land owning households out of the village economy, these households can either sell their land or keep the land fallow or lease out of the land. Given the relative importance of land as a store of value these households do not sell land making the land market inactive. Assuming that these households do not land fallow, the out-migration of land own households creates a space in the production area to be occupied. This space will be occupied by the households who are not migrating but staying in the village and having intention to organize production. So the decision to migrate by labour supplying households to migrate may be dampened if there is out-migration of land owning households. If the above reasoning is even partly true, the decrease in migration rates in the agricultural growth areas can be due to the presence of rich peasantry increasing the demand or due to agricultural led out-migration of land owning households and labour supplying households who could be potential migrants consolidate their position as cultivators and do not migrate. In other words migration of one class may lead to occupational mobility for another class in the village. An economy witnessing agricultural growth might witness lower migrations but the structures which get generated with importance of tenancy might constrain the very process of growth of the village economy. So may be literature on migration should study the interaction of different classes of migrations on the resultant reallocation in the village economy in the context whether the structure generated are conducive for growth or hamper long-term growth.

Table A7.1

Land-based importance of NCPHs in the surveyed villages

Village	No. of NCPH	Share of NCPHs to Total Households	Share of Land Owned by NCPHs	Share of Land Owned by NCPHs and non-resident HHs
Mentipudi	9	10	38.1	65.4
Kothapalli	6	2.8	15.8	67.8
Seethampet	12	7.1	24.1	24.1
Arepalli	14	4.1	11.5	11.5
Tatiparthy	0	0	0	0
Chinnapur	36	16.7	26.5	26.5
Nagaram	4	2.3	5.8	11.8
Jonanki	13	8.6	49.4	49.4
B. Koduru	3	1.6	60.3	60.3
Total	97	5.5	20.1	25.2

Source: Fieldwork.

Table A7.2

Distribution of leased-in area and leased-out area across the study village (land in acres)

Villages	Leased-in		Leased-out		Difference between Extent of Leasing-in and Out	Difference as Share of Operated Land
	Number	Extent	Number	Extent		
Mentipudi	37	98.5	5	18		
	(41.11)	(46.63)	(5.56)	(8.52)	80.5	0.38
Kothapalli	78	201.4	8	26.5		
	(37.5)	(66.51)	(3.85)	(8.75)	174.9	0.58
Seethampet	27	62.8	14	75.1		
	(15.88)	(15.49)	(8.24)	(18.05)	−12.3	−0.03
Arepalli	18	54	14	76		
	(5.33)	(5.31)	(4.14)	(7.47)	−22	−0.05
Tatiparthy	14	66	2	12		
	(6.48)	(8.2)	(0.93)	(1.6)	54	0.07
Chinnapur	27	49.45	38	64.85		
	(12.5)	(16.78)	(17.59)	(22.01)	−15.4	−0.05
Nagaram	20	33.5	3	5.625		
	(11.7)	(8.5)	(1.75)	(1.52)	27.87	0.07
Jonanki	42	56.8	13	30.8		
	(27.81)	(28.87)	(8.61)	(11.51)	26.0	0.13
B. Koduru	7	28.65	25	22.74		
	(3.95)	(6.88)	(14.12)	(6.88)	5.91	0.01
Total	270	651.1	122	331.615		
	(15.54)	(16.07)	(7.02)	(8.18)	319.48	0.08

Source: Field survey.
Note: Figures in brackets indicate percentage of the total operated land.

References

Athreya, V.B., Djurfeldt, G., and Lindberg, S. (1990). *Barriers broken: Production relations and agrarian change in Tamil Nadu*. New Delhi: SAGE Publications.

Haque, T. (2001). 'Impact of tenancy reforms on productivity improvements and socio-economic status of poor tenants'. Policy Paper No. 13, NCAEPR, New Delhi.

Murty, C.S. (2004). 'Large farmers in land lease market: Are marginal farmers affected?' *Economic and Political Weekly*, 39(29), 3270–78.

Patnaik, U. (1990). *Agrarian relations and accumulation mode of production debate in India*. New Delhi: Oxford University Press.

Rao, R.S. and Bharathi, M. (2010). 'Comprehensive study on land and poverty in Andhra Pradesh: A preliminary report'. In M. Bharathi (ed.), *In search of method*. Hyderabad: B-1 Collective and Center for Documentation, Research and Communication.

Rao, Y.V.K. and Subrahmanyam, S. (2002). *Development of Andhra Pradesh: 1956–2001: A study of regional disparities*. Hyderabad: N.R.R. Research Center.

Human Development Report. 2009. (2009). *Overcoming barriers: Human mobility and development*. Human Development Report, published by UNDP, New York, USA.

Upadhya, C.B. (1988). 'The farmer-capitalists of coastal Andhra Pradesh'. *Economic and Political Weekly, 23*(27), 1376–82.

Vijay, K. (2011). 'Labour Migrations in Mahabubnagar: Nature and Characteristics', Economic and *Political Weekly, 46*(2), 67–70.

Vyas, V.S. (2003). *Indian agrarian structure, economic policies and sustainable development: Variation on a theme*. New Delhi: Academic Foundation.

World Development Report (2009). *Reshaping economic geography*. World Development Report. Washington, DC: The World Bank.

8

Migration from Contemporary Bihar[1]

Amrita Datta

Introduction

Bihar has a long history of migration. In the 1830s, a significant
wave of migration began; Biharis were taken as indentured labour
(*girmitiya*) to sugarcane and rubber plantations in the British colonies
of the Caribbean—Guyana, Suriname, Trinidad and Tobago, Fiji and
Mauritius, and this migration lasted for almost a century. In the second
half of the nineteenth century, there were two major migration streams
from the state—to the tea gardens in Assam and to the urban labour
markets in Calcutta, both of which were prominent for a century. In
the post-independence period, the spread of the green revolution since
the late 1960s in north-western India led to a surge in the demand for
agricultural labour. Bihar, mired in economic stagnation and poverty,
saw a massive outflow of agricultural labourers to the states of Punjab and
Haryana, which continued for a long time (Rodgers and Rodgers, 2001;
Sharma, 2005). More recently, migrant streams have become prominent
in other distant urban areas in the country, particularly in the southern
states. It is argued that 'variations in employment prospects and uneven
levels of urbanization would continue to drive migration from Bihar'
(Singh and Stern, 2013).

The last few decades have witnessed a change in the nature and pattern
of migration. Micro-studies reveal that out-migration from Bihar has
shifted from rural–rural migration towards rural–urban migration, and

from predominantly short-term flows to relatively longer-term flows. There has been an increase in the incidence of migration from the state, as well as an expansion of the footprints of the Bihari migrant workers. These workers, spread across the length and breadth of the country are engaged in diverse occupations predominantly in urban locations and contribute to the growth and development of these destination economies. The circularity of migration, that is, the workers' eventual return to rural areas, is closely intertwined with the nature of urban labour markets characterized by work in the informal economy, with little or no social protection. It is this pattern of economic growth and development in urban India that thrives on migrant labour; it not only drives but also defines the nature of migration from rural Bihar (Datta, 2016).

At the same time, migration contributes to the economic development of Bihar; it is a common livelihood strategy of the rural households, and the remittances sent by migrant workers support their families back home. In short, migration is a contemporary reality that affects a large number of individuals and families; it is a way of life in Bihar. It is embedded in the psyche of the state and its people, and this, in turn, has ramifications on the labour markets, social structures, gender relations and a myriad of other areas.

This chapter aims to present an account of migration from Bihar which is not captured in official statistics.[2] It draws from a primary dataset of a longitudinal study in seven districts of rural Bihar that is part of an ongoing research programme on inclusive development in Bihar at the Institute for Human Development (IHD), New Delhi as well as the results from other micro-studies in the state. The chapter also draws from fieldwork experiences of the author as part of the aforementioned research programme. The chapter is divided in five sections. Post-introduction, the second section examines the role of migration as one of the most important livelihood strategies among households in the rural areas, focusing also on the role of remittances in source households. The third section concentrates on migration at destination, focusing on the work and living conditions of migrant workers and highlights the special problems that they face. The fourth section engages with various perspectives of the state, its complexities and peculiarities, as far as migration from Bihar is concerned. The last section summarizes and concludes the study.

Migration as a Livelihood Strategy

Migration has become an increasingly important livelihood strategy for households in rural Bihar. Data from the IHD's longitudinal study in seven representative districts of Bihar reveals that the incidence of migration, measured by proportion of households with at least one migrant member substantially increased from 45 per cent in 1998–99 to about 62 per cent in 2011. Another recent micro-study in the state estimates that one-fourth to one-third of all households has migrants (IIPA, 2010).

Migration from Bihar fits well in the framework of the New Economics of Labour Migration (NELM), wherein, migration decisions are made, not at the individual level (as posited by neo-classical economic theory), but at the household level; migration is undertaken by the households for income enhancement and the diversification of risks in the context of poorly functioning or missing markets (Stark, 1991). Migration leads to a bi-locational residence, where some members of the household migrate, while others stay back in the village (Datta et al., 2012).

In the context of Bihar, de Haan (1997) argues that migration is a family strategy that results from economic as well as cultural considerations. It is men who go out to work, and women are restricted within the village. In fact, the demographic characteristics of migration are such that migration peaks for young adult males; about three quarters of all migrants are men between the ages of 15 and 35 years (Rodgers et al., 2013).

Table 8.1 presents workers disaggregated by sex and residential status for ages 15–59 years. It can be clearly seen that migration levels are quite high—only about half of the total workers are residents, the others migrate. There is also a stark differentiation by sex; while more than half of the

Table 8.1

Workers disaggregated by sex and residential status, age 15–59 years

Residential Status	Male	Female	Total
Resident	45.20	91.30	51.00
Migrant; away for 0–3 months	3.50	0.50	3.20
Migrant; away for 3–8 months	20.90	1.00	18.40
Migrant; away for 8+ months	30.40	7.20	27.50
Total	100	100	100

Source: Calculated from unit-level household data, IHD (2011).

adult male workforce is away from the village in the case of women, this figure is less than 10 per cent. In other words, migration for work is a sex-selective phenomenon—men go out to work while women stay back in the village. This sex selectivity of migration has gendered implications, which have been discussed later.

Table 8.1 also reveals that the most dominant migration stream is that of more than 8 months in a year, followed by migration which is of 3–8 months in a year. Very short-term migration, that is migration for less than 3 months in a year is quite low. This pattern of migration, where, a considerable proportion of the working population is engaged in labour markets away from the village for substantial periods of time indicates that migration is an important livelihood strategy. That it is also a vital source of income will emerge from the discussion in the next section, when we examine the extent of remittances in the rural economy.

Figures 8.1 and 8.2 present the various sources of income for migrating and non-migrating households. We have seen earlier that households with migrants are the most common household type in rural Bihar. The average annual remittance received by households with migrant members is quite high, and thus, it is no surprise that average household

Figure 8.1

Sources of income for non-migrating households

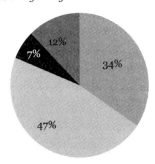

- ▨ Income from agriculture and allied activities
- ▨ Income from non agriculture
- ■ Income from govt transfers casual labour in govt programmes
- ▨ Income from other sources

Source: Calculated from unit-level household data, IHD (2011).

Figure 8.2

Sources of income for migrating households

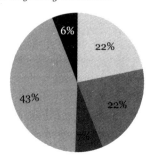

- Income from agriculture and allied activities
- Income from non agriculture
- Income from govt transfers casual labour in govt programmes
- Income from remittances
- Income from other sources

Source: Calculated from unit-level household data, IHD (2011).

incomes are considerably higher in households with migrant members, vis-à-vis households that do not have migrants. In fact, the practice of sending remittance to the source household back in the village is near universal. A look at the composition of income for these households reveals that remittances are the most important source of income in these households; these contribute up to 43 per cent of the total household income in households with migrant members (see Figure 8.2). The share of agriculture is only 22 per cent in the total income in these households. What is even more striking is that the share of agriculture in the total incomes of households with no migrant members is quite low (34 per cent; see Figure 8.1). Lack of work in agriculture, aversion to agricultural work by the youth, and the lack of options in non-agricultural work in rural Bihar are closely intertwined with out-migration.

According to micro-studies in the late 1990s, the main reasons of migration were search of employment and better wage (IHD, 2004; Karan, 2003). Today, out-migration from rural Bihar continues to be driven by a combination of lack of employment and livelihood opportunities in the rural areas, on the one hand, and a demand for cheap labour in urban areas across India, on the other. In other words, migration can be attributed to 'both' distress and developmental reasons. In the backdrop of the state's economy characterized by low industrialization, high population pressure on land and low investments in agriculture, IIPA (2010) argues that out-migration occurs, not because of floods and droughts, but because of 'structural imbalance' in the state's economy, migration is the common villager's solution to the existential challenge.

There is an excessive dependence on remittances; one study estimates that 4.5 to 5 million migrant Bihari workers send remittances equivalent to about five per cent of the state's GDP (IIPA, 2010). Another estimate finds that remittances could amount to 4 to 7 per cent of the state's net domestic product (Rodgers and Rodgers, 2011). However, consumption and subsistence dominate remittance use in source areas, and very little is used for production or investment (IIPA, 2010, Karan, 2003).

Micro-studies also reveal that permanent out-migration from rural Bihar is not the norm, but an exception. In other words, there is a permanence of circular migration. Migrants have one foot in the city and the other in the village (Datta et al., 2014). They continue to maintain links with the village and return after their working life expires. Thus, it is the rural areas that bear the cost of production and reproduction of labour; in other words, they subsidize urbanization and other development projects elsewhere in the country that thrive on migrant labour. While return migration has the potential to act as a catalyst of economic change in the source (rural) areas, as of now, there is scant evidence for this in Bihar.

What are the implications of this form migration on gender relations? First, it creates a gender imbalance in the rural areas, where women far outnumber men. In some of the north Bihar villages, out-migration is so rampant that few able-bodied men are found in the villages, especially in the peak agricultural season in northwest India. Out-migration of men has ramifications on women's work both within and outside the household. Women are more involved in agriculture, and there is evidence towards a feminization of agriculture, which may be attributed to the out-migration of men from rural areas. Household work, especially raising children, now completely falls in the women's domain. In addition, women are more involved in making decisions and managing money in the household. Increased mobility of women is also associated with out-migration of men in general, and in some conservative communities, in particular (Datta and Mishra, 2011).

There is a clear caste pattern in migration that emerges from several studies. Migration is higher among Muslims and OBC I households. Castes which are involved in agriculture and tied to land, be it by cultivation of own land, or leasing in of land, such as the Yadavs and the Kurmis, not surprisingly, have lower rates of out-migration from rural Bihar. As far as landownership is concerned, migration is higher among the highest and the lowest rungs of landownership (Karan, 2003; Rodgers et al., 2013).

A few decades ago, caste-based antagonism and violence in the state contributed to the out-migration, especially of the lower castes. Their motivation, apart from earning a livelihood was to break free from the shackles of the semi-feudal society based on the exploitation of their labour. Ironically, overtime, the upper castes started migrating too, in search of work, and often undertook occupations outside the village that are considered derogatory and shameful to undertake within the village. Scholars have argued that migration indeed weakens ties of the old feudal order (Oberai, Prasad, and Sardana, 1989). It triggers the breakdown of the feudal system, based on economic exploitation, and erodes the stronghold of the upper castes in the agrarian setting. In Bihar, migration has provided a route to 'work with dignity and freedom' (Deshingkar et al., 2006).

Another much talked about, but less studied form of out-migration is the massive outflow of students in the state. Albeit migration for work is most prevalent, migration for education and for skill development is substantial. A. N. Das, in the 1990s argued that brain drain from the state, migration of young men and women to the metropolises, to modernity, has ramifications, just like brawn drain (to the fields of northwestern India, then) (Das, 1998).

Migration at Destination

We discussed that the nature of migration from Bihar has undergone major change. Earlier streams of migration were predominantly to the rural areas of northwestern India. The low growth of agriculture and decline in agricultural income since the 1990s in Punjab has been a major disincentive for migratory labour (Singh, Singh and Ghuman, 2007). This has led to shifts in migrant destination overtime, and, migration, now is predominantly to urban areas outside the state (see Figures 8.3 and 8.4).

Figure 8.3

Destination: Rural or urban

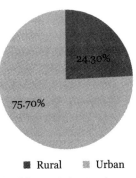

Rural   Urban

Source: Calculated from unit-level data, IHD (2009–10).

Figure 8.4

Where do migrant workers go?

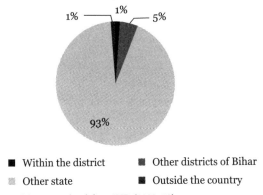

■ Within the district   ■ Other districts of Bihar
▓ Other state   ■ Outside the country

Source: Calculated from unit-level data, IHD (2009–10).

The National Capital Region in Delhi is the most popular destination of migrant workers from Bihar; about one in four migrant workers go there. Punjab and Haryana continue to be important, but now, workers are moving from the rural to the urban areas in these states. West Bengal and Assam are old destinations; migrants still go there, but their numbers are dwindling. High growth states such as Maharashtra and Gujarat, as well as the southern states have also witnessed Biharis migrating for work in large numbers (Figure 8.5).

Figure 8.5

Distribution of migrant workers by state

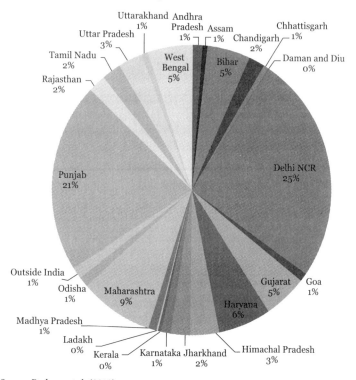

Source: Rodgers et al. (2013).

However, be it in the village or in the city, the migrants generally live in the margins at the place of migration. While their economic contribution to the city is immense, they are not considered part of the city's physical and social fabric (Datta, 2014). This section highlights the vulnerabilities migrant workers face, and the problems that emerge by way of migration. An engagement with these is crucial to understand migrant perspectives, to understand migration, and for policymaking and action.

We address first, work undertaken by Bihari migrants. Casual wage workers are the most dominant stream of workers from rural Bihar. Construction, industry and agriculture are the three main sectors where migrant workers are employed (Rodgers et al., 2013). Each of these sectors present unique vulnerabilities for migrant workers. Employers prefer migrant workers since they provide cheap labour, and can easily be hired and fired (Deshingkar and Akter, 2009). The construction sector is notorious for the middlemen and contractors who exploit workers. In addition, lack of physical safety at construction sites make the workers particularly vulnerable (Pattanaik, 2009).

In agriculture, in particular, mechanization on a large-scale has led to a decline of work in Punjab; paddy transplantation is the only labour-intensive task that creates a demand for (migrant) labour (Singh, 2012). The number of days of work available now lasts only about a month in a year, and there seems little economic viability of the long journey for this 'short' migration for the Bihari migrant worker.

There are some occupations where migrants are particularly at risk. Brick-making is one such occupation where Biharis are employed in large numbers, mainly from the districts of Madhubani, Gaya and Nalanda. The construction boom has created a massive demand for bricks within and outside Bihar. These brick kilns thrive on cheap migrant labour, which predominantly belong to the lower castes. The mode of migration, unlike in other occupations, is where families migrate; together, men, women and children work and live at the kilns. The sector is dominated by middlemen who go to the villages to recruit workers. Wages are paid on piece rate, and deducted from an advance made to the family, leaving much scope for exploitation (Deshingkar et al., 2006).

Trafficking of children, especially from north Bihar to brick-kilns and other diverse jobs and occupations, such as mining, quarrying, loading, agriculture, tea shops, domestic labourers is also prevalent. Trafficking is quite widespread; a recent study estimated that 7.7 per cent of children in two districts of north Bihar are trafficked. Trafficking was found in landless households, predominantly Muslims and scheduled castes. The children lived and worked in pathetic conditions, knew little of education or recreation, and faced ill-treatment and abuse by contractors and employers (Mitra and Mishra, 2011).

The life of the Bihari migrants at destination is not easy. They live in the fringes of societies where they have migrated. Migrants in rural destinations, live not in the village, but the agricultural fields. They have little interaction with the host population, and keep to themselves and other migrant workers. In towns and cities, migrants live mostly in slums, in cramped living conditions, often 4–5 Bihari men in a small room with shared or no toilet facilities. They pay high rates for amenities such as water and electricity. They have no access to their food entitlements, and often pay much more than the market rate for groceries and other essentials (Datta, 2014; IIPA, 2010). In short, their work is precarious and their lives often lonely. Labour migration also needs to be viewed from the lens of class, where white-collar educated workers and certain professions in the new economy, such as security guards and others, are acceptable, while others are not. Given the hardships associated with migration, it is pertinent to ask 'why' people (still) migrate. In the context of Bihar, it appears that most people exercise their choice in the decisions related to migration. They perceive migration to be beneficial for them and their families. Migration offers opportunities for not just more income but also (the possibilities of) a better life.

At the same time, in recent years, many host locations have witnessed an anti-migrant sentiment, and migrants from Bihar have faced a backlash in destinations such as Maharashtra and Assam, among others. In Maharashtra, for instance, in 2008, there was severe anti-Bihari backlash fuelled by local 'son of the soil' political parties, and a prominent leader of one of these parties made statements such as:

> A guest is welcomed if he adjusts himself to the host's house. But if he tries to change the host's house through dadagiri, we won't tolerate it. And no means no! (*The Indian Express*, 2008)

Often, this backlash is rooted in ethnocentric movements (as in the case cited above), while, at other times, it is brought about the state and its agents. For instance, the chief minister of the Indian capital state has said in a public meeting: [t]hese people come to Delhi from Bihar and Uttar Pradesh but don't ever go back causing burden on Delhi's infrastructure. (Sethi, 2009)

Similarly, in the southern state of Tamil Nadu, where Bihari migration is a relatively recent phenomenon, migrant profiling by creating a database of migrant workers, including their biometric identity is underway. Migrants are perceived to be a 'law and order problem', and views like the one below, by a police officer are common.

> We have asked firms employing migrant labourers to submit their details. Our data collection would convey a strong message to them that if they are involved in any kind of anti-social activities, they will be traced.... (*The Times of India*, 2012)

Indeed, migrants are often linked with rising crime in the city, and the backlash is severe. Cases such as the recent gang rape in Delhi, where the accused are Biharis, have ramifications for all migrant Bihari workers. Migrants live in fear, and a culture of fear is created and perpetuated by the dominant social and cultural agendas in host locations. These are manifested in various forms, through means, physical or otherwise. The lines below were a part of a mass SMS that went viral in 2008, when anti-Bihari sentiment reached a high in Maharashtra. The first line (below) was the title of an editorial by a revered leader of a political party in its political mouthpiece; a classic example of how fear is created and sustained.

Ek Bihari, Sau Bimari.
Ek Bihari, Sau Bimari. Do Bihari Ladai ki taiyari,
Teen Bihari train hamari aur paanch Bihari to sarkar hamaari. One Bihari,
a hundred diseases.
One Bihari, a hundred diseases. Two Biharis, preparation for a battle,
Three Biharis, the train is ours and five
Biharis, the government is ours. (The Times of India, 2012)

Thus, while Article 19 of the Indian Constitution guarantees freedom of movement throughout the territory of India, and the freedom to reside in any part of the country to every citizen, living with these xenophobic vibes in host locations is an everyday reality for the Bihari migrant worker. They have little option but to work, as their earnings in the host location sustains their families, and their lives back home in Bihar.

Perspectives of the State

In the meantime, Bihar is booming. For almost a decade, the economy of the state has experienced one of the highest growth rates in the country. There is a school of thought that contends that out-migration from the state is on the decline, in the backdrop of this high growth and development 'within' the state in recent years. The Labour Department of the Government of Bihar claims that migration from the state declined by 35–40 per cent between 2008 and 2012. The Department estimates that 1.5 to 2 million interstate migrant labourers have returned to Bihar due to availability of work within the state (Gupta, 2014).

Other evidences for such contention include the following: first, media reports that throw light on labour shortage at specific destinations, such as the paddy fields in Punjab and the diamond industry in Surat. Second, it is asserted that:

> The situation in Bihar has changed for better as there are abundance of job opportunities here due to ongoing development works....the people need not go outside to earn two square meals... (Kumar)

There is a fallacy in both lines of argument. In the first case, labour shortage in destination is considered synonymous with a decline in migration, while the second (dangerously) assumes that development in source areas is necessarily associated with a reduction in migration. However, various scientific micro-studies (including the one on which this chapter is based), as well as reports in the mass media have found that out-migration from Bihar is high and continues to increase. The failure of the Mahatma Gandhi National Rural Employment Guarantee Act (MGNREGA) in the state also provides some hints that migration trends have not been reversed.

How does the state engage with migration? Is it considered benign, or is it looked down upon? To address these questions, it is useful to engage with the various actors that comprise the state. Three such actors may be:

  i. The provincial government of Bihar (source of migrants)
 ii. The provincial governments of other states (destination of migrants)
iii. The national government, which is supposed to look at internal migration in the country as a whole.

Each one of these three actors is likely to have a different perspective on migration. At times, they may contradict one another. Let us take the case of the source government, the Government of Bihar. There is a sense at the level of the provincial government that migration from the state is declining. This is reflected not just in the political rhetoric (as discussed earlier) but also in official documents of the state. This denial of (the extent of) migration leads to the invisibility of migrant workers and thus, has (adverse) ramifications for their well-being.

What about the state at destination? The Inter-State Migrant Workmen Act, 1979, mandates the host state to protect migrant workers and safeguard rights such as wage equality with local labourers, the provision of suitable residential accommodation and free medical facilities, protective clothing and suitable conditions of work. One of the major shortcomings of the Act is that it only has under its purview interstate migrant workers brought in by contractors. In other words, it does not cover workers that voluntarily migrate. Specific sectors, like construction and brick-kiln, where migrant workers are concentrated also remain outside the ambit of the Act. The Act remains largely on paper as few contractors take out licences and very few enterprises employing interstate migrant workers are registered under the Act (International Organisation for Migration, 2008). The Report of the Second National Commission on Labour has found the Act to be futile due to the reluctance of the state labour departments to cooperate with labour departments of the origin state, ineffective enforcement and the ignorance of workers. It also notes that trade unions have neglected the plight of migrant workers. It argues that well-to-do destination states owe their prosperity to migrant workers and advocates that it is only legitimate to demand that migrant workers receive fair treatment, housing, adequate wages, social security and similar benefits, and they should not be subjected to discriminatory or exploitative conditions (National Commission of Labour, 2002). It is ironic, therefore, that host governments are generally infamous for their hostility to migrant workers. There is no acknowledgement of the migrants' contribution to the local economy; it is absent in the development discourse of the destination state.

Now, what about the central government? The official data collection machinery, such as the Census and National Sample Survey Office contribute to the gross underestimation of migrant workers. It is these 'national statistics' that lead to the invisibility of migrant workers. It is paradoxical then, that the state, at all levels, be it the province of Bihar, the province of destination, or the centre desire to manage, control and contain migration. Plans and policy documents articulate the negative connotations attached with migration; migration is essentially bad, and it must be curbed. Albeit, there are different perspectives on other aspects of migration, there is a clear consensus of state actors on the values attached with migration, both at source and destination.

The state's perspective is one of non-acknowledgement and denial of the contributions of migrant labour at both source and destination. It is from this lens that migration is essentially viewed as a 'problem', and there is a stress on curbing migration in various policy documents. Take the Twelfth Five Year Plan, for instance. Migrant labourers are clubbed in a working group of child labourers and bonded labourers—perceived as entities to be eliminated, with no agency of their own. In a similar vein, government programmes such as the Provision of Urban Amenities in Rural Areas (PURA) aim to prevent the migration of the working populations to the urban areas. Similarly, the annual plan of the government of Bihar (2009–10) highlights that one of the main expected results of the flagship programme, MGNREGA, is to reduce out-migration from the rural areas.

Scholars have argued that it is naïve to assume that migration can be controlled (IIPA, 2010). Migration is a deeply entrenched livelihood strategy in Bihar. It is built on long-sustained social networks, as well as past migration experiences, which are accumulative in nature. Thus, schemes like MGNREGA are unable to address the structural and historical bases of most migration streams that are a way of life in Bihar.

Conclusion

We have seen that migration has played a significant role in the economic development and social change in Bihar. Migration offers livelihood options to rural households; households transfer a part of their productive labour to other rural and urban labour markets to enhance and often diversify their income. The sex and age selectivity of labour migration in Bihar implies a massive out-migration of males, especially of young men from the rural areas, while the women, children and elderly are left behind in the village. This leads to a spatial distribution of the household. It results in a bi-locational or a multi-locational household, whereby the members of the household live in different locations; the household has one foot in the village and the other outside (mostly in the city).

Migration is no longer just a pathway out of poverty, but a pathway to be connected to a modern world, to be a part of a modern life. Migration from Bihar can be classified as what Deshingkar and Grimm call, 'accumulative kinds of migration' that contributes to economic development and poverty reduction (Deshingkar and Grimm, 2005).

But, migration is not easy. The journey of migration is long and arduous. Often, it lasts a few days. Migrants contribute to the growth and development of host locations, yet face systematic exclusion from access to entitlements. Not only do migrants contribute to the growth processes at destination, but they subsidize this growth too as it is the rural economy that bears the cost of production and reproduction of labour. This is the paradox of the Bihari migrant—he is a symbol of resilience within the state, but that of hostility outside.

The core of our argument is that development is linked with more, not less mobility. It is associated with an expansion of capabilities, with increasing aspirations. In Bihar, migration has contributed to poverty reduction and to economic development. Outside Bihar, Bihari migrant labour has contributed to and subsidized the growth process, particularly in other urban destinations in the country. But, migration is precarious at every step, starting from the journey itself, in the work and in the living conditions. The exclusionary nature of migration is embedded in the very process of migration itself.

If the state (at various levels) negates the very existence of migrants, their vulnerabilities are further accentuated. The paradox of the state is its denial of migration on the one hand, and the need to manage it, on the other. It is in this paradox that migrants traverse the state; they survive in the interstices of state, its policies.

In this backdrop, there is a dire need to give visibility to migration, to migrant workers. A strong policy focus on migrants' rights and a decent work agenda is urgently required. The only legislation, the ISMW Act, 1979, needs an overhaul and laws for the protection of migrant workers need to be implemented in both letter and spirit. And this can only happen if mobility is accepted as a means of human development and migrant rights, a part of the inclusive growth paradigm.

Notes

1. I am grateful to Jesim Pais and Irudaya Rajan for their comments on an earlier version of the chapter and to the participants of the conference, Internal Migration in Contemporary India held at the Rajiv Gandhi Institute for Contemporary Studies, New Delhi on 22 and 23 February 2013.
2. Official statistics such as the Census and NSS are unable to accurately capture migration from rural Bihar. For details, see Rodgers et al. (2013).

References

Das, A.N. (1998). 'India in the image of Bihar'. *Economic and Political Weekly, 33*(49), 3103–04.

Datta, A. (2016). 'Migration from rural Bihar: Insights from a longitudinal study (1981–2011)'. In Himanshu, Praveen Jha and Gerry Rodgers (eds.), *Longitudinal research in village India: Methods and findings*. New Delhi: Oxford University Press.

———. (2014). 'Strangers in the city? Young Bihari migrants in Delhi'. Paper presented at Emotions of Migration in Asia Workshop, York University, Toronto.

Datta, A., Rodgers, G., Rodgers, J., and Singh, B.K.N. (2012). 'A tale of two villages: Contrasts in development in Bihar'. IHD Working Paper No. 5, Institute for Human Development, New Delhi.

Datta, A. and Mishra, S.K. (2011). 'Glimpses of women's lives in rural Bihar: Impact of male migration'. *The Indian Journal of Labour Economics, 54*(3), 457–77.

Datta, A., Rodgers, G., Rodgers, J., and Singh, B.K.N. (2014). 'Contrasts in development in Bihar: A tale of two villages'. *Journal of Development Studies, 50*(9), 197–208.

de Haan, A. (1997). 'Migration as family strategy: Rural-urban labor migration in India during the twentieth century'. *The History of the Family, 2*(4), 481–505.

Deshingkar, P. and Akter, S. (2009). 'Migration and human development in India'. Human Development Research Paper 2009/13. New York: UNDP.

Deshingkar, P. and Grimm, S. (2005). *Internal migration and development: A global perspective.* International Organization for Migration, Geneva.

Deshingkar, P., Kumar, S., Chobey, H.K., and Kumar, D. (2006). *The role of migration and remittances in promoting livelihoods in Bihar.* London: Overseas Development Institute.

Government of India. (2002). Report of the Second National Commission on Labour, Government of India, New Delhi.

Gupta, A. (2014). Destination Bihar. *Down to Earth.* Retrieved from http://www.downtoearth.org.in/coverage/destination-bihar-46655 (accessed on 15 January 2016).

IHD (Institute for Human Development). (2004). *Dynamics of poverty, employment and human development in Bihar.* New Delhi: Institute for Human Development.

IIPA (Indian Institute of Public Administration). (2010). *A study of Bihari migrant labourers: Incidence, causes and remedies.* New Delhi: Author.

International Organisation for Migration. (2008). *Migration, development and poverty reduction in South Asia.* Geneva: Author.

Karan, A. (2003). 'Changing patterns of migration from rural Bihar'. In G. Iyer (Ed.), *Migrant labour and human rights in India* (pp. 102–39). New Delhi: Kanishka.

Kumar, N. (2012). 'No need to migrate for work: Nitish Kumar'. Retrieved from http://ibnlive.in.com/news/no-need-to-migrate-for-work-nitish-kumar/268547-37-64.html (accessed on 16 January 2016)

Mitra, M. and Mishra, S.K. (2011). *Stolen childhoods: A study of child trafficking in the Kosi region of Bihar.* New Delhi: Save the Children.

Oberai, A.S., Prasad, P.H., and Sardana, M. (1989). *Determinants and consequences of internal migration in India: Studies in Bihar, Kerala, and Uttar Pradesh.* USA: Oxford University Press.

Pattanaik, B.K. (2009). 'Young migrant construction workers in the unorganised urban sector'. *South Asia Research, 29*(1), 19–40.

Rodgers, G., Datta, A., Rodgers, J., Mishra, S.K., and A.N. Sharma (2013). *The Challenge of Inclusive Development in Rural Bihar.* New Delhi: Institute for Human Development and Manak Publications.

Rodgers, G. and Rodgers, J. (2001). 'A leap across time: When semi-feudalism met the market in rural Purnia'. *Economic and Political Weekly, 36*(22), 1976–83.

———. (2011). 'Inclusive development? Migration, governance and social change in rural Bihar'. *Economic and Political Weekly, 46*(23), 43–50.

Rodgers, G., Datta, A., Rodgers, J., Mishra, S.K., and Sharma, A.N. (2013). *The challenge of inclusive development in rural Bihar.* New Delhi: Institute for Human Development and Manak Publications.

Sethi, Sunil (2009). 'The Crisis of Identity Proofs', *The Business Standard,* 14 November.

Sharma, A.N. (2005). 'Agrarian relations and socio-economic change in Bihar'. *Economic and Political Weekly, 40*(10), 960–72.

Singh, L., Singh, I., and Ghuman, R.S. (2007). 'Changing character of rural economy and migrant labour in Punjab'. MPRA Paper 6420, University Library of Munich, Germany.

Singh, M. (2012). 'Preference for migrant agricultural labour in Punjab'. *Economic and Political Weekly, 47*(29), 27–28.

Singh, N.K., and Stern, N. (2013). *The new Bihar, rekindling governance and development.* India: HarperCollins Publishers.

Stark, O. (1991). *The migration of labour.* Cambridge: Basil Blackwell.

The Indian Express. (2008). 'Do political movements need to obey the law? What about Advani rath yatra, Modi's Godhra outrage?' Retrieved from http://www.expressindia. com/latest-news/do-political-movements-need-to-obey-the-law-what-about-advani-rath-yatra-modis-godhra-outrage/276266/ (accessed on 16 January 2016).

The Times of India. (2012, 3 Mar). *Tamil Nadu begins enumeration of migrant labourers.* Retrieved from http://articles.timesofindia.indiatimes.com/2012-03-03/chennai/31119210_1_migrant-labourers-labour-department-migrant-workers (accessed on 16 January 2016).

———. (2012, November 21). *Tale of the Tiger.* Retrieved from http://lite.epaper.timesofindia. com/getpage.aspx?articles=yes&pageid=12&max=true&articleid=Ar01202&sectid=6 edid=&edlabel=TOIBG&mydateHid=18-11-2012&pubname=Times+of+India+-+Bangalore+-+Ek+Hi+Tha+Tiger&title=TALE+OF+THE+TIGER&edname=&pu blabel=TOI

9

Migration and Punjab: Some Perceptions

Surjit Singh

Punjab is a state in the northwest India, bordering Pakistan in the west, Jammu & Kashmir in the north, Himachal Pradesh in the northeast, Haryana in the south and southeast and Rajasthan in the southwest. It occupies merely 1.6 per cent of the total land area of the country and only 0.33 per cent of the world area (50,362 sq. km). It is the most prosperous state of India with the highest per capita income and has the distinction of having one of the lowest proportions of population living below the poverty line. Punjab is basically an agrarian economy and is endowed with abundant resources and an enthusiastic farming community. Punjab has the country's 2.6 per cent cropped area and lies between the great system of rivers Indus and Ganges. Most of the state is an alluvial plain, irrigated by canals. It has more than 4 million hectares of well-irrigated land, with cropping intensity of 186 per cent. Over 95 per cent of food grains that are moved interstate to feed deficit areas through the Public Distribution System (PDS) are the stocks produced from this state. The Gross State Domestic Product (GSDP) of Punjab during last few years has grown over 6 per cent.[1] Uneven development across states, whether in terms of economy or culture, creates movement of people and is the main reason for migration[2] along with factors like poverty, landholding system, fragmentation of holdings, lack of employment opportunities, large family-size and natural calamities. The high land–man ratio, caste system, lawlessness and exploitation at native places speed up the breakdown of traditional socio-economic relations in the rural economy and people decide to migrate to relatively prosperous regions in search of better employment and income. Besides, diversification of economy and increased land productivity in certain areas, rapid improvement in transport and communication means, improvement in education, increase in population pressure and zeal for improving living add momentum to the mobility of population. In this regard, Bihar and Punjab are two extremes of socio-economic index; Punjab stands at the top and Bihar touches the bottom. Primarily because of this, Punjab supplies agricultural produce to the rest of the country and Bihar supplies labour. The Marxists call this 'enclave hinterland relation' that is not merely economic, but social too.[3] This chapter looks at the migration issues in the context of Punjab. It deals with both internal and external migration in Punjab.

Demographic Changes in Punjab

Table 9.1 presents decadal changes in population of Punjab. In the recent past, the population has been growing at a rate of more than 2 per cent per annum; the highest growth was observed during 1971–81 and the lowest during 1991–2001. However, rural population growth has been below 2 per cent since 1961–71 and has stood at 1.23 per cent during 1991–2001. On the other hand urban growth has been high, ranging between 4.451 per cent during 1971–81 and 2.527 per cent during 1961–71.

Table 9.1

Decadal change in population: Punjab

Periods	Total	Rural	Urban
1901–11	−10.78	−10.46	−13.00
1911–21	6.26	6.17	6.92
1921–31	12.02	8.92	34.37
1931–41	19.82	16.06	41.85
1941–51	4.58	−9.71	20.02
1951–61	21.56	19.47	29.06
1961–71	21.70	20.63	25.27
1971–81	23.89	17.48	44.51
1981–91	20.81	17.69	28.95
1991–01	19.76	12.28	37.58

The urban population growth throughout has been higher than the rural population growth, indicating increasing urbanization.

Why People Move

Migration is not new to the human race. Individuals driven by adventure, hope, desperation, searching for the ideal place to work and live have always travelled the world over (Singh, 2000). The main driving force behind migration is a better standard of living away from home. The decision to move is complex; it is not a simple rational choice by individuals seeking to maximize incomes. It is a decision rooted in social relations and influenced by history, culture and policy regimes as researches have shown amply. The push-and-pull analysis is a too simple way to explain new pushes and pulls that people living in marginal areas of India are facing today. Surplus labour arising from the scarcity of cultivated land, inequitable land distribution, low agricultural productivity, high population density and the concentration of the rural economy almost exclusively on agriculture has contributed to a continuous increase in out-migration. In an agrarian society, with little access to land leaves the landless and marginal farmers with few alternatives to migration. We have more than 80 per cent of holdings that are small and marginal and per capita net sown area is below 0.2 hectare. Droughts and poor mountain and forest economies are the other push factors. The dry areas of Bihar, ecological fragile lands of Uttarakhand with little diversification and deteriorating access to common property resources lead to out-migration. There is a positive relation between degradation and out-migration. Migration is also due to distress phenomenon (Reddy, 1990). Singh and Karan (2001) for Bihar find that remittances accounted for one-third of the average annual income of landless and marginal households sending migrants. Migration worsens poverty because migrant households are often in debt. However, this relation is not straightforward. Debt incurred is also due to high transit cost and higher cost of living at the destination, but migration also improves creditworthiness of the households and they are able to borrow more because of that. The Human Development Report of Punjab notes that many migrants are Dalits and tribals.

Punjab has historically been associated with tremendous population movements both national and international. It became the pioneer in Green revolution in 1960s and with it, the scope for the industrial development increased and created the need for strengthening infrastructure facilities. With the dominant pattern of rural to urban migration within Punjab and inflow of migrant labour from other backward states, there was a simultaneous increase in out-migration of Punjabi workers to other developed countries for still better economic prospects. A major proportion of the migrant labour force working in the industrial sector of Punjab hails from Uttar Pradesh and Bihar. These migrants are attached to Punjab because of better employment opportunities, higher wages, lower economic and social exploitation and the near absence of caste oppression. Migrants are not only employed in the agricultural and the industrial sectors, but also in other occupations such as building and road construction, brick-making, rickshaw pulling and so on.

Economic history of the world, however, shows that human migration is the natural manifestation of socio-economic and technological growth/ development. The normal course of migration is that it takes place from relatively less developed to high-developed regions/countries. The in-migration to Punjab, from other states of India, especially, from Uttar Pradesh and Bihar should be viewed in this context. The incidence of rural poverty in Bihar and Uttar Pradesh in 1993–94 was 58.2 and 42.3 per cent, respectively, which is higher than the national average (37.3 per cent). The corresponding poverty incidence was 42.1 and 33.4 per cent in 2004–05 in Bihar and Uttar Pradesh respectively. In Punjab, the proportion of rural people living below the poverty line was 9.2 per cent during 2004–05 (Table 9.2). Thus, Punjab is economically better off than Bihar

Table 9.2

Some features

Items	Uttar Pradesh	Bihar	Punjab
Gross irrigated area as % to GCA (2007–08)	76.17	60.56	97.70
Demography and Employment			
Urbanization (2001)	20.8	10.5	34.0
% of agricultural labour to total working force (2001)	65.9	77.3	39.0
Statutory minimum wages of agricultural labourers (2008–09)	115.9	89.0	104.3
% of population below poverty line (2004–05) (rural)	42.7	55.7	22.1

Source: CMIE.

and Uttar Pradesh. And it is, thus, the obvious reason for the migration of these poor rural migrants to Punjab (Government of India, 2008).

Migration Status

Punjab is one of the agriculturally most advanced states of India. Since mid-1960s, with the evolution of high yielding varieties (HYVs) of crops and the adoption of modern and improved farm practices, agriculture in the state witnessed an unprecedented growth. With the increase in cropping intensity and farm output along with shift of cropping pattern towards labour intensive crops, like paddy, during the late 1970s, the state witnessed manifold increase in demand for farm labour. As sufficient local labour was not available, farmers of the state had to depend on the migratory labour for various agricultural operations, especially during peak seasons (Sidhu et al., 1997). There were other factors too that compelled labour movement from eastern India into Punjab, like incidence of floods, droughts, non-availability of jobs, poverty and indebtedness back home (Gupta, 1991; Gupta and Bhakoo, 1980). Punjab, thus, has been a favourite destination for a long time, first for jobs in agriculture and recently for industrial jobs. The Human Development Report of Punjab identifies migration streams into the state from the poor areas of all north-western states as well as eastern and central states. Wage rates are double than that in Bihar and Uttar Pradesh. Agriculture attracted 700,000 (mainly seasonal) migrants each year in the 1990s but other sectors attracted a further 14 lakh migrant workers. In the early 1980s, 40 per cent of the workers in the unorganized hosiery sector were migrants. Numbers have increased steadily since the 1970s. Migrant workers also form a large proportion of the workers in the 22 sugar mills in the state. The transport sector, like rickshaw-pulling is now largely the domain of this labour in all the cities.

Migration Inflow in Punjab

The dramatic improvement in agricultural productivity, with the advent of green revolution resulted in the increase in per capita income. The successful and sustained agricultural transformation widened the gap in per capita income between Punjab and other states, especially in the eastern and western India (Ghuman, Brar, and Singh, 2007). This created a route of migration for poor people from rural areas of these regions into Punjab. The total migrants reported in the Census 1981 were of the order of 822,377 persons. This increased to 1,126,149 persons in 1991 and then to 1,752,718 in 2001 (Table 9.3). The annual growth of migrants in Punjab during the period 1981 to 1991 was of the order of 2.59 per cent. The inflow of migrants increased sharply during the decade of 1991 to 2001. The rise in the flow of migrants in Punjab during the period 1991–2001 was quite sharp. The annual rate of growth comes out to be 4.52 per cent, which is higher than the previous decade. The compound growth rate of migrant inflows to Punjab was 3.55 per cent per annum during the period 1981 to 2001. The overall growth rate is higher than the first decade that is 1981 to 1991 compared with the 1991 to 2001. This implies that the migrant flow to Punjab was higher in the decade of 1991 to 2001 than that of the 1981 to 1991. However, similar trends occurred so far as the growth rates of migrants coming from other important states are concerned.

Table 9.3 shows an important fact that the growth rate of migrant inflows from Bihar was the highest compared to other major states. There

Table 9.3

Trend in migration in Punjab

State/Year	Census Years						Growth Rate (%/Annum)		
	1981	%	1991	%	2001	%	1981–91	1991–2001	1981–2001
Bihar	50,235	6.43	90,732	9.20	267,409	17.01	6.09	11.42	8.72
Haryana	248,043	31.74	298,192	30.41	361,766	23.02	1.85	1.95	1.90
HP	112,289	14.37	136,134	13.80	165,158	10.51	1.94	1.95	1.94
Rajasthan	91,879	11.76	110,853	11.24	136,168	8.66	1.90	2.08	1.99
UP	220,216	28.18	280,350	28.42	517,351	32.92	2.44	6.32	4.36
MP	15,556	1.99	15,717	1.58	30,559	1.95	0.10	6.87	3.43
West Bengal	12,970	1.66	18,635	1.89	45,902	2.92	3.69	9.43	6.52
J&K	30,223	3.87	36,108	3.66	47,349	3.01	1.80	2.75	2.27
Total of eight states	781,411	95.02	986,621	87.61	1,571,662	89.67	2.36	4.77	3.56
Total	822,377	100	1126,149	100	1,752,718	100	2.59	4.52	3.55

Source: Government of India, Population Census (various years).

was a sharp rise in the migrant inflows from Bihar to Punjab. Comparing the structure of migrant inflows, Haryana tops in **1981** sending 31.74 per cent of migrants to Punjab. Uttar Pradesh with 28.2 per cent followed it. Himachal Pradesh and Rajasthan, the two other neighbouring states, sent 14.4 and 11.8 per cent migrants, respectively to Punjab. Bihar ranked 5th so far as migrant inflow to Punjab was concerned in 1981. The eight major sending states accounted for 95.02 per cent of migrant inflows to Punjab in **1981**. In **1991**, Haryana was still at the top by sending 30.41 per cent of migrants to Punjab. Uttar Pradesh with 28.42 per cent followed it. Himachal Pradesh and Rajasthan, the two other neighbouring states, sent in 13.8 and 11.24 per cent migrants, respectively into Punjab. Bihar again ranked 5th so far as migrant inflow to Punjab was concerned in 1991. The percentage from the eight major sending states came down to 87.61 per cent of migrant inflows to Punjab in 1991. In **2001**, Haryana sent the second highest percentage of migrants to Punjab (23.02 per cent) as Uttar Pradesh topped by sending 32.92 per cent of migrants. Migration from Bihar increased as it ranked 3rd in 2001 with 17.01 per cent migrants. Himachal Pradesh and Rajasthan sent in 10.51 and 8.66 per cent migrants, respectively into Punjab. The eight major sending states accounted for 89.67 per cent of migrant inflows to Punjab in 2001. Thus, Bihar enhanced its stakes in migrants to Punjab and the other states, Haryana, Rajasthan and Himachal Pradesh reduced their contribution as these states developed and the nature of employment changed too.

Urban Migration

Table 9.4 shows an important fact that the growth rate of urban migrant inflows from Bihar was the highest compared to other major states. There was a sharp rise in the migrant inflows from Bihar to Punjab. Comparing the structure of urban migrant inflows, Uttar Pradesh topped in 1981 sending 38.02 per cent of migrants to urban Punjab. Haryana with 25 per cent followed it. Himachal Pradesh and Rajasthan sent in 14.44 and 9.37 per cent migrants respectively into urban Punjab. Bihar ranked 5th so far as migrant inflow to urban Punjab was concerned in **1981**. In **1991**, Uttar Pradesh again topped by sending 38.49 per cent of migrants to urban Punjab followed by Haryana with 21.92 per cent. Himachal Pradesh and Rajasthan sent in 13.2 and 8.5 per cent migrants, respectively into urban Punjab. Bihar moved one position up by ranking 4th so far as migrant

Table 9.4

Trend in urban migration in Punjab

State/Year	1981	%	1991	%	2001	%	1981– 91	1991– 2001	1981– 2001
			Census Years					Growth Rate (%/Annum)	
Bihar	26,039	6.41	58,348	10.88	184,992	19.42	8.40	12.23	10.30
Haryana	101,607	24.99	117,582	21.92	162,931	17.10	1.47	3.32	2.39
HP	58,719	14.44	70,812	13.20	93,063	9.77	1.89	2.77	2.33
Rajasthan	38,092	9.37	45,603	8.50	59,632	6.26	1.82	2.72	2.27
UP	154,568	38.02	206,480	38.49	381,625	40.05	2.94	6.39	4.62
MP	6,125	1.51	9,537	1.78	16,749	1.76	4.53	5.79	5.16
West Bengal	6,297	1.55	10,255	1.91	30,553	3.21	5.00	11.53	8.22
J&K	15,092	3.71	17,822	3.32	23,265	2.44	1.68	2.70	2.19
Total	406,539		536,439		952,810		2.81	5.91	4.35

Source: Government of India, Population Census (various years).

inflow to urban Punjab was concerned in 1991. In **2001**, Uttar Pradesh still sent the highest number of migrants with a share of 40.1 per cent of migrants to urban Punjab. Haryana with 17.1 per cent was followed by Bihar which ranked 3rd so far as migrant inflow to urban Punjab was concerned in 2001 with 19.42 per cent migrants. Himachal Pradesh and Rajasthan sent in 9.77 and 6.26 per cent migrants, respectively into urban Punjab. Thus, Bihar enhanced its stakes in migrants to urban Punjab and Haryana, Rajasthan and Himachal Pradesh reduced their contribution. Bihar observed growth of 8.40, 12.23 and 10.3 per cent respectively during 1981–91, 1991–2001 and 1981–2001. West Bengal also has emerged as one of the states sourcing migrants to Punjab and most of the migrants are from Cooch Bihar district.

Rural Migration

Table 9.5 shows an important fact that the growth rate of rural migrant inflows from Bihar was the highest compared to other major states. There was a sharp rise in the migrant inflows from Bihar to rural Punjab. Comparing the structure of rural migrant inflows, Haryana tops in **1981**

Table 9.5

Trend in rural migration in Punjab

State/Year	Census Years						Growth Rate (%/Annum)		
	1981	%	1991	%	2001	%	1981–91	1991–2001	1981–2001
Bihar	24,196	6.45	32,375	7.19	8,2417	13.32	2.95	9.79	6.52
Haryana	146,436	39.06	180,519	40.10	198,935	32.15	2.11	0.97	1.54
HP	53,570	14.29	65,322	14.51	72,095	11.65	2.00	0.99	1.50
Rajasthan	53,787	14.35	65,250	14.49	76,536	12.37	1.95	1.61	1.78
UP	65,648	17.51	738,701	16.41	135,726	21.93	1.19	6.62	3.70
MP	9,431	2.52	6,181	1.37	13,810	2.23	−4.14	8.37	1.92
West Bengal	6,673	1.78	8,380	1.86	15,349	2.48	2.30	6.24	4.25
J&K	15,131	4.04	182,86	4.07	24,084	3.87	19.91	2.79	2.35
Total of eight states	374,872	92.64	450,182	90.52	618,852	93.13	1.85	3.23	2.54
Total	404,657	1,000	497,312	100	664,468	100	2.08	2.94	2.51

Source: Government of India, Population Census (various years).

sending 39.1 per cent of migrants to rural Punjab followed by Uttar Pradesh with 17.51 per cent migrants. Himachal Pradesh and Rajasthan sent in 14.29 and 14.35 per cent migrants, respectively into rural Punjab. Bihar ranked 5th so far as migrant inflow to rural Punjab was concerned in **1981**. In **1991**, Haryana topped in sending 40.1 per cent of migrants to rural Punjab. Uttar Pradesh with 16.41 per cent followed it. Himachal Pradesh and Rajasthan, the two other neighbouring states, sent in 14.51 and 14.50 per cent migrants, respectively into rural Punjab. Bihar ranked 5th so far as migrant inflow to Punjab was concerned in 1991. In **2001**, Haryana tops in sending 32.15 per cent of migrants to rural Punjab. Uttar Pradesh with 21.93 per cent followed it. Bihar again ranked 3rd so far as migrant inflow to rural Punjab was concerned in 2001 with 13.32 per cent migrants. Himachal Pradesh and Rajasthan sent in 11.65 and 12.37 per cent migrants, respectively into rural Punjab. Thus, Bihar and Uttar Pradesh enhanced their stakes in migrants to rural Punjab and other states Haryana, Rajasthan and Himachal Pradesh reduced their contribution. Bihar observed growth of 2.95, 9.79 and 6.53 per cent respectively during 1981–91, 1991–2001 and 1981–2001. West Bengal gained in growth during 1991–2001 (6.24 per cent from 2.3 per cent). The gainer is Madhya Pradesh during the nineties compared to the eighties significantly. Thus, sources of rural in-migration to Punjab have been changing during the last two decades (till 2001).

It may be pointed out here that Rajasthan and Himachal Pradesh, though important sources for rural in-migration, do not send migrants for agricultural purposes. Himachal Pradesh migrants are in service sector as cooks mainly and in lower jobs in irrigation and such related activities. Rajasthan is famous for sending labour for brick kilns and West Bengal migrants mainly work in urban areas as domestic workers and rickshaw/ cycle cart pullers in cities. Thus, who works where is also determined by what they do back home. It is culturally determined too.

Table 9.6 reveals the major internal migration streams, especially of duration 0–9 years. If we consider rural–rural stream of internal migration is dominated by Bihar and West Bengal is at the bottom of top 10 states. Considering rural–urban stream, Mizoram tops with 39.1 per cent and at the bottom is J&K with 21.1 per cent. In case of urban–rural migration

Table 9.6

Migration streams for top ten states for intrastate migration by last residence (duration 0–9 years) in India: 2001

Rank	Rural–Rural	Rural–Urban	Urban–Rural	Urban–Urban
1	Bihar (79.9%)	Mizoram (39.1%)	Goa (26.7%)	Tamil Nadu (27.4%)
2	Jharkhand (75.8%)	Meghalaya (27.4%)	Kerala (13.3%)	Mizoram (25.5%)
3	Assam (73.0%)	Nagaland (26.8%)	Nagaland (13.2%)	Goa (21.9%)
4	Himachal Pradesh (71.8%)	Arunachal Pradesh (25.9%)	Sikkim (11.8%)	Nagaland (20.3%)
5	Sikkim (70.8%)	Gujarat (25.9%)	Tamil Nadu (11.5%)	Maharashtra (19.2%)
6	Uttar Pradesh (69.8%)	Tamil Nadu (23.3%)	Meghalaya (11.0%)	**Punjab (15.5%)**
7	Rajasthan (69.7%)	Haryana (21.9%)	Mizoram (8.5%)	Karnataka (15.3%)
8	Chhattisgarh (69.2%)	Maharashtra (21.2%)	Andhra Pradesh (8.4%)	Gujarat (14.6%)
9	Orissa (67.5%)	Karnataka (21.2%)	Maharashtra (8.2%)	Arunachal Pradesh (12.9%)
10	West Bengal (66.5%)	J&K (21.1%)	Karnataka (7.4%)	Manipur (12.5%)

Source: Census of India, 2001.

stream, Goa tops with 26.7 per cent of intrastate migrants (could be due to various reasons such as retirement, illness or returning to the parental home and other factors could be better communication to commuters from adjacent areas to urban centres for work) and Karnataka is at the bottom with 7.4 per cent among the top 10 states. As regards the urban to urban internal migration, Tamil Nadu tops with 27.4 per cent and Manipur is at the bottom with 12.5 per cent. In all, these streams of internal migration, Punjab figures in urban to urban stream only with 15.5 per cent figure and ranks 6th among the top ten states.

Migration by workers is mostly a well-considered economic decision and not a random one, a rational and not a rash move. The process of migration being a selective process, it often results from imbalances of economic change and chances. Punjab had a total population of 20,281,969 in 1991 and in-migrants from other states stood at 811,060 while the out-migrants were 501,285. This gave a figure of 336,636 net in-migrants in 2001. The migration rate (per 100) during 1991–2001 was 1.7. In contrast, in case of Bihar, the corresponding figures were 460,782, 2,241,413 and –1,722,907.

Punjab is a state with an interesting migration profile (Table 9.7). Though the total number of migrants from outside the state and outside the country is 8.1 lakh and 0.27 lakh, respectively, there is significant out-migration from the state (5 lakh). The number of male out-migrants is less than female out-migrants. As a result, the net migrants into Punjab are only 3.3 lakh, the sex ratio stacked highly in favour of males (313 females per 1000 males). States from where sizeable number of in-migrants came to Punjab are: Uttar Pradesh (2.42 lakh—28.9 per cent), Bihar (1.49 lakh—17.83 per cent) and Haryana (1.14 lakh—13.61 per cent).

The two other neighbouring states, namely, Himachal Pradesh and Rajasthan had sent in 6.66 and 6.17 per cent migrants to Punjab in 2001, while 3.21 per cent came from other states. In case of male in-migrants Uttar Pradesh had sent in 33.68 per cent, Bihar had sent in 25.0 per cent and Haryana sent in 6.84 per cent. The two other neighbouring states, namely, Himachal Pradesh and Rajasthan had sent in 4.95 and 4.15 per cent migrants to Punjab in 2001, while 3.87 per cent came from other countries. As regards the female in-migrants, Uttar Pradesh had sent in 23.02 per cent, Haryana sent in 21.87 per cent and Bihar sent in 9.08 per cent. The two other neighbouring states, namely Himachal Pradesh and Rajasthan had sent in 8.74 and 8.64 per cent migrants to Punjab in 2001, while 2.39 per cent came from other states. Thus, there is gender differential in in-migration from the same source state.

Table 9.7

Migration profile (0–9 years) Punjab: 2001

Migrants	Total			Rural			Urban		
	Persons	Males	Females	Persons	Males	Females	Persons	Males	Females
Total Population	24,358,999	12,985,045	11,373,954	1,609,6488	8,516,596	7,579,892	8,262,511	4,468,449	3,794,062
From within the state	1,712,627	397,678	1,314,949	1,134,471	180,486	953,985	578,156	217,192	360,964
Total in-migrants from outside	837,921	460,497	377,424	309,791	146,412	163,379	528,130	314,085	214,045
From other states- Total	811,060	442,664	368,396	300,208	140,002	160,206	510,852	302,662	208,190
Rural	571,036	331,376	239,660	247,152	116,775	130,377	323,884	214,601	109,283
Urban	221,768	101,328	120,440	46,647	19,967	26,680	175,121	81,361	93,760
Uttar Pradesh	241,987	155,103	86,884	72,777	43,607	29,170	169,210	111,496	57,714
Haryana	114,031	31,482	82,549	60,167	11,542	48,625	53,864	11,940	33,924
Bihar	149,375	115,102	34,273	46,317	36,039	10,278	103,058	79,063	23,995
Himachal Pradesh	55,795	22,808	32,987	24,756	7248	17,508	31,039	15,560	15,479
Rajasthan	51,710	19,092	32,618	29,850	9874	19,976	21,860	9218	12,642
From other countries	26,861	17,833	9,028	9,583	6,410	3,173	17,278	11,423	5,855
Total out-migrants	501,285	204,152	297,133	262,476	98,509	163,967	224,644	99,087	125,557
Net migrants	336,636	256,345	80,291	47,315	47,903	-588	303,486	214,998	88,488

(Table 9.7 Continued)

(Table 9.7 Continued)

Migrants	Total			Rural			Urban		
	Persons	Males	Females	Persons	Males	Females	Persons	Males	Females
Distribution of in-migrants (%)									
Total in-migrants from outside	837,921	460,497	377,424	309,791	146,412	163,379	528,130	314,085	214,045
From other states- Total	96.79	96.13	97.61	96.91	95.62	98.06	96.73	96.36	97.26
Rural	68.15	71.96	63.50	79.78	79.76	79.80	61.33	68.33	51.06
Urban	26.47	22.00	31.91	15.06	13.64	16.33	33.16	25.90	43.80
Uttar Pradesh	28.88	33.68	23.02	23.49	29.78	17.85	32.04	35.50	26.96
Haryana	13.61	6.84	21.87	19.42	7.88	29.76	10.20	3.80	15.85
Bihar	17.83	25.00	9.08	14.95	24.61	6.29	19.51	25.17	11.21
Himachal Pradesh	6.66	4.95	8.74	7.99	4.95	10.72	5.88	4.95	7.23
Rajasthan	6.17	4.15	8.64	9.64	6.74	12.23	4.14	2.93	5.91
From other countries	3.21	3.87	2.39	3.09	4.38	1.94	3.27	3.64	2.74

Source: Census of India, Migration Tables, 2001.

Reasons for Migration

Census also enquires about why people migrate, but lists only six reasons. Table 9.8 shows that the reasons for migration in case of males and females vary significantly (migration duration 0–9 years). At aggregate level, 40 per cent of migrants moved in because of employment/work into Punjab,

Table 9.8

Reasons for migration in Punjab: 2001

Reasons	Migrants (Duration 0–9 Years)			Per cent Migrants		
	Persons	Males	Females	Persons	Males	Females
All States	811,060	442,664	368,396	100.0	100.0	100.0
Work/employment	323,688	290,938	32,750	**39.9**	**65.7**	8.9
Business	5,306	3,769	1,537	0.7	0.9	0.4
Education	8,933	5,874	3,059	1.1	1.3	0.8
Marriage	160,193	2,264	157,929	19.8	0.5	**42.9**
Moved after birth	21,405	11,866	9,539	2.6	2.7	2.6
Moved with HHs	225,057	88,499	136,558	27.7	20.0	37.1
Others	66,478	39,454	27,024	8.2	8.9	7.3
Uttar Pradesh	241,987	155,103	86,884	100.0	100.0	100.0
Work/employment	125,309	111,873	13,436	**51.8**	**72.1**	15.5
Business	1,479	1,125	354	0.6	0.7	0.4
Education	1,364	955	409	0.6	0.6	0.5
Marriage	22,043	451	21,592	9.1	0.3	24.9
Moved after birth	3,803	2,093	1,710	1.6	1.3	2.0
Moved with HHs	68,251	26,526	41,725	28.2	17.1	**48.0**
Others	19,738	12,080	7,658	8.2	7.8	8.8
Haryana	114,031	31,482	82,549	100.0	100.0	100.0
Work/employment	14,757	12,458	2,299	12.9	**39.6**	2.8
Business	662	406	256	0.6	1.3	0.3
Education	1,509	937	572	1.3	3.0	0.7
Marriage	59,651	649	59,002	**52.3**	2.1	**71.5**
Moved after birth	5,658	3,186	2,472	5.0	10.1	3.0

(Table 9.8 Continued)

(Table 9.8 Continued)

Reasons	Migrants (Duration 0–9 Years)			Per cent Migrants		
	Persons	Males	Females	Persons	Males	Females
Moved with HHs	23,662	9,645	14,017	20.8	30.6	17.0
Others	8,132	4,201	3,931	7.1	13.3	4.8
Bihar	149,375	115,102	34,273	100.0	100.0	100.0
Work/employment	99,642	94,631	5,011	**66.7**	**82.2**	14.6
Business	771	627	144	0.5	0.5	0.4
Education	580	468	112	0.4	0.4	0.3
Marriage	8,476	291	8,185	5.7	0.3	23.9
Moved after birth	1,486	803	683	1.0	0.7	2.0
Moved with HHs	27,835	10,772	17,063	18.6	9.4	**49.8**
Others	10,585	7,510	3,075	7.1	6.5	9.0
West Bengal	25,484	15,847	9,637	100.0	100.0	100.0
Work/employment	12,018	11,227	791	**47.2**	**70.8**	8.2
Business	174	133	41	0.7	0.8	0.4
Education	313	255	58	1.2	1.6	0.6
Marriage	2,961	52	2,909	11.6	0.3	30.2
Moved after birth	382	209	173	1.5	1.3	1.8
Moved with HHs	7,622	2,706	4,916	29.9	17.1	**51.0**
Others	2,014	1,265	749	7.9	8.0	7.8
Assam	5,774	2,660	3,114	100.0	100.0	100.0
Work/employment	1,165	1,043	122	20.2	39.2	3.9
Business	32	19	13	0.6	0.7	0.4
Education	112	64	48	1.9	2.4	1.5
Marriage	656	12	644	11.4	0.5	20.7
Moved after birth	77	35	42	1.3	1.3	1.3
Moved with HHs	3,211	1,181	2,030	**55.6**	**44.4**	**65.2**
Others	521	306	215	9.0	11.5	6.9

Sources: Tables D1, D2 and D3, Census of India 2001.

In case of female in-migrants across states, marriage dominates as the major reason for migration with Haryana at the top (71.5 per cent), followed by West Bengal (30.2 per cent), Uttar Pradesh (25 per cent), Bihar (24 per cent) and Assam (20.7 per cent). The other reason why female in-migrants moved into Punjab is moving with the household: Assam 65.2 per cent, West Bengal 51.0 per cent, Bihar 49.8 per cent, Uttar Pradesh 48.0 per cent and Haryana 17.0 per cent. As regards in-migration of females into Punjab due to work/employment is concerned the percentages are: Uttar Pradesh 15.5 per cent, Bihar 14.6 per cent, West Bengal 8.2 per cent, Assam 3.9 per cent and Haryana 2.8 per cent. Thus, the reasons why females moved into Punjab are largely different from male migrants.

65.7 per cent males did so compared to mere 8.9 per cent females. Among male migrants, the second most important reason is moved with the household (27.7 per cent) followed by marriage (19.8 per cent) while in case of female migrants, marriage is the most important reason (42.9 per cent) followed by moved with the household (37.1 per cent). For male in-migrants from Uttar Pradesh, employment/work is the most important reason (72.1 per cent) compared to 82.2 per cent male in-migrants from Bihar cited work/employment as the main reason for migration. These proportions are 70.8 per cent males from West Bengal, 39.6 per cent from Haryana and 39.2 per cent from Assam. In case of Bihar, 9.4 per cent male migrants moved with the household compared to 17.1 per cent in case of West Bengal migrants, 44.4 per cent from Assam, 30.6 per cent from Haryana. There are 10 per cent migrants from Haryana who migrated because they moved after birth.

Recent Evidence on Migration

In India, as per the NSSO survey of 2007–08, there were 33.4 per cent of migrants compared to 28.5 per cent of migrants (Table 9.9). The estimated

Table 9.9

Proportion of migrants (per 1,000)

Migrants	Punjab	India	Punjab Migrants (00)	India Migrants (00)	% Share in Total Migrants, Punjab	% Share in Total Migrants, India
Rural Male	74	54	6,104	206,186	7.66	7.16
Rural Female	571	477	43,658	1,731,934	54.76	60.17
Rural male + female	312	261	49,762	1,938,120	**62.42**	**67.33**
Urban Male	223	259	9,571	357,044	12.00	12.40
Urban Female	565	456	20,393	583,225	25.58	20.26
Urban male + female	379	354	29,964	940,269	**37.58**	**32.67**
Rural + urban male	124	109	15,675	563,229	19.66	19.57
Rural + urban female	569	472	64,051	2,315,160	80.34	80.43
All	334	285	79,726	2,878,389	100	100

Sources: NSSO, *Migration in India: 2007–08,* 64th round (July 2007–June 2008), NSS report No. 533 (64/10.2/2).

number of migrants was 79.73 lakh persons in Punjab. Further, 31.2 per cent of the persons were rural migrants compared to 37.9 per cent of urban migrants. A higher percentage of urban males were migrants compared to rural male migrants in Punjab, though a slightly higher percentage of rural females were migrants compared to urban female migrants. Finally, a higher percentage of females were migrants as compared to male migrants. An estimated 80.34 per cent migrants in Punjab were females while this proportion was marginally higher at 80.43 per cent in India. Also 62.42 per cent migrants are from rural areas in Punjab, which is lower than the national proportion of 67.33 per cent. Thus, there are significant rural–urban and male–female differentials in migrants.

Educational Base of Migrants

It is found that 39.0 per cent migrants are not literates in Punjab while in India this proportion was 44.8 per cent (Table 9.10). About 7.6 per cent migrants were literate but below primary pass, 24 per cent were primary or middle class educated, 21 per cent were secondary/higher secondary pass and only 7.5 per cent migrants were with educational level 'graduate and above'. Thus, in Punjab, a much greater proportion of migrants were with educational level of secondary/higher secondary or below and about 47 per cent are below primary educated. In case of male migrants in Punjab,

Table 9.10

Distribution (per 1,000) of migrants by educational level

	Punjab	India	Punjab	India	Punjab	India
	Rural Male		**Rural Female**		**Rural Persons**	
Not Literate	258	233	502	592	472	554
Literate but below primary	120	156	61	95	68	102
Primary or middle	200	333	253	225	246	236
Secondary/HS	344	187	157	71	180	84
Diploma/certificate	23	24	4	3	6	5
Graduate +	55	66	24	13	28	19
All	1,000	1,000	1,000	1,000	1,000	1,000
Estimated migrants (00)	6,104	206,186	43,658	1,731,934	49,762	1,938,120

(Table 9.10 Continued)

(Table 9.10 Continued)

	Punjab	India	Punjab	India	Punjab	India
	Urban Male		**Urban Female**		**Urban Persons**	
Not Literate	211	117	274	298	254	230
Literate but below primary	179	100	48	89	90	93
Primary or middle	246	289	221	279	229	283
Secondary/HS	213	265	283	211	261	231
Diploma/certificate	12	39	12	12	12	22
Graduate +	136	189	162	110	154	140
All	1,000	1,000	1,000	1,000	1,000	1,000
Estimated migrants (00)	9,571	357,044	20,393	583,225	29,964	940,269
All	**All Male**		**All Female**		**All Rural+Urban**	
Not Literate	230	160	429	518	390	448
Literate but below primary	156	121	57	94	76	99
Primary or middle	228	305	243	238	240	251
Secondary/HS	264	236	197	107	210	132
Diploma/certificate	16	33	6	6	8	11
Graduate +	104	144	68	37	75	58
All	1,000	1,000	1,000	1,000	1,000	1,000
Estimated migrants (00)	15,675	563,229	64,051	2,315,160	79,726	2,878,389

Sources: NSSO *Migration in India:* 2007–08 64th round (July 2007–June 2008), NSS report No. 533 (64/10.2/2).

23.0 per cent migrants are not literates while in India this proportion was 16.0 per cent. About 15.6 per cent migrants were literate but below primary pass, 22.8 per cent were primary or middle class educated, 26.4 per cent were secondary/higher secondary pass and only 10.4 per cent migrants were with educational level 'graduate and above'. Thus, in Punjab, a much greater proportion of male migrants were with educational level of secondary/higher secondary or below and about 39 per cent had below primary level education.

In case of female migrants in Punjab, 42.9 per cent migrants are not literates while in India this proportion was 51.8 per cent. About 5.7 per cent migrants were literate but below primary pass, 24.3 per cent were primary or middle class educated, 19.7 per cent were secondary/higher secondary pass and only 6.8 per cent migrants were with educational level 'graduate and above'. Thus, in Punjab, a much greater proportion of male migrants were with educational level of secondary/higher secondary or below and about 48 per cent had below primary level education.

Almost 47.2 per cent of rural Punjab migrants are not literate and 6.8 per cent are literate but below primary pass. However, one fourth of the rural migrants are primary/middle pass with another 18 per cent having educational level 'secondary/higher secondary. Just 2.8 per cent have educational level 'graduate or above'. It is further observed that a greater percentage of rural female migrants are not literates; almost double the proportion. However, rural female migrants have less higher level of educational qualifications. It is also found that a higher proportion of urban female migrants have higher educational qualification compare to urban male counterparts.

Migration Rate

The migration rate (proportion of migrants in the population) in the urban areas (35.4 per cent) was higher than the migration rate in the rural areas (26.1 per cent) in India while the corresponding rates were 37.9 and 31.2 per cent (Table 9.11). At the aggregate level the migration rate in Punjab was 33.4 per cent compared to national migration rate of 25.5 per cent. Magnitude of male migration rate was far lower than female migration rate, in both rural and urban areas in India and Punjab. However, the difference in rural male–female migration rates in Punjab is much greater compared to that in the urban areas.

Migration rate is found to be lowest for bottom monthly per capita expenditure (MPCE) two deciles in both rural and urban Punjab (26.1 per cent and 31.6 per cent respectively). There is an increasing trend in rate

Table 9.11

Migration rate (per 1,000 persons)

	Rural		Urban			
Rural	*Punjab*	*India*	*Punjab*	*India*	*Rural + Urban*	
Male	74	54	223	259	124	109
Female	571	477	565	456	569	472
Both	312	261	379	354	334	285

Source: NSSO *Migration in India: 2007–08.*

of migration with the increase in level of living, with the migration rate attaining peak in the top two decile classes in both rural and urban areas (Table 9.12). Further, migration rate for rural male for the bottom two deciles was 4 per cent while it was 16.8 per cent in case of urban males. In case of rural females, migration rate was high at 46.6 per cent when it was even higher for urban females at 50 per cent. On the other side, the migration rate for rural males for top two deciles was almost half the urban male migrants (13.5 per cent and 26.7 per cent respectively). Even at the aggregate level, the migration rate of rural males was three times lesser than the urban males (7.4 per cent and 22.3 per cent respectively). On the other hand, migration rate for rural females was slightly higher than urban females' migration rate. Thus, migration rates of females in both rural and urban areas are much higher than male migration rates across the MPCE deciles, which mean more women, migrate than men. This is primarily because of two causes, marriage and movement because of parents/earning member moving from usual place of residence.

Table 9.12

Migration rate (per 1,000 persons) in different MPCE quintile class: Punjab

MPCE Quintile Class/Migration Rate	Rural Male	Rural Female	Rural All	Urban Male	Urban Female	Urban All
0–20	40	466	261	168	499	316
20–40	61	570	296	172	561	346
40–60	41	580	292	250	553	387
60–80	87	606	340	260	577	408
80–100	135	644	371	267	634	439
All	74	571	312	223	565	379
Distribution of Migrants (per 1,000)						
0–20	103	178	169	155	175	169
20–40	170	190	188	158	195	183
40–60	115	198	188	226	194	204
60–80	233	215	217	226	206	213
80–100	378	218	238	235	229	231
All	1,000	1,000	1,000	1,000	1,000	1,000

Source: NSSO, *Migration in India: 2007–08.*

Further, equal percentages of rural and urban migrants come from lowest MPCE two deciles (17 per cent each). There is not much difference in percentages of migrants from various MPCE deciles, though for the top two deciles rural migrants outscore the urban migrants. It is also found that there were 10.3 per cent rural male migrants from lowest two deciles as against 37.8 per cent from top two deciles while these percentages are 15.5 and 23.5 per cent, respectively for urban male migrants. Similarly, these percentages are 17.8 and 21.8 per cent respectively for rural female migrants and 17.5 and 23.0 per cent respectively for urban female migrants.

Nature of Movements

Table 9.13 shows that permanent migrants constitute a major proportion of migrants from Punjab (90.9 per cent) while another 8.9 per cent are temporary migrants for 12 months or more. Percentage of permanent migrants (64.4 per cent) is much higher compared to percentage of urban migrants (85.1 per cent). However, percentage of rural male and urban male permanent migrants is almost equal (68.9 per cent and 68.1 per cent respectively). But, percentage of rural female permanent migrants is much higher compared and urban female permanent migrants (98 per cent and 93 per cent, respectively). Finally, percentage of female permanent

Table 9.13

Distribution (per 1,000) of migrants by nature of movements in Punjab

Regions	Temporary with Duration of Stay		Permanent	All
	<12 Months	*12 Months or More*	*Permanent*	*All*
Rural male	10	301	689	1,000
Rural female	0	20	980	1,000
Rural all	**1**	**55**	**944**	**1,000**
Urban male	10	309	681	1,000
Urban female	0	69	931	1,000
Urban all	**3**	**146**	**851**	**1,000**
Rural–urban male	10	306	684	1,000
Rural–urban female	0	36	964	1,000
Rural–urban all	**2**	**89**	**909**	**1,000**

migrants is much higher compared with male permanent migrants (96.4 per cent and 68.4 per cent, respectively). In case of temporary migrants, percentage of male migrants (30.6 per cent) is significantly higher than the female temporary migrants (3.6 per cent) in the 12 months or more. The wide differences exist in rural and urban areas too. And the percentage of female migrants is insignificant in case of less than 12-month temporary migrants' category. This shows that females do not move as temporary migrants and remain behind at the place of residence to look after the family. The major movement of females is because of marriage or moving of the family.

Migration Streams

About 62 per cent migrants are from rural to rural areas at the national level and this percentage is much lower at 55 per cent in case of Punjab (Table 9.14). Also, a significantly higher percentage of rural female migrants move within rural areas compared to rural male migrants (61 per cent and 27 per cent, respectively). The migration stream of significance is rural to urban areas wherein 19 per cent of all migrants move in Punjab and this percentage is slightly lower than the national figure of 19.5 per cent. Further, a higher percentage of male migrants are rural to urban migrants (41.7 per cent) compared to female migrants (14 per cent). It is also observed that 18.4 per cent migrants are urban to urban areas and this percentage is again higher among male migrants (20.8 per cent) than the female migrants (17.8 per cent). Finally, urban to rural migration is minimal in Punjab (7.7 per cent migrants only). The percentage of male

Table 9.14

Distribution (per 1,000) of internal migrants by four types of rural–urban migration streams

Migration Streams	Male		Female		All	
	Punjab	India	Punjab	India	Punjab	India
Rural–rural	269	272	611	700	547	617
Urban–rural	106	89	71	49	77	57
Rural–urban	417	390	140	148	192	195
Urban–urban	208	248	178	103	184	131
All	1,000	1,000	1,000	1,000	1,000	1,000

migrants is higher at 10.6 per cent than the female migrants (7.1 per cent). This shows that in Punjab rural to rural migration dominates and more males than females are involved in migration movements other than rural to rural. A similar pattern is observed in case of national migration streams too.

Table 9.15 reveals that in the case of rural male migrants, basic movement is towards the rural areas (75 per cent) be it same district (23.6 per cent), other districts (13.6 per cent) and other states (28 per cent) while in case of rural female migrants, the movement is greater within the rural

Table 9.15

Per 1,000 distribution of migrants by location of last usual place of residence

Rural Male	Punjab	India	Rural Female	Punjab	India	Rural Person	Punjab	India
Rural areas of			Rural areas of			Rural areas of		
Same State			*Same State*			*Same State*		
Same District	236	462	Same District	501	683	Same District	469	639
Other District	136	180	Other District	318	214	Other District	296	211
Other States	280	86	*Other States*	74	35	*Other States*	99	40
Urban areas of			Urban areas of			Urban areas of		41
Same State			*Same State*			*Same State*		
Same District	72	77	Same District	40	36	Same District	44	41
Other District	106	91	Other District	46	21	Other District	53	28
Other States	78	72	Other States	17	8	Other States	25	15
Other countries	92	32	Other Countries	3	2	Other Countries	14	6
All	1,000	1,000	All	1,000	1,000	All	1,000	1,000

(Table 9.15 Continued)

(Table 9.15 Continued)

Urban Male	Punjab	India	Urban Female	Punjab	India	Urban Person	Punjab	India
Rural areas of			Rural areas of			Rural areas of		
Same State			Same State			Same State		
Same District	71	197	Same District	181	272	Same District	146	244
Other District	54	188	Other District	154	206	Other District	122	199
Other States	519	218	Other States	103	107	Other States	236	149
Urban areas of			Urban areas of			Urban areas of		
Same State			Same State			Same State		
Same District	40	79	Same District	164	132	Same District	124	112
Other District	137	197	Other District	255	196	Other District	218	196
Other States	144	109	Other States	138	81	Other States	140	91
Other Countries	35	12	Other Countries	5	5	Other Countries	15	8
All	1,000	1,000	All	1,000	1,000	All	1,000	1,000

Source: NSSO. 2001, *Migration in India: 1990–2000*, 55th Round (July 1999–June 2000), September.

areas (89 per cent) be it the same district (50.1 per cent), other districts (31.8 per cent) and other states (7.4 per cent). Rural male migrants also move to urban areas, but a majority of them move to is urban area of other districts (10.6 per cent), though 9.2 per cent migrated to other countries and 7.8 per cent to other states. However, only 11 per cent rural female migrants moved into urban areas but largely within Punjab and only 0.3 per cent migrated abroad. Finally, rural migration is rural to rural within Punjab (76.5 per cent) and only 14 per cent towards urban areas with 1.4 per cent going abroad.

In case of urban male migrants, basic movement is towards the rural areas (64 per cent) with major movement towards rural areas of other states (52 per cent) while in case of urban female migrants, the movement is largely within the urban areas (66 per cent) be it the same district (16.4 per cent), other districts (25.5 per cent) and other states (13.8 per cent). Urban male migrants also move to urban areas but major proportion is urban areas of other districts (13.7 per cent) and other states (14.4 per cent), though 3.5 per cent migrated to other. However, 18.1 per cent urban females migrate into rural areas of the same district and another 15.4 per cent move to urban areas of other districts with 10.3 per cent migrating into other states. Only 0.5 per cent migrated abroad. Finally, urban migration is towards rural areas in Punjab (50 per cent) and only 1.5 per cent going abroad. It is a pointer towards better rural infrastructure and rural–urban continuum being created.

Reasons for Migration

The most prominent reason for migration in Punjab for rural male migrant is employment related reasons followed by movement of parents/earning member (20.7 per cent) and other reasons (18.6 per cent) while for rural females it is marriage. Ninety-two per cent followed movement of parents/earning member (4.5 per cent) (Table 9.16). Rural migrants mainly move for marriage (82.3 per cent). The other reasons of some significance are movement of parents/earning member (6.5 per cent) and employment related reasons (5 per cent). The reason for migration for urban male migrants was dominated by employment related reasons (67.8 per cent) followed by movement of parents/earning member (18.6 per cent) and 4.6 per cent were forced to migrate. In case of urban female migrants, marriage dominates as a reason (76.3 per cent) followed by movement of parents/earning member (16.2 per cent). Urban migrants primarily move because of marriage (52.4 per cent) and employment related reasons (22.8 per cent) and movement of parents/earning member (17.0 per cent). Overall migrants in Punjab move because of marriage (71 per cent), employment related reasons (11.8 per cent) and movement of parents/ earning member (10.4 per cent). Thus, there are gendered reasons for migration in both rural and urban areas. It is observed that male migrants do move because of 'being forced' reasons, which could be economic

Table 9.16

Distribution (per 1,000) of migrants by reason for migration: Punjab

	Employment Related Reasons	Studies	Forced Migration	Marriage	Movement of Parents/ Earning Member	Others	All
Rural male	380	69	74	71	207	186	1,000
Rural female	4	0	3	928	45	15	1,000
Rural all	50	8	12	823	65	35	1,000
Urban male	678	10	46	14	186	61	1,000
Urban female	19	14	10	763	162	25	1,000
Urban all	228	13	21	524	170	36	1,000
Rural–urban male	561	33	57	37	194	109	1,000
Rural–urban female	9	5	5	875	82	18	1,000
Rural–urban all	118	10	16	710	104	35	1,000

Source: NSSO. 2001, *Migration in India: 1990–2000*, 55th Round (July 1999–June 2000), September.

distress in the family. Most male migrants must be first member of the household migrating for better living and livelihood for the family and this is also entrenched in social structure of Punjab. It is surprising that females do not largely use employment opportunities for migration and this again because they are not allowed to go out.

Economic Activities

The 2007–08 NSSO survey on migration collected information on usual principal activity status of the migrant before and after migration. It is observed that in case of Punjab, across area and gender, the percentage of migrants not in labour has reduced after migration but this percentage is still very high except in case of urban male migrants and to some extent rural male migrants.

In case of rural male migrants, prior to migration 47.8 were engaged in economic activities and their percentage went up to 68.8 per cent after migration while in case of rural female migrants the corresponding

Table 9.17

Distribution (per 1,000) of migrants by their usual principal activity status before and after migration: Punjab

	Self Employed	Regular Wage/ Salaried	Casual Labour	Total Employed	Unemployed	Not in Labour Force	All
Rural male: Before	221	160	96	478	38	485	1,000
Rural male: After	225	268	165	658	16	326	1,000
Rural female: Before	34	5	2	41	0	958	1,000
Rural female: After	31	21	22	73	1	925	1,000
Rural all: Before	57	24	14	95	5	900	1,000
Rural all: After	54	52	40	146	3	851	1,000
Urban male: Before	126	157	130	413	279	308	1,000
Urban male: After	199	502	86	787	19	194	1,000
Urban female: Before	5	28	3	35	2	963	1,000
Urban female: After	20	78	8	106	1	894	1,000
Urban all: Before	43	69	43	156	90	753	1,000
Urban all: After	77	213	33	324	6	670	1,000
Rural urban male: Before	163	158	117	438	185	377	1,000
Rural urban male: After	210	411	117	736	18	246	1,000
Rural urban female: Before	25	12	2	40	1	960	1,000
Rural urban female: After	27	39	17	84	1	915	1,000
Rural urban all: Before	52	41	25	118	37	845	1,000
Rural urban all: After	63	112	37	212	4	783	1,000

Source: NSSO, 2001 *Migration in India: 1990–2000*, 55th Round (July1999–June 2000), September.

change was from 4.1 per cent to 7.3 per cent (Table 9.17). In the case of male migrants, it is interesting to observe that self-employment increased marginally but casual labour went up from 9.6 per cent to 16.5 per cent when regular wage/salaried employed increased from 16.0 per cent to 26.8 per cent. This means quality of employed declined after migration for rural males in quite a large number. However, unemployment reduced for them. It could be that unemployed migrants got into casual jobs after migration. In case of female rural migrants, self-employed reduced while regular wage/salaried jobs per cent increased and so did the casual labour.

In the case of urban male migrants, unemployment drastically went down after migration (27.9 per cent to 1.9 per cent) while employment improved from 41.3 per cent to 78.7 per cent after migration. Here a significant decline in percentage of urban male migrants going into causal labour after migration is observed (13 per cent to 8.6 per cent), though percentage of urban male migrants increased to 50.2 per cent from 15.2 per cent in regular wage/salaried activities after migration. Urban male migrants in self-employment increased though.

Now, in the case of urban female migrants, percentage of employed migrants increased from 3.5 to 10.6 per cent and regular wage/salaried improved from 2.8 to 7.8 per cent after migration. Self-employment also increased in case of urban female migrants (0.5 per cent to 2.0 per cent). However, even in urban locations, female migrants are mainly not in labour force, though the proportion of urban female migrants reduced from 96.3 per cent to 89.4 per cent after migration. This female labour force participation is such because most moved because of marriage and not for economic activities per se. Finally, in the case of urban migrants, regular wage/salary based economic activities participation after migration increased from 6.9 per cent to 21.3 per cent, though self-employment too improved from 4.3 per cent to 7.7 per cent. This shows that there is no doubt that after migration greater percentage of migrants are engaged in economic activities, it is more prominent in the case of urban migrants and male migrants.

Return Migrants

Rate of return migration (proportion of return migrants in the population)[4] for males in rural areas is significantly higher than that for females, namely 14.1 per cent for males and 3.6 per cent for females (Table 9.18). The corresponding figures for India are 23.7 per cent and 10.6 per cent. In urban areas, the rate of return migration did not differ much for males and females, that is, 7.1 per cent for males and 6.0 per cent for females. Overall, male return migration is more than double the female return

Table 9.18

Number of return migrants per 1,000 migrants

Out-migrants	Male		Female		All	
	Punjab	India	Punjab	India	Punjab	India
Rural	141	237	36	106	49	120
Urban	71	117	60	104	64	109
All	98	161	44	106	55	116

Source: NSSO. 2001 Migration in India: 1990–2000, 55th Round (July 1999–June 2000), September.

migration at 9.8 per cent for males and 4.4 per cent for females. Besides, rate of return migration in urban areas is higher than the rate in rural areas in Punjab while it is reverse in case of India.

Out-migrants

Out-migrant is defined as any former member of a household who left the household, any time in the past, for staying outside the village/town was considered as out-migrant provided he/she was alive on the date of survey. Out-migration rate (proportion of out-migration in the population) for males was 9.2 per cent from rural areas and 5.1 per cent from urban areas at the national level while the corresponding percentages are 6.1 per cent and 3.4 per cent for Punjab, respectively (Table 9.19). In case of females, out-migration rate was 16.6 per cent from rural areas and 11.0 per cent from urban areas at the national level while the corresponding percentages

Table 9.19

Number of out-migrants per 1,000 persons (Rural)

	Rural Punjab	Rural India	Urban Punjab	Urban India	All Punjab	All India
Male	62	92	34	51	52	81
Female	170	166	109	110	151	152
All	114	128	68	79	99	115

Source: NSSO. 2001 Migration in India: 1990–2000, 55th Round (July 1999–June 2000), September.

are 17.0 per cent and 10.9 per cent for Punjab, respectively. At the aggregate level, out-migration rate for rural areas is higher (11.4 per cent) compared to urban Punjab (6.8 per cent). This means that migrants who once enter Punjab would not like to leave as prosperity of the region holds them back and most might also have made investment in fixed assets.[5]

A relatively higher percentage of female out-migrants from both the rural and urban areas, took up residence within the state: Nearly 89 per cent rural female out-migrants and 80 per cent urban female out-migrants had residence within the state at the national level (Table 9.20). In Punjab too, a relatively higher percentage of female out-migrants from both the rural and urban areas, took up residence within the state: Nearly 87.5 per cent rural female out-migrants and 69.6 per cent urban female out-migrants had residence within the state. Further, 95 per cent of rural female out-migrants in Punjab took up residence within the country compared to 94 per cent urban female out-migrants. A slightly higher percentage of urban female out-migrants took up residence outside the country compared to rural female out-migrants.

Table 9.20

Per 1,000 distribution of out-migrants by present place of residence

Rural Male	Punjab	India	Rural Female	Punjab	India	Rural Person	Punjab	India
Same state	265	466	Same state	875	890	Same state	703	734
Within same District	116	173	Within same District	562	614	Within same District	436	452
Another District	149	293	Another District	313	276	Another District	267	282
Outside the state	249	458	Outside the state	74	102	Outside the state	123	233
Within the country	515	924	Within the country	949	992	Within the country	826	967
Another country	485	72	Another country	49	7	Another country	173	31
All	1,000	1,000	All	1,000	1,000	All	1,000	1,000
Urban Male	Punjab	India	Urban Female	Punjab	India	Urban Person	Punjab	India

(Table 9.20 Continued)

(Table 9.20 Continued)

Rural Male	Punjab	India	Rural Female	Punjab	India	Rural Person	Punjab	India
Same state	377	499	Same state	696	797	Same state	609	699
Within same District	120	143	Within same District	405	425	Within same District	327	332
Another District	257	356	Another District	291	372	Another District	282	367
Outside the state	265	333	Outside the state	245	176	Outside the state	251	228
Within the country	642	832	Within the country	941	973	Within the country	860	926
Another country	339	159	Another country	59	27	Another country	135	71
All	1,000	1,000	All	1,000	1,000	All	1,000	1,000
Rural + Urban Male	Punjab	India	**Rural + Urban Female**	Punjab	India	**Rural + Urban Person**	Punjab	India
Same state	290	471	Same state	833	873	Same state	681	728
Within same District	117	168	Within same District	525	578	Within same District	411	430
Another District	173	303	Another District	308	294	Another District	270	298
Outside the state	253	438	Outside the state	114	116	Outside the state	153	232
Within the country	543	909	Within the country	947	988	Within the country	834	960
Another country	453	86	Another country	52	11	Another country	164	38
All	1,000	1,000	All	1,000	1,000	All	1,000	1,000

Source: NSSO. 2001. *Migration in India: 1990–2000*, 55th Round (July 1999–June 2000), September.

A relatively lower percentage of male out-migrants from both the rural and urban areas, took up residence within the state: Nearly 26.5 per cent for rural male out-migrants and 38.7 per cent urban male out-migrants had residence within the state in Punjab. Further, 51.5 per cent of rural male out-migrants in Punjab took up residence within the country compared to 64.2 per cent urban male out-migrants. A slightly higher percentage of rural male out-migrants took up residence outside the country compared to urban male out-migrants.

Further, a relatively lower percentage of male out-migrants took up residence within the state compared to female out-migrants, that is 29.0 per cent male out-migrants and 83.3 per cent female out-migrants had residence within the state in Punjab. Further, 54.3 per cent male out-migrants in Punjab took up residence within the country compared to 94.7 per cent female out-migrants. A significantly higher percentage of male out-migrants took up residence outside the country compared to female out-migrants: 45.3 per cent male out-migrants and 5.2 per cent female out-migrants.

Finally, a relatively lower percentage of urban out-migrants (60.9 per cent) took up residence within the state compared to rural out-migrants (70.3 per cent) in Punjab. Further, 12.3 per cent of rural out-migrants in Punjab took up residence outside Punjab compared to 25.1 per cent urban out-migrants. A significantly higher percentage of urban out-migrants took up residence within the country compared to rural out-migrants, namely 82.6 per cent for rural out-migrants and 86.0 per cent urban out-migrants. Also a higher percentage of rural out-migrants took up residence outside the country compared to urban out-migrants, that is 17.3 per cent for rural out-migrants and 13.5 per cent urban out-migrants. Finally, the table shows that 68.1 per cent of out-migrants took up residence within Punjab, with another 15.3 per cent going to other states and 16.4 per cent took up residence outside the country. Thus, out-migration is largely within the country and within the state of Punjab too.

Reasons for Out-migration

Table 9.21 shows that 65.2 per cent out-migrants migrated because of marriage followed by employment related reasons (22.9 per cent). However, in case of rural out-migrants, 66.1 per cent out-migrants migrated because of marriage followed by employment related reasons (24.4 per cent) while in case of urban out-migrants, 62.3 per cent out-migrants migrated because of marriage followed by employment related reasons (17.6 per cent). Urban out-migration is also due to studies (8.9 per cent) and movement of parents/earning member (8.1 per cent) while these factors

Table 9.21

Distribution (per 1,000) of out-migrants by reason for out-migration

Punjab	Rural Male	Rural Female	Rural All	Urban Male	Urban Male	Urban All	Rural Urban Male	Rural Urban Female	Rural Urban All
Employment related reasons	831	16	**244**	598	17	**176**	779	16	**229**
Studies	59	11	**25**	193	51	**89**	89	20	**40**
Forced migration	0	8	**6**	46	9	**19**	11	8	**9**
Marriage	20	913	**661**	16	849	**623**	19	899	**652**
Movement of parents/ earning member	48	39	**41**	123	65	**81**	64	45	**50**
Others	39	12	**20**	23	8	**12**	36	12	**18**
All	1,000	1,000	**1,000**	1,000	1,000	**1,000**	1,000	1,000	**1,000**

Source: NSSO. 2001 *Migration in India: 1990–2000*, 55th Round (July1999–June 2000), September.

have much lower influence for rural out-migrants. Forced out-migration is relatively higher in case of urban areas compared to rural areas. Further, employment related reasons dominate significantly in case of rural male compared to rural female out-migrants (83.1 per cent and 1.6 per cent) while marriage is significant factors for rural female compared to male out-migrants (91.3 per cent and 2.0 per cent). Rural males out-migrate in greater proportion than rural females. In urban areas, 59.8 per cent males out-migrate due to employment related reasons than female out-migrants while 19.3 per cent males do so because of studies compared to just 5.1 per cent females. Similarly, 12.3 per cent males do so because of movement of parents/earning member compared to just 6.5 per cent females. Thus, reasons for female out-migration are varied compared to male out-migrants.

It is further found that (Table 9.22) rural male out-migrants, residing abroad, 91.7 per cent are economically active compared to 75.6 per cent residing within the country while of urban male out-migrants, residing abroad, 92.7 per cent are economically active compared to much lower percentage of 55.0 per cent residing within the country. In case of all male out-migrants, residing abroad, 91.9 per cent are economically active

Table 9.22

Number of economically active (per 1,000) out-migrants

Male	Rural Punjab	Urban Punjab	All Punjab
India	756	550	702
Another country	917	927	919
All	834	668	797
Female			
India	15	174	52
Another country	479	604	512
All	38	199	76
Both			
India	146	250	170
Another country	827	824	827
All	263	326	278

Source: NSSO. 2001 *Migration in India: 1990–2000*, 55th Round (July 1999–June 2000), September.

compared to 70.2 per cent residing within the country. Thus rural male out-migrants in Punjab are more economically active within the country compared to those in another country, but overall rural male out-migrants are more economically active compared to urban male out-migrants. Now coming to female rural out-migrants, residing abroad, 47.9 per cent are economically active compared to just 1.5 per cent residing within the country while of urban female out-migrants, residing abroad, 60.4 per cent are economically active compared to much lower percentage of 17.4 per cent residing within the country. In the case of all female out-migrants, residing abroad, 51.2 per cent are economically active compared to 5.2 per cent residing within the country. Thus, urban female out-migrants in Punjab are more economically active in both another country and within the country.

Out-migrant Remittances

A higher percentage of male out-migrants from another country remit money compared to those within the country: 69.2 per cent from another country and 45.4 per cent from India. A similar pattern is observed in case of both rural male and urban male out-migrants, but a greater percentage of rural male out-migrants remit money home compared to urban out-migrants. In case of female out-migrants, a very low percentage remits money home, though urban female out-migrants out do their rural counterparts. Finally, in case of both rural and urban out-migrants from Punjab, a much higher percentage of those residing abroad sent money home (Table 9.23).

Finally, the net migration rate for Punjab is 13 (Table 9.24). There are 18,586 in-migrants, while out-migrants to other states are 11,697

Table 9.23

Number of remitter out-migrants (per 1,000)

Male	Rural Punjab	Urban Punjab	All Punjab
India	521	266	454
Another country	712	595	692
All	614	373	560
Female			
India	3	5	3
Another country	62	108	74
All	6	11	7
Both			
India	94	58	86
Another country	578	440	552
All	177	109	162

Source: NSSO. 2001 *Migration in India: 1990–2000*, 55th Round (July1999–June 2000), September.

Table 9.24

Net migration rate (per 1,000 of population)

In-migrants	18,586
Out-migrants to another state	11,697
Out-migrant to abroad	3,864
Net Migration	3,025
Population	238,582
Net Migration rate	13

Source: NSSO. 2001, *Migration in India: 1990–2000*, 55th Round (July 1999–June 2000), September.

and out-migrants to abroad are 3,864. Thus, net migration is 3,025 per 1,000 of population.

Migrant Labourers in Punjab: Local Level Concerns

Movement of living beings in search of better environments is a natural phenomenon and man is no exception to it. Migration of human beings is a complex phenomenon. In the present era of globalization and liberalization, the study of migration has become one of the most dynamic aspects of human beings. The World Development Report 1999–2000 (World Bank, 2000) estimates that more than 13.0 crore people now live outside the countries of their birth. India as a nation has seen a high migration rate in recent years. Over 9.8 crore people migrated from one place to another in 1990s, the highest for any decade since independence (GoI, 2001). While freedom to migrate within the country is an enshrined right, uneven regional development, levels of desperation and other factors have created friction points. Most people migrate because of a combination of push and pull factors. Lack of rural employment, fragmentation of land holdings and declining public investment in agriculture create a crisis for rural Indians. Urban areas and some rural areas with industrial development or high agricultural production offer better prospects for jobs or self-employment (Deshingkar, 2009).

The large-scale in-migration to Punjab by labourers/workers is more seasonal than permanent and it is a matter of concern for policy makers and academia. The pros and cons of this migration, situation of these migrant labourers, influence of this in-migration on state economy and also on local labour and their interests, all are issues of concern. There are quite a few studies related to this. For instance, Ghosh and Sharma (1995) revealed that feudal exploitation and acute poverty are the main factors for distressed migration from Bihar. It is a survival strategy for people of landless households. Though, a new trend of migration is observed in Bihar where people/some members of families belonging to upper castes with small landholdings from rural Bihar are migrating to supplement their family incomes for better socio-economic condition. A few studies also have indicated the attitude of local employers who generally prefer migrant workers for their tolerant attitude towards low wage, more difficult task as well as for non-unionization practices. Various other studies have looked at problems faced by such workers, social tensions, unionization issues; changing status of local agricultural labour, casualization of labour in Punjab's agriculture, seasonality issues and so on. Some have even tried to address the issue of slow process of peasantization of small and medium farmers in Punjab, issues concerning presence of migrant labour and huge surplus workforce in Punjab—a paradox. The Human Development Report (2004) of Punjab devoted a chapter on migration. Migrants are looked upon more as a problem and a threat to the locals. At the same time, various studies state that Punjab needs outside workers for various reasons, like green revolution. Whereafter the agricultural boost created peak season labour requirements, which were difficult to fill with local labour. Simultaneously, small manufacturing in urban centres generated demand. Service activities too that were required in the growing and crowded industrial belt required additional labour. The influx also started as Punjab agriculture offered higher wages to migrant labour. Additional labour was required for brick kilns, rickshaw-pulling, contract workers, workers in grain markets, textile factories, and so on. Ludhiana alone is estimated to have more than 2.0 lakh migrant workers.[6] Long terms studies conducted by Institute of Human Development in 18 villages of Bihar show that problems of caste hierarchies, flood proneness and risky agriculture and low wages has led to an increase in long-term migration. Labour migration data for 1981–83 and 1999–2000 showed that increasing rural–urban migration to work in the non-farm sector was a new trend. The traditional destinations of rural Punjab and Haryana are not as popular as they were 20 years ago because fewer jobs were available as agriculture became more mechanized (Dayal and Karan, 2003). A study by Singh (1995) had shown that in 1980–81, in two districts of Punjab, namely Ludhiana and Hoshiarpur, there were two different streams of migrant labour flowing from Bihar to Punjab. From the districts of Monghyr, Saharasa, Darbhanga, Muzaffarpur and Samastipur in north Bihar seasonal migrants to work on peak agricultural operations. Their total number ranged between 4–5 lakh. These were not the poorest persons and 14 per cent were scheduled caste, 84 per cent were from backward castes and 2 per cent were from upper caste. They mainly worked on three operations, namely, wheat harvesting, paddy transplantation and paddy harvesting. The second stream hailed from

Table 9.25

Impact of labour migration on wage rate for different agricultural operations in Punjab: 2011

Operation	Without Migration	With Migration	Amount ₹	Per cent	t-value
Harvesting of wheat (₹/ha)	6,710	5,407	1,303	19	5.96*
Transplanting of paddy (₹/ha)	6,321	4,426	1,896	30	7.65*
Rate of contract (₹/annum)	61,000	44,286	16,714	27	7.44*

Source: Kaur et al. (2011).

tribal belt of Chhotanagpur; their number was small. They more or less worked as indenture labour in Hoshiarpur. Punjabi farmers went all the way to Chhotanagpur to get this labour and took care of all the transaction costs. A revisit to same village in 1990–91 by Singh showed that slowly the gap between the wage rates of local and migrant labour was being bridged, but there was a clear hierarchy in the direction of changes. The local labour completely withdrew from the labour-intensive agricultural operations and left the same for the migrant workforce.[7] It is observed that triangular intense competition took place between migrant labour, local labour and machinery. Migrant labour was displacing local labour and started working as attached labour too; on the other hand, workers were being displaced by combine harvesters in paddy harvesting cum threshing. However, the well-organized trade in tribal labour from Bihar vanished. A recent study on impact of migrant labour (Kaur et al., 2011) shows that migrant labour did compress wages/cost for certain operations in Punjab (Table 9.25).

Kalyan Das, a landless agricultural worker of Rampur village in Araria district of Bihar, migrates to Punjab every year.

I saw my father leaving our home every year when I was a child, not once, but thrice in a year. That was back in the 1980s. He used to go to Punjab. When he grew old, he stopped and I started going. At least two members of each family in this village go to Punjab at least twice every year. We go in groups of 14 or 15 people and mostly around the time of sowing or harvesting. We do not get more than ₹80 a day here for our work on the fields. But in Punjab, we are hired on contract by a farmer and get paid on the amount of work done and not on daily basis. For example, we get ₹2200 for sowing one acre of land there. Around sowing and harvesting seasons, the farmers wait for us at every railway station in Punjab and Haryana and pick us up from there. They arrange for our stay and provide us one meal a day and tea. We work more than 12 hours a day, but at least we get the money. Usually, one season of sowing or harvesting lasts 25 days. By the end of the season, we come back with anything between ₹10,000 and ₹15,000 after expenses. And we are treated much better there. The landlord here exercises his upper caste rights a lot. We being scheduled caste are looked down upon. But there, if the landlord drinks tea, he offers us tea too. The Sikh landlords treat us like their own sons. Because of two sowing and two harvesting seasons in a year, we have the option of going four times in a year. But we usually go twice except when we are in dire need. The farmer gives all of us one hall-like room to stay in. Taking the family along is impractical. (Frontline, 2012, p. 25)

Conclusion

Migration issues in the context of Punjab are straightforward and linked to its history, adventurous people and risk taking population, especially the Sikh. Its productive land has attracted lakhs of people to eke out their livelihood, some settle here and others return home. Many poor households across the country have not only eaten the food grains produced on the fertile lands of Punjab, but also have removed their poverty, moved out of indebtedness. Migration has been a powerful mechanism in Bihar's agrarian society, giving the poor a collective voice against exploitation and Punjab has contributed to this voice.[8] Many have undergone upward social and economic mobility. The major senders of migrants are Uttar Pradesh, Bihar, Haryana, Rajasthan, West Bengal and Assam. Over the years there have been changes in inflows of migrants to Punjab. The major reason for migration for males is employment and for females it is marriage or the movement of the family/earner. There are not many differences between census and NSSO patterns. There are gender differentials in movement by source state and reasons too. Rural–rural migration dominates in Punjab and that too within the state. However, in Punjab's case international migration is significant in the sense that it has history and Punjabis, especially Sikhs have been pioneers in migration abroad. Migration both into and outside to other states and other countries has contributed vitally to Punjab's economy and society.

Notes

1. Growth was 5.9 per cent in 2005–06, 10.18 per cent in 2006–07, 9.05 per cent in 2007–08, 5.85 per cent in 2008–09, 6.29 per cent in 2009–10, 6.81 per cent in 2010–11 and 5.68 per cent in 2011–12 (Government of Punjab 2013).
2. It is also considered at the root of capitalist growth.
3. Singh (1997) argues that the success of green revolution enclave in the Punjab region is instrumental in reinforcing semi-feudalism in Bihar.
4. Those migrants who had reported that the present place of enumeration was UPR any time in the past was considered as return migrants.
5. Punjab is a state with an interesting migration profile. Though the total number of migrants from outside the state and outside the country is 8.1 lakh and 20,000 million respectively, there is significant out-migration from the state (5 lakh). The number of male out-migrants is less than female out-migrants. As a result, the net migrant into Punjab is only 3.3 lakh, the sex ratio is stacked highly in favour of males (313 females per 1,000 males). States from where sizeable number of in-migrants came to Punjab are: Uttar Pradesh (2.4 lakh), Haryana (1.1 lakh) and Bihar (1.4 lakh). Male in-migrants from Uttar Pradesh and Bihar cited work/employment as the main reason for migration (72.1 per cent and 82.2 per cent, respectively).
6. In the late 1990s, the estimated migrant labour in Punjab stood at: Agriculture 7 lakh; brick kilns 2 lakh; manufacturing industries 6.5 lakh; service industries 1.5 lakh; rickshaw pulling 1 lakh; domestic workers 0.5 lakh; construction industry 3.5 lakh (total 21.65 lakh) (Government of Punjab, 2004).
7. Wage increase for local labour was 186 per cent while it was 138 per cent for migrant labour.
8. Almost 26.36 per cent of migrants from Bihar in 2001 came to Punjab. This is because Punjab's agricultural cycle begins one month after Bihar and this helps seasonal migrants to migrate from Bihar to Punjab.

References

Dayal, H. and Karan, A.K. (2003). *Labour migration from Jharkhand.* New Delhi: IHD.

Deshingkar, P. (2009). *Circular internal migration and development.* London: ODI. Retrieved from http://essays.ssrc.org/acrossborders/wp-content/uploads/2009/08/ch8.pdf

The Frontline (2012). Special Issue on Migration, *29*(18), 25.

Ghosh, P.P. and Sharma, A.N. (1995). 'Seasonal migration of rural labour in Bihar'. *Labor and Development, 31*(50), 118–36.

Ghuman, R.S., Brar, J.S., and Singh, I. (2007). *Status of local agricultural labour in Punjab: The Punjab state farmers commission.* Chandigarh: Government of Punjab.

Government of India. (2008). *Eleventh Five Year Plan:* 3: *2007–2012.* New Delhi: Planning Commission.

Government of Punjab (2004). *Punjab Human Development Report.* Retrieved from http://www.in.undp.org/content/dam/india/docs/human_development_report_2004_punjab_full_report.pdf (accessed on 1 February 2014).

Government of Punjab. (2013). *Economic Survey of Punjab 2012–13*, Economic and Statistical Organisation, Department of Planning, Government of Punjab, Chandigarh.

Gupta, A.K. (1991). 'Migration of agricultural labour from Eastern to North Western region'. *Social Change, 21*(6), 85–90.

Gupta, A.K. and Bhakoo, A.K. (1980). 'Rural to rural migration and characteristics of migration in Punjab'. *Social Change, 10*(3–4), 18–22.

Kaur, B., Singh, J.M., Garg, B.R., Singh, J., and Singh, S. (2011). 'Causes and impact of labour migration: A case study of Punjab agriculture'. *Agricultural Economics Research Review,* Conference Issue, *24,* 459–66.

Reddy, D. Narasmiha (1990). 'Rural Migrant Labour in Andhra Pradesh'. Report submitted to the National Commission on Rural Labour, Government of India, New Delhi.

Singh, M. (1995). *Uneven development in agriculture and labour migration: A case of Bihar and Punjab.* Shimla: IIAS.

———. (1997). 'Bonded migrant labour in Punjab agriculture'. *Economic and Political Weekly, 32*(11), 518–19.

Singh, M. and Karan, A.K. (2001). *Rural labour migration from Bihar.* New Delhi: IHD.

Singh, Surjit (2000). 'Immigration Policies and Earning Behaviour of Immigrants in Canada'. *IASSI Quarterly 19*(1), 1–15.

World Bank. (2000). *World Development Report 1999/2000: Entering the 21st Century.* Washington, DC: Author.

10

Seasonal Migration from Odisha: A View from the Field

Deepak K. Mishra[1]

Introduction

Seasonality associated with rain-fed and subsistence agriculture is intrinsically linked to household vulnerability.[2] There is increasing recognition of the linkages between poverty, vulnerability and seasonality (Chambers et al., 1981; Devereux, 2010; Gill, 1992, pp. 44–79). Several recent studies have brought out the significance of seasonal migration as a livelihood strategy in rural India (Deshingkar et al., 2008; Harriss-White and Garikipati, 2008). However, seasonal migration has been ignored or underestimated in the official statistics in India.[3] Recent evidences point out the increasing relevance of seasonal or circular migration not only as a coping or survival mechanism for the poor households, but also as part of the accumulative strategies of the relatively better off households (Deshingkar and Start, 2003). Seasonal migration has been found to be highly segmented, regionally uneven and deeply embedded in the caste/class/gender and ethnic networks. Micro-studies from different regions of India suggest that in the backdrop of increasing regional disparity and spatial concentration of poverty, seasonal migration has become part of the coping strategies of rural households in the relatively backward and remote regions of the country. Seasonal migration is known to be a complex phenomenon having varied impacts on different categories of migrating households and individuals even within the same region.

Seasonal migration in India has long been seen as a response of the poor to extreme poverty, lack of employment and limited livelihoods options.

With expansion of communication networks and rising demand for casual labour in the expanding informal sector in urban India, seasonal migration has expanded into new areas and more and more labour, particularly from ecological fragile and poor regions, has been joining the circuits of circular migration. There is, however, a new literature suggesting that such periodic migration, and the consequent dependence on multiple livelihoods, opens up new opportunities for the poor to get out of the poverty trap.[4] While there is considerable evidence to argue that seasonal migration, essentially, is an exploitative phenomenon driven by extreme poverty and distress, this increasingly influential body of research has stressed the beneficial outcomes of such migration through its direct and indirect impacts in reducing rural poverty in less developed, remote and ecologically fragile regions. In such a framework, the rural areas get the benefits of increased employment opportunities that are compatible with local agricultural cycles, inflow of remittances, investment of non-agricultural surplus in agriculture and in asset creation and also the associated shifts in outlooks, knowledge and information flows as a result of out-migration, while the urban areas enjoy the fruits of cheap labour, without bearing the social and economic cost of creating a labour force. This kind of a win–win situation is increasingly conceived as one of the ways in which benefits of globalization and spatially uneven economic growth percolates down to the rural areas and the poor through the mediating influences of the labour market. The informality of such labour contracts and the spatial labour reallocations has been credited with making the seasonal labour market flexible enough to adjust to the needs of the global production regimes.

This chapter seeks to examine the contention that labour migration to expanding cities in India has opened up new channels of opportunities for the rural poor. Based on a field survey in Balangir and Nuapada districts of Odisha and supplementing the arguments with indirect evidences from secondary data, the chapter provides evidence on the nature, extent and conditions of seasonal migration in one of the poverty-stricken belts in India. The study investigates the process of migration of the landless and the small farmers from Odisha to various destinations within and outside Odisha through in-depth interviews and argues that seasonal migration from these belts need to be understood in the historical context of evolution of agrarian relations in the region. In the backdrop of increasing regional disparity and spatial concentration of poverty in some distinct regions of Odisha, seasonal migration has become part of the coping strategies of rural households. The linkages between poverty and seasonal migration get mediated through structural inequalities of various kinds, including those based on land ownership, caste, gender and ethnic hierarchies.

Seasonal Migration in Globalizing India: An Overview

Migration studies have a long tradition in many academic disciplines. Early theorizations such as by Lewis (1954) emphasized uneven and dualistic nature of development as the main reasons for labour mobility.[5] Lee's (1966) emphasis on push and pull factors and Todaro's (Harris and Todaro, 1970; Todaro, 1969) explanation in terms of expected income differentials between rural and urban areas have remained influential for long. The widespread experience of proliferation of low and semi-skilled migrant workers in the expanding urban informal sector in a number of developing countries has raised serious questions about the traditional view that explained migration in terms of smooth inter-sectoral labour flows. More recently, the New Economics of Labour Migration (NELM) school has attempted to explain migration as the outcome of different kinds of market failures including absent or underdeveloped capital and insurance markets (Stark, 1980, 1991; Stark and Bloom, 1985). Such theorizations have broadened the scope of analysis to incorporate transaction costs, imperfect information along with market imperfections in explaining the decisions of households and individuals to migrate. More importantly, this school of thought has emphasized that migration decisions are not taken by isolated individuals, but by families or households collectively so as to maximize the expected income, minimize risks and to partially circumvent incomplete and/or absent markets.

The neo-classical theories of migration have typically emphasized the voluntary and self-interest, maximizing behaviour of agents as the underlying causes for decisions to migrate. Critics have pointed out the flaws in such assumptions both on theoretical and empirical grounds (Breman, 1985; McDowell and de Haan, 1997; Sasikumar, 2004; Standing, 1985). Studies in the Marxist framework have typically emphasized the coercive nature of labour contracts through which the capitalists and intermediaries exploit migrant labourers. The role of wider structures in perpetuating such exploitation of migrant workers has received much attention in the literature[6] (Breman, 1996). The presence of extra-economic coercion in such labour relations has been widely noted. Breman (1985) and Olsen (1998) have drawn attention to the elements of bondage and unfreedom involved in migration labour contracts negotiated through debt. The main criticism against the Marxian analysis of migration is that it takes a deterministic view of a highly diverse phenomenon. With its stress on structural factors, it tends to underplay or ignore the agency of migrants.

Some recent studies on migration have analyzed migration within the overall framework of livelihood diversification (Deshingkar and Farrington, 2009). Livelihood approach considers migration as a response to diversifying the earnings portfolio of the households. The multiplicity of causal mechanisms underlying the decision to migrate is perfectly compatible with this view on migration (de Haan et al., 2002).

Studies on migration in India have noted the relatively low levels of mobility in rural India. One possible reason[7] could be the underestimation of migration as official statistics, with some notable recent exceptions, ignore seasonal migrants. Although there have been very few attempts to theorize seasonal or circulatory migration, few recent studies have brought in a variety of perspectives to explain seasonal migration (de Haan and Rogaly, 2002; Deshingkar and Farrington, 2009; Deshingkar and Start, 2003; Kothari, 2002).

Rogaly (1998, 1999) in a study on seasonal migration in West Bengal found evidence of seasonal migration-induced agrarian change in both origin and destinations. While competition and lack of collusive arrangement among employers at the destinations enhanced choices and bargaining power of the migrant labourers, labour outflow from the destinations led to higher wages and better working conditions at the origin areas.[8] In contrast, Mosse et al. (2002) find that in western India, because of its tie to long-term debt, migrant labour is often extremely unproductive and unprofitable for those involved. The outcome of migration was found to be varied depending upon the economic and social resources that the household can command. Even in the context of West Bengal, Rogaly et al. (2001) note that although migration has expanded the choices of migrants, 'the process is still driven by an economic compulsion and the choices remain small'. Joshi and Verma (2004) in a study on labour migration from Chhattisgarh found that seasonal migration contributes significantly to the household economy of the marginal farmers and landless labour households. Deshingkar and Start (2003), in a comparative analysis of seasonal migration from Andhra Pradesh and Madhya Pradesh note that the distinctive features of accumulative and coping migration streams, although migration options were found to be more secure and more attractive over time. Badiani and Safir (2009) using panel data from six villages find that circular migration is responsive to climatic variation at the village level. Households having a larger reliance on agriculture were found to be most responsive to such climatic variations. The poverty-reducing impact of circular migration has been noted in Deshingkar et al. (2009). While the diversity in outcomes for different groups of migrants noted in several studies bring out the significance of structural inequalities, often migration paves the way for loosening of the oppressive structures (de Haan and Rogaly, 2002).

After the availability of data on short-term migration from recent NSS data, several distinctive features of seasonal migration as opposed to migration, in general, has been noticed by scholars. Mishra and Bose (2013) point out the following distinguishing features of seasonal migration. Firstly, while migration as a livelihoods strategy is opted by both the poor and relatively better-off sections of the rural society, seasonal migration is mostly the strategy of the relatively marginalized groups. Persons belonging to deprived social groups and those with poor asset base and low-earning occupations at origin have greater chances of migrating seasonally. Not only that long-term and seasonal migration are very different kinds of groups in terms of their capabilities and socio-economic background, but also the occupational composition of the seasonal migrants at the destination, especially in the urban and the rural areas, clearly brings out that these are essentially two distinct processes. Long-term migrants are found to be better off than the seasonal migrants with respect to consumption expenditure, employment status, job quality and educational levels. Seasonal work is more about low-paid, insecure and casual work. The urban construction sector, in particular, has employed a large number of seasonal migrants through a series of sub-contractors and middlemen. Secondly, in terms of regional dimension, the incidence of seasonal migration is relatively higher from the regions with low levels of development (Keshri and Bhagat, 2012; Srivastava, 2011, p. 425–26) and land productivity (Mishra and Bose, 2013; Shah, 2010). However, seasonal migration also takes places some of the relatively better endowed and developed regions and in some cases regions serve both as origins and destinations of seasonal migration. Mapping the seasonal migration rates from NSS regions further substantiates such a complex spatial pattern (Figure 10.1). The central Indian regions emerge as a contiguous region with high incidence of seasonal migration, although some relatively better-off regions also report a relatively high incidence of seasonal migration (Mishra and Bose, 2013).

Figure 10.1

Seasonal migration in India: NSS regions

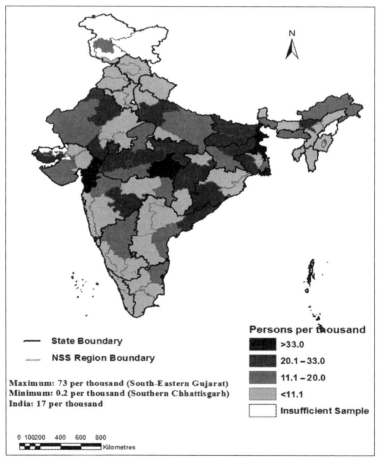

Source: Mishra and Bose (2013).

Poverty and Seasonal Migration from Odisha

Odisha is not only the poorest state in India, but it is also at the bottom in terms of many indicators of social and economic development.[9] Poverty in the state has declined at a remarkably slower rate than in many other poorer states in India. As per the National Human Development, 2001, Odisha's rank was among the lowest. Odisha has the highest IMR among the major states. On many other aspects of social sector development, its performance has been dismal. Odisha's track record in poverty eradication has been one of the worst in the country (Table 10.1). Until recently, in comparative terms, Odisha's track record in fighting poverty has been dismal.[10] In recent years, there has been a dramatic decline in the levels of poverty in Odisha; however, the overall context of poverty and deprivation continues to be worse than the average for the country. As against the national average of 29.8 per cent, Odisha has registered a poverty percentage of 37 per cent as per the 2009–10 figures released by the Planning Commission (2001). The percentage of rural people below the poverty line was 39.2 per cent in Odisha, while it was 33.2 per cent at the all India level. Although the analysis is based on figures based on earlier rounds of NSS,[11] the broad characterization of the nature and pattern of poverty in Odisha remains valid, despite the recent claims of reduction in its extent.

Poverty in Odisha is spatially and socially concentrated.[12] There are distinct regional patterns in the concentration and inter-temporal trends

Table 10.1

Poverty in Odisha and India, 1973–74 to 2004–05

Year	Odisha			India		
	Rural	*Urban*	*Total*	*Rural*	*Urban*	*Total*
1973–74	67.28	55.62	66.18	56.44	49.01	54.88
1977–78	72.38	50.92	70.07	53.07	45.24	51.22
1983	67.53	49.15	65.29	45.65	40.79	44.48
1987–88	57.64	41.53	55.58	39.09	38.20	38.85
1993–94	49.72	41.64	48.56	37.27	32.36	35.97
2004–05	46.80	44.30	46.40	28.30	25.70	27.50

Source: Mishra (2009) and http://pib.nic.in/archieve/others/2007/mar07/2007032102.xls.
Note: The above are official estimates given by the Planning Commission.

in the incidence of poverty. Poverty in coastal Odisha has declined to comparatively low levels, while that in the north and south Odisha, it has continuously remained high. Regional and social concentration of poverty reinforces each other—SCs and STs have higher rates of poverty than others, but STs/SCs of interior Odisha have a remarkably higher probability of being poor than their counterparts in coastal Odisha (de Haan and Dubey, 2005; Mishra, 2009; Panda, 2008; Shah et al., 2005). This spatial and social concentration of poverty in Odisha is rooted in the historical processes of economic transformation and stagnation. The structural inequalities in the distribution of assets and entitlements mirror the underlying processes of social hierarchies, discrimination and exclusion. The agrarian economy of Odisha and the way it has been transformed since the colonial period provides clues to the regionally and socially differentiated poverty regime in rural Odisha.

It is precisely in the two poorest regions of Odisha (Northern and Southern), where an overwhelming majority of SC and SC population lives. For Odisha as a whole, the incidence of poverty among the ST and the SC is higher than that among the others. Between 1993–94 and 2004–05, poverty ratio, in fact, has increased among the STs and SCs in the northern and southern districts. This spatial and social concentration of poverty among the tribals and Dalits living in interior districts of Odisha is the outcome of the historical processes of exclusion and discrimination that have been among the pronounced features of the social economy of the region. But the exclusion from and unequal access to state-initiated anti-poverty measures also has significant bearing on such outcomes (Shah et al., 2005).

Historically, the regions of northern and southern Odisha has been the home of a number of tribal groups, which were gradually brought under the direct and indirect political control of British colonialism. Many of these areas were ruled by small princely states under the patronage of the British colonial government, while much of coastal Odisha was under the direct rule of the British government. While migration of the people from the plains to these hinterlands had a long history, during the colonial period, the rulers of these tribal-dominated states, in an effort to raise more revenue, started providing incentives to cultivators and traders to settle in their kingdoms. Simultaneously, there was a gradual attempt to change the property rights structures over land, forest, water bodies, and so on, in favour of the state. Access to forests and other common property resources were restricted and regulated. There is some evidence to show that the caste composition of the zamindars and *gauntias*, the village-level representatives of the state, also underwent some changes. Gradually, the upper castes started taking control from the tribal chieftains. The response of the tribals took various forms, from rebellion to gradual submission. During the colonial period, there were a series of tribal rebellions in these princely states, which were basically protests against encroachments by the state and outsiders upon what the tribals thought as their traditional sources of livelihood. Faced with severe and recurrent droughts, some of the tribals also migrated to the distant tea plantations in Assam.

In the post-independence period, a remarkable aspect of the 'transfer of power' in the *garjats*, as these princely states were known, was the continuity of the structure of authority and control. The feudal rulers of the princely states simply reinvented themselves as leaders of their erstwhile subjects and started controlling political power in this region for many decades. In more than one sense, this continuity of political leadership has been influencing the political developments of this region till date.

After independence, starting with the Hirakud multi-purpose dam on Mahanadi and a steel plant at Rourkela, a number of development projects were launched by the government in this area. It was expected that these projects, through various forward and backward linkages, would create prosperity in this backward region. To a limited extent, it did act as the catalyst for agricultural and industrial development in parts of the state, but for the people who lost their land, these projects became symbols of domination of the state and outsiders. Factories and roads came up, but a large section of the local inhabitants, particularly tribals, continued to remain as victims rather than participants in the onward march of development. Forests, which were so central to the livelihood security of the people, thanks to state's apathy and greed of the few, disappeared. The state policy of supplying forest products at a low price to the industrialists made matters worse. Although, some of the Non-Timber Forest Products (NTFPs) were nationalized, the operations of the state agencies, instead of helping the producers and collectors of these products, actually penalized them. The traditional irrigation systems, such as community tanks and wells in Balangir and Kalahandi, died a slow death, thanks to the government's apathy and clash of interests at the local level. Agricultural productivity, barring a few areas, remained stagnant. The processes of land alienation through debt bondage continued unabated (Sarap, 1991b). And finally a stage came where Kalahandi, Balangir and Koraput (KBK) region came to be recognized as synonymous with mass poverty, starvation and hunger deaths (Curie, 2000; Lokadrusti, 1993;

Mishra and Rao, 1992). The varied kinds of state intervention, in favour of capital, and against the poor and marginalized have been mediated through unequal power relations at the grassroots. The development projects have not been able to create alternative sources of livelihood for those who were displaced. Again, because of various reasons including resource degradation, diversion of resources for industrial, mining and conservation projects, those sections of the society who are dependent upon natural resources such as land, forest and water find it increasingly difficult to sustain their livelihood. Lack of education, poor resource base and slow expansion of alternative employment opportunities have restricted the possibility for alternative livelihood within the region. It is this combination of these two processes, namely dispossession and differentiation, which have created the current crisis of livelihood in parts of Odisha. Seasonal migration from interior Odisha needs to be viewed as an outcome of these histories of dispossession, marginalization and exploitation. That the extent of out-migration has increased in recent decades highlights the deepening of these processes of dispossession.

Seasonal Migration from Odisha: An Analysis of NSS Data

In this section, an attempt has been made to understand the characteristics of seasonal migrants from Odisha on the basis of the NSS 64th round data. The percentage of short-term migrants is low at 1.7 per cent in India. In Odisha, it is 1.34 per cent, where the percentage of short-term migration of males is higher at 2.3 per cent than that of females, which is only 0.5 per cent (Tables 10.2 and 10.3). Region-wise, the highest percentage of short-term migration in Odisha is found in the Southern Region at 71.4 per cent (Table 10.4). The southern districts of Odisha are also known for its highest incidence of poverty among rural regions in India. As NSSO data suggests, although a small percentage of population is engaged in short-term migration, it is interesting and important to know the characteristics of the population engaged in it because analysis reveals that it is a distress-induced livelihood option of the poorest in the rural population. Although given the limitations of sample size, it would be difficult to generalize the results, it provides important insights into the background characteristics of seasonal migrants in Odisha.

Table 10.2

Seasonal migrants, all states/UTs

States/UT	Seasonal Migrants as Percentage of Population	States/UT	Seasonal Migrants as Percentage of Population
Jammu & Kashmir	1.35	**West Bengal**	**2.44**
Himachal Pradesh	0.51	**Jharkhand**	**2.61**
Punjab	0.71	**Odisha**	**1.33**
Chandigarh	0.00	Chhattisgarh	1.66
Uttaranchal	0.43	**Madhya Pradesh**	**2.58**
Haryana	0.40	**Gujarat**	**3.38**
Delhi	0.22	Daman & Diu	1.27
Rajasthan	1.52	Dadar & Haveli	0.01
Uttar Pradesh	1.37	Maharashtra	1.18
Bihar	**3.04**	**Andhra Pradesh**	**1.38**
Sikkim	0.37	Karnataka	1.12
Arunachal Pradesh	1.80	Goa	0.93
Nagaland	**3.00**	Lakshadweep	0.41
Manipur	0.47	Kerala	0.49
Mizoram	0.41	Tamil Nadu	1.14
Tripura	0.30	Pondicherry	1.09
Meghalaya	1.27	Andaman & Nicobar	0.54
Assam	1.16	Total	1.69

Source: Unit level Data, NSSO, 64th Round.

Table 10.3

Seasonal migration, Odisha (rural)

Sex	Migrant	Non-Migrant	Total
Male	(2.22) [82.55]	(97.77) [48.96]	(100) [49.41]
Female	(0.46) [17.45]	(99.54) [51.04]	(100) [50.59]
Total	(1.32) [100]	(98.67) [100]	(100) [100]

Source: Same as in Table 10.2.
Note: Figures in parentheses refer to percentage to row totals and those in square brackets refer percentages to column totals.

Table 10.4

Seasonal migration, region-wise Odisha (rural)

Sex	Coastal	Southern	Northern	Total
Male	(11.76)	(72.72)	(15.51)	(100)
	[97.37]	[84.11]	[68.66]	[82.55]
Female	(1.50)	(64.99)	(33.50)	(100)
	[2.63]	[15.89]	[31.34]	[17.45]
Total	(9.97)	(71.38)	(18.65)	(100)
	[100]	[100]	[100]	[100]

Source: Same as in Table 10.2.
Note: Figures in parentheses refer to the percentage to row totals and those in square brackets refer percentages to column totals.

Table 10.5

Seasonal migrants by social category, Odisha (rural)

Social Category	In Percent
ST	40.83
SC	23.58
OBC	23.49
Others	12.11
Total	100.00

Source: Same as in Table 10.2.

Table 10.5 shows the distribution of short-term migrants by social category. It is the highest among the ST at 41 per cent followed by SC and OBC at 24 per cent.

Destination during longest spell: The destination of short-term migrants shown in Table 10.6 reflects that the males mostly migrate to urban areas either within the state or outside it. Female migrants, on the other hand, migrate to rural areas. 52 per cent females had migrated to rural areas outside the state. Short-term migration of female members to urban areas outside the state is very low at 5 per cent, whereas the same for males is the highest at 28 per cent.

Short-term migration is highest among households engaged in agricultural labour (38 per cent) and other non-farm labour (28 per cent). Households that are self-employed in agriculture constitute 20 per cent of the total migrants (Table 10.7). Such households, though possessing

Table 10.6

Seasonal migrants, by destination during longest spell (rural)

Destination Duration Longest Spell	Male	Female	Total
Same district rural	7.98	5.02	7.46
Same district urban	14.56	3.19	12.58
Inter-district rural	10.83	25.97	13.47
Inter-district urban	23.15	8.84	20.66
Interstate rural	15.84	52.16	22.17
Interstate urban	27.64	4.84	23.66
Total	100	100	100

Source: Unit level Data, NSSO, 64th Round Migration.

Table 10.7

Seasonal migrants, by household type (rural)

Household Type	Short-term Migrants
Self-employed in non-agriculture	10.64
Agricultural labour	38.09
Other labour	28.08
Self-employed in agriculture	20.55
Others	2.64
Total	100

Source: Unit level Data, NSSO, 64th Round Migration.

land, belong to the category of small and marginal farmers as evident from Table 10.8. Over 80 per cent of short-term migrants belong to households possessing land less than or equal to just an acre. Although the percentage of migrants out of total population is low, and a large percentage of land poor have not migrated, what is clear is that the incidence of short-term migration declines sharply among those who have more land. Landlessness, thus, appears to be a vital push factor for migration.

Table 10.9 is an interesting one as it is observed that migration is highest among the illiterate. It increases for persons having some kind of primary and lower primary education and again sharply declines for higher levels of education. Short-term migration in Odisha is, therefore, an option either for the illiterate seeking low-end jobs or for those with a little education, which may or may not facilitate a more remunerative migration.

Table 10.8

Seasonal migrants, by total land possessed (rural)

Land Holding (in Acres)	Percentage of Total Migrants
less than 0.01	25.64
0.02–1.00	57.03
1.01–2.0	16.01
2.01–4.00	1.25
4.01 and above	0.06
Total	100

Source: Unit level Data, NSSO, 64th Round Migration.

Table 10.9

Short-term migrants, by literacy status (rural)

Literacy/Educational Status	Total
Not literate	38.36
Below primary (and others)	19.10
Primary	14.05
Upper primary/middle	17.77
Secondary	5.95
Higher secondary and above	2.99
Total	100

Source: Unit level Data, NSSO, 64th Round Migration.

The Usual Principle Activity Status (UPAS) of migrants, both male and female, suggests that they are dominantly engaged in 'casual wage' at the source areas/village (Table 10.10). This phenomenon is highly prevalent among the females as 88 per cent of females out of the total labour force belong to the 'casual wage' category compared to 66 per cent for males. The characteristics of land poorness, low literacy levels, engagement in casual wage labour (both agricultural and other labour) together reflect the poverty vulnerability of short-term migrants of Odisha.

The distribution of migrants across industries shows that they are mostly engaged in construction (36 per cent) and manufacturing (38 per cent). More females (25 per cent) than males are also seen to participate in agricultural activities at destination places.

Table 10.10

Seasonal migrants, by UPAS of those in labour force at origin (rural)

Usual Principal Activity Status	Male	Female	Total
Self-employed	28.14	11.63	25.73
Regular wage/salaried	2.96	0	2.53
Casual wage	66.05	88.37	69.3
Unemployed	2.85	0	2.44
Total labour force	100	100	100

Source: Unit level Data, NSSO, 64th Round Migration.

There are strong linkages between short-term migration and poverty because the phenomenon is mostly prevalent among the population which belongs to the lower MPCE class as shown in Table 10.11. This is true for both male and female migrants as 66 per cent of these migrants belong to the lowest MPCE classes (bottom 30 decile group) (Table 10.11).

To sum up, there is a neat correspondence between the spatial and social concentration of poverty on the one hand and that of seasonal migration, on the other. It is precisely in those regions where poverty ratios are higher and seasonal migration is more prevalent. Similarly, it is the SCs and STs of Odisha who have a higher share both in the population below the poverty line and also among the seasonal migrants. Seasonal migrants typically belong to the marginalized sections in terms of land ownership and employment patterns and also they are over-represented among the poor. In other words, unlike the case with migrants, in general, seasonal migrants are, by and large, a more vulnerable and disadvantaged group.

Table 10.11

Seasonal migrant households in different MPCE decile classes

MPCE Decile Classes	Male	Female	Total
Bottom 3 (0–30)	66.37	65.67	66.26
Middle 3 (30–60)	24.51	16.09	23.05
Top 4 (60–100)	9.1	18.25	10.69
All total	100	100	100

Source: Unit level Data, NSSO, 64th Round Migration.

The Drivers of Seasonal Migration from Odisha: Insights from Field Survey

This section is based on our field survey in six villages in Nuapada, Kalahandi and Balangir districts. Apart from in-depth interviews with migrant workers, members of families of migrant workers who are left behind, non-migrant labour and farmer households, labour contractors and their agents, NGO activists, journalists, traders, lawyers, local officials and politicians, we have also conducted focus group discussions with different groups in these villages. These findings on the nature, causes and implications of seasonal migration in the study region have been cross-checked and/or supplemented with two other micro-level information: (a) the migration register maintained by local NGOs[13] and (b) a study sponsored by the district administration of Nuapada (Tripathy and D.J. Research and Consultancy, n.d.).

The migration process starts months before the actual migration takes place, in the month of September and October, during the *nuakhai* festival. Labour contractors, *sardars,* and their agents start advancing small sums of money as advance to labour families in exchange for their promise to migrate. Generally, the advance is given to a household group called *pathuria,* consisting of a man, his wife and a young child. The lump-sum money advance that they get ranges from 8,000–10,000 per person.[14] In the last one year, there has been an increase in the amount of advance money. In most cases, this advance is spent in paying off old debts, social ceremonies, like marriages, and in repairing and construction of houses. Very rarely we have found evidences of the money being spent in acquiring new productive assets such as land or bullocks.

Destinations of Seasonal Migrants

Seasonal migrants from this region go to few specific locations and work in particular industries, although, in the past five years or so there has been a significant increase in the destination as well as in the number of occupations in which the migrants work. Some of the significant streams of seasonal migration have been noted below.

Brick-kilns of Andhra Pradesh/Uttar Pradesh

More than two lakh labourers migrate to the brick kilns of Andhra Pradesh every winter, immediately after the harvesting season. Mostly, they migrate to the brick kilns in the vicinity of Hyderabad, Sikanderabad, Vijayanagaram and Vishakhapatnam. From parts of Nuapada district, migrants go to the brick kilns of Faizabad and other districts of Uttar Pradesh. The history of this migration is at least two decades old, but it was the severe drought of 1996–97 that was the turning point in the history of this migration. This migration starts during November–December and continues up to May–June. Another group of migrants, who mostly intend to find work in the brick industry as loaders, start late, that is around late December and stay until July. These migration contracts are negotiated through contractors and often the workers do not have any idea about the destination in which they are going to work. Most of the migrants return within six months. There are migrants who go to different towns of Uttar Pradesh as well. In recent years, some workers have started migrating to Chennai and Bengaluru.

Brick Kilns within Odisha

Of late, many migrants have started going to brick kilns in various urban centres of coastal Odisha, such as Bhubaneswar, Cuttack, Jagatsinghpur and Puri. In most cases, the workers find work through *dalals* and contractors, but in some cases, they search for work independently. Here, there is a lot of variability in the period of migration: it varies from one to six months.

Agricultural Labour in Irrigated Belts of Odisha

In the neighbouring districts of Bargarh and Sambalpur, irrigation from Hirakud dam project has facilitated intensive wet rice cultivation. The demand for labour picks up during the periods of transplantation, weeding and harvesting. Groups of relatively young men and women move together to work under piece-rate contracts for specific types of farm work. At times, farmers visit their villages, pay an advance and seal a contract before the group travels to the destination, and at times, the workers travel to key points like Bargarh bus stand where prospective employers or contractors negotiate the deals with them.

Rickshaw-pulling, Hotels in Chhattisgarh

There is a long history of migration from these districts to cities like Raipur and Bilaspur. Many of the rickshaw pullers in the capital city of Raipur are from these districts of Odisha. There is a large population from these areas in the slums of Raipur. However, apart from the permanent migrants to Chhattisgarh, many seasonal migrants also find work in the towns of Chhattisgarh.

Agricultural Farms in Chhattisgarh

A comparatively new phenomenon is the creation of large horticultural and agricultural farms in Chhattisgarh by farmers from Rajasthan, Gujarat, Punjab and Haryana. These farms mostly supply vegetables to different cities like Nagpur and Raipur. Seasonal migrants, particularly those belonging to the *mali* caste, have started going to these farms in recent years.

Construction Work

In recent years, many of the seasonal workers have started working in the construction sector in cities like Chennai, Mumbai, Delhi, Bengaluru and Thiruvananthapuram. Some of them are attached to specific labour contractors or employers and they keep on working wherever they are sent to work. Some of these mobile workers have moved to interior areas of Jammu and Kashmir, Himachal Pradesh and Arunachal Pradesh, particularly to work in the road construction sector. Those who are migrating alone or with families have a distinct advantage over those who have migrated under contracts with labour agents or *sardars*. Those negotiating the terms of employment directly with prospective employers have a chance of getting better wages and more freedom in terms of leaves.

Urban Informal Service Sector

In recent years, there has been a significant rise in the number of seasonal migrants who work in the urban informal sector in various cities of India. Although their numbers are still very small in comparison with those who are going for work in the brick kilns, this group of relatively young and better-educated seasonal migrants mostly work in the hotels and restaurants, transports, catering and security services, in major cities of south India. Many of them aspire to be long-term migrants, have better earnings than other seasonal migrants and have been able to save and remit more than other categories of seasonal migrants.

Elements of Unfreedom in Seasonal Migration

As more and more people have started leaving these migration-prone districts, serious concerns have raised about the implications of such seasonal out-migration. The debate on this at the village level was found to be a highly polarized one. All seasonal migrants and members of their households expressed seasonal migration as a 'choice under compulsion'. They are all aware of the fact that they have to live under very difficult situations, work very hard for unusually long hours (10–14 hours) and are aware that they are not paid what is their due. Yet, they prefer to go every year, as the alternative is unemployment and even hunger. It is true that over the years, there have been attempts to provide employment through Mahatma Gandhi National Rural Employment Guarantee Act (MGNREGA), and distributing rice at subsidized rates through Public Distribution System (PDS). Still this is not sufficient for the migrants to survive for the entire period. For many of them it is the question of repayment of past debts that forces them to go. In all the interviews and group discussion that we conducted, it was clear that seasonal migration (particularly to brick kilns of Andhra Pradesh) was a less preferred option for the migrants.

There are several elements of bondage that could be noticed in these seasonal migration contracts.

(a) Migrants and their families have taken money in advance, which makes their choices limited in the end. They have to go and often these commitments are strictly monitored by a chain of intermediaries—including labour contractors, sub-contractors and their agents—right up to the village level. Also, there are severe spillover effects of not honouring the contracts as a defaulter is easily discoverable by labour contractors in the area.

(b) Often migration contracts are limited to the period of work. The rates per thousand of bricks made and the rate that migrant workers are paid are generally not specified by the labour contractors. After reaching the destination, the migrants have no choice but to work as per the rates specified by their employers. Re-negotiation of contracts, at the place of work, after the workers have arrived, puts the migrant worker at obvious disadvantages. At times, when less bricks are made because of factors not in the control of labourers, such as untimely rain or poor quality of soil, the workers are not compensated for their loss.

(c) More often than not, migrant workers are taken to their place of work by the labour contractors or their agents. But the workers are not aware of their destinations. They reach specific railway stations and thereafter the brick kiln owner and their agents/supervisors take them to their work destinations. Workers do not have any information about their place of work, their employers or the rates that have been fixed through negotiations between labour contractors and employers.

(d) If the workers do not want to continue working, for reasons of illness or any other problem, they are subjected to worst forms of coercion and at times violence. They do not have the right to move anywhere or to seek other kinds of employment in their destination sites.

Such instances of bondage are reported primarily from the workers who had gone for work in the brick kilns. However, migrants to other sectors also report such occasional instances of extra-economic exploitation by the employers. There were stories of struggle and collective resistance as well. At the individual level, experience from years of migration has enabled some workers to resist extreme forms of bondage. Access to mobile phone itself has acted as a catalyst for communication and workers have been able to be in touch with their family members and friends, working in other areas or with those staying back in the villages.

Local Dynamics of Seasonal Migration

The linkages between seasonal migration and poverty are too obvious in the region. Firstly, it is the cycles of debt, mostly taken to finance daily consumption needs, catastrophic health expenditures and social ceremonies that has made 'advance money' the cornerstone of household survival. In every year, new debts are taken and the only way to pay this back is through seasonal migration. We got some indirect evidence of this in Botha village, where because of a relatively successful micro-credit programme, the dependence on high-interest informal loan has declined. From this village, fewer people have migrated and those who have done so have bargained for a better deal.

Secondly, low agricultural productivity is at the bottom of the crisis. As such rain-fed, single-crop, subsistence agriculture does not have the capacity to absorb labour particularly in the context of high degree of landlessness. Even today, for small and marginal farmers, migration decisions are linked to crop production. In years of drought or crop failure, more people tend to migrate from this group. However, the situation is far more structural in nature, as an analysis of cotton farming in the region shows. Cotton cultivation is expanding in the region because of the push given by the agriculture department and private traders. The farmers have taken huge loans from the traders, commission agents and informal lenders to purchase seeds, fertilizers and pesticides. Often these loans are inter-linked with product sale arrangements. Thus, small and marginal farmers, through the well-known mechanisms involving inter-linked contracts receive a lower price for the output. In years of crop failure, the situation even worsens. We came across several cases, where failure to get a reasonable earning from cotton cultivation has forced small farmers to go for seasonal migration.

Thirdly, employment generation, either through government-sponsored programmes, like MGNAREGA or through access to non-farm sector in nearby areas, has an impact on migration decisions. In Tentulimunda village, around 20 landless families have stopped migrating because they have been assured of 100 days of work through employment guarantee programme. 'I did not want my child to discontinue his studies', was the response of one of the workers. But almost in every village, there was demand for more work during the lean period.

To a limited extent, the seasonal out-migration of labour has disturbed and altered the established structures of power in the villages. As a large number of labour households have found a source of sustenance during the lean season, they have been able to free themselves from the clutches of exploitative moneylenders and employers in agriculture. Permanent labour contracts, with varying degrees of unfreedom, which were part of the agrarian relations, have almost disappeared. Access to lump-sum cash, once a year has allowed some of the labour households to repair or built their houses. In some cases, particularly in the case of those who have migrated to the cities, migration has brought visible changes in lifestyles and consumption patterns. Mobile phones and jeans have become a marker of the changed social status of migrants. To the extent that most labour migrants belong to the lower castes and tribes, such changes have altered the caste relations in the villages, up to an extent.

Finally, the suggestion that 'seasonal migration can act as a poverty-reduction strategy' needs serious reconsideration. Even though the average income of the households who migrate seasonally tend to be higher than that of labour households who do not go out, even after years of seasonal migration, the conditions of the migrating households have not improved much. There are only few exceptions to this: (a) Seasonal migrants, who have become labour agents have been able to break this cycle of debt-induced migration and have become relatively better-off and (b) households or individuals who migrate to urban construction sector in cities (often through family contacts, but not through agents) have been able to save some money and their conditions are much better than those migrating to the brick kilns.

As of now, such seasonal migration has led to several adverse outcomes for the migrants and the families. The worst victims are old parents, children and women. The seasonal migration for work has meant disruption of studies for the children and the situation has not improved much even after some innovative interventions by NGOs. The denial of access to education acts as a key factor forcing children to depend on seasonal migration, when they grow into adults. Women, when they migrate with their families, are subjected to a number of different kinds of problems apart from long hours of work, including sexual violence. When they stay back, they have to take extra work burden to manage the households. We encountered many women who found the situation difficult to cope up with. It was also difficult for the elderly people to survive this long spell without any help. Some of them did not get health care or even food during this period.

The initial response of the state was to ignore the problem. However, repeated media attention, video footages of large number of migrants leaving railway stations and cases of torture at worksites created awareness about the problem, the response was to criminalize seasonal migration, often through sporadic arrests of agents and labour contractors. While there has not been any systematic attempt to implement the Inter-state Migration Act, periodic episodes of police action has made seasonal migrants more vulnerable. They have tried to migrate through alternate routes, often in disguise as marriage parties, and have agreed to work for lower rates and advances. In recent years, the bonded labour act has been invoked to rescue groups of workers. However, the rehabilitation of workers has not been good enough for migrants to stop migration. In specific cases, rescued workers have again migrated to survive the lean season. Over the years, seasonal labour market has created an entrenched network of contractors and agents in the local area, so much so that when police tried to intervene and arrest labour contractors from a hotel in Kantabanji, the hub of labour trade in the region, the local politicians, including an MLA gheraoed the police station demanding their quick release.[15]

The local political economy of accumulation is deeply entrenched in the seasonal labour process. Although Kantabanji has emerged as a key trading centre since long, the labour migration network has already been established as a key aspect of the local economy. A number of sectors and activities, such as hotel and restaurants, transport, petty and wholesale trading, informal lending and agriculture, have been deeply entrenched in the circulation of the money that flows into the region from employers in faraway cities and worksites. Interviews with labour contractors and journalists revealed that workers receive only a fraction of what is paid as labour costs by prospective employers; a series of middlemen and rent-seekers stake claims over the money flows. Over the years, the flow of money has been increasing in its volume and it has become a durable feature of the local economy. As the previously dominant landlord classes have got fragmented and have moved to various non-farm sources of earnings, labour circulation has become a preferred arena for rent seeking and accumulation for some of them.

Summary of Findings and Policy Implications

Against the claims, first, that seasonal migration results from the optimization strategy of households to combine livelihoods options through temporary spatial reallocation of labour (Hampshire and Randall, 1999) and, second, that since both poor and rich migrate, there is no obvious link between poverty and migration (Kundu and Sarangi, 2007), this chapter provides evidence to suggest that there is a need to distinguish between long-term and seasonal migration. It finds that seasonal migration is more likely to be a distress-driven-coping strategy against poverty and limited options for livelihoods in the areas of origin. What is of particular importance is to note that even in the age of globalization, which is, pulling in labour to India's urban hubs, the traditionally existing pre-capitalist entities are getting reconfigured.

Seasonal migration is not only the outcome of decisions made by individuals, but those who migrate also operate within the local political and economic structures. There are strong linkages between migration and the production relations in agriculture in the origin areas, both as the conditions that trigger seasonal migration and also in terms of the impact of migration on these structures. While out-migration has a long history in the region, known for recurrent drought, chronic poverty and hunger, in the recent phase, seasonal migration has come to be a stable and recurrent phenomenon institutionalized through complex networks of kinship, reciprocity and bondage. The adverse incorporation of migrant labour into the global production networks signals the continuing significance of *unfreedom* under global capitalism. The study also brings out the diversity in the outcomes of seasonal migration, both at the inter-household as well as intra-household levels, in terms of its manifold implications for food security, gender equity and well-being. Low productivity of agriculture, landlessness, low levels of education, limited access to alternative livelihoods and food and employment insecurity during the lean period emerge as significant determinants of seasonal migration. However, the key element of distress that drives the desire to migrate is the loans advanced by labour contractors and their agents. Hence, seasonal migration contracts have been analyzed in the context of the changing informal credit market operating in the region. Improved communication networks, civil society interventions and rising labour demand in urban India have resulted in significant changes in the bargaining power of the rural labour in comparison to the past, but the primary motive for such migration continues to be distress driven. The study also brings out the significance as well as the limitations of employment guarantee programmes in reducing the vulnerability of migrant households.

Notes

1. The author wishes to thank Dinesh Kumar Nayak and Rukmini Thapa for their assistance in this research. Thanks are due to Lokadrusti, Yuva, Abani Panigrahi and Sanjay Mishra for their generous help during the field survey.

2. '[S]easonality "in itself" implies an increase in the degree poverty' (Gill, 1992, p. 11, *emphasis in original*).
3. See for example, Breman (1985), Rogaly (1999), Rogaly et al. (2001), Deshingkar and Start (2003), Deshingkar and Farrington (2009) among others.
4. While there is a well-documented research on the 'unfreedom' that characterizes, much of such labour migration from relatively less developed areas to cities and fields (Breman, 2007), this recent research views seasonal migration as a 'voluntary response' of the poor to escape out of poverty. It is seen as part of the livelihoods strategy of the poor that is, at least partly, seen as an response to increasing opportunities in a growing economy. In fact, such temporary migration is seen as part of the 'trickling down' of economic prosperity to the bottom through spatial adjustments in the labour market. This study presents results of a field survey in interior Odisha that questions this optimistic view on seasonal migration.
5. These models explain migration as an equilibrating mechanism, which, by transferring labour from the traditional labour-surplus, low-productive agricultural sector to the modern, labour-deficit, highly productive, industrial sector, brings about wage equality in the two sectors.
6. Chandra (2004, p. 28) notes 'migration serves capital by providing cheap labour and it increases competition among workers putting downward pressure on wage level of indigenous workers.' Olsen and Murthy (2000), in their study on the plight of Palamur labourers from Mahbubnagar district in Andhra Pradesh suggest that exploitation is both direct and indirect—wages are lower than market wages and there is extraction of overtime and child labour.
7. Munshi and Rosenzweig (2009) attribute this to the presence of sub-caste networks that provide mutual insurance to their members.
8. Srivastava (1999) also finds a similar result for Uttar Pradesh.
9. This section is based on Mishra (2011).
10. 'State level income poverty data reveal that in 1999–2000 Odisha has become India's poorest state, surpassing Bihar that was still the poorest in 1993–94 but showed a substantial decline in poverty during the late 1990s. At the end of the 1990s, Odisha agricultural wages also were lower than in any other state. Odisha's poverty headcount stagnated around 48–49 per cent between 1993–94 and 1999–2000, while at all-India level, the headcount declined markedly, in Andhra Pradesh poverty halved, and even Madhya Pradesh showed a decline of 5 percentage points. For Odisha, the trend of falling behind the Indian average has a longer history, but is particularly marked during the 1990s.' (de Haan and Dubey, 2005).
11. The latest rounds of NSS data (2009–10) were not available at the time of writing of this report. For a comparative understanding of poverty in the districts of Odisha, see Chaudhuri and Gupta (2009).
12. *NSSO Regions*: Odisha.
Coastal: Baleshwar, Jajapur, Bhadrak, Nayagarh, Kendrapara, Khordha, Jagatsinghapur, Puri, Cuttack.
Southern: Ganjam, *Nuapada*, Gajapati, *Kalahandi*, Kandhamal, Rayagada, Phoolbani, Nabarangapur, Baudh, Koraput, Sonapur, Malkangiri, *Balangir*.
Northern: Bargarh, Kendujhar, Jharsuguda, Mayurbhanj, Sambalpur, Dhenkanal, Debagarh, Anugul, Sundargarh.
13. Migration records have been maintained by several NGOs working in the region including Lokadrusti, Adhikar, Yuva, Vikalpa and so on. These records are often scattered in village-level offices of the organization and have not yet been consolidated, codified and

analyzed. But these are a more or less reliable source of information on the people who have left the village for seasonal work. Sometimes labourers have left the village without informing the NGO/panchayat representatives and to that extent, these are not complete census of seasonal migrants.

14. In 2013, the rates have gone up to ₹12000. (author's subsequent visit; Vakulabharanam, 2013).

15. The incident was reported in several local newspapers, including *The Samaj*, 19 November 2012.

References

Badiani, R. and Safir, A. (2009). 'Circular migration and labour supply: Responses to climate shocks'. In P. Deshingkar and J. Farrington (eds). *Circular Migration and Multilocational Livelihood Strategies in Rural India* (pp. 37–57). Delhi: OUP

Breman, J. (1985). *Of peasants, migrants, and paupers*. Delhi: Oxford University Press.

———. (1996). *Footloose labour: Working in the Indian informal economy*. Cambridge: Cambridge University Press.

Breman, J. (2007). *Labour bondage in West India: From past to present*. New Delhi: Oxford University Press.

Chambers, R., Longhurst, R., and Pacey, A. (eds) (1981). *Seasonal Dimensions to Rural Poverty*. London: Frances Pinter.

Chandra, N. (2004). 'Economics and politics of labour circulation'. In K. Gopal Iyer (ed.), *Distressed Migrant Labour in India: Key Human Rights Issues* (pp. 22–33). *New Delhi: Kanishka.*

Chaudhuri, S. and Gupta, N. (2009). 'Levels of living and poverty patterns: A district-wise analysis for India'. *Economic and Political Weekly*, 44(9), 94–110.

Curie, B. (2000). *The politics of hunger in India*. Chennai: Pan Macmillan.

de Haan, A. and Dubey, A. (2005). 'Poverty, disparities, or the development of underdevelopment in Orissa'. *Economic and Political Weekly*, 40(22/23), 2321–29.

de Haan, A. and Rogaly, B. (2002). 'Introduction: Migrant workers and their role in rural change'. *Journal of Development Studies*, 38(5), 1–14.

de Haan, A., Brock, K., and Coulibaly, N. (2002). 'Migration, livelihoods and institutions: Contrasting patterns of migration in Mali'. *Journal of Development Studies*, 38(5), 37–58.

Deshingkar, P. and Farrington, J. (eds.). (2009). *Circular migration and multilocational livelihood strategies in rural India*. Delhi: Oxford University Press.

Deshingkar, P. and Start, D. (2003). 'Seasonal migration for livelihoods in India: Coping, accumulation and exclusion'. Working Paper No. 220. London: Overseas Development Institute.

Deshingkar, P., Farrington, J., Rao, S.L., and Akter, S. (2009). 'The evolving pattern of circular migration and commuting: Household surveys in Andhra Pradesh'. In P. Deshingkar and J. Farrington (eds), *Circular migration and multilocational livelihood strategies in rural India* (pp. 58–87). *Delhi: OUP.*

Deshingkar, P., Sharma P., Kumar S., Akter S., and Farrington J. (2008). 'Circular migration in Madhya Pradesh: Changing patterns and Social Protection Needs'. *The European Journal of Development Research*, 20(4), December 2008, 612–28.

Dev, S. Mahendra, Panda, M., and Sarap, Kailas (2004). 'Poverty reduction strategies for Orissa', Report prepared for the Government of Orissa.

Devereux, S. (2010). 'Seasonal food crisis and social protection in Africa'. In B. Harriss-White and J. Heyer (eds.), *The comparative political economy of development*. Abingdon: Routledge.

Gill, G.J. (1992). *Seasonality and agriculture in the developing world: A problem for the poor and powerless*. Cambridge: Cambridge University Press.

Hampshire, K., and Randall, S.C. (1999). 'Seasonal Labour Migration Strategies in the Sahel: Coping with Poverty or Optimising Security?' *International Journal of Population Geography* 5, 367–85.

Harris, J., and Todaro, M.P. (1970). 'Migration, unemployment and development: A two sector analysis'. *American Economic Review*, 60(1), 126–42.

Harriss-White, B., and Garikipati, S. (2008). 'India's semi-arid rural economy: Livelihoods, seasonal migration and gender'. *The European Journal of Development Research*, 20(4), 547–48.

Joshi, Y.G., and Verma, D.K. (2004). *In search of livelihood: Labour migration from Chattishgarh*. New Delhi: Manak.

Keshri, K., and Bhagat, R.B. (2012). 'Temporary and Seasonal Migration in India: Regional Pattern, Characteristics and Associated Factors'. *Economic and Political Weekly*, 47(4), 81–88.

Kothari, U. (2002). *Migration and chronic poverty* (Working Paper No. 16). Manchester: University of Manchester.

Kundu, A., and Sarangi, N. (2007). 'Migration, employment status and poverty: An analysis across urban centres', *Economic and Political Weekly*, 42(4), 299–306.

Lee, E.S. (1966). 'A theory of migration'. *Demography*, 3(1), 47–57.

Lewis, W.A. (1954). 'Economic development with unlimited supplies of labour'. *The Manchester School of Economic and Social Studies*, 22(2), 139–91 (Reprinted in Agarwala and Singh (eds) 1958).

Lokadrusti (1993). *Boden: A societal appraisal (A socio-economic study of twenty hamlets in Boden block, Kalahandi District, Orissa)*, Lokadrusti, Khariar.

McDowell, C., and de Haan, A. (1997). *Migration and sustainable livelihoods: A critical review of the literature* (IDS Working Paper No. 65). Brighton: University of Sussex.

Mishra, D., and Rao, R.S. (1992). 'Hunger in Kalahandi: Blinkered understanding'. *Economic and Political Weekly*, 27(24–25), 1245–46.

Mishra, Deepak K. (2011). 'Behind dispossession: State, land grabbing and agrarian change in rural Orissa', Paper presented at the International Conference on Global Land Grabbing, 6-8 April 2011, Institute of Development Studies, University of Sussex, Sussex.

Mishra, Deepak K., and Bose, D. (2013). 'Seasonal Migration from Rural India: Emerging Patterns and Characteristics', CSRD, JNU, New Delhi.

Mishra, Srijit (2009). 'Poverty and agrarian distress in Orissa', Working Paper, WP-2009-006, IGIDR, Mumbai.

Mosse, D., Gupta, S., Mehta, M., Shah, V., Rees, J., and the KRIBP Project Team. (2002). 'Brokered livelihoods: Debt, labour migration and development in tribal western India'. *Journal of Development Studies*, 38(5), 59–87.

Munshi, K., and Rosenzweig, R. (2009). 'Why is mobility in India so low? Social insurance, inequality and growth'. NBER Working Paper No. 14850, April 2009. Retrieved from http://www.nber.org/papers/w14850.pdf (accessed on 28 January 2016).

Olsen, W.K., and Murthy, R.V. (2000). 'Contract labour and bondage in Andhra Pradesh (India)'. *Journal of Social and Political Thought*, *1*(2). Retrieved from http://www.yorku.ca/jspot/2/wkolsenrvramana.htm (accessed on 28 January 2016).

Olsen, W.K. (1998). 'Marxist and neo-classical approaches to unfree labour in India'. In T. Brass and M. Van der Linden (eds), *Free and Unfree Labour: The Debate Continues* (pp. 379–404). Berlin: Peter Lang.

Panda, M. (2008). 'Economic Development in Orissa: Growth without Inclusion'. Working Paper, WP-2008-025, IGIDR, Mumbai.

Planning Commission. (2001). *Odisha state development report*. Retrieved from http://planningcommission.nic.in/plans/stateplan/index.php?state=sp_sdrorisa.htm (accessed on 28 January 2016).

Rogaly, B. (1998). 'Workers on the move: Seasonal migration and changing social relations in rural India'. *Gender and Development*, *6*(1), 21–29.

———. (1999). 'Dangerous liasons? Seasonal migration and agrarian change in West Bengal'. In B. Rogaly, B. Harriss-White and S. Bose (eds), *Sonar Bangla? Agricultural growth and agrarian change in West Bengal and Bangladesh*. Delhi: SAGE Publication.

Rogaly, B., Biswas, J., Coppard, D., Rafique, A., Rana, K., and Sengupta, A. (2001). Seasonal migration, social change and migrants rights, lessons from West Bengal. *Economic and Political Weekly*, *36*(49), 4547–59.

Sarap, K. (1991b). *Interlinked Agrarian Markets in Rural India*. New Delhi: SAGE.

Sasikumar, S.K. (2004). 'Theories of internal migration: A critique'. In Iyer K. Gopal (ed.). *Distressed Migrant Labour in India: Key Human Rights Issues* (pp. 34–43). New Delhi: Kanishka.

Shah, A. (2010). Land degradation and migration in a dry land region in India: Extent, nature and determinants. *Environment and Development Economics*, *15*(2), 173–96.

Shah, Amita, Nayak, Saroj Kumar and Das, Bipin (2007). 'Remoteness and chronic poverty in forest region of southern Orissa: A tale of entitlement failure and state's apathy'. Working Paper 34, Chronic Poverty Research Centre and IIPA, New Delhi. Retrieved from http://www.chronicpoverty.org/publications/details/remoteness-and-chronic-poverty-in-a-forest-region-of-southern-orissa-a-tale-of-entitlement-failure-and-state-s-apathy/ss (accessed on 28 January 2016).

Srivastava, R. (1999). 'Rural labour in Uttar Pradesh: Emerging features of subsistence, contradiction and resistance'. *Journal of Peasant Studies*, *26*(2–3), 263–315.

———. (2011). Labour migration in India: Recent trends, patterns and policy issues. *Indian Journal of Labour Economics*, *54*(33), 411–40.

Standing, G. (1985). 'Circulation and the labour process'. In G. Standing (ed.), *Labour circulation and the labour process* (pp. 1–4). London: Croom Helm.

Stark, O. (1991). *The migration of labour*. Cambridge: Basil Blackwell.

———. (1980) 'On the role of urban–rural remittances in rural development'. *Journal of Development Studies*, *16*(3), 369–74.

Stark, O., and Bloom, D.E. (1985). 'The new economics of labour migration'. *The American Economic Review*, *75*(2), 173–78.

Todaro, M.P. (1969). 'A model of labour migration and urban unemployment in less developed countries'. *The American Economic Review*, *59*(1), 138–49.

Tripathy, Damodar, and DJ Research and Consultancy (n.d.). *Study on migration in Nuapada District*. A Report for District Administration, Nuapada.

Vakulabharanam, V. (2013, June 19). 'Building blocks of servitude'. *The Hindu*. Retrieved from http://www.thehindu.com/opinion/lead/building-blocks-of-servitude/article4827450.ece (accessed on 29 January 2016).

11

Internal Labour Migration in India: Emerging Needs of Comprehensive National Migration Policy

Anjali Borhade

Introduction

The goal of this chapter is to provide a snapshot of internal labour migration in India that includes the volume of migration, its linkages with development and emerging needs for national policy to address labour migration. The chapter examines how some states and civil societies in the source and destination level have responded to reduce the vulnerabilities of interstate migrant workers and faced challenges in the absence of exclusive policies for migrant workers while addressing migrants' needs. The chapter also compiles pioneering policies for migrants at international level and further suggests recommended framework for comprehensive national policy for migrant workers in India.

This chapter addresses voluntary internal labour migration (within the country, interstate and intrastate) for paid work, which includes both permanent (residing in undeclared urban slum areas) and seasonal and circular migration (for 2–8 months in a year) from rural–rural, urban–urban, urban–rural and rural–urban areas of India.

Overview of Internal Labour Migration

Evidence shows that more people migrate internally in many countries. Internal migration is important almost everywhere and in some countries it is far greater than international migration. But, international migration has received more attention than internal migration in most of the countries. Seasonal internal migration is a growing phenomenon in India too. Interstate and interstate labour migration is an important feature of the Indian economy. But there is scant official data available on internal migration, especially from all major official data sources such as Census of India, National Commission on Rural Labour (NCRL) and National Sample Survey data. The NCRL estimates the number of internal labour migrants in rural areas in India alone at around 10 million (including roughly 4.5 million interstate migrants and 6 million intrastate migrants). The 2001 census has recorded about 53.3 million rural to rural migrations within the country. While the latest 64th round NSS survey puts a figure of 30 million on internal migration, various estimates based on micro-level studies (Deshingkar, 2004) suggest that the figure is close to 100–120 million (10–12 crores or roughly 10 per cent of India's population). This increase in migration is essentially due to regional differences in the population pressure on land, drought and inequality of infrastructure industrial development and modernization of agriculture. In particular, the developed areas have increased demand for labour during specific seasonal activities, especially sowing and harvesting in the case of agricultural activities. As this demand often supersedes the availability of local labour, these developed regions offer a higher wage rate and/or greater number of days of employment. The agriculturally developed regions are invariably areas, which have extensive canal irrigation and high yielding variety technology. The demand for labour also exists in seasonally based agro-industries, for example, rice mills, sugar factories, canal construction, road construction and so on (Deshingkar and Grimm, 2005).

Most of this movement has been from the most populous and poorest states with net in-migration being higher for the more developed states. States, such as Uttar Pradesh (UP), Bihar, Rajasthan, Odisha, West Bengal, Jharkhand, with laggard economies and a surplus of labour, send millions of migrants every year. Maharashtra, Gujarat, Haryana, Punjab and Tamil Nadu, known for their robust and flourishing local economies, attract a large number of workers. There are certain conspicuous migration corridors within the country—Bihar to national capital region (NCR), Bihar to Haryana and Punjab, UP to Maharashtra (Mumbai), Odisha to

Gujarat (Surat), Odisha to Andhra Pradesh (Hyderabad) and Rajasthan to Gujarat (Ahmedabad).

According to NCRL, a large number of migrants are employed in cultivation and plantations, brick kilns, quarries, construction sites and fish processing. A large number of migrants also work in the urban informal manufacturing construction, services or transport sectors and are employed as casual labourers, head loaders, rickshaw pullers and hawkers (NCRL, 1991). Some of the highest employers of migrants are the construction sector (40 million), domestic work (20 million), textile (11 million), brick kilns (10 million), transportation, mines and quarries and agriculture (Deshingkar and Akter, 2009). Within these sectors, migrants are mostly employed to fulfil the bottom-end tasks which entail back-breaking labour and maximum risk, tasks which the local labour would not be willing to undertake (Breman, 1996).

Internal Labour Migration, Poverty Alleviation and Development Linkages

Migration has become an important livelihood diversification strategy for many poor groups across India. Internal migration is an activity undertaken primarily by young adults in India followed by teenagers and children along with their parents. Migration is a routine livelihood strategy of poor households, which helps to smooth seasonal income fluctuations and earn extra cash to meet contingencies or increase disposable income. There seems to be little doubt that migration can reduce poverty and stimulate economic growth. The evidence is most clear in situations where economies are growing rapidly as in Asia. While many studies on migration have tended to emphasize the impoverishing effects of migration, they have rarely posed the question of what these households and individuals would have done in the absence of the opportunity to migrate (Borhade, 2011; Deshingkar, 2009).

The analysis of[1] remittance flows has tended to focus on flows between rich and poor countries. But, internal remittances (sending earnings/money to home towns by migrant workers) have not received much attention. The strongest evidence of internal remittances contributing to poverty reduction is from economies where urbanization and manufacturing have increased significantly and where rural–urban migrants earn substantially more than they would in rain-fed farming.

In situations where urban wages are high and employment is regular (even if informal), remittances can be significant. A study of migration in Madhya Pradesh, Rajasthan and Gujarat in India found that 80 per cent of cash income in project villages was derived from migration (Mosse, 2002). Karan's study in Bihar showed that remittances accounted for one-third of the average annual income of landless and marginal households sending migrants. By caste, the scheduled castes (SCs), scheduled tribes (STs) and Muslims earned 29 per cent of their income through migration (Karan, 2003). These evidences confirm that internal migration can play an important role in poverty reduction and it should not be controlled.

It is evident that migration can have multiplier effects on the entire sending area through stimulating land and labour markets, increased agricultural production and improved nutrition, health and education (Deshingkar and Grimm, 2005). There is compelling evidence (Chatterjee, 2006) showing that the returns from migration can improve over time as migrants acquire more knowledge, confidence and skills when they can cut out exploitative middlemen and contractors.

Migration also plays an important role in social developments, such as women empowerment. It is evident that migration of women has increased in informal economy due to availability of women-oriented jobs, such as domestic work, garment industry, construction and agriculture (Deshingkar and Grimm, 2005). It was noted among women who do not migrate and stay back in their villages that the prolonged absence of male decision-makers can result in a change in the social order with women becoming more vocal in village 'decision-making' and participating more often and openly. It was also pointed out in the synthesis report of the PPA[2] (participatory poverty assessment) that family dissolution is not necessarily a disempowering experience for women, and it is certainly empowering for some women (Deshingkar, 2009).

These evidences confirm that internal migration can play an important role in development. But migration has not understood at programme and policy level and, hence, issues of migrants are remained unattended and it remained a neglected sub-group of the population in India.

Vulnerabilities of Migrants

While migration has been shown to have economic and other development benefits, it also has serious negative repercussions (Borhade, 2011).

Migrants are inherently vulnerable as subjects of human rights from the time they leave home to initiate their migration. In other words, any human being is less vulnerable at home than right after he leaves it to become a migrant (Bustamante, 2011). Migrant's vulnerability is shaped by many factors, including political and social marginalization and a lack of socio-economic and societal resources (Derose, Escarce and Lurie, 2007) while living in host states where migrants may not master the official language(s), are unfamiliar with the workings of the legal system and administration, detached from traditional support and family networks (Varennes, 2003). Thus, vulnerability of the migrants arises because of living in a place which is different in culture, language, social settings, legal protection, entitlements and consumption habits from their native places and the loss of the traditional support system they enjoyed before migration (Devi and Kumar, 2011). This section explores different vulnerabilities faced by migrants during migration.

- Poverty, powerlessness
- Language barriers
- Alien states, lack of identity
- Discrimination
- Lack of access to (education, health, livelihood, food security)
- Inability to access assistance and government programmes and services
- Unreliable and unsafe savings and remittance facilities.
- Poor living conditions without basic amenities
- Unsafe and hazardous working conditions
- Less or no legal protection
- Lack of information about rights, entitlements and application of laws in general

Legal Protection

The degree of vulnerability in which migrants find themselves depends on a variety of factors, ranging from their legal status to their overall environment. The hiring of migrants in an irregular situation allows employers to escape providing basic minimum services to them including health, education of children, living and working conditions, and more so that the labour force becomes cheaper than recruiting locals/natives.

These migrant workers fall under category of unorganized sector and are eligible for coverage of all existing labour laws, but because they do not have one fixed employer, it is difficult for Labour Department to provide them coverage of these existing labour laws. In the case of internal migrants, their fluidity in terms of movement and their working conditions in the informal work arrangements in the city debar them from access to adequate care (Borhade, 2011; WHO, 2003, 2008).

Identity and Access to Entitlements

Usually, the benefits of the schemes run by individual state governments are available to persons having resident status and/or legal identity in the respective state that includes range of documents for residential proof, such as local ration card, electricity bill, PAN card, passport and the newly launched Aadhaar card. Migrants, in general, do not have resident status in the destination state. Lack of legal identity of destination state is major problem for migrant workers while accessing basic entitlements including social security, health insurance, education of children, financial inclusion and basic services during their migration period. Identity issue remains cross cutting for access to all these services.

In such a situation, the migrants (both intrastate and interstate) lose their entitlements when they cross borders of their native state or district. For instance, a migrant labourer from states such as Bihar, Odisha, West Bengal or Assam migrates to Kerala, who has been availing rice or wheat and other provisions at subsidized price through the Public Distribution System (PDS) in the home state, is unlikely to benefit from the PDS in Kerala. Some states have also been providing essential consumption items at subsidized rates through its outlets; for example, by the Kerala State Civil Supplies Corporation, an apex federation of Cooperatives for which also a local ration card is necessary. Thus, the migrants have to depend solely on the open market and become more vulnerable to the price differences in the open market compared to the local community (Devi and Kumar, 2011). The situation is the same in almost all states for interstate migrants.

A similar situation exists in accessing state-specific health insurance programmes. Generally, native states do not provide coverage of insurance to migrants in other host states. Rashtriya Swasthya Bima Yojana (RSBY) is the only national health insurance scheme benefitting migrants anywhere in the country, but the scheme has few major limitations. The restriction of RSBY to Below Poverty Line (BPL) households is a considerable problem for migrant families. Migrants may not be able to register in their source village. Migrant families often do not have location-specific identity documents. They are casual labourers who earn their income in cash and they have no means to establish income proof. Similarly, access to other entitlements has same problems that are linked to identity. All of the above has clear links to their vulnerabilities related to identity (Borhade, 2011).

Education

Migration is a leading cause for high drop-out rate of children from schools. These children face vulnerability being out of their domain and peer development process in source areas. At the workplace, the children are mostly away from care and protection, health and nutrition, learning and exposure and overall childhood well-being in comparison with their peers in the source village. Education system at destination cities presents school enrolment problems for these children due to their mobility, language barriers (in case of interstate migration) and availability of resources for inclusion of migrant children.

Financial Vulnerability

Once migrants leave their home area, they are often no longer eligible for social insurance, health benefits or entitlements to livelihood support systems, or even formal welfare schemes. Given the greater risks they are exposed to, their vulnerability and financial exclusion increase (Deshingkar and Start, 2003). Due to lack of identity at destination cities, migrants are not able to open their bank accounts. They mostly have to carry all their money with them since their dwelling at destination locations are not safe enough. This also makes them vulnerable to being robbed. As stated by one of the migrant labourers in Delhi, Avadhesh Kumar from Bihar, 'They consider us outsiders here. We can't keep our money at home due to security reasons. So we carry it all with us. Often local rowdies beat us up and snatch our money.' Migrant labourers also face a number of problems when it comes to sending money back to their source villages. To send money back to their villages, migrants use few available options (Ghate, 2005),

1. Carrying it back themselves or sending it through friends and relatives visiting home
2. Sending it through the post office by a money order
3. Sending it through a bank by bank draft
4. Sending it through an informal remitter

Among these options, the first and the last involve the informal market; the second is seen as expensive and sometimes difficult by remitters (a form has to be filled out in the language of the destination). Finally, sending money through a bank is rarely feasible since most migrants do not have a bank account, either at origin or destination or both. Because of this lack of options for money transfer, migrants cannot send money home as regularly as necessary. A study of remittances to Andhra Pradesh has shown that only 15 per cent of remittances are sent to families on a regular monthly basis. Instead, 35 per cent are irregular and 44 per cent are sent only every three to four months (Samal, 2006). For sending remittances, the transaction costs are of concern to most migrant labourers with the cost of doorstep delivery being quite high. The post office, for instance, charges five per cent, while clients reportedly have to travel to the post office to pick up the remitted amount (Ghate, 2005). In this situation, most of the migrants prefer to send their money through friends and relatives visiting home, which has major risk of robbery or even cheating. From these evidences, it is clear that migrants are most vulnerable and including them in the formal financial system would be a step towards integration and towards economic betterment.

Health

The morbidity patterns among migrants vary with the type of migration and its potential for generating health risks. For instance, in the case of migration into big cities like Mumbai, which takes place on a more or less permanent basis, the susceptibility of the migrants to health problems stems from their peripheral socio-economic existence in the host areas (Ray, 1993;

Sundar, Mahal and Sharma, 2000). In the case of migration for agricultural labour for three or four months, returning home after the harvest, such as those who go from Nandurbar (Maharashtra) to Gujarat, specific problems for the migrants include infectious diseases, chemical- and pesticide-related illnesses, dermatitis, heat stress, respiratory conditions, musculoskeletal disorders and traumatic injuries (Phoolchund, 1991). Itinerant sugarcane harvesting groups in Maharashtra and other states differ enormously from other migrant categories. Sugar-cane workers have a high level of occupational accidents and are exposed to the high toxicity of pesticides. They may also have an increased risk of lung cancer, possibly mesothelioma. This may be related to the practice of burning foliage at the time of cane-cutting. Bagassosis is also a problem specific to the industry as it may follow exposure to bagasse (a by-product of sugar cane). The workers may also be affected by chronic infections, which reduce their productivity (Phoolchund, 1991; Weill et al., 1996). All over India, there are migrants working in stone quarries and work-related illness endemic to stone industry include the respiratory diseases of silicosis and tuberculosis (TB) due to prolonged inhalation of silica dust (Tribhuwan and Patil, 2009).

It has become clear from the study that migrants suffer from lack of knowledge and poor utilization of health services. Since they are away from their usual place of residence, the dependence on their regular system for seeking health care is compromised. The most important aspect of the migrants' vulnerability is that they are staying in open spaces and migrant camps (provided by employer), where they do not have basic amenities like sanitation, bathroom, drinking water and so on. Many adult and young women face risks related to maternal health issues (including sexual and reproductive health) and lack of knowledge and skills to make informed choices and use these services effectively. Since they come from the villages and are away from their traditional systems of health care, invariably, there is a sense of resistance to use services from providers of modern medical care. Migrant women are particularly isolated with respect to health care, including during pregnancy. Providing accurate information about maternal health and facilitating access to services is clearly necessary (from primary findings of National Taskforce Study on Migrants Access to Health Care and responsiveness of health system, ICMR study).

A combination of factors at the area of destination complicates migrant's vulnerability, which is primarily premised on the alien status of the migrants. Limited choice and reduced capacity to negotiate result in increased discrimination in life chances. A migrant is considered an 'outsider'. Various surveys and studies have shown that migrants are disadvantaged relative to the native population regarding employment, education and health. It is difficult to pinpoint specific separate reasons for this, such as deficient education, inferior health care provision, absence of outreach programmes for them, poor wages, initial prejudice and sustained discrimination of health providers, but these factors mutually reinforce each other. For instance, a bias against the migrants may translate into health providers' neglect, which in turn perpetuates poor migrant health.

Evidences suggest that internal migration can play an important role in poverty reduction and economic and social development, hence positive facilitation of safe migration should be specially emphasized which mainly includes access to basic public services mainly health, education and livelihood. Further, the high volume of migration and inter-linkages of the health needs of migrants with all Millennium Development Goals and national policies (Gupta 2002; National Health Policy, 2001; National Population Policy, 2002) means that success in meeting these needs can help support the achievement of the MDGs and these policies. Hence increased emphasis is required to address the special health needs of the migrant population, which can help to improve their health indicators as well the overall experience of migration (Borhade, 2011; Usher, 2005).

Like a lot of other countries, Indian government so far has had a history of trying to restrict migration through a variety of means. However, a paradigm shift in thinking is required among the policymakers, which needs to envisage the fact that migration is a reality that is here to stay. Instead of restricting it, Indian policy makers must look towards countries, such as China and Vietnam where a national policy towards internal migration is in place as there needs to be a shift in favour of encouraging internal migration in order to boost economic development (Ping, 2003).

Current Policy Level Initiatives and Challenges in India

Until recently policy attitude towards internal migration has been mostly reserved, if not entirely negative. A number of programmes and policy dialogues have been initiated by different states to address internal migration as shown in Table 11.1. Some states, such as Maharashtra and

Kerala, are actively trying to engage migrants in development policies, while states, such as Odisha Andhra Pradesh Rajasthan and Bihar are in the process to address specific issues of migrants such as identity, insurance and education of children. Currently, at the central level, there are only two programmes that can be migrant-friendly, subject to its effective implementation: Aadhaar card which promises only nationally credible identity and RSBY which assures national health insurance coverage. All these existing initiatives have functional complexities and challenges that are captured in this section.

Although these programmes and policies may result in reduction of distress migration to some extent, in future migration is expected to increase. This will call for a comprehensive policy to reduce regional and sectoral balances in the development of the sending and receiving states. Overall, there is a need for greater recognition of internal migration and its linkages with development at the policy level for comprehensive migration policy and this policy discourse needs to be backed by solid research of internal migration and development (Srivastav, 2012; Deshingkar, 2009).

Legal Protection

Although India does not have a comprehensive policy on internal migration, fragmented policies for the protection of migrants do exist (Borhade, 2006). The Indian constitution contains basic provisions relating to the conditions of employment, non-discrimination, right to work and so on (For example Article 23 (1), Article 39, Article 42, Article 43), which are applicable for all workers, including migrant workers within the country. Migrants are covered under various labour laws. However, those[3] laws, which do exist to protect the rights of migrant workers, are widely disregarded by employers and intermediaries because of a lack of political will to implement them and ignorance among illiterate migrants of their rights as workers. Additionally, as migrants do not have fixed employers, the latter escape from their responsibilities to provide various benefits to migrants that are mandatory under the existing laws. These laws hold the government as well as the employers responsible for contributing financially towards providing benefits, such as basic health care, insurance and an education allowance for children of workers. The Interstate Migrant

Worker Act has been in force since 1979, which is the only piece of legislation that has great potential to address interstate migration issues, but is not implemented due to lack of awareness among migrants as well non-governmental organizations (NGOs) and the lack of willpower among politicians and government officials dealing with interstate alliance. It is crucial to activate and implement the available laws to address migrants' issues related to exclusion of services.

Health Insurance

Other examples of policies that have helped migrants include the government health insurance in a few states of India. An example is the Jivan Madhur Yojana (insurance programmes) where the government and the migrants each contribute half the insurance premium which covers health problems and accidental death of the worker and also provides an education allowance for the children of workers studying in the 8th to 10th standard of school. These programmes have been effective and helpful for poor migrants but the eligibility criteria are different in different areas, and the workers from host state are not covered if they move to a different state. This needs to be looked into, in order to foster collaboration between the different state governments and insurance companies.

Bihar government has schemes for the migrants 'Bihar State Migrant Labour Accident Grant scheme' which provides compensation to the deceased migrant family up to ₹1 lakh in the event of death; ₹75,000 for permanent disability and ₹37,500 for partial disability. A joint labour commissioner has also been positioned at New Delhi for handling issues of Bihari migrant workers. Government of Bihar has ensured fast-tracking mechanism for processing the policy benefits.

Another example is the RSBY scheme (http://www.rsby.gov.in) launched on 1 April 2008 by the Ministry of Labour and Employment, Government of India, to provide health insurance coverage for BPL families. RSBY is a smart-card based health insurance system with unique portability of access to healthcare services. Thus this scheme can be used by migrant labour at source and at destination.

The scheme has few major limitations. A major limitation is its restriction to hospitalization benefits and the absence of provision for outpatient treatment. This is an extremely critical limitation because the majority of the medical expenses of the poor are incurred for outpatient treatment. Even for hospitalization the coverage is low. Migrant workers face the risk of occupational injuries and in the absence of workplace coverage the low amount of coverage is a bigger problem. It is worth noting that the poor may be willing to pay more for better coverage as experienced by the NGO Nidaan in Bihar.

The restriction of RSBY to BPL households is a considerable problem for migrant families. Migrants may not be able to register in their source village. Migrant families often do not have location-specific identity documents. They are casual labourers who earn their income in cash and they have no means to establish income proof. Further, most seasonal migrants are attached to contractors and are dependent on them for services at destinations. It is extremely difficult to reach out to them.

Migrants also have difficulty in accessing the RSBY because the local administration in many areas does not recognize the presence of seasonal migrants. For example, in Gujarat, the brick kiln workers were denied access to RSBY because they were told that enrolment in the scheme is to be done only in the home state.

Despite the drawbacks of RSBY it must be recognized that there have been some changes made in the scheme based on the learning from implementation and feedback from the field. To enable greater utilization, there is the facility to get a 'Split Card' for migrant families, which can be used by migrant workers at destination, as well at source by his family members. Some state governments have linked their Emergency Transport System with RSBY; some are about to hire civil society organizations for increasing awareness. Recently, Ministry of Labour and Employment has conducted a pilot to test RSBY for OPD use in Odisha, if it is successful, RSBY will be made available for OPD use nationwide (Personal communication with Mr Anil Swaroop, DG, Ministry of Labour and Employment).

Identity

Movement of people from one state to another can lead to loss of certain entitlements they enjoyed in the state where they lived before migration. In the Indian federal system, people derive their entitlements through the fundamental rights conferred on them by the Indian Constitution and the various laws enacted by the Union government and the state governments. Apart from these rights and legal protection, people are eligible to make use of various programmes/schemes executed by the central and state governments. Most of the central government schemes are applicable throughout the country. Even in central government schemes, the benefits reach the people through the state or local government. Unless otherwise specified, such benefits are available only to the permanent residents of the respective state. In such a situation, the interstate migrants lose their entitlements when they cross borders of their native state, as local identity card is a cross cutting issue, as currently there is no national identity mechanism other than the newly launched Aadhaar card.

Enthused by the promise of a nationally credible identity for migrant workers, the[4] the National Coalition for Security of Migrant workers (NACSOM) signed a two year Memorandum of Understanding (MOU) with Unique Identity Authority of India (UIDAI) in June 2010 for widening the spread of Aadhaar among migrant groups. This MOU created a broad framework for collaboration between NGOs working with migrant workers and the UIDAI. On the part of the NGOs with NACSOM the hope was that Aadhaar will become a gateway to services for migrants—especially those services that are denied to them because of their mobility. This includes entitlements such as a bank account at the point of their work or access to portable PDS or universal health coverage and so on. In order to test whether Aadhaar is actually able to link migrants to services, Disha Foundation in Nasik undertook a small pilot. Disha Foundation is the convener organization of NACSOM and in some ways its experience was to be seen as a learning ground for other members of NACSOM at large.

In 2011,[5] Disha Foundation enrolled about 100 migrant workers in Nasik in Aadhaar. Once this enrolment was completed Disha helped the migrants apply for bank accounts in State Bank of India and Maharashtra Bank. However, the applications of the migrants quoting the Aadhaar number were categorically rejected and bank accounts could not be opened. Disha attempted to argue on behalf of the migrant applicants but the bank branches where adamant that Aadhaar was not a suitable Know Your Customer (KYC) document. This became a contentious point between Disha and the local banks but the banks argued that they do not have instructions to use Aadhaar as a KYC document. Finally, the applications became invalid and were withdrawn by Disha. Local leaders among migrant community informed Disha about it (Personal communication with migrant's peer leaders, Ms Vimal Pagar and Ms Suman in Nasik).

NACSOM's association with UIDAI created a high level of hope and expectation. However, the UIDAI promise is yet to be kept on Aadhaar turning into a fool-proof method of accessing services for migrants. The MOU with UIDAI has now concluded but NACSOM is hopeful that Aadhaar will deliver on the high hope for migrant workers—it has also communicated the results of this small pilot to the UIDAI and there is as yet uncertain assurance of how these problems can be overcome. The involvement and authority of NACSOM in the roll out of services for migrants needs to be an important one, otherwise the interest among constituent teams will slowly fade away.

Education

Few state governments have joined their hands for mainstreaming migrant children into education such as Andhra Pradesh Sarva Shiksha Abhiyan (SSA) along with active support of NGOs, such as Aide et Action, have done comprehensive mapping of intrastate and intrastate migrant children in Andhra Pradesh and have developed school enrolment mechanism for them through setting up of units via SSA. Disha foundation in Nasik has done mapping of migrant children and based on mapping, bridge schools have been started by SSA for migrant children at their halt points and work sites. There are few other examples of NGOs having initiated good education system for migrant children, especially for sugarcane cutters and brick-line workers. Some models which are worth looking into are: Learning And Migration Programmes (LAMPs) promoted by America India Foundation in western Odisha through organizations, such as Lokadrusti for children of brick kiln workers, Setu in Gujarat for children or migrants working in salt pans. But even after enactment of Right to Education Act 2010 there are still a large number of migrant children not mainstreamed into education due to variety of reasons, such as lack of resources, difficulty in tapping migrant children, their mobile status, language barriers in case of interstate migrants and so on. It is important that every state government adapts similar initiatives, like Andhra Pradesh, for education of migrant children.

A special focus under the Right to Education Act has to be made for ensuring access to migrant children in schooling all over the country.

Health

Studies show that currently there are no structural policies or programmes targeting the urban migrant's issues in totality and this segment of the population still faces exclusion from the various mainstream programmes. It is clear that public health services need to initiate and reinforce more 'migrant friendly' approach focusing on the health of the underserved poor urban migrant population dwelling in slums and other temporary sites (like construction sites).

The existing central government guidelines allow all migrant children to avail of nutritional supplementation under the Integrated Child Development Scheme (ICDS) at destination cities irrespective of whether or not they are registered in the area (see Appendix). As a result, all migrant children can benefit from the childcare centre (*anganwadi*) services in or near where the migrants reside (*nakas*). Pregnant women can also avail of antenatal and post-partum care through these *anganwadis*, which will be linked to government health services. Adolescent girls can be given treatment for anaemia at these *anganwadis* and, in addition, be provided life skills and sex education through the ICDS programmes.

Disha Foundation, has played a significant role in identifying sites for the establishment of such *anganwadis* that are convenient for migrants, as well as in encouraging migrants to make use of the facilities. Disha has experienced that though the guideline is very pro-migrants, but officials of ICDS at source and destination are not aware about it, and resource allocation for its implementation has not made by the government. This guideline has tremendous potential to address the health concerns of migrant children, adolescents and women; hence its effective implementation is of the utmost importance.

Some currently functioning programmes, such as the National AIDS Control Programmes (Borhade, 2011), have recognized migrant's vulnerability for HIV infection and made a mandate to provide outreach services for migrant. This programme has adopted an outreach approach for HIV/AIDS prevention and treatment for few categories of the migrant population, namely truckers, sex workers and construction workers in India (NACO, 2007).

Migrant populations often cannot access the services/programmes due to their migration status, timings of their work and distance to services and language barriers. In addition, there is also lack of outreach of the health system to such migrant workers, which further distances them from accessing any kind of healthcare adequately. Studies show that urban local bodies (ULBs) and state both do not have focused programmes to address health problems among for urban migrants (NUHM 2008). At present, these bodies undertake very limited outreach activities pertaining to health mainly focused on polio immunization. ULBs are statutorily responsible for provision and maintenance of basic infrastructure and services in cities and towns. The local urban administration, that is, municipality is expected to provide both preventive and curative health services to the urban population. However, the infrastructure and manpower of municipalities are not sufficient to cater to the needs of the growing urban population, particularly the migrant influx. Sometimes, lack of funds and political will are other reasons for insufficient healthcare by urban administration.

However, a number of institutions run by industries, private and non-governmental organizations have been providing health facilities to the urban settled population to some extent. Despite the growth of health institutions under non-governmental agencies and private sector, the state remains the major provider of healthcare services. These existing infrastructures and services are hard-pressed to cater to the growing urban poor population.

Financial Inclusion

Some studies have tried to understand the financial inclusion of migrants and related challenges. There are many challenges to the effective financial inclusion of migrants in India. These challenges exist at the regulatory, institutional and individual levels. Know your customer norms, though implemented through necessity and with the best of intentions, have the unintended consequence of excluding poor migrants from opening bank accounts. In recognition of these difficulties, modifications to KYC procedures have been made but are yet to be implemented in practice. India's financial sector is impressive in terms of scale and the diversity of institutions. Each type of financial institution has its own culture, characteristics and level of ability to provide the frequent and often small-value financial services required by poor migrants. The sheer size of the institutional sector, suggests that opportunities exist for achieving more effective remittance services, through innovations and improvements within the sector. These could take many forms, for example, through technology developments (bearing in mind these would need to be pro-migrants) and business correspondent schemes, to name but two. Finally, social challenges should not be underestimated. Poor migrants typically face different forms of social exclusion, not just financial exclusion. This can negatively affect how they perceive themselves and how others, including banks, perceive them (Thorat et al., 2009).

Very recently, Ministry of Finance has initiated special measures for financial inclusion of migrants, particularly for opening their bank account and remittance services. The ministry is in the process of banking sector convergence for remittance and also simplifying the process of account opening. The pilot for the same has been successfully conducted in Delhi and Pune. The ministry has contacted NACSOM for coordinating better outreach with migrants in different states (Personal communication with Director, Financial Inclusion, Ministry of Finance, New Delhi). A pilot for it has been planned in collaboration with Disha Foundation in Nasik.

Response of Planning Commission

Planning Commission invited NACSOM for presenting recommendations for migrant workers for 12th five year plan. It was assured by the Planning Commission that all key ministries—Ministry of Education, Ministry of Women and Child Welfare, Ministry of Health and Family Welfare, Ministry of Labour and Employment, Ministry of Rural Development—remain present for this meeting. NACSOM has made a comprehensive presentation on the required response needed from various ministries and government departments to create migrant inclusive programmes and policies. The Commission responded very well with the recommendations, and after this meeting, these recommendations have been sent to the respective ministries for further action. As a result, Finance Ministry has contacted NACSOM to lay down strategies for financial inclusion of migrants nationwide. NACSOM and Finance Ministry is in the process of finalizing these strategies.

Some Key State Initiatives to Address Migrants' Needs

Andhra Pradesh and Odisha

The Governments of Andhra Pradesh and Odisha, being concerned about the prevalence of exploitative labour practices including bondage situations in brick manufacturing activities that engage poor and vulnerable migrant workers, organized workshops with stakeholders in collaboration with the Ministry of Labour and Employment, Government of India and the International Labour Organization in 2010 and in 2012 (the author has participated in 2012 workshop). During these workshops, it was decided to prepare and implement a time-bound and result-oriented project to benefit workers in the identified sector, namely, brick kilns that have intrastate and interstate migrants, mainly from Odisha and other states working in Andhra Pradesh. As a result, a MOU was drafted, with inputs from Ministry of Labour and Employment, Governments of Andhra Pradesh and Odisha, to facilitate the strengthening of interstate coordination mechanism for smooth implementation of the activities in source and destination areas of migrant workers such as education of children, occupational health, grievances handling and so on. The purpose of the MOU is to facilitate effective coordination and mutual understanding between the parties for smooth implementation of agreed activities, under this project (Personal communication with Mr Anil Swaroop, Director General, Ministry of Labour and Employment).

Maharashtra State Response to Migration

Setting up of migration receiving research and resource centre by Government of Maharashtra:

Maharashtra state has been working to develop and implement an integrated, convergence-based approach to facilitate and mitigate distress migration in Nasik district. The approach also addresses the need to strengthen rural–urban development link. The state is in the process to set up a dedicated 'migration receiving, research and resource centre', towards addressing scheduled caste and scheduled tribe migration, which involves the active role of Tribal Department and supportive role from Revenue, Urban Land Ceiling, Municipal Corporation and Public Works departments. The centre intends to address the migration at destination and source end. It plans to generate migration data for more informed programmes and policies. The centre will facilitate migration at Nasik city destination during the migration period via livelihood skill building and job linkages, education and health services. On the other hand emphasis would be provided for urban and tribal development linkages, better implementation of available government programmes at source villages of migrants in Nasik district for sustainable development with the goal to reduce distress migration for livelihood.

Through a special drafted scheme via incentive grant, the Central Tribal Ministry has sanctioned grant for the construction of the centre and the Maharashtra state government will finance the programme cost for three years. The land for construction of the centre has been allotted by urban land ceiling department. The migration centre seems to be very promising towards mainstreaming migration issue at programme and policy level at source and destination end. The tribal ministry wishes to pilot this initiative in Nasik and based on the results it has wider replication possibilities in high migration pockets at the state/national level.

Disha Foundation has facilitated the entire process since 2004 and it is the technical partner of Tribal Ministry and Government of Maharashtra for conception of said centre and effective operation of the same. It has taken nearly seven years' long advocacy efforts for Disha to create positive response on migration issue at government level.

Similarly, various government departments have initiated special measures to address various needs of migrants in Nasik city such as grievances handling centres by Labour Department, temporary ration cards by PDS, education of migrant children by SSA, livelihood trainings by Industrial Training Institute and comprehensive response to address SC/ST migration by Tribal Department.

Disha Foundation has remained a bridge between these departments and migrant communities during creating such positive response towards migration. It is apparent that the administration will need pressure as well support while developing institutional framework for migrant inclusive programmes till the mainstream of migration happens at larger scale (the author is the key advocate for and is closely involved during the process of setting up of the centre and the initiatives of other key departments).

Bihar

Government of Bihar has initiated Jeevika (Bihar Rural Livelihoods Project) a community driven poverty alleviation project. It works in 400 villages covering 700,000 households and facilitates creation of an institutional platform of communities of the migrant poor. Plans are to reach 12.5 million households forming them into 1 million self-help groups through the National Rural Livelihoods Mission (NRLM). This community platform is leveraged for a wide variety of interventions ranging from health, education to employment, making the poor the heart of the change. Financial inclusion is facilitated by working with banks. Social indicators are improved by dovetailing government schemes and working with NGOs. At the supply side, at the block level, Migration Resource Centres are planned. Community professionals will help build the database of migrants with details of their destinations, incomes and name of the contractor. Jeevika will converge with the labour department for issuing of identity card to ensure government entitlements, like social security and pensions and prevent exploitation by police, on buses and trains. Government of Bihar also plans to intervene and offer above mentioned services to Bihari migrants at major destination states, mainly NCR Delhi and Maharashtra (Personal communication with CEO, Jeevika).

Migrant Labour Welfare Boards

Punjab Migrant Welfare Board

Punjab is the first state in the country, which constituted the board for the welfare of migrant labourers coming in Punjab from other states. The board looks after the rights and interests of migrant labours. A significant migrant labour population lives in Punjab's industrial hub Ludhiana and in the state capital Chandigarh. They are also significantly contributing in the agriculture, industry and other sectors of economy of Punjab. The board plans to take full care of the rights of migrant labour coming to Punjab and already living in Punjab. The board ensures to coordinate the endeavour of the government in giving a new push to the economy of Punjab by involving migrants in the mainstream.

Kerala State Government Initiative (Devi and Kumar, 2011)

The Kerala state government introduced a welfare scheme for the migrant workers on the May Day of 2010. Under the scheme titled 'Inter-State Migrant Workers Welfare Scheme', a membership card is issued to each migrant worker who gets enrolled. Each registered worker would get up to ₹25,000 as healthcare assistance for in-patient care in empanelled hospitals in case of accidents or chronic diseases. The scheme is implemented through the Kerala Construction Workers Welfare Fund Board The scheme, though pioneering, has certain inherent weaknesses. The programme targets to enrol half a million workers, which is much lower than the total number of migrant workers in the state, indicating that most of the migrant workers remain outside the protective umbrella. One reason for the failure to enrol most of the migrant workers is the lack of awareness about the welfare scheme among the target group. There was no strategy to communicate directly with the migrant workers coming from different regions of India and speaking different languages and dialects. Most of the communication was through advertisements in the print media, which was in Malayalam, the local language or English, which is also different from the language of the migrant workers. There is very little chance that migrants take note of these advertisements.

As noted above, the scheme is administered by the Board, which operates the welfare scheme for construction workers. As of now they are primarily targeting the builders. They contact the builders and ask them to enrol the migrant workers working with them. For registration, the workers have to furnish copy of the identity cards, which majority of migrants do not have, so the builders register only migrant workers who have a proof of their identity. Another reason for exclusion of a significant section of the migrant population arises from the stipulation that the employer has to certify that the worker is working with him, which many of the employers are unwilling. A large section of the migrant workers are employed in the plywood industry. But the owners of plywood units are not willing to certify the employment of the worker for registration under the scheme. The above requirements also prevent the casual migrant labourers who do not have a permanent employer from availing the benefits of the scheme. Similar is the situation with domestic workers and seasonal workers employed in plantations, agricultural farms and so on. As a result, the enrolment is only less than two per cent of the estimated migrant labour force in the state 18 months after the initiation of the scheme.

The initiative of the state government to institute a welfare scheme for migrant workers, in spite of its weaknesses, needs to be appreciated. It also indicates that the visibility of these 'invisible people' has increased in administration and governance aspects in the state. The state government, in the future, may have to think about constituting a separate mechanism to implement the scheme as presently the scheme is faced with constraints due to inadequate personnel. Currently, the staff of the Construction Welfare Fund Board is implementing this additional scheme without any change in the staffing pattern. They are also constrained because of the non-availability of vehicles and other facilities necessary for undertaking the fieldwork. It is also important that the representatives of the migrant labourers are present in the monitoring committee. Situation is same in other states of India.

Punjab is a state where a migrant welfare board was constituted; similarly Kerala has constituted special scheme of migrant workers. But other states have not constituted any separate welfare board or welfare scheme for migrant workers. Instead, it is assumed that the welfare of migrant workers will be taken care through existing construction workers welfare boards. In such a situation, issues of migrant workers such as their rights to PDS, membership in community health insurance scheme, grievance handling do not receive attention. The absence of a representative of the migrant workers in the monitoring committee eliminates the possibility of their voices being heard in the implementation of the scheme under welfare boards.

Policy for Internal Labour Migration: Some Innovative Solutions from International Communities

Some governments, including that of India, are still following the fallacious mindset that internal migration needs to be curbed through a variety of means. The realization hasn't sunk in yet that internal migration is

Table 11.1

Existing central/state government policies and programmes for migrants

Sr No	Ministry/ Government Department	Available Policy/ Programme	What it Ensures	Challenges	Recommendation (What is Lacking)
		Central Government Programmes that may Include Migrants/Address Migrants Needs			
1.	Office of Registrar General and Census Commissioner and National Sample Survey Organization (NSSO), Ministry of Statistics and Programme Implementation	National level surveys to capture socio-demographic, employment profiles of citizens of India	To capture socio-demographic profile of citizens of all states of India	No special strategies to capture seasonal and circular migrants, Lack of official data on seasonal and circular Internal Migration	Adopt the special methodology to capture seasonal and circular migrant populations, include special variables in the questionaries' of these survey to capture seasonal and circular migrants.
2.	Ministry of labour and employment	Legislation on interstate migration called as Inter-state Migrant Workers Act, 1979	Ensures rights and entitlements of interstate migrants	Ineffective Legislation, covers only interstate migrants & lack of implementation of the act by labour department	Amendment in the legislation—keeping in mind the rising incidence and complexity of interstate migration. (Proposed amendments are attached in the Appendix)
3.	Ministry of Women and Child Welfare	Scheme for migrant children and women provides health care services to migrant women, children and adolescents at destination cities	Seamless access to nutrition and informal education services to migrant women and children at source and destination in any state of India	Poor implementation due to lack of awareness among implementing officials of ICSD, as well as community and NGOs	Stricter implementation and budget allocation

4.	Ministry of Health and Family Welfare. (Previously Ministry of Labour and Employment)	'Rashtriya Swastha Bima Yojana' Scheme provides portable access to health care specially for hospitalization	Portable National health insurance programme 'Rashtriya Swastha Bima Yojana' that can be accessed in any city/state of India	Scheme is available only for BPL families, registration needs to be done at source. Benefit can be received only for the hospitalization. OPD use is not covered	Scheme should be universal for BPL/non BPL families, OPD use must be covered in the insurance. Scheme should be widely implemented in all states of India.
5.	Ministry of Health and Family Welfare	National Urban Health Mission 2013	Mission plans to cover urban migrant population for preventive and curative health services via outreach services.	No specific guidelines to tap migrant population	Development of specific guidelines and strategies to capture migrant population in various health programmes for- outreach and enabling access to services
6.	Ministry of Human Resource Development Department of Education & Literacy Department	Right to education Act, aims to provide universal education for all children of India	Education for migrant children	High School Dropout ratio of migrant children, and inability to capture migrant children in mainstream of education at destination level	Early Childhood Care and Education for migrant children, Mapping of migrant children, initiate mobile education system for migrant children, addressing language barriers of interstate migrant children, recruitment of same language teacher for migrant children.

(Table 11.1 Continued)

(Table 11.1 Continued)

Sr No	Ministry/ Government Department	Available Policy/ Programme	What it Ensures	Challenges	Recommendation (What is Lacking)
7.	AADHAR	National Identification number	Only National identity card available for migrants	Lack of Identity proof and other documents for migrants inclusion in AADHAR	Strengthening enrolment process of migrants into AADHAR, linking AADHAR with social security programmes that can be accessed anywhere in India
8.	Ministry of Finance	Financial Inclusion of migrants through Jan Dhan Yojana	Compulsory financial inclusion of interstate migrants through opening a bank account in nationalized banks with special relaxation in documents.	Tapping mobile migrants in cities	Co-ordination with local NGOs working with migrants for outreach. Close co-ordination with banks for Raising Awareness among migrants
9.	Ministry of Rural Development	Maintaining migration register and database creation as a part of MNREGS (MNREGS)	Documentation of migrant workers moving out of panchayat for livelihood.	Lack of registration & accurate data of out-migrants at panchayat level	To involve the PRIs to initiate mandatory documentation of migrant workers moving out of rural areas

Special Initiatives Taken By State Governments

1.	**Maharashtra:** Development Department (TDD), Government of Maharashtra	Migration research and resource centre to address tribal migration for livelihood in two blocks and one city of Nasik district. Setting up of convergence with other key line departments such as labour, health, education, municipal corporation etc.	• Migration Data management— source and destination • Facilitation of migration for public services at Nasik city- destination • Individual family development plan at source areas—targeted implementation of existing tribal programmes for sustainable development of the region to reduce distress migration for livelihood.	Currently Close coordination and handholding is provided to TDD by an NGO Disha Foundation. Disha faces challenges in convergence with other key line department, as there is no institutional framework that exists to define roles of these departments.	The initiative taps only scheduled tribe population.

(Table 11.1 Continued)

(Table 11.1 Continued)

Sr No	Ministry/ Government Department	Available Policy/ Programme	What it Ensures	Challenges	Recommendation (What is Lacking)
	Maharashtra Pubic distribution systems, Maharashtra	Government resolution to issue temporary ration cards to temporary migrant population in cities	Portability of Food security services to migrants.	Documentation proofs of migrants mainly residence proof, income certificate to acquire ration cards Tedious process to cancel original ration card at source and get temporary ration card at destination	Low cost food option for migrant workers Portability of PDS for Migrant workers across district borders. A national roaming (mobile) temporary ration card for such migrants can be provided to migrant workers
2.	**Bihar:** Ministry of Labour & Employment, Government of Bihar	Bihar State Migrant Labour Accident Grant scheme, (Amendment) Rules, 2011—Bihar Notification No: S.O. 395 (15-Nov-2011)	Provides compensation to the deceased migrant family up to Rs. 1 lakh in event of death; Rs. 75,000 for permanent disability and Rs. 37,500 for partial disability. A joint labour commissioner has also been positioned at New Delhi.	The scheme coverage is only in Bihar, if migrants are moved out of Bihar state, they are not covered in the scheme. Tapping of migrants is another challenge for their inclusion in the scheme	Greater awareness among migrants about the scheme. Coverage of scheme in other states of India.

	Rural Development, Government of Bihar	Jeevika, rural livelihood and skill building and job placement initiative for Bihari migrants in Bihar.	Jeevika will converge with the labour department for issuing of identity card to ensure government entitlements like social security and pensions and prevent exploitation by police, on buses and trains	Market linkages and matching labourers skills for better employability	Better database of migrants based on skills and available options of employability in the market
10.	**Punjab & Kerla** Migrant welfare board–Punjab and Kerala states' Labour and Employment Department	Welfare board for migrant workers	Inclusion of migrants in construction workers welfare boards	Lack of effective registration of migrants & portability of benefits of welfare boards	Universalization of these boards—Inclusion of migrants from other sectors other than construction sector
11.	**Rajasthan Department of Labour and Employment**	Registration of out migrants at panchayat level	Labour department ensures registration of out-migrants at panchayat level, and provides identity card to migrants	Department has to depend on NGOs for registration process, hence sustainability of the initiative is questionable.	Panchayats should make it mandatory to register outgoing migrants.
12.	**Odisha–Andhra Pradesh** Labour & Employment Departments MOU	Migrant Assistance Centres	Providing assistance and support to migrant workers in brick-line sector at the source and destination area	Implementation, tapping of migrants, lack of co-operation of employers of migrants	Registration of migrant at source and destination. Employers increased participation

Source: Borhade 2015 (unpublished)

in fact a reality, which is here not only to stay but also to increase. Not only that, the realization also needs to emerge that internal migration is an essential factor for the country's economic development and as such needs to be encouraged. The most important step in that direction will be the formation of a national policy towards internal migration as has been the case in China and Vietnam. One of the initiatives being pilot tested in China is agreement between the source and destination provinces so as to make the rural to urban transition of migrants more seamless. In addition, steps have been taken in China to remove working card requirements for migrant rural workers to create conditions for free population movements and settlement. The belief behind these initiatives is the fact that migration will continue and people will use irregular channels if legal channels are not available. The Chinese ILO CP-TING project aims to develop cheap, fast and transparent labour migration channels on a large scale, geared especially towards those with low education and skill levels. Creation of legal channels for migration is directly linked to the vulnerability of migrants related to their identity and loss of entitlements upon migration. Other policies also exist for increasing human capacity of migrants, such as a joint circular released in 2004 by Chinese Ministries of Agriculture, Finance, Labour and Social Security, Education, Science and Technology and Construction urged local governments to launch training programmes for the local rural migrant labour force. This was known as the Sunshine Programme and is a major initiative across the six ministries on vocational training of 10 million rural labourers to plan to migrate to cities. This initiative also emphasizes the need for cross-cutting and holistic approaches for addressing the various vulnerabilities of the migrants.

India has ratified many of the International Labour Organization's conventions but is neither a signatory nor has ratified the[6] Convention of Migrant Workers (CMW), which provides the formal sanction for protection of the migrants. Similarly,[7] the UN Convention of Migrant Workers clearly spells the global focus on the human rights of migrants, but India has not adopted either of them and hence interests, including health of migrants are not protected.

There are also examples of policies targeted at maximizing the benefits of migration, such as the work supported by the Asian Development Bank in the Greater Mekong Subregion involving countries of Vietnam, Lao PDR, Cambodia and Thailand.

India also need better policies related to urban and rural development and better integration of policies for urban and rural areas instead of statements like 'We have started NREGA then why is migration still occurring'. For example, the Lao PDR has committed itself towards strengthening rural to urban market links as a part of its rural development plan. Vietnam is also recognizing the need for rural–urban linkages through its Central Region Development Strategy, 2000, and the Vietnam Urban Forum.

Suggestive Framework for National Policy for Internal Migrant Workers

With the background discussed in this chapter, this is suggestive policy framework, which is based on series of consultations among NACSOM members, workers and employer's organizations and various government officials who have initiated efforts to address migration issue in their respective states in past years. The policy framework is therefore a comprehensive and integrated reference document. The document provides a broad range of recommendations on various migration issues.

The framework required to be divided into two sections;

1. Policies to support migrants during migration period.
2. Development polices for sending and receiving states of migration

Suggestive Framework for Policy to Support Migrants during Migration Period

1. Research on Internal Migration
   The policy should address the serious need to enhance national and regional labour migration data collection, analysis and exchange of information to build database and address the knowledge gap on internal migration. The knowledge gap includes the conditions and needs of migrant workers and their families, labour needs and supply in states of origin and destination in order to match labour skills with labour demand through comprehensive regional approaches, institutional mechanisms and best practices to address migration issues by government and civil societies. This can be achieved in two ways

a. Promotion of a national policy think-tank: The Ministry of Labour and Employment should fund a national think-tank for advice on matters of migration and labour. The think-tank should also take up research activities.

b. Resources for research on internal migration and labour issues: State level research institutions should be encouraged to develop state migration profiles which feed into the policy-making process. This research could look into the nature, trends of migration and problems associated with access to benefits for migrants both at the source and destination.

2. Ensuring Access to Basic Entitlements
   A major focus of policy must be to ensure migrants' identity and citizenship rights in transit and at destination during their migration period. A national mechanism needs to be introduced to address identity and citizenship issue which can directly benefit migrants to avail access to basic entitlements mainly food security, education, health, shelter and financial inclusion. There are some best practices adopted by few state administration and civil society organizations that can be reviewed and adopted for implementation.

3. Universalization of Social Security Benefits
   Policy needs to provide social protection and social security benefits to migrants before, during and after migration period irrespective of their state of origin and destination. A fool-proof mechanism needs to be developed for universal access to social security benefits, particularly unemployment, insurance, compensation for employment injury and old age pension, education of migrant's children, maternity benefits to women (migrant or migrant's spouse) and remittance and savings services by migrants.

4. Skill Up-gradation and Market Linkages
   Policy should focus on building robust system for skill up-gradation and market linkages for employment in the unorganized sector. Lately, there is a heavy emphasis on skilling up of the large pool of young workers in the unorganized sector. It is also well known that a significant part of the unorganized sector is constituted by migrant workers who are in many cases barely equipped to enrol or benefit from the existing skill up-gradation programmes because of various reasons—no or less education, already in labour

market with no time to spare for long duration (6 months to 1 year) courses and so on. A number of civil society organizations and some corporate bodies have been making efforts in this regard but suffer from problems of certification. It would be important to review the experiences of civil society members working with the migrant youth and mainstream their concerns in the National Skill Development Corporation.

5. Legal Aid and Redressal of Legal Disputes
   Fast track legal response for cases of minimum wage violation, accidents and workplace abuse—The policy should ensure fast track legal response systems to expedite case resolution. The present legal machinery is less sensitive to the nature of legal disputes in the unorganized sector where labour has little documentary proof of his/her employment. It is seen that many disputes never make their way to the court or keep languishing for lack of proof. The jurisdiction of the Labour Courts, which is mandated to look at labour disputes, is also limited within a state.

   a. Creation of migration resource centres: Policy should promote setting up of migrant resource/assistance centres at the major source and destination locations which provide information, counselling and respond in case of emergencies. The NACSOM members have set up such assistance centres by the name of Shramik Sahayata evam Sandarbha Kendras that provide such services to migrant workers both at source and destination. These centres are being run in five states including UP, Odisha, Maharashtra, Rajasthan and Gujarat by 31 organizations.

   b. Creation of a national labour helpline: In cases of long distance interstate migration, cases of harassment, abuse and cheating in transit are frequently reported. At the destination, migrant workers often get into trouble with police for inability to produce a valid identity. At work place, instances of abuse and exploitation by way of withholding of wages, less or non-payment of wages also abound. It would be important to set up a national labour helpline supported by a network of migration resource centres set up in major source and destination locations (mentioned earlier). This labour helpline should be managed by labour departments and civil society organizations working on the issue of labour and migration.

c. Formation of interstate migration management bodies: Given the high rate of migration across certain corridors, such as eastern UP–Mumbai, Bihar–NCR, Western Odisha–Andhra Pradesh, Rajasthan–Gujarat and Odisha–Gujarat, there is a need to institute processes involving labour departments of both source and destination states.

   i. A migrant worker cell should be established within each state labour department which specifically addresses issues concerning migrant workers

  ii. A labour officer from the source state can be deputed at the destination to look into matters concerning migrant workers and work collectively with labour officers at the destination.

      Example: Bihar has experimented with deputing a Joint Labour Commissioner at Bihar Bhawan in Delhi. That experience can be looked at and build on.

6. Political Inclusion of Migrant Communities

Policy should emphasize on political inclusion of migrants. A large number of migrants are unable to cast their vote as they are away from their native place during elections in search of livelihoods. There is a need to create mechanisms to enable voting from this population.

7. Inter-sectoral Convergence

There are a number of government programmes and policies, which need to build convergence for the migrant community for their effective utilization. Various ministries should be part of this convergence, such as Ministry of Rural Development, Ministry of Women and Child Welfare, Ministry of Health and Family Welfare, Ministry of Urban Development, urban local bodies and so on. Policy should promote the building of national capacity to manage labour migration by developing national labour policies and legislation consistent with overall population policy and government structures to manage labour migration. The latter should include the creation of focal points within relevant ministries to handle labour migration issues and establish institutional mechanisms for enhanced co-operation between government authorities, worker organizations, employer associations and civil societies.

8. Resource Allocation

   Much of the execution of existing provisions depends on the human resource capacity available with the labour departments and the total fund allocation made to them. The importance of labour ministry in a growing economy cannot be understated and there is a need to take serious cognizance of the resource and capacity needs of state labour departments.

   a. Infusion of funds for better and speedier operations: The labour department needs an urgent infusion of resources both human and capital. It would be important to create more provisions for an effective functioning of the labour departments.

   b. Provision for creating facilities on labour *nakas/chowrahas*: Processes should be instituted for greater involvement of urban local bodies in ensuring basic facilities for migrants such as drinking water, temporary shelter, sanitation, education, health, sheds at labour *nakas*.

9. Legislation on Migration

   There is a need to design a legislation to bring the aforementioned guidelines into force. The legislation should lay out a roadmap for implementation of the policy, giving details of the provisions, process of execution and the details of the governing institutions. The policy should serve as a guiding light for the legislation, which would in turn ensure that all the provisions under the policy are brought to life.

10. Key Stakeholders

    The key stakeholders in this process should be the Ministry of Labour and Employment and its entire machinery including the welfare bodies and the network of labour departments in each state. Among the elected representatives, an active involvement would be required from Panchayat officials and members of the Urban Local Bodies, that is the municipalities. In addition to above, the civil society organizations working with unorganized sector workers would be close partners in the design and implementation of the migration policy and the legislation, both.

11. Governance

    The implementation of the policy should be done under the guidance of the Ministry of Labour and Employment. A special unit should be set up at Ministry of Labour and Employment. The unit should work closely with other ministries such as Ministry of Rural Development, Ministry of Women and Child Welfare, Ministry of Health hand family welfare, Ministry of Urban Development, urban local bodies and so on for effective convergence within state policies.

Special unit should be created to perform the functions given:

(a) Collection, management and collation of migration data.

(b) Operation of migration resource centres created in the high migration zones within the country.

(c) Operation of interstate migration management bodies, such as the migrant workers' cell, instituted within state labour departments.

(d) Operation of national labour helpline.

(e) Linkages of migrant workers and their households with existing government schemes.

(f) Incorporate mechanisms that monitor the provision of decent work for migrants and enable them to access legal provisions for social protection.

(g) Set up national and sub-regional social dialogue mechanisms to address migrant labour issues.

(h) Promote equality of opportunity by strengthening gender-specific approaches to policies and activities concerning labour migration, particularly in recognition of the increasing feminization of labour migration.

(i) Facilitate technical co-operation activities with international agencies, including ILO, IOM, WHO, UNAIDS and others concerned.

Development Polices for Sending and Receiving States of Migration

1. Inclusive Urban Development Policies:
   Though the constitution of India gives right to citizens to travel, reside and carry out any trade, profession or business in any part of the country, this right can be undermined by governments and urban bodies, which do not implement enabling development

policies and measures. Current urban policies are becoming more exclusionary, that leads to increase the cost of migration for the poor and the anti-migrant rhetoric is becoming more strident in many states and urban metropolises (Bhagat 2011).

Migration should be acknowledged as an integral part of development. Government policies should not hinder but should seek to facilitate internal migration. It should form the central concern in city planning and city development agenda should seek to include and integrate migrants politically, economically, socially, culturally and spatially. There should be integration with other existing policy documents such as the Twelfth Five Year Plan, JNNURM and City Development Plans, which should recognize the value of migration in very explicit terms and address migrants' concerns and their rights unequivocally. The centre, states and urban bodies need to pursue coherent urban development policies in this regard.

2. Development Policies in Sending States of Migration:
   To alleviate distress migration, a foremost set of policy initiatives has to aim for a more vital pro-poor development strategy in the sending areas/states of migration that can strengthen the livelihood base in these areas. These should be in the form of agriculture, land and water management, improved infrastructure and the creation of non-farm employment and self-employment. These strategies need to be accompanied by changes that improve the access for the poor to land, social and physical infrastructure and government institutions. But as this could be long-term plan, meanwhile policies should promote role of Panchayats as the focus of the resource pool for migrant workers residing in their sending area. They should maintain a database of migrant workers through 'migration register' and issue identity cards and pass books to them before migration. Further, panchayats should initiate migration management and governance including training, placement and social security benefit assurance for migrants before and during migration. With growing IT-based communication, it should become possible for panchayats or NGOs play this role.

Overall India needs better integration of urban and rural policies towards strengthening the need for rural–urban linkages.

Conclusion

India is facing migration challenges and has an increasing need to formulate and implement strategies to improve migrants' condition. Governments must ensure coherence between national policies for migration and development. Currently, India has less or no structural policies or programmes targeting the migrant's issues in totality. The Indian Government can borrow from the evidence-based policies and programmes prevalent worldwide and adapt them to the Indian scenario. There is a need to modify the existing policy structure and programmes so that the needs of this marginalized group are accommodated in the various national programmes. Effective implementation of the available programmes, as well convergence of that programme as source and destination level, both inter and intrastate level would be important to improve the status of migrants. For this, interstate collaboration is required among government departments, to assess and subsequently tackle risks and their consequences before, during and after migrants' period of work, both in their origin or return and destination. The provision of basic services would require better coordination among departments located in different sectors and different areas. The central government has major role to play in the whole process including alliance among key services providers and their respective department and their capacity building and resource allocation. Development of a national migration policy would be proactive step towards it.

Appendix

Interstate Migrant Workers Act, 1979 (Regulation of Employment and Conditions of Service): Necessity for Amendment

The system of employment of interstate migrant labour is an exploitative system prevalent in many states of India. Such migrant labour is recruited from various parts of a particular state through contractors or agents for work outside that state in large construction and other projects.

The Inter-state Migrant Workers Act (ISMWA), 1979 (Regulation of Employment and Conditions of Service) was enacted to protect the rights and safeguard the interest of migrant workers. The Act intends to regulate the employment of interstate migrant workmen and to provide their conditions of service. It applies to every establishment and the contractor, who employs five or more interstate migrant workmen. The act exists, but is poorly implemented or not implemented at all due to many reasons. Since it is the only legal piece available in India to address migrant workers' rights and entitlements, it must be amended in the most urgent manner to ensure migrant workers' welfare seamlessly before and during migration.

The ISMWA needs to be reoriented in the context of contemporary trends in labour mobility. The broad trends in internal labour mobility in India are as follows:

- Rural to rural migration is still the dominant form of labour mobility.
- However, there has been an increase noted with respect to rural to urban migration and urban to urban migration during 1999–2000 to 2007–08.
- There has been an increase in long distance (interstate migration) in recent years.
- Economic reasons is one of the most important factors influencing migration of males.
- There has been an increase in short duration migrants in the last decade.
- Of the short duration migrants, majority are engaged in the construction sector.
- Informal networks, including personal networks, are emerging as the dominant agency facilitating contemporary migration. Accordingly, a significant proportion of migrants are not recruited through the contractors.
- Some of the major problems faced by migrants include: Many migrants are denied benefits of social and economic security; they are often denied entitlements under public distribution system in the destination regions; prospects for upward mobility is more or less absent for migrant workers; and awareness among the migrant workers on their rights and entitlements is relatively very low.

Key Recommendations for Amendment in ISMWA 1979

Recently Ministry of Labour and Employment had formed a working group for amendment in ISMWA 1979. Based on the detailed discussions among the working group members (author was one of the group member) and consultations with NGOs and workers organizations, the following recommendations can be made for amendments in the ISMWA.

- It must be noted that given the current trends, there is a pertinent need to revise the ISMWA in the context of:
  - Inadequate coverage of legislation
  - Lack of benefits accruing to the migrant workers
  - Problems related to the portability of benefits
  - Lack of guidelines for interstate coordination
  - Delays in settlement of claims

    Subsequently, it is recommended on the basis of various issues related to the amendment, particularly in relation to coverage of the Act, registration of workers, extent of social protection/rights to be provided, modalities for ensuring portability of benefits, role of concerned stakeholders and measures for ensuring effective coordination between different centre/states/districts and setting up of migration facilitation centres and developing co-ordination among source and destination for better facilitation of migration (preferably through NGOs).

- There is a pertinent need to look at the definition of migrants. The duration and patterns of migration must be taken into account while finalizing definition of migrants. The group has come to the agreement that people who migrate for more than one month period should be considered as migrants for the Act.
- The Act should cover both interstate as well as intrastate migrants.
- Registration of migrants must get universal, at both ends—source as well destination. The local administration (rural and urban) could be the nodal points for facilitating registration.
- Registration of contractors is also equally important and must get done similar to migrants (contractors, who have received licenses at source area, must be validated at destination areas. Labour

department must appoint NGOs as a nodal agency for the validation of licenses).

- Minimum five labourers criterion should be removed from the ISMWA 1979 to get coverage and benefit of the Act, as most of workers travel for work individually as well.

- Regarding the benefits/entitlements for migrants, below key areas should be mandatory:

  - Health insurance- registration under RSBY
  - Food security (PDS access)
  - Formal education and nutrition for children of the migrant workers
  - Basic amenities including housing and sanitation, for example, a suggestion for migrant hostels can be made. Some of the states are considering this idea, like Uttar Pradesh.
  - Old age pension benefits
  - Fast track grievance settlement in case of compensations (wage), accidents and harassment
  - Right to get unionized
  - Inclusion within Employment State Insurance Corporation (institute mechanism to provide provident fund)

- This act should ensure portability of all above-mentioned entitlements. These core benefits should be portable to migrants all over India. Mechanism for portability of these entitlements should be developed, such as issuance of smart card during registration process and linking it with portability of these entitlements.

- For accessing these entitlements, migrant workers should be authorized to provide self-declaration about their status as migrant workers.

- A single window should be set up for migrants to access all the above-mentioned entitlements.

- There is also a need to develop appropriate grievance settlement systems particularly to ensure that the claims of the short-term migrants are settled at the earliest. There should be a fast-track court for handling migrant's cases at block and district level, with joint involvement of labour department and the National Legal Services Authority of India.

- There is a strong need to set up migration facilitation centres at the source and destination levels. This should include a setup for legal aid for migrant workers. This should converge with Legal Service Authority Act 1987/DALSA and so on.

- It was also noted that the certain existing institutions, like Construction Workers Welfare Boards could be used as effective instruments for facilitating the transfer of benefits to the migrant workers. This is very important considering that a large section of the migrant workers are engaged in construction sector. It was also discussed that many migrants are working in other sectors and mechanism should be developed for their registration.
- Involvement of urban local bodies is recommended in ensuring the basic needs of the migrants such drinking water, shelter and so on for migrant workers.
- Sheds should be provided at labour markets in each city/town.
- ESI benefits should be provided to migrant families.
- Migration allowance should be introduced in the Act.
- Travelling allowance for family of migrants must be revised in the Act.
- Dearness allowance must be provided to migrants.
- Minimum wages must be ensured to migrants.
- 24×7 Helpline for migrants in cities/district level/block level should be started.

Notes

1. A *remittance* is a transfer of money by a foreign worker to his home country. In this chapter it refers to the transfer of money by migrants from destination to their home/source area.
2. A Participatory Poverty Assessment (PPA), is an iterative, participatory research process that seeks to understand poverty in its local, social, institutional and political contexts, incorporating the perspectives of a range of stakeholders and involving them directly in planning follow-up action. PPAs can be defined as an instrument for including poor people's views in the analysis of poverty and the formulation of strategies to reduce it through public policy.
3. Existing Central and State legislation for unorganized sector migrant workers in India include: National Employment Guarantee Act 2005, The Minimum Wages Act (1948); the Inter-State Migrant Workmen Act (1979); the Contract Labour System (Regulation & Abolition Act) (1970), the Bonded Labour System (Abolition) Act (1975), for women under the Equal Remuneration Act (1976), the Construction Workers Act (1996), or the Factories Act (which for example, sets a handling limit for women of 20 kg).

4. The National Coalition for Security of Migrant Workers (NACSOM) is a collective forum of organizations working to support migrant workers and advocate for their services and entitlements in India. The coalition is formed of nearly 30 organizations across the country–mostly grassroots organizations from of Maharashtra, Uttar Pradesh, Rajasthan, Bihar, Odisha, Madhya Pradesh and Gujarat who have direct work with migrant workers. It aims to highlight gaps in the policies for migrants and also work collectively to respond to their unique and complex demands. NAC-SOM hopes to become a powerful platform on issues of internal migration and migrants' inclusion in urban governance and policies.

5. Disha Foundation is a Nasik based NGO from Maharashtra state of India. Being a pioneer NGO working with migrants since 2002, Disha has facilitated the internal labour migration via direct intervention with migrants and policy dialogue with governments, to address migration and different needs of migrants, including health, education, livelihood and rights, in general.

6. The Hague Declaration focused on adopting a more humane approach to migrants and migration, have two sets of international instruments for migrants rights: first the core human rights treaties such as the International Covenant on Civil and Political Rights, whose provisions apply universally and thus protects migrants; and second CMW and the ILO conventions which specifically apply to migrants. Despite several attempts, migrants continued to be protected under an amalgam of general internal law, human rights law, labour law and international law, but with CMW, the provision for the protection of the migrants' received formal sanction. CMW was adopted by General Assembly at its 45th session on 18 December 1990.

7. The United Nation's International Convention on the Protection of the Rights of All Migrant Workers and Members of Their Families entered into force on 1 July 2003. It constitutes a comprehensive international treaty regarding the protection of migrant workers' rights. It emphasizes the connection between migration and human rights, which is increasingly becoming a crucial policy topic worldwide. The Convention aims at protecting migrant workers and members of their families; its existence sets a moral standard and serves as a guide and stimulus for the promotion of migrant rights in each country.

References

Borhade, A. (2006). *Addressing needs of seasonal labour migrants in Nasik, Maharashtra, India* (Working Paper No. 2). Delhi: Population Council.

———. (2011). 'Health of internal labour migrants in India: Some reflections on the current situation and way forward'. *Asia Europe Journal, 8*(4), 457–60.

Borhade A. (2015). 'Internal Labour Migration and Policy Review of India', Unpublished.

Bhagat, R.B. (2011). *Migrant's denied right to the city, UNESCO/UNECEF Internal Migration in India Initiative 2011*

Borhade A. (2015). 'Internal Labour Migration and Policy Review of India', Unpublished. Pune: Center for Enquiry into Health and Allied Themes (CEHAT).

Breman, J. (1996). *Footloose labour: Working in India's informal economy*. Cambridge: Cambridge University Press.

Bustamante, J.A. (2011). Report of the Special Rapporteur on the human rights of migrants; Human Rights Council Seventeenth session, United National General Assembly A/ HRC/17/33, 21 March 2011. Retrieved from http://www.refworld.org/pdfid/4eef13fb2. pdf

Chatterjee, C.B. (2006). *Identities in motion: Migration and health in India.*

Devi, R.D. and Kumar, N.A. (2011). *Population pressure on land in Kerala* (Working Paper No. 24). Kochi: Centre for Socio-economic and Environmental Studies.

Derose, K.P., Escarce, J.J. and Lurie, N. (2007). 'Health care: Sources of vulnerability'. *Health Affairs*, 26(5), 1258–68.

Deshingkar, P. and Akter, S. (2009). 'Migration and Human Development in India', Human Development Research Paper 2009/13, UNDP. Retrieved from http://hdr.undp.org/ sites/default/files/hdrp_2009_13.pdf

Deshingkar, P. and Grimm, S. (2005). 'Voluntary internal migration: An update'. Paper commissioned by the Urban and Rural Change Team and the Migration Team, Policy Division, DFID. ODI. September 2004. Retrieved from http://www.odi.org.uk/plag/ RESOURCES/reports/0509_voluntary_internal_mi gration_update.pdf

Deshingkar, P. and Start, D. (2003). *Seasonal migration for livelihoods in India: Coping, accumulation and exclusion.* London: Overseas Development Institute.

Ghate, P. (2005). 'Serving migrants sustainably: Remittances services provided by an MFI in Gujarat'. *Economic and Political Weekly*, 40(17), 1740–46.

GOI (2002). National Population Policy, Ministry of Health and Family Welfare, GOI.

Gupta, S.P. (December 2002). Retrieved from http://planningcommission.nic.in/reports/ genrep/pl_vsn2020.pdf *Report of the Committee on India Vision 2020.* Planning Commission, Government of India.

Karan, A. (2003). 'Changing patterns of migration from rural Bihar'. In G. Iyer (ed.), *Migrant labour and human rights in India.* New Delhi: Kanishka Publishers.

Malaysia National Stakeholder Conference. (2008). *Developing a comprehensive policy framework for migrant labour.* Paper presented at National Conference 'Developing a Comprehensive Policy Framework for Migrant Labour, International Labour Office, Jakarta.

Mosse, D., Gupta, S., Mehta, M., Shah, V., Rees, J., and the KRIBP Project Team (2002). 'Brokered Livelihoods: Debt, Labour Migration and Development in Tribal Western India', *Journal of Development Studies*, 38(5), 59–87.

NACO (National AIDS Control Organization). (2007). *Targeted Intervention for Migrants under NACP III.* Ministry of Health and Family Welfare, GOI.

NCRL (National Commission on Rural Labour). (1991). *Report of the study group on migrant labour* (Vol. II, Part II). New Delhi: Ministry of Labour, GoI.

National Health Policy. (2001). Ministry of Health and Family Welfare, GoI.

National Population Policy. (2002). Ministry of Health and Family Welfare, GOI.

National Urban Health Mission. (2008). Ministry of Health and Family Welfare, GoI.

Phoolchund, H.N. (1991). 'Aspects of occupational health in the sugar cane industry'. *Journal of the Society of Occupational Medicine*, 41(3), 133–36.

Ping, H. (2003). *China migration country study.* Paper presented at the Regional Conference on Migration, Development and Pro-poor Policy Choices in Asia organized by the Bangladesh Refugee and Migratory Movements Research Unit, Dhaka and DFID, UK.

Thorat Y.S.P., Ramana, N.V., Ramakrishna, R.V., Koshy, Anne and Zak, Therese (2009). *Remittance needs in India* (NABARD GTZ Technical study).

Samal, C.K. (2006). 'Remittances and sustainable livelihoods in semi-arid areas'. *Asia Specific Development Journal, 13*(2). Retrieved from http://www.cgg.gov.in/workingpapers/ Remittances%20Paper.pdf

Ray, D.B. (1993). 'Basic issues and real challenge: Health of urban poor'. In P.K. Umashankar and G.K. Mishra (eds), *Urban health system.* New Delhi: Reliance Publishing House and IIPA.

Srivastava, R. (2012). 'Internal Migration in India: An overview of its features, trends and policy challenges'. In *National Workshop on Internal Migration and Human Development: Workshop Compendium, Vol. 2, Workshop Papers,* UNESCO and UNICEF, New Delhi, pp. 1–47.

Sundar, R., Mahal, A., and Sharma, A. (2000). *The burden of ill-health among the urban poor: The case of slums and resettlement colonies in Chennai and Delhi.* New Delhi: National Council of Applied Economic Research.

Tribhuwan, R.D. and Patil, J. (2009). *Stone quarry workers: Social insecurity and development issues.* New Delhi: Discovery Publishing House.

Usher, E. (2005). *The millennium development goals (MDGs) and migration.* Geneva: International Organization for Migration.

Varennes, F. de. (2003). 'Strangers in foreign lands: Diversity, vulnerability and the rights of migrants'. Retrieved from http://www.unesco.org/most/paper_devarennes.pdf (accessed on 24 December 2015).

Weill, H., Beuchner, H.A., Gonzalez, E., et al. (1996). 'Bagassosis: A study of pulmonary function in 20 cases'. *Annals of Internal Medicine, 64*(4), 737–47.

WHO (World Health Organization). (2003). *International migration, health and human rights.* Geneva: Author.

———. (2008). *61st World Health Assembly: Resolutions and decisions.* Geneva: Author.

Websites Accessed:

World Health Organization. http://www.who.int/en/ (accessed on 3 November 2012).

International Organization for Migration. http://www.iom.int/ (accessed on 18 October 2012).

International Labour Organization. http://www.ilo.org/global/lang--en/index.htm (accessed on 20 October 2012).

Census of India. http://www.censusindia.net/ (accessed on 16 November 2011).

National AIDS Control Organization, India. http://www.nacoonline.org/NACO (accessed on 10 October 2012).

Sussex Centre for Migration Research. www.migrationdrc.org (accessed on 16 November 2012).

Website of DFID. http://www.dfid.gov.uk/ (accessed on 1 January 2013).

Website of Ministry of Health and Family Welfare. Government of India (accessed on 11 January 2012).

Website of Ministry of Labour, Government of India (accessed on 19 October 2012).

Website of Rashtriya Swasthya Bima Yojana, Ministry of Labour and Employment, Government. http://www.rsby.gov.in (accessed on 21 October 2012).

Solution Exchange for the Work and Employment Community Consolidated Reply on Increase Utilization of RSBY by Migrant Workers and BPL Households. ftp://ftp. solutionexchange.net.in/public/emp/cr/cr-se-emp-28011001.pdf (accessed on 2 November 2012).

World Health Assembly (2008). The 61st World Health Assembly, Migrants health, WHA61.17. http://apps.who.int/gb/ebwha/pdf_files/A61/A61_R17-en.pdf (accessed on 10 November 2011)

National Health Policy. 2002 (India). http://www.mohfw.nic.in/NRHM/Documents/National_Health_policy_2002.pdf (accessed on 10 December 2012).

Employment State Insurances Corporation, Extension of ESI scheme to the construction site workers. http://www.esic.nic.in/CIRCULARS/RevII-030111.pdf (accessed on 12 November 2012).

Eleventh Five Year Plan. 2007–2012. Planning Commission of India, GOI. http://planningcommission.nic.in/plans/planrel/fiveyr/11th/11_v1/11th_vol1.pdf (accessed on 20 November 2012).

About the Editor and Contributors

Editor

Deepak K. Mishra is currently Professor of Economics at the Centre for the Study of Regional Development, School of Social Sciences, Jawaharlal Nehru University, New Delhi. He has worked in the areas of agrarian change, livelihood, labour and employment and economic transformation of mountain economies. He has co-authored *The Unfolding Crisis in Assam's Tea Plantations: Employment and Occupational Mobility* (Routledge, 2012). He was a Commonwealth Visiting Fellow at Oxford University during 2008–09. In 2012, he was Visiting Professor at the International Centre for South Asian Studies, Russian State University for the Humanities, Moscow.

Contributors

R.B. Bhagat is a Professor and Head, Department of Migration and Urban Studies, International Institute for Population Sciences, Mumbai. He has authored six books and more than 70 research papers in reputed journals. Professor Bhagat is currently working with UNESCO-UNICEF India Migration Initiative.

Anjali Borhade is an Associate Professor, Indian Institute of Public Health, Gurgaon and Technical Director, Disha Foundation, Nasik. She is the founding director of the pioneering Disha Foundation, an NGO that supports migrant rights, including health.

Rikil Chyrmang is currently associated with O.K.D Institute of Social Change, Guwahati. At the time of writing this chapter, he was a Doctoral Scholar at the Centre for Development Studies, Thiruvananthapuram.

Amrita Datta is an Associate Fellow, Institute for Human Development, New Delhi and a PhD researcher at the International Institute of Social Studies, Erasmus University Rotterdam.

Elizabeth Williams-Oerberg is a Postdoc scholar at the Department of Cross-Cultural and Regional Studies, University of Copenhagen. She is currently working on the research project 'Buddhism, Business and Believers'.

S. Irudaya Rajan is a Professor, Centre for Development Studies, Thiruvananthapuram. He is the editor of the Annual Series *India Migration Report* since 2010 and also Editor-in-chief of the international journal *Migration and Development*.

Babu P. Remesh is currently in charge of *Director* of the School of Interdisciplinary and Transdisciplinary Studies, Indira Gandhi National Open University (IGNOU), New Delhi.

Anshu Singh is a doctoral candidate at the Department of Sociology, Delhi School of Economics, University of Delhi.

Late Surjit Singh was Director and Professor, Institute of Development Studies, Jaipur until his untimely death in 2013. Professor Singh was a prolific scholar with 13 books and over 90 articles in national and international journals on diverse themes ranging from agricultural economics, rural and agricultural credit to globalization, trade and climate change.

Nidhitha Sreekumar is a doctoral scholar (UGC Senior Research Fellow) at the Department of Sociology, Delhi School of Economics, University of Delhi. She has successfully completed her tenure as Fulbright-Nehru Doctoral Research Fellow (2014–2015).

Meenakshi Thapan is Professor of Sociology at the Delhi School of Economics, and Co-ordinator of the D.S. Kothari Centre for Science, Ethics and Education, University of Delhi since 2012. Her first book was *Life at School: An Ethnographic Study* and the most recent are *Ethnographies of Schooling in Contemporary India* (SAGE, 2014), *Living the Body: Embodiment, Womanhood and Identity in Contemporary India* (SAGE, 2009).

R. Vijay is a Professor of Economics, School of Economics, University of Hyderabad. He has published articles on changing nature of agrarian structure, land and lease market as well as on costs and consequences of different types of migrations on agrarian economy.

Index

A Participatory Poverty Assessment (PPA), 332

Bhagalpur riots, 52, 57

census and NSSO, 32, 260

Danish Research Council for Culture and Communication (FKK), 175
death rate, 40
Disha foundation, 304–06, 308, 310

educational migration among Ladakhi youth, 157
  academic disadvantages, 165–68
  contradictory resource, 17, 168, 169, 171
  historical development of, 157, 158
  internal migration as transnational migration, 163
  migration for higher education, 161, 162
  policy recommendations, improvement for, 64, 171–74
emergence of Noida and Gurgaon, 22
employment, 7, 12, 16, 21, 30, 31, 34, 37, 40, 47, 49, 53, 55, 61, 63, 64, 66, 73–75, 90
estimated birth rate
  1997-2010 in, 139

four patterns of urbanization, 45

Hague Declaration, 333

Infant Mortality Rate (IMR), viii, 139
institutional support and migrants, 89, 90
internal labour migration
  overview of, 292, 293

policy for, 319–21
poverty alleviation and development linkages with, 293, 294
vulnerabilities of migrants, 294–99, 306–08
internal labour migration in India
  existing central/state government policies and programs, 314
  key state initiatives
    Andhra Pradesh and Odisha, 309
    Bihar, 311
    Maharashtra state response to migration, 309, 310
  migrant labour welfare boards, 312
    Kerala state government initiative, 312, 313
    Punjab migrant welfare board, 311
internal migrant workers
  development polices
    sending states of migration in, 326
    urban development policies, 326
  suggestive framework for national policy for
    basic entitlements, 320, 322
    governance, 325, 326
    inter-sectoral convergence, 324
    key stakeholders, 325
    legal aid and redressal of legal disputes, 323, 324
    legislation on migration, 325
    political inclusion of migrant communities, 324
    resource allocation, 325
    skill up-gradation and market linkages, 322
    universalization of social security benefits, 322

internal migration
  contemporary India, book, 13, 15–18,
    20
internal migration in India
  agrarian questions of labour, 2–5
  economic reasons for, 11–13
  informalization and migration, 7, 8
  migrant populations
    internal and international,
      percentage of, vii, 9
    size and growth rates of, migration
      stream, vii, 9
    size and growth rates of, type of
      movement, vii, 10
  policy concerns, 20, 21
  trends and patterns, 2
  uneven development, poverty and
    migration, 5–7
Inter-State Migrant Workers Act, 1979,
  328, 329
inter-state migration
  ethnic conflict and, 35, 36

labour migration in North-East
  projected population in North East,
    2020, vii
land based importance of NCPHs
  surveyed villages in, 182

migrant labourers in Punjab, 257, 258
  wage rate, impact of, 259
migration, 1
  birth, rural and urban areas, 41
  components of urban growth, in India
    contribution of, 41
  death and natural increase rate in India
    rural and urban areas, 41
  household remittances, uses of, viii
  in urban growth
    contribution of, 40
  migrants, percentage of
    selected million plus cities, 43f, 39
  urbanization, linkages between, 38
migration and marginalization
  North East migrants in Delhi
    determinants and unique aspects,
      73–75
    profile of migrants, 72, 73

migration development and poverty
  relationship between, 36, 37
migration from contemporary Bihar, 204,
  205
  destination, 210
  livelihood strategy, 206–10
    migrating households, 207, 208
    New Economics of Labour
      Migration (NELM), 206
    non-migrating households, 207
    workers disaggregated by sex and
      residential status, ix
  role of migration, 205
migration in Agrarian classes, 180–82
  classes of migration on local structures,
    implication
    agricultural labour households and,
      ix, 199
    Non farm sector (NFS), 198
  cropping pattern, 187
  households and owned land, viii, 190
    in different study villages,
      distribution, 34
  implicit opinion, 199
  inter village differences in, 192
  intra-village trends in migrations, 195
  sources of irrigation, 182
  surveyed villages, viii, ix, 183, 184, 188,
    195, 198, 199
migration in India
  development and poverty, relationship
    between, 36, 37
  faster urbanization, 43, 44
  government policies and programmes,
    44
  historical perspective, 28
  internal and international, percentage,
    vii, 9
  inter-state migration and ethnic
    conflict, 35, 36
  migrants' contribution, 44, 217
  percent distribution of
    distance categories and steams of
      migration by, 34
    steams of migration and gender
      by, 33
  push and pull factors, 43, 257
  Rajiv Awas Yojana (RAY), 45

reasons of rural and urban areas
  gender by, 33
  recent trend and pattern of, 30
  The Jawaharlal Nehru Urban Renewal
    Mission (JNNURM), 44

National Capital Region (NCR)
  bleak employment, 74
  educational and employment
    considerations, 73
  emerging occupational profile and
    accessing jobs process, 74–76
  migration and migrant
    neighbourhoods, 78, 80
  political unrest, violence and poverty,
    74
  profile of migrants, 71, 72
  working in cities, charm of, 74
National Coalition for Security of Migrant
  Workers (NACSOM), 333
natural growth rate, 139
net migrants rate, viii
North East migrants in Delhi
  cultural gap, 90, 91
  media, migrant collectives, centrality
    of, 91
  media, role of, 91
  negotiating city life, 72
    cultural gap, 90, 91
    discriminations in daily life, 82
    faulty notions and social labeling,
      81
    illegality as means of exploitation,
      84
    racial discrimination and violence,
      85, 86
    verbal abuse, 85, 86
  workplace, discriminations and
    harassment, 87–89
number of persons living below poverty
  line (BPL), viii, 142

Place of Enumeration (POE), 45
Place of last residence (POLR), 45
population dynamics
  population by age group, viii
  public and private employment
    organised sector, xi

race, 176
Rajiv Awas Yojana (RAY), 44
Rashtriya Swasthya Bima Yojana (RSBY),
  296
rural migration in Punjab, ix, 230
  economic activities, 247
  migration profile, ix, 232, 233, 261,
    322
  migration rate, 240
  migration streams, 243
  nature of movements, 242, 243
  out-migrants, x, 250–53
  proportion of migrants, 237, 242
  reasons for migration, 246
  return migration, 249

seasonal migration
  Odisha
    destination during longest spell by,
      rural, x, 274, 275
    findings and policy implications,
      285, 286
    households in different MPCE
      deciles classes, x, 277
    household type by, rural, 124–25t,
      275
    migrants, Al States/UTs, x, 273
    region-wise, rural, x, 274
    short term migrants, 276
    social category by, rural, x, 274
    total land possessed by, rural, 276
    UPAS, 276
seasonal migration in India, xi, 268

The Jawaharlal Nehru Urban Renewal
  Mission (JNNURM), 44

Udalguri district of Assam, survey
  language spoken, percentage
    distribution, xi
urban local bodies (ULBs), 307
urban migration in Punjab
  trend in, ix, 229
usually employed by category of
  employment
    distribution of, viii, 144
Usual Principal Status Unemployment
  Rate, viii, 146

women's mobility and migration
    gender and migration, 47
        case study, 51–53
        perspectives, 50
        statistics, 48, 49
    muslim women in Jamia Nagar, Delhi, 53

change, 62, 64
community spaces, ghettoization,
    57–61
freedom and social mobility, 54,
    56, 57
policy recommendations, 64, 66, 67